Richard Hooker and the Vision of God

Richard Hooker and the Vision of God

Exploring the Origins of 'Anglicanism'

Charles Miller

James Clarke & Co

Filio amato amicoque Michaeli
cuius fides intellectum quaerens

James Clarke & Co
P.O. Box 60
Cambridge
CB1 2NT

www.jamesclarke.co
publishing@jamesclarke.co

ISBN: 978 0 227 17400 5

British Library Cataloguing in Publication Data
A record is available from the British Library

Contents

Preface

I owe the origin of this book to Archbishop Michael Ramsey who, in his retirement, came each year to my theological college to lecture between 1979 and 1982. One autumn his lectures were on the Anglican tradition; he began with the theology of Richard Hooker.[1] Canon Donald Allchin, another visiting lecturer, stimulated further interest in Hooker and made me aware of the important study by Olivier Loyer, *L'Anglicanisme de Richard Hooker*. I am grateful to The Revd Dr Andrew Louth, who sold me his copy of Loyer's two-volume study at a bargain price. It is a rare treasure.

In 1994 Fr John Paul kindly invited me to give the Adult Sunday School afternoon lectures at St Andrew's-by-the-Wardrobe in the City of London; with the preparation of those lectures the gestation of the present study really began. Subsequent teaching at Nashotah House, The General Theological Seminary, and Yale Divinity School in the United States gave me occasion to widen my reading and delve more deeply into Hooker's theological world.

Beginning in 2002, and henceforth while increasingly immersed in parochial ministry, I took advantage of periods of annual leave to return to the work. I am grateful to Dr Marjorie Reeves (*requiescat in pace*) formerly of Norham Road, Oxford, Bp Geoffrey Rowell of Bishop's Lodge, Worth, Michael and Mary Jenkins of the Old Library, Ilminster, and the Abbot and community of the Monastery of St John the Baptist, Tolleshunt Knights, without whose hospitality and occasions of retreat this book would not have been written.

Thanks are due to the staff of the Bodleian Library, Oxford, and to Mr David Sherwood, Director of the Frances Donaldson Library, Nashotah House, USA, and his assistant Ms Laura Hummer, for their help in providing electronic resources.

Particular thanks are due to Ms Rachel Hayden without whose able and generous assistance this manuscript would not have been submitted on time, to the Reverend Douglas Dales for his encouragement, to Michael Miller in the final stages of manuscript preparation, and to Mr Adrian Brink and Ms Emily Reacher of James Clarke & Co for their interest, support and guidance.

St Helen's Rectory
Abingdon-on-Thames
17 December 2012

---

1. The notes of the lectures were subsequently transcribed and edited by Dale Coleman as Michael Ramsey's *The Anglican Spirit* (Cambridge, MA, 1991).

Sources and Abbreviations

The Sources for Hooker's Writings

Whenever possible, Hooker texts are taken from the second edition of John Keble's *The Works of that Learned and Judicious Divine Mr Richard Hooker with an account of His Life and Death by Isaac Walton* (Oxford, 1841).

Citations from that edition give the books of the *Laws* in upper case Roman numerals, followed by the chapter in lower case Roman numerals, followed by the section of the chapter in Arabic numerals, e.g.: III, vi, 2. The location in the three-volume Keble edition follows in brackets, e.g., [I, pp. 361-2].

Where necessary, texts are cited from the modern critical edition under the general editorship of W. Speed Hill, *The Folger Library Edition of the Works of Richard Hooker in 6 volumes* (Cambridge, MA/London, 1977).

Citations from this edition give the work in abbreviated form followed by its location in the edition's volume given in upper case Roman numerals and the page number in Arabic numbers, e.g., V: 250.

Abbreviations

ANC – Ancient Christian Writers series
CRH – Companion to Richard Hooker
DF – Dublin Fragments
DEC – Decrees of the Ecumenical Councils
FLE – The Folger Library Edition
FSJ - First Sermon on a Part of St. Jude's Epistle
LCC – Library of Christian Classics
LDJ – A Learned Discourse of Justification, Works, and How the Foundation of Faith Is Overthrown
CPF – A Learned and Comfortable Sermon of the Certainty and Perpetuity of Faith in The Elect
RHCCC – Richard Hooker and the Construction of Christian Community
RHER – Richard Hooker and the English Reformation
SNP – A Learned Sermon on the Nature of Pride
SRH – Studies in Richard Hooker
SSJ – Second Sermon on a Part of Jude's Epistle
ST – Summa Theologiae

A Note on Terminology

The term 'non-conformist' is used throughout this study. It does not reflect the nuances of churchmanship and ideological concern which characterised the inhabitants of the Elizabethan church. Taking a cue from Peter Lake's analysis of Puritanism, by 'non-conformist' I mean all those who, along a spectrum of intensity and extremity of views, either refused to be part of, or were unhappily implicated in, the 'allegedly corrupt and corrupting' elements of the Elizabethan church as established by law.[1] The term therefore excludes 'papists' with whom, despite their own refusal to conform, the established church's critics associated many of the unreformed aspects of the Church of England.

A Note on Quotations

Because of their abundance, chiefly from Hooker texts, and to save encumbering the pages, I have omitted the ' . . . ' at the beginning and end of quotations. It is used, however, within quotations to indicate parts of the text that have been omitted.

The two-volume study by Olivier Loyer accompanies us through the pages that follow. Citations from his *L'Anglicanisme de Richard Hooker* appear simply with volume number and page, e.g. I, p. 355. (Although the pagination is continuous through them the volume number is given; this is very helpful if one is consulting the original version of the thesis published the University of Lille, as is the case in this study).

Paget's Taxonomy of Laws

In his Introduction to the Fifth Book of Hooker's Treatise of the Laws of Ecclesiastical Polity, Francis Paget provides a detailed 'pedigree' of Hooker's hierarchy of laws as they appear in the Laws of Ecclesiastical Polity. In some cases the laws in question are overtly understood as such by Hooker; but in many cases Paget has rendered them as 'laws' in his interpretation of Hooker's use and argument. Paget's taxonomy, or 'pedigree' (as he calls it) is reproduced on pp. 66-7 of this study as part of the discussion of Hooker's theology of creation. There are, to be sure,

---

1. Peter Lake, *Moderate Puritans and the Elizabethan Church* (Cambridge, 1982), pp. 1-7, provides a foothold on the issues of nomenclature vis-à-vis the late Elizabethan church of Hooker's public life.

other ways to structure the derivative elements of Hooker's taxonomy than the one proposed by Paget. But no interpreter of Hooker has provided as detailed or compelling a taxonomy as Paget's, and it is highly useful in grasping both the richness of Hooker's concept of 'law' and the integrated character of his world-view. For that reason, footnote references to parts of the taxonomy are given so that the reader can locate particular discussions within the taxonomy as a whole.

Introduction
Why Study Richard Hooker?

The readers invited to enter the intellectual and theological world of Richard Hooker might well ask 'Why?' During most of the last century, it has been claimed, Richard Hooker was more honoured than read, and the flow of Hooker scholarship was little more than a trickle.[1] However, since the 1980s something of an industry has developed so that now, among a rather small but growing international group, Hooker scholarship has well and truly entered the academy. With this entrance there has been both loss and gain. On the positive side we now have the results of a wide spectrum of detailed studies of Hooker's life, his historical context, his contributions to literature, politics and thought. On the negative side the conversation has largely forsaken the vicarage and entered the lecture hall. The scholarly circle is enlarged but, as so often happens, those writing are increasingly talking only to themselves. As a result, expensive monographs and cumbersome, intimidating compendia are available for the learned. They present rich but competing views; they give the reader some purchase on the subject but with a narrow view of the terrain around him. Naturally, this study makes use of them.

That growth of interest in Hooker among specialists has been accompanied by an abandonment of serious study of Hooker's thought among theological students, clergy and theologians. That is surely part of the drift in Anglican theology in the English-speaking world, but it is also a global trend. Among this constituency it is very true that the name of Hooker is more honoured than read; and even here it is questionable whether the name of Hooker is even known. Something needed to be done to bridge the gap. This study is the result.

There are, to be sure, reasons why Richard Hooker might be forgotten in the daily distribution of theological food to Christian people. When we realise how non-theological – though not *un*-theological – so many of Hooker's concerns and insights seem to be, we might well wonder what could be gained by a study of Richard Hooker *as a theologian*? There are, it seems to me, four responses to that question.

First, Hooker teaches us to think theologically. That may not be readily apparent when reading his great work, the *Laws of Ecclesiastical Polity*.

1. So the author of the essay 'Richard Hooker' in the *Times Literary Supplement* claimed (30 April 1954, p. 281).

But when we begin to discern the taut lines that connect his discussion of disputed particulars with basic principles, and when we recognise the ground into which his principles are anchored, we realise that every aspect of reality and experience with which Hooker is concerned has theological significance. He is a vivid witness to the comprehensive extent of theology's reach and implications. In that sense theology is still for Hooker the 'queen of the sciences'. Hooker helps us think theologically in another way too. He encourages his readers always to relate principles to particulars and vice-versa. That is most obvious in the *Laws* whose very conception and execution seeks to honour such an approach. Hooker objected to contemporary styles of thinking, even by theologians, which sought short cuts and valued speed in articulating or resolving the often intricate issues of doctrine and ecclesial life.

Second, Hooker exemplifies how Christians should comport themselves in religious controversy. Admittedly, there is a question among Hooker scholars as to the genuineness of his eirenic rhetoric, and it is probably the case that pressure from collaborators as well as polemical expediency occasionally gave Hooker's pen a harsh argumentative edge. He sometimes betrays peevishness at ignorance among those who should know better or whose arguments are transparently self-serving and manipulative. Still, by the standards of his age, and in comparison with other defenders of the established church, Hooker's writings manifest a restraint, a humility, and an honest desire to persuade by reasoned argumentation. 'My whole endeavour is to resolve the conscience', Hooker insists in the Preface to the *Laws*, and we have no reason to doubt him. Richard Church remarked, in keeping with this view, that Hooker is more eager to show his adversaries *why* they are wrong than *that* they are wrong.[2]

In line with that approach, Hooker takes seriously the need to represent his adversaries' positions accurately. He is keenly aware of how easily lesser motives can drive an honest argument off course: 'when stomach doth drive the wit, the match is not equal'.[3] It is true that Hooker's adversaries are hard to identify from the pages of the *Laws*, but, where they can be, it is clear that Hooker tries to represent accurately the views of critics of the established church.[4] He is loath to erect straw men, and that characteristic, among others, has led some to view the *Laws* as representing a new and higher stage in English religious controversial literature.

---

2. R. W. Church, *Introduction to Book One of Hooker's Treatise of the Laws of Ecclesiastical Polity* (Oxford, 1896), p. xvi; emphasis his.
3. Preface, ii, 6 [I, p. 137].
4. An example is his treatment of Thomas Cartwright; see John Luoma's article 'Restitution or Reformation? Cartwright And Hooker On the Elizabethan Church', *Historical Magazine of the Protestant Episcopal Church*, XLVI: 1 (1977): 85-106.

A third reason to study Hooker's writings, and the *Laws* especially, is the dialogic character of his approach to theology. There will be occasion to return to this idea and expand upon it since it relates to the character of Hooker's thought and theological style. It deserves mention here because Hooker challenges an increasingly time-bound, relativistic approach to doctrine and truth. Hooker, who was more aware of what we call 'historical development' than we might at first suppose, was extraordinarily effective in constructing a theological vision by means of a dialogue with Christian and philosophical traditions extending widely both in time and space. His sources, about which more will be said elsewhere, are as wide, as ancient, and as modern as Hooker could make them. While his theological 'project' was very much of its own time and place, he brought to it as many useful insights as he could muster. He has set a standard which theology is ever challenged to meet and, if possible, surpass.

A fourth and final reason to study Hooker as a theologian is that he exemplifies a responsible, constructive, and pastorally accountable inter-play between theology and spirituality. Hooker, of course, lived and theologised in an age that was at once more religiously attuned and more serious than our own. But the issue goes deeper than that. It has to do with Hooker's high evaluation of reason in the thought and practice of the Christian religion, and with the need for aided reason endued with the gifts of grace in the consideration of it. It also has to do with what one writer calls Hooker's 'spirituality of truth', his sense, we might say, that the knowledge of God and love for God (and therefore for God's truth) go together. Hooker thus challenges his readers not just intellectually and theologically but also spiritually. In his own way he confronts us with the ancient maxim of the spiritual theologian Evagrius, that a theologian is one whose prayer is 'strong'.

But there are, equally, aspects of the study of Hooker's writings of which we must beware.

First, it is important to see Richard Hooker and his writings as part of an emerging English religious tradition, and as a contribution to it. His writings form a stage, but only one stage, in its development. However perennial the quality of that contribution may be, however enduring the tone and direction he has given to Anglicanism as a theological culture, we are not on that account obliged to follow the specific form of his arguments, or to embrace all of his conclusions, or to justify to ourselves or to others his various accommodations to the circumstances in which he found himself.[5] Perhaps we should simply beware of seeing Hooker after the fashion of the so-called 'magisterial reformers' Martin Luther and John Calvin. Despite its many worthies through the centuries, English theology

---

5. And accommodations there were: see Christopher Morris' 'Introduction' to *Of the Laws of Ecclesiastical Polity*, 2 vols (London, 1965), pp. vi-vii.

has never been determined by a single, luminary figure as was reform in Germany and France. We must appreciate Hooker's contribution in relation to its historical context since only then can we assess it in relation to actual possibilities and alternatives.

Yet we can also discern within his writings insights and creative trajectories which may help us still. Henry McAdoo sums it up well when, after describing the broad historical context, he insists that 'out of all this something time-defying was created.'[6] That 'something' is not a set of fixed viewpoints but a less precise quality and character of thought: values and priorities he brought to the theological task. In a small way this introduction to Hooker's writings seeks to elucidate them and, in so doing, I hope it will extend his creative legacy into our age and beyond.

Our aim in this study is to present Hooker's theology, and in so doing to explore the origins of what came to be called 'Anglicanism'. The descriptive term 'Anglican' will not generally be used to describe Hooker in the pages that follow. At the end we will return to the matter of nomenclature since it is a matter of dispute which this study as a whole should help clarify. Our concern is with ideas, so while allusions will be made to historical context and ecclesiastical affairs, those are not our focus. We want instead to grasp Hooker's vision of God so as to understand what lies before, within, and beyond the particular expression of Christian faith and ecclesial life that he defends and advocates. Hooker is a theologian not because he knows the sources, uses the concepts and fashions the language, but precisely because, as Egil Grislis reminds us, his focus is *God*.[7]

Theology has been defined as study which, through participation in and reflection upon a religious faith, seeks to express the content of that faith in the clearest and most coherent language available.[8] That definition would suit Hooker, and so we are approaching his writings with it in mind. While we will be trying to understand the mind of one of the most profound Elizabethan divines in the formative years of the independent life of the English Church, we will at the same time be surveying the science of theology as a distinct field of study. We will be experiencing the shape of theology as it seeks to give coherence to the mystery of God and God's action in the world, and we will enter into concept and language worlds that connect us not just with Hooker and his age, but with the great Christian tradition. To enliven that encounter, the Appendix provides passages from Hooker's writings – mostly from the *Laws* but not exclusively – so that his 'voice' can still be heard in its difference, its richness, and in its power of inspiration.

---

6. 'Richard Hooker', in Geoffrey Rowell, ed., *The English Religious Tradition and the Genius of Anglicanism* (Wantage, 1992), p. 106.

7. Egil Grislis, 'Hooker among the Giants: the Continuity and Creativity of Richard Hooker's Doctrine of Justification', *Cithara*, XLIII: 2 (2004): 12.

8. John Macquarrie, *Principles of Christian Theology* (New York, 1966), p. 1.

Part One

Orientation

Chapter 1
'That Glorious Beam of the English Church'
The Man and his World

In a significant measure theology is a matter of biography. The theological vision a person constructs and espouses, together with the form of its expression, are deeply related to personal life and circumstances. Certainly that is so of Richard Hooker.

Hooker's biographers, though, have often obscured that. This is partly owing to the fact that the first biography of Hooker by the somewhat sympathetic bishop of Exeter, John Gauden, was written in the year of the Restoration, a lengthy sixty years after Hooker's premature death in 1600. It is also the result of the complex motives which surrounded the writing and publication in 1665 of what might be called the official *Life of Mr Richard Hooker* by the seventeenth-century biographer Izaac Walton. Walton was already well known for his lives of eminent clerics John Donne and Robert Sanderson, so he was the obvious candidate when Archbishop of Canterbury Gilbert Sheldon, unhappy with Gauden's portrait of Hooker, sought to replace it with something more satisfying.[1] Walton could be relied upon to depict Hooker in terms wholly consonant with the interests of the neo-Laudianism of the restored Church of England: learned, reasonable, prayerful and, more to the point, utterly committed to royal supremacy, the *Book of Common Prayer*, and episcopacy by divine right.[2]

Walton's *Life*, however, was thin on sources. Never mind that long periods of Hooker's bookish life were uneventful; even where his life was worth recording documentary evidence was in short supply. So Walton was often left to construct his picture from an oral history available to him from his wife's relatives. In some cases that made for erroneous facts and an innocently misleading picture of Hooker. Nor was Walton's *Life* free from ideological bias. His appended discussion of the last three books

---

1. Lee Gibbs cites, for instance, Gauden's assertion of Hooker's academic mediocrity ('Life of Hooker', *CRH*, pp. 3-4).
2. Walton's *Life* was published in 1666 and then in all subsequent editions of Hooker's works through the nineteenth century (Gibbs, 'Life', p. 5). Texts cited here are from Walton's *Life* in *The Lives of John Donne, Sir Henry Wotton, Richard Hooker, George Herbert, Robert Sanderson* (Oxford, 1927). On the conservative shape that the Restoration Church took and why, see I. M. Green, *The Re-Establishment of the Church of England 1660-1663* (Oxford, 1978).

of the *Laws of Ecclesiastical Polity*, for instance, tried to undermine their authenticity, and so their authority, in an effort to 'neutralise' Hooker's advocacy of the principle of consent in governance.[3] Something like hagiography was the result. Still, Walton's classic displaced the preceding biography and shaped generations of readers' picture of the learned and judicious Hooker: less a defender of the Elizabethan Church than of its neo-Laudian Restoration version.

As part of the nineteenth-century Tractarians' return to the sources and a wider English cultural tendency toward 'imaginative historical reconstruction'[4], John Keble published the first critical edition of Hooker's works in 1838. He revisited Walton's *Life* for inclusion among its introductory material and added his own theological assessment of Hooker's place and value as an 'Anglican' authority. Keble's special interest was episcopacy and its origin by divine right.[5] Keble's own investigation into the textual history of Hooker's *Of the Laws of Ecclesiastical Polity* and other writings prompted questions about the adequacy and accuracy of Walton's picture. Thus began what Arthur McGrade has called the 'deflationary trend' especially notable in recent Hooker scholarship, a steady displacement of Hooker from his role as a Restoration icon on a near-saintly pedestal.[6]

The critical posture begun by Keble has gathered such momentum in the intervening century and a half that it has become possible to construct a life of Hooker which, while not free of some probably insurmountable uncertainties, gives us a far more reliable account of Hooker's life and of the context and development of his thought than has hitherto been possible.[7] There is no need to repeat those biographical results in detail. It is important at the start of this theological study, however, to relate with broad brush stroke the circumstances, issues, institutions and associations that helped generate Hooker's theological vision, and then elicit its exposition.

---

3. Gibbs, 'Life', p. 6. See also Michael Brydon, *The Evolving Reputation of Richard Hooker* (Oxford, 2006), pp. 105-20.

4. So Peter Nockles in his essay 'Survivals or New Arrivals? The Oxford Movement and the Historical Reconstruction of Anglicanism', in Stephen Platten, ed., *Anglicanism and the Western Christian Tradition* (Norwich, 2003), p. 144.

5. He concluded that Hooker's views were so contradictory as to 'neutralise' his testimony one way or another; see Keble's Editor's Preface [I, p. lxxvii].

6. In his editor's introduction to *Richard Hooker and the Construction of Christian Community* (Tempe, AZ, 1997), p. xiii.

7. Philip Secor has capitalised on this in his biography *Richard Hooker Prophet of Anglicanism* (London/Toronto, 1999), but readers must be aware of significant amounts of conjecture; Lee Gibbs' essay 'Life of Hooker' cited in note 1 above draws upon the close but unfinished biographical research of George Edelen.

Early Life and Education

Richard Hooker was probably an only child born on or near Easter Day in 1553 or 1554 in Heavitree, a suburb of the prosperous and proud cathedral city of Exeter in Devon.[8] His father, Roger, was of a prestigious local family though he himself did not inherit either the family property or the strong family tradition of involvement in local civic affairs. That was the good fortune of his brother John.

From the point of view of Richard Hooker's eventual contribution as a theologian, his uncle John was an important influence both materially and ideologically. John Hooker was an Oxford-educated, successful, civic-minded man who also theologically aware. His friendship with Bishop John Jewel went back to the days of the Marian exile when John Hooker joined Jewel and the roughly eight-hundred English religious exiles in Switzerland and the Rhineland. By the time of Elizabeth's settlement of religion in 1558, John Hooker was what we would now consider a committed Protestant of the magisterial sort, that is, in the stream of Martin Luther and John Calvin.

He was also a thorough-going Erastian. He viewed religious refor-mation as a small price to pay for civic peace and the good order of the commonwealth. When it came to the relationship between church and state his was a 'broad and pragmatic route' which viewed religion as a prop and servant of a prior political good.[9] From both civil and ecclesiastical ministers, therefore, loyalty to the crown was an essential requirement. He once asserted that:

> Preposterous, then, is the judgment of those who would have [it] that religion should pertain only to the bishops and clergy, and the chief magistrates should deal only in matters of policy. But the law of Moses and the law of the Gospel, doth determine the contrary.[10]

'Magistrates are God's ministers' too, he insisted, 'substitutes, and vicars, upon earth from whom all power and authority is ordained.'[11] Those, to be sure, were not the precise sentiments of his nephew in later years, but the theme of a variegated and over-lapping jurisdiction between civil and ecclesiastical spheres surely was.

Given John Hooker's intellectual commitments (he wrote several books on ecclesiastical and local history) it is no surprise that he sponsored his nephew's tuition at the Exeter Grammar School from the age of eight.

---

8. March 25th, the probably day of Hooker's birth, was the day on which the new calendar year began; but Gibbs, following Edelen's carefully researched chronology, gives April 1554 as the time of birth ('Life', p. 8). The matter remains unsettled.

9. Secor, *Prophet*, p. 35.

10. *Ibid.*

11. *Ibid.*

Richard Hooker was an able student. Walton wrote that as a school-boy 'he was an early Questionist, quietly inquisitive'. 'Why this was and that was not to be remembered? Why this was granted, and that denied?'[12] That description surely fits the probing habit of the mature Hooker. Whether or not the education provided by his uncle at the Grammar School was sufficient preparation for admission to an Oxford college, John Hooker intended it to be so. Did his well-placed friend, John Jewel, play a part? We do not know. But Richard Hooker was admitted to Jewel's own Oxford college, Corpus Christi; he arrived late in 1569 at the age of fifteen.

Oxford

Perhaps the two university towns of Oxford and Cambridge experienced the traumas and transitions of the era of church reform even more than London. When it is remembered how thoroughly ecclesiastical the origins and subsequent habits of the universities were, it follows that the consequences of religious upheaval and change would be deep and wide for their colleges and halls. Although Oxford was never as bent on reform as Cambridge, it too felt the stresses and strains.[13]

Corpus Christi College had been founded early in the sixteenth century by Richard Fox, who was deeply imbued with the spirit of the 'new learning' of Renaissance humanists like John Colet and the Dutchman Desiderius Erasmus. Indeed, Erasmian humanism profoundly influenced Oxford throughout the first half of the sixteenth century. The inherited emphasis on Aristotelian, or 'scholastic', logic was enriched by the new rhetorical aspects of the curriculum. With the help of Erasmus' interpretation of classical Ciceronian rhetoric, Hooker's education at Corpus was a powerful combination of logical rigor and rhetorical precision.

Corpus was founded before the formal separation from papal jurisdiction. Its founding religious perspective was liberal, humanist, and Roman Catholic. Despite subsequent formal acts of separation at the national level, and in the face of widening currents of reformed theological ideas within the university as a whole, Corpus continued (as did many other English institutions) to include Roman Catholic sympathisers among its fellowship. In fact, such was the strength of this sympathy that William Cole, president of the college at the time of Hooker's admission, had to be forcibly installed by the Bishop of Winchester on the Queen's personal order in the face of staunch resistance by the fellows who preferred their own pro-Roman Catholic candidate. Later, when a replacement for Cole himself was proposed, Hooker and other fellows were temporarily expelled from the

---

12. *Life*, pp. 162-3.
13. See, for instance, C. M. Dent, *Protestant Reformers in Elizabethan Oxford* (Oxford, 1983), pp. 47-73.

college.[14] Corpus was hardly the 'Garden of Piety, Peace, and Pleasure' that Walton's *Life* of Hooker had described;[15] although periods of discord were, of course, due to internal politics as well as national religious reform.

Intellectual and Practical Influences

Hooker's collegiate and university years between 1569 and 1583 formed the first half of his short life and a key phase of philosophical, rhetorical and theological training. In addition, he made contacts that had a determining impact on his intellectual posture and profession course. Three major influences and two minor ones deserve mention.

First among the major influences stands John Rainolds. When Hooker arrived at Corpus he was put under the tutorial care of Rainolds who, at the age of twenty, was already well known and highly respected in the university. He was an able mixture of Renaissance learning and strong Reformed theological commitment – an advocate of John Calvin's theological system as found, say, in his *Institutes of the Christian Religion*, as well as of the writings of Oxford's Reformed professor of divinity, Peter Martyr Vermigli. We cannot doubt the impact on Hooker of Rainold's intellectual world.

Another influence was the dashing, brilliant Henry Saville.[16] Saville was, among many intellectual strengths, an eminent Greek specialist. He edited the first critical edition of St John Chrysostom's works and was a likely promoter of Greek patristic interest among Hooker's cohort. Another influence – and here too we must emphasise likelihood rather than certainly – was Antonio del Corro, a one-time Spanish monk who had become a keen advocate of Luther's theology. It is impossible to trace his influence with certainty, but it is noteworthy that at least one of Hooker's later critics likened Hooker's views on predestination to those of del Corro.[17] It is reasonable to suppose that, broadly speaking, the influence of both Saville and del Corro enabled Hooker to consider wider theological options than those of the increasingly regnant English Calvinism.

Two other figures, who were to exert influence of a different kind, appeared on the scene during Hooker's years as tutor and lecturer: George Cranmer and Edwin Sandys.[18] Both, it seems, were intentionally put under Hooker's care. The close friendship that grew between them had huge consequences for Hooker's later career and on the writing and character of his great work, *Of the Laws of Ecclesiastical Polity*.

---

14. Gibbs, 'Life', p. 9.
15. *Life*, p. 178.
16. See Church's comments, *Introduction*, p. viii.
17. Walter Travers in his *Supplication* (III, pp. 558-9).
18. Cranmer was the grand-nephew of the Archbishop by the same name; Sandys was the son of the Bishop of London who later became the Archbishop of York.

We know little of the particulars of Hooker's collegiate and university life apart from the general duties expected of college tutors and university lecturers. In 1579, the year in which Hooker was made a deacon, he began deputising for Thomas Kingmill, the professor of Hebrew. Two years later, in 1581, he was ordained as a priest. College fellows were also expected to preach learned sermons. From this period we have Hooker's earliest extant writing: his two sermons on the Letter of Jude.[19] Soon the offer of the parochial living of Drayton Beauchamp allowed Hooker to leave the college.[20] But Hooker continued his studies. It is likely that in this period Hooker resided in the London home of the wealthy merchant John Churchman, whose daughter Joan Hooker soon married.[21]

Preferment

But Hooker was not destined for obscurity. In the same year he left Oxford, Hooker was invited to preach at the famous outdoor pulpit at St Paul's Cross, close by St Paul's Cathedral in the City of London. For several centuries it had been the recognised platform for the dissemination and debate of issues of church and state especially during periods of religious reform or political uncertainty.[22] It could reasonably be counted the most famous pulpit in England; sermons preached there were often an 'event'. The great and the good, the powerful and the weak, statesmen, churchmen, commoners, and even royalty, attended. Whatever the audience, the atmosphere could be raucous, combustible, and confrontational. That Hooker would even face the prospect belies Walton's picture of him as a dove-like, softly-spoken saint. Hooker must have possessed a convincing pulpit presence, oratorical forcefulness, and just plain nerve.[23] No text of that sermon exists. However, we can reasonably suppose that his views, however much they may have dissatisfied non-conformists like Walter Travers, found a favourable hearing among some highly-placed and influential churchmen.[24]

---

19. For the text see III, pp. 659-99; the sermons are interesting at various levels, not least in that they reveal Hooker's basically Reformed view of the Church of England at that time.
20. The Buckinghamshire parish was located about 20 miles northeast of Oxford. There is no evidence that Hooker ever took up residence in the parish.
21. On the significance of the marriage see C. J. Sisson, *The Judicious Marriage of Mr. Hooker and the Birth of the Laws of Ecclesiastical Polity* (Cambridge, 1940), pp. 1-2, 17-44.
22. See Secor, *Prophet*, pp. 105ff.
23. On Hooker as a preacher, see *ibid.* p. 127, note 7.
24. Critical comments on the content of the sermon were later made by Travers in his *Supplication to the Privy Council*; for that text see note 17, above.

At the time of the St Paul's Cross sermon Hooker's cousin, Walter Travers, was Reader of the Temple Church at the inns of court.[25] Despite his unhesitating advocacy of further reform in the Church of England, Travers had, with the patronage of Lord Burghleigh, been appointed as Reader to support the ailing Master of the Temple, Dr Alvey. It was Travers' expectation that, upon the retirement of the Master, he would be succeed him.[26]

Archbishop Whitgift, unlike Bishop Aylmer of London, was all too familiar with Travers. As Vice-Chancellor Whitgift had expelled him from Cambridge for abetting Thomas Cartwright in sowing Puritan discontent among the fellowship at Trinity College, and, more impertinently, for refusing episcopal ordination as a requirement for a full college fellowship.[27] By any reckoning the Mastership was a prestigious post with an influential pulpit; it was, after all, at the heart of England's legal world.[28] Both Whitgift and Burghleigh realised its strategic importance as a platform of advocacy for competing visions of the church among the increasingly influential corps of London's common lawyers.[29] In the end Whitgift convinced the Queen to disallow Travers' appointment to the Mastership, although he continued as Reader.[30] However, a concession was exacted from the Archbishop in that he had to settle for a compromise candidate. Hooker was appointed Master in March 1684/5. It is important to note that Hooker was not Whitgift's first choice. That fact weakens the argument that Hooker was appointed precisely as an apologist for the Archbishop's views and policy and that his *Laws*, as it began to take conceptual shape in the Temple years, was simply a conformist manifesto.

Master of the Temple

The time of Hooker's Mastership was contentious. While there was personal respect between Hooker and Travers, their public and professional relations were often highly oppositional. From the start it was clear that Hooker was unsympathetic to the creeping Presbyterianism that

25. These inns were the centres of England's legal culture and practice. At the centre of the Temple was its chapel, originally a church of the order of the Knights Templar.
26. The post of Master of the Temple was a crown appointment.
27. After a period in Geneva Travers had gone to Antwerp where he was ordained by elders and appointed as pastor to the English congregation there. Upon his return to England he aimed to complete the reformation of the church along a Genevan model.
28. On the post see W. Speed Hill, 'The Evolution of Hooker's *Of the Laws of Ecclesiastical Polity*', *SRH*, p. 120.
29. On a possible influence on the Laws of the 'new learning' of the common lawyers, see H. C. Porter, 'Hooker, the Tudor Constitution, and the *Via Media*', *SRH*, pp. 86-9
30. The disallowance was based on the fact that he had not been canonically ordained, i.e., by a bishop.

Travers was advocating.[31] Hooker's perceived unsoundness on issues of polity engendered suspicion about Hooker's theology in general; whence Walton's description: 'The Forenoon Sermon spake Canterbury, and the Afternoon Geneva.'[32]

Walton's simple characterisation of the divergent perspectives in play raises an important question about Hooker's role and intent during those years at the Temple: did Hooker speak for Canterbury? That is, in the Temple debates with Travers did Hooker represent the establishment position pure and simple? And, beyond that, was he acting intentionally and by arrangement on behalf of Whitgift, his strategists and his operatives? Was the composition of the Laws of Ecclesiastical Polity planned from the start as part of Hooker's role in facing down non-conformism both in one of the capital's premier pulpits and more widely?[33] Interpreters of Hooker are not wholly agreed about this. But there seems to be enough evidence in Hooker's Temple sermons, for instance, to indicate his independence from establishment support and guidance. Far from preaching Canterbury, Hooker preached Hooker.[34] The debate ended when Archbishop Whitgift suspended Travers.

The Temple period was an intellectually rich and active period for Hooker. He was, for instance, in the midst of a dynamic renaissance of the English common law tradition associated with Sir Edward Coke. Echoes of that appear in the Laws. From this period too we have sermonic evidence of Hooker's theology. His Sermon Of the Certainty and Perpetuity of Faith in the Elect was composed then, as were the two sermons that now form A Learned Discourse of Justification, Works, and how the Foundation of Faith is Overthrown, and A Learned Sermon of the Nature of Pride.[35]

Then another question arises: did Hooker begin consideration and even planning of the Laws while he was Master of the Temple? The issue cannot be fully settled. However, some important issues that later figure in the Laws made their appearance in the extant works of the Temple period.[36] What Hooker's Temple writings illustrate most importantly is his

31. For instance, Travers advised Hooker not to act officially until his call had been ratified by the congregation.

32. Walton, Life, p. 200.

33. Sisson, for instance, takes the view that the Laws was a joint effort with George Cranmer and Edwin Sandys planned from the start; but that is a minority view. See pp. 32-3, 45-7. 'Hooker's great book was born under his father-in-law's roof. John Churchman's hospitality in Watling Street was the common meeting-place for those with whom Hooker wished to consult...and the scene of frequent discussions between Hooker and Edwin Sandys, George Cranmer, and Dr John Spenser' (p. 45).

34. See Richard Bauckham, 'Hooker, Travers, and the Church of Rome', Journal of Ecclesiastical History, 29: 1 (1978), 41.

35. See, respectively, III, pp. 469-81; pp. 483-547; pp. 597-642.

36. For instance, the hierarchy of laws and the foundational role of reason.

willingness to take an independent line, chiefly from his non-conformist critics, but also, albeit to a lesser extent, from conformist orthodoxy. So his departure from the Temple in 1591 gave Hooker the chance to develop and weave his distinctive considerations and trajectories into something more coherent and comprehensive.

The Appearance of the *Laws*

Appointments in the Salisbury diocese gave Hooker the income to support his growing family, and insofar as the posts did not require residency or actual pastoral work, Hooker was free to pursue his large project.[37] While the Archbishop was attempting to find Hooker a more suitable permanent post, Hooker himself was working on the Preface and first four books of his proposed eight books *Of the Laws of Ecclesiastical Polity*. It is reckoned that the Preface and Books I-IV were ready for the printer by the end of 1591.

But which printer? It seems that by the early 1590s the non-conforming Puritan movement had already crested and that the publication of numerous anti-Puritan rebuttals by conformist polemicists like Richard Bancroft, Thomas Bilson and Hooker's friend Hadrian Saravia had flooded the market. There was simply no will on the part of printers to assume the risks of publishing a work as large as that which Hooker was proposing, especially when it had no archiepiscopal backing.

At the point of this practical *impasse* Hooker's former pupil Edwin Sandys took a decisive step: he offered to underwrite the publication of the *Laws*. This offer meant that the Preface and the first four books could be printed immediately, in time for the Parliamentary session of late winter 1593/4 which would consider important anti-presbyterian, non-conformist legislation.[38] Thanks to Cranmer, Hooker's relation, the printer John Windet, entered the proffered portion of the *Laws* at the Stationers Hall at the end of January 1593. About six weeks later Lord Burghleigh received a copy in readiness for the parliamentary session.

The fact that the first published parts of the *Laws* were slow to sell did not hinder Hooker's intention to complete and publish books V through VIII. But George Cranmer's involvement did.[39] His overtly political concerns, coupled with his view that effective polemic meant point-by-point engagement with the opponents' arguments, compelled Hooker

---

37. Hooker was appointed Sub-dean of the cathedral, and Rector of St Andrew, Boscombe, and Prebendary of Netheravon. Secor thinks that Hooker, with his wife and two daughters, resided in London at the home of his father-in-law John Churchman (*Prophet*, pp. 249-50). That would have given Hooker access to sources relevant to his writing.

38. On the Sandys-Cranmer involvement see Hill, 'Evolution', pp. 131ff.

39. I follow Hill's rendition of events here; *ibid.*

to rework the material in hand and chiefly Book V. 'Remember your adversaries', Hooker was advised. 'Cranmer and Sandys were absorbed', Speed Hill has written, 'in the immediacy of an explosive political situation', so they advocated a direct and forthright rebuttal.[40] Indebted as he was to them, Hooker gave way. As a result Book V grew to a size equal to the previous four books altogether, and it took four more years to complete; it finally appeared in 1597. It meant too that, although they were probably completed, Hooker himself never saw the publication of Books VI through VIII.

Self-Defence and Death

Amid the writing and re-writing of Book V Hooker at last received a benefice suitable to his needs. St Mary's, Bishopsbourne, lay some three miles from Canterbury. In 1594 its incumbent was appointed bishop of Norwich and the living, which was in the Queens' gift, was offered to Hooker.[41] In January 1594/5 Hooker was appointed, and instituted in early July 1595. The spacious rectory was well suited to this rather prosperous clerical family. The parish itself was accessible to the cathedral in Canterbury and its chapter library; Hooker's Dutch friend Hadrian Saravia was a canon there. In this idyllic rural setting Hooker devoted himself to his family, his pastoral work, and to the remaining books of the *Laws*.[42]

In 1598 Hooker made his one appearance as preacher at Court. His distance from the cut and thrust of London life notwithstanding, Hooker was not wholly exempt from the continuing controversies of the time. One or two churchmen, who were unhappy with Hooker's defence of the established church in the published portions of the *Laws*, published in 1599 an attack on Hooker's theological soundness *vis-à-vis* the formularies of the Church of England entitled *A Christian Letter of certain English Protestants*. It elicited from Hooker a robust, incisive rebuttal of which only portions remain.[43] As far as its topics of comment, it gives important evidence of Hooker's theological views at the end of his life. *The Dublin Fragments* will be important at points during this study.

Hooker was struck down with sickness, having contracting a fever in the course of a journey to and from London. In the latter half of October 1600 Hooker registered his will. Thenceforth confined to bed, he received

---

40. *Ibid.*, p. 136.
41. Dr William Redman was Hooker's immediate predecessor in Bishopsbourne.
42. Gibbs relates two incidents that marred Hooker's final years ('Life', p. 15).
43. The so-called *Dublin Fragments* discovered by Keble in the library of Trinity College, Dublin [II, pp. 537-97]. On this episode and speculation as to the author of *A Christian Letter*, see Secor, *Prophet*, pp. 317-21.

the sacrament and made a final confession to Dr Saravia. He died on November 2nd. Walton tells us he died contemplating the angels and their marvellous order.

Upon hearing of Hooker's death, it was a matter of utmost importance to his friends and colleagues in London and Oxford that his papers be kept safe and secure. John Churchman immediately dispatched one of his household to Bishopsbourne to secure Hooker's papers. In the spring of 1601 those friends, Hooker's executor and others, examined the cache of papers and found among them Books VI and VII of the *Laws* in almost final form, and Book VIII incomplete. The manuscripts were distributed among the group with the intent of completing, editing and publishing them. Thus began the dispersal of Hooker's literary remains which has given to the *Laws* and the other minor works their complex and at times baffling textual, publishing and interpretive history.[44]

Our purpose in this study is not to wade too far into those technical waters. Bearing in mind Stephen McGrade's evocative suggestion that in Hooker's extant corpus we have what he calls a 'church-in-text',[45] we will look to those texts to reveal the building's shape and content. To do so we must turn to the foundations upon which Hooker builds and the materials with which he works.

---

44. On that see Gibbs' concise review ('Life', pp. 18-23).
45. Stephen McGrade, 'Classical, Patristic and Medieval Sources', in Torrance Kirby, ed., *A Companion to Richard Hooker* (Leiden/Boston, 2008), p. 85.

Chapter 2
'The Weight of this Requireth Largnesse'
The Big Picture

In 1924 Lionel Thornton wrote an introduction to Richard Hooker's theology in a series devoted to 'Masters of English Theology'. In a final chapter, 'Hooker and Ourselves', he wrote this:

> Though history repeats itself, certain types of thought have a strangely persistent tendency to recur in forms superficially new yet in a profounder sense unchanged by the lapse of time. In this respect Hooker undoubtedly stands at the head of a line of thought which has left its mark deeply upon English theology through successive centuries.[1]

In Hooker's case that influence has been as recurrent as it has been diverse. A theologian, a philosopher, an historian, a political theorist, a controversialist, a stylist wholly equal to the cultural achievements of the Elizabethan age – Hooker is all these. In theology he has been called a Thomist, a Calvinist, a quintessential 'Anglican'; in politics an Erastian, the first Whig, an absolutist, and the father of modern social contract theory; in philosophy a Platonist, an Aristotelian, and a rationalist.[2] We will not tackle all the issues which those various, indeed divergent, viewpoints raise. What we must acknowledge behind them all, though, is a subtle, versatile and immensely creative mind. To some readers that mind has given rise to irreconcilable oppositions; to others it has generated a unique, comprehensive synthesis.

The purpose of this chapter is to position ourselves for what follows. A credible preliminary posture is important for anyone entering into Hooker's intellectual world, so our aim more specifically is to paint in broad brush-strokes the kind of mind at work and the intellectual sensibilities with which it works. In that sense our concern is with 'the big picture'.

The basis of this study is the view reached by the French Roman Catholic scholar Olivier Loyer, who concluded his comprehensive theological analysis by saying that 'we are confronted with a spirit accustomed to go to the root of a problem, to recognise the manifold aspects of the issue,

---

1. L. S. Thornton, *Richard Hooker. A Study of His Theology* (London, 1924), p. 101. Thornton himself became a distinguished theologian who began a multi-volume systematic exposition of theology in the 1940s.
2. These diverse views are expounded in the various works which are cited throughout this and the chapters that follow.

and then to try to reconcile the differences on that basis'.[3] As we approach Hooker's thought, then, the twin ideas of *root* and *reconciliation* will help us gain a sense of the synthesis that he sought to achieve in his vision of God, the world, the church and the human community.

Root

At the root of Hooker's rich, comprehensive thought is theology. 'Theology' here means the consideration of God and of God's ways with and in the world and with humankind as creator, redeemer, sanctifier and consummator.[4] However much we might admire Hooker's genius in the many domains of thought mentioned earlier, like politics and philosophy, Hooker is a theologian through and through. While for Hooker the heart of theology is Trinitarian – the Father's saving manifestation in Christ actualised through history by the Spirit – its circumference is without limit; its concern is nothing less than everything.

When a reader opens the pages of Hooker's chief work, *Of the Laws of Ecclesiastical Polity*, that is not immediately clear. In Book I of the *Laws* Hooker explains why he has composed his treatise:

> The Laws of the Church, whereby for so many ages together we have been provided in the exercise of Christian religion and the service of the true God, our rites, customs, and orders of ecclesiastical government, are called into question . . . therefore we offer the laws whereby we live unto the general trial and judgment of the whole world.[5]

Those words, which at first remind us of the origin of the debates of the 1580s and 1590s in those among the English community in Frankfurt forty years before, in fact declare the overarching theme, the fundamental issue, that occupies Hooker's mind: law. Hooker means, to be sure, the laws of the Church of England since they were the flashpoint of contemporary debate with the established church's critics. But beneath those particular laws to which exception had been taken by non-conformists there lay the basic issue of law itself: first, law in general as conceived philosophically and theologically, and second the manifold laws that splay outward like the spokes of a wheel or the finely balanced descending parts of a mobile.

Some have argued that Hooker's *Laws* marks a decisive new stage both in the debates with non-conformists and in the emergence of 'Anglicanism'.[6] According to that view, although he built upon a body of establishment

---

3. *L'Anglicanisme de Richard Hooker*, 2 vols. (Lille, 1978), II, p. 663; all translations from this work are my own.
4. Later in this study we will distinguish 'theology' and 'economy', but not here.
5. I, i, 3 [I, p. 199].
6. See Peter Lake's study *Anglican and Puritan? Presbyterian and English Conformist Thought from Whitgift to Hooker* (London, 1988), pp. 145-230.

apologetic that preceded and flourished around him, Hooker made a distinctive, indeed unique, breakthrough in the nature and the style of the debate. The hilltops, if you like, where the battle between defenders of the established church and non-conformists had hitherto been fought were forsaken for a different field: a more subtle kind of intellectual combat down in the valleys. C. S. Lewis put it well when he remarked that 'the *Polity* [viz. *Laws*] marks a revolution in the art of controversy. Hitherto, in England, that art had involved only tactics; Hooker added strategy'.[7]

What drew a donnish, peaceable clergyman into fierce combat for the mind, soul and body of the Church of England as established by law in the reign of Elizabeth I? No matter how much regard he may have had for its non-conformist critics personally, Hooker found upon consideration that their whole case for further reform was based upon misconceptions of principles and their application. That is, Hooker discerned in the non-conformists' case what Peter Lake describes as 'a central epistemological lapse', a basic and far-reaching mistake about the right relations between reason and scripture.[8] That surely is the real presenting issue that Hooker discerned and upon which he focused his rebuttal. But there is more. In Hooker's view the non-conformists' lapse skewed not only their views of scripture and reason, but their interpretation of God and God's relation to the world, to humankind, and to the church. We must account for the comprehensive and creative strategy in Hooker's response in large measure because he saw, as few if any others did, the full implications of the non-conformist critique. Hooker's wide field of vision lay behind C. S. Lewis' description of the 'great flanking movements' in the early books of the *Laws* and especially in Book I.[9]

So Hooker begins the first book of his *Laws* with a theoretical argument arising, one might feel, from a different world,

> because the point about which we strive is the quality of our laws, our first entrance hereinto cannot better be made, than with consideration of the nature of law in general, and of that law which giveth life unto all the rest, which are commendable, just and good; namely the law whereby the Eternal himself doth work.[10]

However, that is but the start. Proceeding, Hooker tells us, 'to the law, first of Nature, then of Scripture, we shall have the easier access unto those things which come after to be debated, concerning the particular cause and question which we have in hand'.[11]

A key aim of the strategy in the *Laws*, then, is to give its readers a God-view and a world-view from which to engage and assess the particular issues in debate.

---

7. *English Literature in the Sixteenth Century, Excluding Drama* (Oxford, 1954), p. 458.
8. *Anglicans and Puritans?*, p. 147.
9. *Literature*, p. 458.
10. I, i, 3 [I, p. 200]. See the Eternal Laws of Paget's taxonomy (p. 66).
11. *Ibid.*

Reconciliation: Three Working Principles

In searching for a comprehensive description of Hooker's analysis and defence of the established church some have spoken of Hooker's theology, and of the *Laws* in particular, as a system.[12] But that is misleading. Certainly if 'system' means a monolithic philosophical structure informing the exposition or a set of theological categories rigorously applied to any given question, then Hooker's writings do not form a system in any customary sense. We can, nevertheless, see across Hooker's writings a coherence that, as Loyer explains, rises out of 'a core of concepts'. If Hooker does not construct a formal theological system, or *summa*, he works with a 'constellation of fundamental ideas'.[13] This 'core' forms 'a kind of intellectual tool-kit' and with its intellectual tools in hand Hooker approaches the problems of theology and the life of Christians. It is his 'metaphysical and logical base'.[14]

What, then, are those tools? Loyer identifies three principles which in and among themselves give Hooker's thought its 'fundamental coherence'.

First, an intellectual principle informs Hooker's theological vision of God and the world.[15] All of creation is the expression of a divine, rational Mind, and all humanly-perceptible reality is discernible, investigable, and, to some extent at least, knowable by rational human subjects. This intellectualism is wedded to Hooker's concept of law because in the conceptual world in which he stands law is by definition rational. A fuller discussion of that theme must wait until a subsequent chapter. We should note now, however, that Hooker's entire thought-world is pervaded by a sense of the rational character of law, and that the human mind's rational capacity is fulfilled in apprehending and coordinating itself to such laws.

Second, Hooker's thought is imbued with the principle of hierarchy. Here we must be careful; 'hierarchy' can have different meanings. For Hooker, as for medieval predecessors like Thomas Aquinas, the meaning of hierarchy is deeply influenced by that elusive Christian thinker known as Dionysius (or Pseudo-Dionysius) the Areopagite.[16] For Dionysius

---

12. So, for instance, Lewis (see citation above); and John Marshall's chapter 'Hooker as the Author of a Summa' in *Hooker and the Anglican Tradition. An Historical and Theological Study of Hooker's Ecclesiastical Polity* (London, 1963), pp. 66-74.

13. Loyer, II, p. 664.

14. *Ibid.*

15. *Ibid.* II, pp. 664-5.

16. It can fairly be said that Dionysius' works *The Celestial Hierarchy* and *The Ecclesiastical Hierarchy*, written at the end of the fifth or the beginning of the sixth centuries, are the well-spring for the idea of hierarchy influencing both medieval and Byzantine Christian thought. See Andrew Louth, *Denys the Areopagite* (London/Wilton, CT, 1989), pp. 33-57.

hierarchy lay at the centre of his vision of God, the world, and the church; yet for him, as for Aquinas and Hooker whom he inspired, it does not imply distance and separation, connotations 'hierarchy' often has for post-Enlightenment readers. To the contrary, as a 'sacred order' or 'principle', hierarchy refers to the ordered relation of each part to other parts and to the whole. In hierarchy each thing occupies a place and performs a necessary role related to everything else. Its chief value is *connectivity* and, above all, *connection*, even union, with the source of all, God.

The third and final principle of Hooker's thought is participation. This principle complements the second and is, in fact, one of the richest ideas in Hooker's conceptual universe.[17] To complement Aristotle's tendency toward division, distinction and categorisation – a logical method with which Hooker has much sympathy – Hooker adds the dimension of participation derived from Plato and his neo-Platonic successors.[18] So Hooker seeks to balance division and distinction with participation and union. '[A]ll things in the world are said in some sort', Hooker tells us, 'to seek the highest, and to covet more or less the participation of God himself.'[19] As we shall see, that has important bearings upon Hooker's theology of the Trinity, his Christology and anthropology, and flows from there into his doctrine of grace and the sacraments. But it pervades his thought entirely. It is no surprise, then, that it informs Hooker's understanding of law insofar as distinction and difference are balanced by overlap and interaction in the actual spheres of laws' operations, namely, church polity. In all three principles, yet in the third above all, the theme of reconciliation is at work. Distinction and difference are affirmed while mutual influence and constructive interaction are the goal.

So in response to the Church of England's critics Hooker does not just fashion a rebuttal, he articulates a vision of reality shaped by the principles of rationality, hierarchy and participation. By themselves they do not form a 'system' in any technical theological sense. But precisely because they are characteristics of reality, they are basic to his theological task and are ordering features of his thought.

---

17. A point noted by various Hooker commentators through the decades; in addition to Loyer, for instance, see Thornton, *Hooker*, pp. 70-1, A. M. Allchin, *Participation in God: A Forgotten Strand in Anglican Tradition* (London, 1988), pp. 7-14, and John Booty, *Reflections on the Theology of Richard Hooker* (Sewanee, USA, 1998), pp. 169-84.

18. On the Platonist and neo-Platonist strand in Hooker's thought see, for instance, W. J. Torrance Kirby, 'The neo-Platonic Logic of Richard Hooker's Generic Division of Law', in *Renaissance and Reformation/Renaissance et Réforme* 22, 4 (1998): 49-67.

19. I, v, 2 [I, p. 215].

Style

What of Hooker's 'matchless writings'?[20] As we have seen, Hooker was educated by those with a humanist appreciation of the power of rhetoric. While Hooker's writings, especially the *Laws*, are cast in a largely traditional classical model, they express to the full the literary aspirations and capacities of the Elizabethan age.[21]

However, we first meet Hooker as a preacher, not as a writer of extended theological or philosophical prose. His style, which has been described as 'baroque', 'ornate' and 'metaphysical', contrasts sharply with the plain and 'histrionic' style of Walter Travers, for instance, and other Puritans.[22] The historian Thomas Fuller, documenting the Temple controversy, described Hooker's preaching like this:

> Mr Hooker's voice was low, stature little, gesture none at all, standing stone-still in the pulpit, as if the posture of the body were the emblem of his mind, unmovable in his opinions. Where his eye was fixed at the beginning, it was found fixed at the end of his sermon. In a word, the doctrine he delivered had nothing but itself to garrish it. His style was long and pithy, driving on a whole flock of several clauses before he came to the close of a sentence. So that when the copiousness of his style met not with proportionable capacity of his auditors, it was unjustly censured for perplexed, tedious, and obscure. His sermons followed the inclinations of his studies, and were for the most part on controversies, and deep points of school-divinity.[23]

In what contrast to Travers' graceful utterances, plausible gestures and profitable matter! Certainly Hooker's style is copious; readers must grasp from the start that the paragraph, not the sentence, is the natural unit of his prose.[24] Perhaps from the pulpit it demanded more than could be expected from Hooker's listeners. As to the *Laws*, though, the style served Hooker and his readers well in so far as it lent itself to the strictly ordered, hierarchically framed, argumentation. It is true, of course, that, as the author of *A Christian Letter* complained of the *Laws*, it differed from 'the simplicity of the Scriptures', but the style was well suited to

---

20. So Izaak Walton describes them in his *Life* (p. 207)
21. In contrast to the Ramist-inspired rhetoric preferred by non-conformists. On Ramism as a philosophico-logical and rhetorical movement see Lee Gibbs, 'Theology, Logic and Rhetoric in the Temple Controversy Between Richard Hooker and Walter Travers', *Anglican Theological Review*, LXV: 2 (1963): 181-3.
22. *Ibid*: 178.
23. Quoted by Gibbs, *ibid*: 177.
24. Morris, 'Introduction', I, p. vii.

the logical division and development of the subject matter. That may have raised problems as to the immediately polemical effectiveness of the *Laws*, but it ensured a theological legacy of incomparable worth and influence.[25]

It means in consequence that the eight books of the *Laws of Ecclesiastical Polity* form a coherent whole.[26] As a literary embodiment of the hierarchical principle even the small controversial points are related to 'large and luminous principles'.[27] The rhetorical richness, the variety of scope and subject matter together with luminosity in the relation of parts to the whole, make of the *Laws* something profoundly beautiful. With good reason C. S. Lewis described Hooker as an artist; with him English philosophical and theological literature really begins.[28]

Sources

There are many points of entry into the study of Hooker's thought. Our focus on his theology does not spare us from reckoning with the diverse sources and their influence upon him. The declaration attributed to Pope Clement VIII upon reading the *Laws* reminds us that the comprehensive sweep of his learning astounded many contemporaries: 'There is no Learning that this man hath not searcht into; nothing too hard for his understanding'.[29] In some measure that quality of mind and expression is consistent with the kind of education Hooker received, what R. J. Schoek has described as the 'twinning' of Erasmian humanism and Christian theology.[30] Within his magnificent pantheon of sources, though, we can identify five sources that exert a special influence on his theology, especially in the *Laws* and the short writings that followed it.

In Book I of the *Laws* the influence of pagan philosophy is especially strong. Chief among them is that of Aristotle but, as was stated above, Plato and neo-Platonism play their part as balancing factors. The result is a robust fusion of the great schools of classical antiquity.[31]

The Platonist stream continues in a second major influence, the church

---

25. Gibbs, 'Rhetoric': 178-9.
26. We leave aside here the still debated status of Book VI.
27. A. J. Mason's fine phrase in his essay 'Richard Hooker' in William E. Collins, ed., *Typical English Churchmen* (London, 1902), p. 33.
28. *English Literature*, p. 468; Church, *Introduction*, pp. xiv-xv.
29. Walton, *Life*, p. 212.
30. More precisely: 'the Erasmian program of fusing the Christian study and teaching of the Bible and the church fathers with a deeply classical wisdom, both built upon a solid foundation in the liberal arts and especially rhetoric', R. J. Schoek, 'From Erasmus to Hooker: An Overview', *RHCCC*, pp. 59-73.
31. Most expansively, W. J. Torrance Kirby, *Richard Hooker Reformer and Platonist* (Aldershot, 2005).

fathers. Chief among them, from the western tradition, is Augustine whose discrete but profound influence recent research has document.[32] From the eastern Christian tradition two influential Byzantine theologians stand out: Dionysius the Areopagite and the great systematiser John of Damascus.[33] In all three neo-Platonic influence is strong.

Those three writers were themselves co-opted into St. Thomas Aquinas' magisterial thirteenth-century synthesis expounded in treatises like the *Summa contra Gentiles* and above all the *Summa Theologiae*. Admittedly, Hooker does not restrict himself to Aquinas or the Thomist tradition among the schoolmen. There are as many quotations from, for example, the Franciscan Duns Scotus as from Aquinas. But Hooker's eclecticism in reference to the schoolmen cannot hide the 'swing and sweep' impact of Aquinas' theological system and of the *Summa Theologiae* above all.[34] Book I reveals Aquinas' influence on Hooker's exposition of law, of human agency, and 'the good'; some have even detected in the *Laws* overall shape a reflection of the *Summa Theologiae*.[35] However that may be, Hooker's knowledge and appreciation of these theologians establishes 'school divinity', and Aquinas above all, as the third major influence.

As much as Hooker drank deeply from the well of the western tradition in literature, philosophy and theology, he was very much a man of his own times. He was a son of the magisterial Reformation associated with Martin Luther and John Calvin. Like most of his contemporaries, therefore, he breathed the air of Calvinism both in its source documents from the hand of John Calvin and his disciples, and in its particular English form as Marian exiles returned from the continent and re-worked Calvin's legacy.[36] Hooker quotes them: Theodore Beza, Martin Bucer, Henry Bullinger, Peter Martyr Vermigli, Thomas Cartwright and, of course, John Calvin himself, 'incomparably the wisest man the French Church did enjoy since the hour it enjoyed him'.[37] The irony in that remark notwithstanding, Calvinism was as unavoidable an influence in the theological world in which Hooker

---

32. See the contributions of Ranall Ingalls listed in the 'Works Cited' below. For an equivocal view of Augustine's influence on Hooker see Thornton, *Hooker*, p. 35.

33. John Meyendorff treats him thus in his chapter 'An Effort at Systematization: St. John of Damascus' in *Christ in Eastern Christian Thought* (Crestwood, USA, 1975), pp. 153-72.

34. McAdoo, *The Spirit of Anglicanism* (London, 1965), p. 121; on Aquinas' influence, as a start, see Thornton, *Hooker*, p. 29; and more recently Neelands, 'Grace', pp. 301ff. But Aquinas' influence is not straightforward, as references throughout this study reveal.

35. So Marshall reads the overall shape of the *Laws* in *Hooker*, pp. 66-74. But his view has not been well received among Hooker scholars.

36. The aftermath of the exile was a key factor in the demise of Lutheran influence in the reformation of English theology.

37. From the *Laws*, Preface, I [I, p. 127].

lived as neo-orthodoxy and neo-Thomism were in the theological thought of the last century. Still, Hooker is willing to adopt a critical stance toward Calvin and his legacy: he refuses to credit Calvin's views with canonical status; he is determined to go his own way.[38] We will have occasion to note those aspects of divergence, some of them profound, as this study unfolds, although comparisons with Calvin's theology is not our aim. That having been said, the Reformation's stream of evolving theological discourse constitutes the fourth major influence on Hooker.

Fifthly, Hooker was a man and a mind indebted to Renaissance humanism.[39] Its influence appears in three important ways. We see it first in Hooker's own scholarly commitment to the biblical languages, Hebrew and Greek, and to a kind and quality of exegetical scrutiny equal to the then current philological standards. At key points in his writings Hooker employs the heuristic tools of humanism's philological training.

Humanist influence also appears in Hooker's abiding interest in the concept of law, which was a widespread concern throughout Renaissance culture. That stands to reason in an age which saw the old order of Christendom tumble and new, sometimes radical, ideas about civil and religious polity emerge in the context of the new nation-states.[40] England's legal culture, especially its common law tradition, became a focal point of such interests, and that context made its mark on Hooker during his years at the Temple Church.[41]

Humanist culture gave Hooker a keen historical sense, which will become apparent in the following chapters. We will return to it in the consideration of Hooker's practice of theology. At the start, however, we should recognise Hooker's sense of historical perspective and historical process in relation to revelation, theology and polity.[42] In this respect Hooker is certainly no modern; but relative to the theological sensibilities with which he was in debate Hooker displays a distinctive historical awareness. The Preface to the *Laws* is lengthy in large part because Hooker is at pains to show the historically conditioned origins of John Calvin's Genevan polity. Close historical inspection of those circumstances convinced Hooker that there were no clear signs of special divine authority for Calvin's reformation nor,

---

38. Preface II, 8 [I, p. 139]; see Richard Baukham's comments in 'Richard Hooker and John Calvin: A Comment', *JEH*, 32, 1 (1981): 127; and Secor, *Prophet*, pp. 245-6.

39. These influences are many, including John Colet and the Dutchman Desiderius Erasmus. See Peter Munz, *The Place of Hooker in the History of Thought* (London, 1952), pp. 168-172.

40. Thornton, *Hooker*, p. 29.

41. On this see H. C. Porter, 'Hooker, the Tudor Constitution, and the Via Media', *SRH*, p. 86.

42. This point is part of John Luoma's discussion in 'Who Owns the Father?' *Sixteenth Century Journal* 8, 3 (1977) 58.

as a consequence, for the non-conformists' platform against the Church of England.[43] The empirical reference point of history enhances Hooker's sense of historical process and contingency and often helps him avoid a doctrinaire approach in the analysis and evaluation of Christian theology and practice.

Sixthly and finally, there is Scripture itself. In acknowledging Hooker's critique of the non-conformists' biblicism, we must equally recognise the profoundly biblical character of his theology. No single source is more pervasive both in the *Laws* and throughout Hooker's minor writings too; nor does that characteristic lessen over time as Hooker's theology matures. Book I of the *Laws* is a case in point. It is widely viewed as the most philosophical of the *Laws'* eight books, but, as a careful reading makes clear, citations from Scripture dominate.[44] What might obscure that is the fact that Hooker privileges Scripture *within* the rich assemblage of sources and their insights that have been described above. These are issues to which we will return in chapters considering Hooker's doctrine of Scripture and his understanding of theology. Without pre-empting those discussions, it is appropriate to end this description of 'the big picture' with a brief comment on the issue of theological 'method'.

'Liberal Method'

That Hooker sought with a high degree of success to draw such diverse sources into a coherent theological whole is remarkable. However, he has been credited with even more. Many accept that Hooker used his synthesising skill to create what H. R. McAdoo describes as a 'liberal method' in theology.[45] We need to comment here, however, on the appeal to and description of this method as McAdoo presents it. He did not invent it, to be sure; Francis Paget's masterly edition of Book V of the *Laws* includes an extensive introduction in which the three-fold appeal ascribed to Hooker is succinctly presented.[46] It was a short step for McAdoo to render that insight into his own era's interest in 'method' and then survey the field of establishment theology in the century after Hooker to see it at work. The brilliance of *The Spirit of Anglicanism* lies just there, and its influence has been great.[47] Without doubt there is legitimacy to the broad point that McAdoo makes, as the brief survey of Hooker's sources suggests, and as the following chapters will show.

43. Thornton, *Hooker*, p. 23; Preface, I-II [I, pp. 126-42].

44. Lee Gibbs makes this clear in his 'Introduction to Book I' in *FLE*, VI, I, pp. 81-124.

45. *Spirit*, pp. 1-12.

46. *An Introduction to the Fifth Book of Hooker's Treatise Of the Laws of Ecclesiastical Polity* (Oxford, 1899), pp. 226-7.

47. See, for instance, Part Three, 'Authority and Method' in S. Sykes, J. Booty and J. Knight, eds., *The Study of Anglicanism* (London, 1998), pp. 87-128.

At the same time, there are reasons to be wary of his template for reading Hooker and his contribution to subsequent Anglican theology. In the first place we need to ask whether Hooker's approach to the practice of theology really constitutes a method in the strict sense of the word. The three-fold appeal which is commonly credited to Hooker is not in itself a theological method; it refers rather to what might be called spheres of authoritative insight to which the Christian community looks when it seeks to understand truth and 'accordingly' to order its common life. A theological method is, certainly, concerned with sources, but it is concerned too with an articulated conceptual apparatus as the basis for thought and discourse. One feature of this study is to reveal such potential within Hooker's writings and especially his *Laws*, but in so doing we have to alter Hooker's overt arrangement of material and draw lines of connection which are usually implicit rather than overt throughout his corpus.

A second issue concerns the definition of each of the three components of the purported method. For instance, what exactly does Hooker mean by 'reason'? Clearly he does not mean what Englishmen would have meant after Hume, Locke or Butler. And even in his own theological context there is no ready answer to that key question. Hooker simply is not that clear: he gives no prolegomenon to his theological treatises, no clear definition of terms, in the way a modern practitioner would do.

Other aspects of his purported method are problematical also. As we will have occasion to observe later, taken altogether Hooker shows – at first sight, at least – an ambivalent, even uncomfortable attitude towards 'traditions', by which he means the unwritten truths subscribed to by Roman Catholic contemporaries. When he refers positively to traditions Hooker usually has in mind 'matters indifferent' duly decided by ecclesiastical authority.[48] But do such ecclesially approved 'indifferent' matters form what advocates of this method mean by tradition? That is doubtful.

McAdoo's interpretation of Hooker's 'liberal method' eschewing the so-called 'authoritative method'[49] of the theological tradition hitherto ascribes no clearly fixed order to the three components of which, he argues, it is constituted. How, therefore, are Scripture, tradition and reason related? In pursuing the use of this triad in Hooker's 'Anglican' successors, McAdoo in fact admits that they work with those components in significantly different ways. That such a dynamic use of sources created over time a distinctive theological atmosphere in 'English theology' we cannot doubt. We would, however, expect a clear expression of the use of sources and their inter-relation in a proper theological method.

Finally, we must ask how much this assemblage of sources in Hooker

---

48. But see *Laws*, V, lxv, 2 [II, p. 318].

49. McAdoo, *Spirit*, p. 2.

actually distinguishes him from his predecessors and contemporaries within and beyond the shores of England. Certainly neither Hooker nor his English contemporaries had a corner on the expanding market of ancient Christian sources.[50] Equally, Hooker's use of, for example, Aquinas' writings can be seen as part of a sixteenth-century Thomist revival and reveals an appreciation of a distinguished Christian rationalism that long preceded him. Even McAdoo elsewhere describes Hooker's method as a 'threefold dialectic' of the sources cited above.[51] That phrase suggests that in ascribing anything distinctive to Hooker the issue is less about the sources themselves and more their relation in theology's exploratory and explicative programme.

The chapters that follow will, I hope, reveal those relations. In the process, however, we will not gain insight into a method so much as into a theological *style* where tone, proportion, priorities, line, texture and relation prevail. Maybe Porter is right: we should think of Hooker as being among the poets.[52] In that regard – to bring this discussion back to the Elizabethan world – Hooker's theological approach is notable in itself and distinguishable from the theologies of his age. The exploration and explication of Hooker's theology will confirm that in his writings, and chiefly in his *Of the Laws of Ecclesiastical Polity*, the distinctive style of an emerging 'Anglican' identity 'discovered itself'.[53]

---

50. See Luomo, as cited above.
51. 'Hooker', p. 111.
52. 'Tudor Constitution', p. 111.
53. This is the apt phrase of B. M. J. Reardon in his essay 'Richard Hooker's Apology for Anglicanism', *The Hibbert Journal*, LII (1954): 279.

PART TWO

FOUNDATIONS

Chapter 3
'That Light Which None Can Approach Unto'
God

Since Hooker's universe is, as C. S. Lewis has said, 'drenched with Deity', we must consider what sort of deity that is. This chapter, therefore, takes up Hooker's doctrine of God. Every Christian theologian would subscribe in principle to a God-filled universe, for the idea has a firm scriptural basis: 'in him we live and move and have our being' (Acts 17.28). Hooker takes that seriously. But Lewis' arresting phrase suggests more, so a chief concern here is to discover the distinctive Hookerian edge prompting such a description of the relationship between God and the world. There is no doubt that Lewis had a sharp sense of the wider intellectual world which informed Hooker's doctrine of God – he was, after all, a trained philosopher before he became a literary specialist – yet it is equally clear that the actual shape, direction and apologetic purpose of the *Laws* chiefly elicited his description. It is like that among most interpreters of Hooker's thought.

We, however, will take a different approach. Of course we must keep an eye on Hooker's apologetic aims; theology, after all, always has a context. But for great thinkers, more than immediacy informs their intellectual world and its expression. In the case of Hooker's doctrine of God, then, we want to move beyond the strict argumentative sequence of, for example, the *Laws*, to extract the philosophy and theology that support that sequence; at the same time, while the *Laws* by sheer magnitude of conception is the dominant source of Hooker's doctrine of God, we need to look to some of his other writings as well to fill out the picture. This chapter will turn its attention chiefly to the first and fifth books of the *Laws of Ecclesiastical Polity* and to sections of the *Dublin Fragments* with a few glances toward the early sermons. From those portions of Hooker's writings we can lay out the broad contours of his understanding of God in himself, 'theology' most strictly speaking, and of God as he extends himself as creator, what theologians typically call 'economy'.

There are challenges in this approach. One of them is reckoning with Hooker's allusive, even coy, use of sources. Beginning with Keble's edition of his works, and formidably in the latest critical edition and surrounding literature, Hooker's sources have been largely laid open; still, degrees of speculation remain, and nowhere more so than in the themes of this chapter. Reasons for this lay partly in the character of Hooker's apologetic purpose and audiences, partly in the conventions of writing and scholarship – so different from our own – and partly, perhaps, in constraints he may have felt owing to political expedience. We cannot be sure. The result is that we need to be attentive to the covert as well as to the overt clues Hooker gives us as we try to piece together his understanding of God and God in creation. That having been said, the chapter is divided into three parts taking up, first, the question of 'God-talk' and how it can be meaningful; second, four foundational descriptions of God; and third, the relationship between creator and creation.

Saying and Un-saying: The Necessary Dangers of Theology

The first book of Hooker's *Laws* is, among other things, a highly intricate and artfully compressed prolegomenon to all that will follow. At one level Hooker himself had alerted his readers to the fact that Book I would set the stage for the arguments throughout the ensuing books. At this level the overt conceptual focal point in Book I is law, as we might anticipate given the title of the work as a whole. Even at that level of forthright argument, though, Hooker is aware that, as so often in both art and nature, what strikes us most forcefully is what we do not immediately or easily see.[1] In the case of Hooker's doctrine of God what we do not readily see is how he approaches the task of theology in the spirit of Aquinas. He had affirmed, on the one hand, that we could speak truly about God, but that, on the other, 'one reaches the highest point of one's knowledge about God when one knows that one does not know him'.[2]

It is true that others have emphasised Hooker's reliance on the *Summa Theologiae* in Book I's exposition of law, but there is little appreciation of the extent to which Hooker's theological universe is fundamentally shaped by Aquinas' subtle synthesis of the cataphatic and apophatic traditions of theological discourse.[3] The distinction long predated Aquinas, but he worked them into a new synthesis so as to give talk about God rational coherence without losing sight of the unknowability of God in his essence. Hooker's few supporting citations (beyond the scriptural ones which predominate) indicate his embrace of those two theological streams: the cataphatic, emphasising the power to speak positively about God; and the apophatic, refusing to do so on the grounds that God is wholly beyond human conceptual grasp.

---

1. I, i, 2 [I, p. 198].
2. *De Potentia* 7.14; as quoted by Brian Davies, *The Thought of Thomas Aquinas* (Oxford, 1992), p. 58; see pp. 58-60 for his description of Aquinas' appreciation for both traditions.
3. W. J. Torrance Kirby refers to these two streams as a factor in Hooker's theology ('Reason and Law', *CRH*, pp. 251-71); another interesting appeal to those streams is Barry G. Ramsussen's essay 'Presence and Absence: Richard Hooker's Sacramental Hermeneutic', *RHER*, pp. 151-64.

Indeed, an explicit clue comes in the second chapter of Book I of the *Laws* where Hooker, launching into a densely affirmative exposition of God's working, quickly draws himself back from his words and his argument in an unexpected expression of negative reserve:

> Dangerous it were for the feeble brain of man to wade far into the doings of the Most High; whom although to know be life, and joy to make mention of his name; yet our soundest knowledge is to know that we know him not as indeed he is, neither can know him: and our safest eloquence concerning him is our silence, when we confess without confession that his glory is inexplicable, his greatness above our capacity and reach. He is above, and we on earth; therefore it behoveth our words to be wary and few.[4]

There the apophatic sensibility epitomised in Byzantine theologians like Dionysius and John of Damascus comes to the fore.[5] Whatever names for God we use, a Dionysian commentator has said, are 'mere inadequate symbols of That Which transcends all thought and existence'.[6] In Hooker's world, God is 'that light which none can approach unto'.[7]

How, then, is it possible to say anything truly and affirmatively about God? Both Aquinas and Hooker qualify that approach in their understanding of theological language. The opening of Book I makes clear that for Hooker, as for Aquinas, the starting point is the real, albeit limited, knowledge of God that comes from natural theology.[8] Romans 1.20 and 2.15 were commonplaces in the theological tradition's appeal to natural knowledge of God, knowledge, that is, that could be read from the world and human experience apart from revelation. What is striking throughout the *Laws,* beginning in its very first chapters, is the extent of Hooker's appeal to the tradition of natural theology.[9] In this he follows the lead of Augustine, and Aquinas more so, a fact that provoked a rebuke from the author of *A Christian Letter* who suspected Hooker's reliance on

---

4. I, ii, 2 [I, p. 201].

5. See, for instance, the former's treatise *On the Divine Names*, I, and the latter's *On the Orthodox Faith*, I, 1, where apophasis is affirmed. Both sources are significant to both Aquinas and Hooker.

6. So C. E. Rolt in his translation *Dionysius the Areopagite: The Divine Names and the Mystical Theology* (London, 1940), p. 7.

7. III, viii, 9 [I, p. 370].

8. 'For faith', Aquinas declares, 'presupposes natural knowledge just as grace does nature', *ST*, Ia. 2.2; see also Ia-IIae. 103.1 where he speaks of the 'sacraments of the law of nature'.

9. Hooker knew, of course, how much Augustine had contributed to that reliance in writings like his *On Christian Teaching*; on that theme see Ranall Ingalls discussion of Augustine's influence on Hooker in his thesis 'Richard Hooker on the Scriptures' (Ph.D. thesis, Lampeter [2004]), *passim*.

'Philosophy and schoolmen's divinity'.[10] That strand of thought does not suppose that such natural knowledge is saving knowledge, but it is real and useful nonetheless.[11] Book I, then, weaves natural and revealed theology into a concise distillation of insight into the being and working of God. Five couplets of ideas express the doctrine of God as Hooker presents it in the *Laws* and in his other writings.

One and Simple

Torrance Kirby has noted the centrality of God's oneness in the philosophical theology of neo-Platonism.[12] It was therefore readily assimilated by Christian divines as a primary attribute of God in their advocacy of Trinitarian monotheism. Immediately after his expostulation about reserve in humankind's knowledge of God Hooker moves back into an affirmative mode by asserting: 'Our God is one'.[13] In keeping with Aquinas' understanding of terms predicated of God, Hooker qualifies his first statement, 'Our God is one', by adding '*or rather very Oneness*'. His point, of course, is that God is indistinguishable from his attributes: God does not, as we might put it, *have* oneness as a characteristic, God *is* oneness.[14] And since that is partly what is meant by divine simplicity, Hooker continues his sentence by stating that God is also 'mere unity, having nothing but itself in itself, and not consisting (as all things do besides God) of many things'.[15] As we will see later, Hooker's insistence on the oneness of God in no sense rules out Trinitarian faith, but asserts God's numerical unity, uniqueness and indivisibility. Here, however, it is important for Hooker to establish a basis in natural and revealed theology, and to assert God's oneness and simplicity as the basis of coherence and consistency in all that God is and does.

Cause and Agent

If simplicity and oneness establish God's essential difference and distance from what he has made, his being the 'First Cause' sets God in relation to whatever effects flow from their cause. The apophatic tradition of Dionysius and others had, in fact, allowed a meaningful relationship

---

10. *ACL, FLE* IV, p. 72.
11. See Ingalls, 'Scriptures', p. 233.
12. 'Grace and Hierarchy: Richard Hooker's Two Platonisms' in Kirby, ed., *Richard Hooker and the English Reformation* (Dortrecht, Boston, London, 2003), p. 36; see there his note 7.
13. I, ii, 2 [I, p. 201].
14. Hooker's emphasis; I follow Brian Davies, *The Thought of Thomas Aquinas* (Oxford, 1992), pp. 68-9.
15. I, ii, 2 [I, p. 201].

between the divine cause and created effects; Aquinas' Christianised Aristotelianism built upon it, and Hooker embraces it. The relation between cause and effects recurs throughout his writings; for Hooker it is a metaphysical foundation. Here too the natural theology of antiquity's philosophers is Hooker's *point de départ*. After all: '[T]he wise among the very heathens themselves have all acknowledged some First Cause, whereupon originally the being of all things dependeth'. From there Aquinas' metaphysics take over so that Hooker weaves his own theological metaphysics around Aquinas' scheme of first and secondary causes, 'since', as Hooker explains what for him is a commonplace, 'on God as the most high all inferior causes in the world are dependent'.[16]

Yet the relation of first cause to secondary causes and effects is more than a relationship of dependence.

First, God's status as first cause means, by definition, that God is the origin of all activity. In Aquinas' reckoning that means that God is the most actual, so that Aquinas speaks of God as *pure act*, or, as we might put it, total actuality; in God there is no potential yet to be realised, no becoming. Hooker uses Aquinas' language of 'act' and 'potency' enough for us to be confident that he is thinking in Aquinas' terms. He does so further on in Book I when, for instance, he reminds us that in comparison with all created things which 'are somewhat in *possibility*', God alone is excepted 'who *actually* and everlastingly is whatsoever he may be, and which cannot hereafter be that which now he is not'.[17] As pure act God is therefore perfect. Further, God is perfect because he contains the perfections of all his creatures. So Aquinas argues, and Hooker, we can fairly suppose, agrees.[18]

As pure act God is also good. Hooker puts in like this in the *Dublin Fragments*: 'God hath a natural bent only, and infinitely, unto good'.[19] As for Aquinas existence is by definition good, so for Hooker: 'all things that are, are good'.[20] God as fully actualised existence is goodness itself, the cause of all goodness is in the effects that flow from God as first cause. All effects are more or less good to the extent to which they are actualised as themselves, that is, in their existence.[21]

Something of that movement from divine goodness to creaturely goodness, from the first cause to its effects, seems to be implied in what

---

16. V, xxiii, 1 [II, p. 115]; this comes in a discussion on prayer; see also his *Learned Sermon of the Nature of Pride*, III, where he describes the 'resemblance' of all effects to their 'supreme cause' [III, p. 624].

17. I, v, 1 [I, p. 215].

18. So Davies, *Aquinas*, p. 81; 'God is perfect because he is fully actual . . . For things are called perfect when they have achieved their actuality' (p. 85).

19. *DF*, V, App. I [II, p, 563].

20. I, v, 1 [I, p. 215].

21. *Ibid.* p. 66.

Hooker elsewhere calls the 'impartation of virtue'.[22] This is important to note; all effects from the first cause are meant to convey 'virtue' as goodness – both as a moral quality and as energy.

The relation of first cause to secondary causes and effects as Aquinas develops it is basic to the possibility of talking about God. Here we touch upon his use of analogy and analogical language; it is an approach which Hooker accepts, as we will explore in chapter twelve. Here, though, we note one important point: the extent to which it is possible to talk about God at all depends on the relationship between God as first cause to all created secondary causes and effects. The reason is clear both for Aquinas and Hooker: every cause is to some extent in its effect, and every effect to come extent partakes of its cause. Aquinas in fact had developed an insight asserted by Dionysius himself who, in his assertion of God's essential unknowability and the unlikeness of all created things to their creator notwithstanding, taught that created things are to some extent like the creator they seek to imitate.[23] To an extent, then, the limited perfections in creatures tell us something of the perfect attributes of God.

The description of God as 'First Cause' points also to divine freedom. God's freedom arises from the fact that God is *un*caused. But neither Hooker nor Aquinas, nor the writers of antiquity before them, wish to defend an arbitrary divine freedom. That is why Hooker complements his description of God as first cause with an assertion of divine *agency*. The philosophical consensus that Hooker here draws upon and articulates has, he insists, consistently spoken of the first cause 'as an Agent'.[24] That implies the primary attribute of personality by which is meant that the first cause is a self-conscious, intelligent Being with the power of choice. Hooker maintains that in so many words since this divine agent, he explains, 'knowing what and why it worketh, observeth in working a most exact order or law'; hence Hooker's approval of Plato's description of this divine agent as an '*intellectual* Worker'.[25]

Hooker then deduces from that a cadre of words and ideas which he will use as tools in the exposition yet to come, 'counsel' (*boulē*), 'reason' (*logos*), and 'way' (*hodos*), all of them compacted into two English terms comprehending their diverse but related significations: 'Order' and 'Law'.[26] As an intellectual worker, then, the 'First Cause' and 'Agent' regulates itself according to order and law and in the same way accomplishes all its effects.

---

22. *Ibid.*
23. *ST*, Ia. 4.3; the references is to Dionysius' *The Divine Names*, 9 (see Davies, *Aquinas*, p. 67). See the Second Eternal Law in Paget's taxonomy (p. 66).
24. I, ii, 3 [I, p. 201].
25. I, ii, 3 [I, pp. 201-2].
26. I, ii, 3 [I, p. 202].

Reason and Will

Since the relationship between cause and effect enables a degree of meaningful discourse about God on the basis of created reality, humankind offers special insight into who and how God is; after all, the first cause has created humankind in his 'image and likeness' (Genesis 1.26). That is the basis on which Hooker, like so many philosophical and theological predecessors, speaks of God in terms of reason and will. Of course what humans experience of themselves and describe as two distinct modes of activity, two differentiated faculties (to use a traditional nomenclature), are one in God, for God is simple; in him all aspects, like all attributes, are undifferentiated even as they are fully actualised.

The relation of reason and will in God had been periodically the focus of intense theological discussion, debate and development, both in the Byzantine period leading up to Aquinas' important source, John of Damascus, and in the western medieval tradition. It is a complex area into which we cannot wade far; however, several points have a bearing on issues which Hooker has cause to take up in his writings.

God: an *'Intellectual* Worker'

This phrase taken from Plato epitomises the posture Hooker takes in relation to late-medieval and Reformation-era views about divine reason and will. Sometimes the matter is put in these terms: which of the two has priority in God? That is not an accurate way to pose the question regarding divine reason and will, and Hooker does not put it that way. He knows that from the angle of God's simplicity, reason and will are indistinguishable. However, from the perspective of our attempts to decode divine action toward and in creation, Hooker thinks that reason and will relate in God in something like the way they do in human beings: that is, will inclines toward that which reason proposes as good. That, roughly speaking, was the approach taken by the Dominican school of Aquinas.[27]

Calvin and his successors, on the other hand, built upon an alternative emphasis on the primacy of will over reason in God associated with the theology of Aquinas' younger Franciscan contemporary, Duns Scotus. Up to, through and beyond the Reformation a stream of theological 'voluntarism' developed which, at least in caricatured form, credited the divine will with a dominance seemingly disconnected with reason. Calvin himself had declared in his *Institutes*, for instance, that something was just simply because God willed it.[28]

Hooker disagrees with that approach to reason and will in divine action.

---

27. See *ST*, Ia.19. 3.
28. See, for instance, III, 23, 5 [*LCC*, II, pp. 952ff.].

'They err', he says (leaving it tantalisingly unclear to whom he is referring!), 'who think that of the will of God to do this or that there is no reason beside his will'.[29] However far above human comprehension God's purposes may be, we may be sure that God 'worketh all things . . . not only according to his will, but "the Counsel of his own will"'. Hooker is quoting Ephesians 1.11, a text which reprises a key word that Hooker has already invoked in relation to God's ordered working, *boulē*, that is, the 'counsel' or 'wise resolution' in God that guides what God wills.[30] We may say, therefore, that insofar as God is an 'intellectual Worker', God wills intellectually, or reasonably.[31]

God's Two Wills

If the critics of Hooker's *Laws* disliked his scholastic bent, they took specific aim at his assertion that in God two wills operate, a general 'antecedent' will, and a particular 'consequent' will. Those were the terms ascribed to Hooker as early as his St Paul's Cross sermon which Hooker's biographer Walton notes was controversial.[32] Indeed, the terms provoked critical comment both soon after the sermon itself, and then much later in *A Christian Letter*; in each case criticism was connected with Hooker's recourse to scholastic and 'speculative doctrine' whose overall result, they feared, was to 'hoodwink'.[33]

The distinction was certainly scholastic; it appeared as an important distinction in Aquinas' article on predestination in part one of his *Summa Theologiae,* in the fourth Question, 'whether the elect are predestined by God'. In responding in favour of the question, Aquinas had to reconcile two apparently opposing scriptural texts: on the one hand, God's choice of some 'before the foundation of the world' (Ephesians 1.4); on the other, God's desire that 'everyone be saved and come to the knowledge of the truth' (1 Timothy 2.4). To reconcile Scripture's two testimonies Aquinas responded that 'God wills antecedently [*antecedenter*] that all men be saved', but that he does not will the salvation of all consequently [*consequenter*]'.[34] Aquinas emphasised that the distinction is not acceptable on the side of the divine will, which has no 'before and after', but is nevertheless real and meaningful on the side of things willed.[35]

---

29. I, ii, 5 [I, p. 203]; see also his *Learned Sermon of the Nature of Pride*, III [III, pp. 624-5].
30. *Ibid.*
31. Reason appears throughout Aquinas' writings as '*ratio*'.
32. *Life*, p. 177; see W. David Neelands, 'Richard Hooker and the Debates about Predestination, 1580-1600', *RHER*, pp. 45-8.
33. For the text of the 1585 critique see *FLE*, V, p. 286; for deceptive scholastic speculation see *A Christian Letter*, *ibid.* 5, pp. 6, 48-9.
34. *ST*, Ia. 23. 4; translations from Aquinas' works are mine unless otherwise noted.
35. Aquinas thus preserves the attribute of divine simplicity; Hooker surely

Aquinas himself appropriated the distinction from John of Damascus, one of his preferred Byzantine sources. In his own discussion of God's providence and predestination in *On the Orthodox Faith* the Damascene, drawing upon earlier eastern Christian responses to different kinds of necessitarianism in Islamic and pagan forms, had employed that distinction.[36] He likewise was trying to reconcile scriptural texts, and in a fashion less overtly analytic than Aquinas, associated God's antecedent will [*to proēgoumenon thelēma*]with his positive action in the world as the first cause of all goodness, and God's consequent will [*to hetomenon thelēma*] with particular permission to secondary causes. In its origins in eastern theology the distinction was part of a larger concern, namely to assert and defend God as the good and purposeful creator of all while allowing genuine, albeit relative, freedom to his creation and above all to humankind. From that point of view, the conceptual distinction regarding the divine will for John of Damascus, Aquinas, and Hooker allowed a degree of freedom to the created order by means of the notion of concession or permission as a function of God's consequent will.

Provident and Predestinating

From the time of his St Paul's Cross sermon onward, Hooker remained committed to that metaphysical distinction concerning God's will owing to its relevance to the matters of providence and predestination. Those were core biblical concepts which no orthodox theology could dismiss, so Hooker's doctrine of God had to include them.[37] There was, however, scope in *how* providence and predestination were related in God's self and in his workings *ad extra*. We will have occasion to take up these two topics in regard to Hooker's anthropology and Christology; now we must sketch the first steps in Hooker's understanding as a basis for the sharper focus it will take in some of the hotly debated confrontations of the day.

There are challenging interpretative issues in this regard. Did Hooker's view on providence and predestination change? If so, how and when? Above all, where does he stand in relation to alternatives around him?[38] What the growing literature on this vexed and vexing issue has so far not taken sufficient account of is Hooker's dependence on Aquinas for

---

realised that, in contrast to his critics who saw in it precisely a rejection of that primary divine attribute.

36. On this aspect of the thought of John of Damascus, see Andrew Louth, *St John Damascene* (Oxford, 2002), pp. 81-2, 142-3.

37. They were standard topics in doctrinal expositions and had been for centuries in both the Christian East and West.

38. Possible development in Hooker's views is explored by Egil Grislis, 'Providence, Predestination, and Free Will in Richard Hooker's Theology', *RHER*, pp. 79-98.

his view on providence and predestination. Aquinas, of course, worked with prior strands of thought, not least those of Augustine, so in taking inspiration from the angelic doctor Hooker is inserting himself into a rich and long theological tradition.

To help place Hooker's views there are several starting points to note in Aquinas' treatment of providence and predestination as they appear in the twenty second and twenty third articles of the *Summa Theologiae's* first part.

Providence

The content of Aquinas' view of providence is woven from a set of terms which are very much to the fore in Book I of the *Laws* and especially in its first five chapters: reason, order, end, necessity, contingency, freedom and goodness. In article twenty-two Aquinas defines providence as God's 'reason ordering things to an end'.[39] While there may be intermediate ends, every such end (*finis*) is good, and God's own self, 'divine goodness' (*bonitas divina*), is the ultimate end. Hooker understands that when he says in Book I that all perfections, that is, attainments of a providentially ordered end, 'are contained under the general name of Goodness'.[40] Later, in the *Dublin Fragments*, Hooker continues this Thomistic strain of thought when he explains how providence works through laws which are the 'general rules' by which God 'conducts' creatures to the end for which they were made.

Aquinas asserts that all things are under providence since, in light of Romans 13.1, everything is ordered to an end. We recall here Hooker's use of the word 'order' in the discussion of God as cause and agent, now complemented by the idea of end or fulfilment of purpose. In the tradition upon which Aquinas drew, and so for Hooker too, Wisdom 8.1 and 11.20 offered important insight into the way God's providential working orders his infinite power by finite means to finite ends: 'even "all things *chrēstōs*, in most decent and comely sort," all things in Measure, Number, and Weight'.[41] Elsewhere Hooker uses the word 'amiable' to describe God's action, rendering the Latin translation that Aquinas himself used for the same sapiential text.[42]

It is consistent with the subtlety and suppleness of divine providence, with its accommodation to what is not God, that it uses secondary

---

39. *ST*, Ia. 22. 1: '*Ratio autem ordinandorum in finem, proprie providentia est . . . Ipsa igitur ratio ordinis rerum in finem, providentia in Deo nominatur'*.
40. I, v, 1 [I, p. 215].
41. I, ii, 3 [I, pp. 202-3];
42. That is, '*suaviter*'; 'amiably' as Hooker elsewhere renders it (*DF*, V, App. I [II, p. 540]).

causes, some necessary and others contingent, to accomplish its unerring purposes.[43] Aquinas is emphatic about God's use of secondary causes as means in the accomplishment of his providential ends. While the reason according to which God providentially orders is inalienable to God's self, the exercise or governance of things to providential effect makes full use of necessary and contingent secondary causes.[44] Not only is God's use of such causes an expression of his goodness, it also lends dignity to his creatures.[45] In the case of humankind, whose unique place in God's providential scheme we will consider in the following chapter, we must note the following: God's reliance on secondary causes means that providence works *with* not *against* free will.

If, however, God foresees all occurrences, is it not the case that divine prescience in fact imposes necessity on all things, so as to void the contingency or freedom of free secondary causes? Aquinas denies that prescience in itself imposes necessity.[46] Hooker agrees. In things ordered by God's providence 'the foreknowledge which he hath of all things . . . doth not make all things to be of necessity'.[47]

Finally, Aquinas understands God's providence to work seamlessly through its ordering of the varied 'degrees' of creation. It works both universally and in particular, as Aquinas often repeats. It was axiomatic for him, under Dionysius' hierarchical scheme, that the perfection of goodness involved the coherent integration of multiple levels of secondary causes and effects, beautiful and good in their variety precisely because some are higher, some lower.[48] Hooker seems to have that comely gradation of being in mind when he speaks of God's 'abundance' showing itself in 'variety' and what Scripture calls '*riches*'. Thus, he says, all things 'shew beneficence and grace in them'. [49]

Hooker, then, follows Aquinas' closely in understanding the ways of providence. But in addition to all the similarities just described, Hooker follows Aquinas in his placement of predestination as a sub-set of providence.

---

43. God's providential purposes, at least at the general or universal level of the first cause, admit no alteration, a point Aquinas takes from the same Wisdom text cited above that speaks of God working not just *suaviter* but *fortiter*, 'strongly', 'mightily'.
44. Hooker devotes a section on 'The Tenth Article touching predestination' in the *DF* to necessary and contingent causality; his treatment, as I read it, accords with Aquinas' treatment in the relevant question of *ST*, Ia; see *DF*, V, App. I [II, pp. 557-61].
45. *ST*, Ia. 22. 3.
46. *Ibid*. 4.
47. *DF*, V, App. I [II, p. 561].
48. *ST*, Ia. 22. 4. So Paget's taxonomy illustrates (pp. 66-7).
49. I, ii, 4 [I, p. 203].

Predestination

Hooker firmly holds to the conceptual order set out in the *Summa Theologiae* where the question on predestination follows immediately after, and is tightly linked to, providence.[50] For Aquinas it is appropriate that since providence orders all things to an end, providence implies predestination for humankind. '*Predestinatio*', in fact, means for Aquinas being propelled forward toward an end as an arrow is shot toward a target.[51] Just as providence leads involuntary creation toward its appointed ends, so predestination sends humankind, as a voluntary agent, toward its supernatural end.[52] Hooker does not use that precise image but he accepts the same teleological definition, so that for Hooker, as for Aquinas, predestination is a part of God's providential care for humankind.

Two Eternal Laws

All that has been said so far leads to the assertion to which Hooker's opening argument has been leading: 'God therefore is a law both to himself, and to all other things besides'.[53] Torrance Kirby has distilled Hooker's argument in these first two chapters of the *Laws* down to what he calls Hooker's 'legal ontology', namely, 'God is Law'.[54] That overstates the case, I think, for we have seen how Hooker's explicit argument rests upon a doctrine of God in large measure influenced by Aquinas and preceding streams of thought which he himself synthesised and developed. Still, there is no doubt, as Kirby says, that Hooker's apologetic purpose is well served by highlighting the metaphysics of law as a principle for addressing concrete institutional issues.[55]

Having credited Aquinas as the source for so much of what we find in Hooker's treatment of law, there are nonetheless ways in which Hooker departs from his views. Chief among Hooker's divergences is his preference for a twofold division of the 'eternal law' of God. Whereas 'the learned' (and Aquinas among them) understand 'eternal law' as single, namely, 'that which with himself he [God] hath set down as expedient to

---

50. This differs from Calvin's placement in the 1559 edition of his *Institutes*. On this matter, and how Calvin's successors placed it in their doctrinal schemes, see François Wendel, *Calvin* (London, 1963), p. 268.

51. See Davies, *Aquinas*, p. 166, note 20.

52. Humankind is unique is having two basic ends: one proportional to created nature, another exceeding that proportion and so needing a strength from outside itself.

53. I, ii, 3 [I, p. 202].

54. 'Reason and Law', pp. 255, 251; he describes Hooker's approach as a 'radical, foundational proposal'.

55. *Ibid.* p. 252.

be kept by all his creatures, according to the several conditions wherewith he hath endowed them,[56] Hooker proposes another, 'first eternal law' that is prior to what he names the 'second eternal law' of the received tradition. He defines the first eternal law as 'that order which God before all ages hath set down with himself, for himself to do all things by'; it is what 'God hath eternally purposed himself in all his works to observe'.[57] While the formulation is not strictly Thomistic, most of the ingredients for Hooker's distinction are there in Aquinas' exposition in part one of the *Summa Theologiae*: divine reason ordering divine will in the self-diffusion of being and goodness outward in a creation which is ordered to its end in God as its ultimate good.

Such a description is more coherent, perhaps, when we notice how Hooker has enlarged his concept of law in keeping with the cadre of ideas constituting his doctrine of God. Law, he says, is more than 'that only rule of working which superior authority imposeth';[58] rather, law he takes to refer to 'any kind of rule or canon, whereby some actions are framed'.[59] McAdoo has aptly captured Hooker's enlarged sense of law by describing it as an 'inner directive'.[60] God's own unchangeable counsel is the content of the first eternal law. Does the view that God's being is a law to his working violate the freedom of God? No, says Hooker, for 'the imposition of this law upon himself is his own free and voluntary act'.[61]

So, then, Hooker's doctrine of God proposes a twofold eternal law: a first eternal law that is God's own, intrinsic to God's being, a law *ad intra*; and a second eternal law that is the expression of God's will and purpose toward all that is not God, that is, *ad extra*. We may well wonder why Hooker has taken such a step. What difference does it make?

It has been noted that this twofold scheme both widens and decreases the distance between God and creation. On the one hand there is the gathering of all derivative laws into relation with their creator in the second eternal law that draws the many into one. On the other hand, the distinction between that second eternal law and the first may be seen to sharpen the distinction between God and his creation, to preserve what Kirby calls the 'hypostatic distinction' between God and everything else. [62] That is a very useful insight.

We cannot be sure what Hooker's reasoning was. It may be that by the innovation he sought to guard against the erosion of apophatic sensibility among both the Thomists of his day and among his English co-religionists.

---

56. I, iii, 1 [I, p. 205].
57. I, ii, 6, and iii, 1 [I, p. 204]. See the First and Second Eternal Laws (p. 66).
58. See *ST*, Ia IIae. 90. 4.
59. I, iii, 1 [I, p. 205].
60. 'Richard Hooker', p. 121.
61. I, ii, 6 [I, p. 204].
62. So Kirby, 'Reason and Law', p. 254.

It may also be that, along those same lines, he felt that it honoured the primary apophaticism of the Byzantine sources to which Aquinas pointed him. Byzantine theology leading up to and beyond John of Damascus, for instance, was exploring what one interpreter has called 'two modes of eternity': one mode is the 'essential eternity' in which only the divine Trinity lives, the other mode is the 'contingent eternity' of the free acts of divine grace.[63] Hooker's two eternal laws bear a striking likeness to that paradigm. However that may be, Hooker's scheme of two eternal laws establishes a dynamic relationship between God, creation and humankind. It preserves God's radical otherness and freedom, and yet acknowledges the real connection and involvement with God in his creation not just as cause in its effects but as good and provident guide bringing what he has lovingly created to a good end.

A Triune Identity

Olivier Loyer tells us that Hooker's treatment of the Trinitarian mystery of God is brief, traditional and oriented toward his treatment of Christ and the sacrament of the Eucharist.[64] It is true that Hooker's most expansive treatment of this comes in the midst of Book V as a preface to Christological concerns relating to the sacrament.[65] In fact, though, God's Trinitarian identity is assumed throughout Hooker's discussions of God and, indeed, his entire field of theological exposition. Given one of Hooker's aims in Book I, namely to exemplify in his own argument how the sources of reason and revelation are mutually supportive in the grasp of truth, it figures that Hooker's treatment of God appears largely contained within the limits of natural religious apprehension. But throughout the *Laws* Hooker builds his case as an orthodox Trinitarian Christian; God's being and working is always the being and working of a tri-personal deity.

Early in Book I of the *Laws* Hooker makes clear that, given the 'compass' of his argumentative purpose there, he will not provide an account of the 'natural, necessary, and internal operations of God', the Trinitarian life of God *ad intra*; instead he will focus on God's voluntary operations, that is, God's free divine action 'by a voluntary purpose', the expression of Trinitarian life *ad extra*.[66] So we must go to Book V first to gain a clearer sense of Hooker's thinking about what it means for God to be Trinity.

63. So John Meyendorff explains the development in the chapter on 'Creation' in *Byzantine Theology* (New York, 1979), p. 131; his phraseology is that of George Florovsky in 'The Idea of Creation in Christian Philosophy', *Eastern Churches Quarterly*, 8 (1949): 67.

64. I, pp. 476-7.

65. V, li [II, pp. 220-22].

66. I, ii, 1 [I, p. 200].

The Master Theme: 'Being in'

Hooker's short but pointed descriptions of God's Trinitarian being and action look to Aquinas' important development of Trinitarian doctrine as it was distilled in his *Summa Theologiae*.[67] He took full stock of his Latin predecessors and then added to that patrimony two key themes from the Byzantine theology of John of Damascus: relations and '*perichoresis*'.[68] In the pertinent articles of the *Summa* Aquinas brings the three distilled insights of his Trinitarian thought together under the theme of 'being in' (*esse in*), based on John 14.11: consubstantiality, relation and procession or origin.[69]

Consubstaniality

The 'foreground' of the triune identity is the shared divine nature.[70] It follows from the simplicity of God and means too the indivisible unity of the nature and the person. For instance, wherever the Father's nature is, the Father's person is, and vice-versa. In Aquinas' reckoning the notion of perichoresis, or 'being in', does not displace the foreground of consubstantiality.

Hooker too emphasises consubstantiality as the first word in his Trinitarian theology. 'The Lord our God is but one Lord'. The Son is the 'consubstantial Word'; the Spirit whom we bless and magnify is 'co-essential'.[71]

Relations

Aquinas uses the word 'relation' to signify the distinct and unique mode of existence of each divine person. In his account the divine being of each person *is* the relation; it is a 'subsistent relation'.[72] Hooker explains Aquinas' teaching simply and concisely, like this: 'Every person hath his own subsistence which no other besides hath'.[73] The point of 'his own subsistence' is to confirm that in their reciprocal relating the divine persons relate *as themselves*, so that what is distinct about them as persons

---

67. Ia, 37-43. But Ingalls emphasizes Augustine's tacit influence ('Scriptures', p. 235).
68. For this term in the Damascene's thought see Andrew Louth, *St John Damascene* (Oxford, 2002), pp. 112-13, 174-5.
69. I am indebted here to the superb study by Gilles Emery, *The Trinitarian Theology of St. Thomas Aquinas* (Oxford, 2007), pp. 298-311. Aquinas does not use the inherited Latin terms for John of Damascus' perichoresis, e.g., *circumincessio*, but prefers the more biblical 'being in', inspired by John's Gospel.
70. Emery, *ibid*. p. 303.
71. V, li, 1 [II, p. 220].
72. A relative reality cannot exist without its correlative (Emery, *Trinitarian Theology*, p. 304).
73. *Ibid*. p. 221.

is not compromised by their mutual 'being in' one another. 'So that in every Person', Hooker explains, 'there is implied both the substance of God which is one, and also that property which causeth the same person really and truly to differ from the other two.' In such an account of 'relation' both Aquinas and Hooker are debtors to John of Damascus who introduced this important aspect into Trinitarian thought.

Procession or Origin

The third aspect of the triune identity is what Aquinas calls 'procession', referring to the distinct origin of each divine person. Succinctly, Hooker renders Aquinas' third element as follows: 'Seeing therefore the Father is *of none*, the Son is *of the Father* and the Spirit is *of both*, they are by these several properties really distinguishable each from other'.[74] One feels Hooker wishes to emphasise this aspect of origin. 'For', he continues

> The substance of God with this property *to be of none* doth make the Person of the Father; the very self-same substance in number with this property to be *of the Father* maketh the Person of the Son; the same substance having added unto it the property of *proceeding from the other two* maketh the Person of the Holy Ghost. So that in every Person there is implied both the substance of God which is one, and also the property which causeth the same person really and truly to differ from the other two.[75]

In reflecting on Hooker's theology at this point in Book V Loyer suggests that when he treats of the divine persons Hooker is less interested in what distinguishes them – though he wishes to be clear and orthodox on that – and more interested in their reciprocity and mutual relation.[76]

The Economic Trinity

Hooker's apologetic aims, however, focus his interest in Trinitarian theology not on the 'natural, necessary, and internal operations of God' which we have been describing, but on God's operations *ad extra*. We will take the subject up in detail in the next chapter. We now note a final element in the teaching of Aquinas which we find in Hooker also. God's life of 'being in' one another, or perichoresis, pertains in God's action toward and in the world as well. The persons, explains Gilles Emery, are inseparably present in the gift they make of themselves: 'in the same way that the persons *exist* indivisibly, so they *act* undividedly'.[77] For his part, Hooker explains that outward perichoretic action like this:

74. V, li, 1 [II, p. 220].
75. *Ibid.* pp. 220-1; Hooker's emphasis.
76. I, p. 477.
77. *Trinitarian Theology*, p. 308.

The works which outwardly are of God, they are in such sort of Him being one, that each Person hath in them somewhat peculiar and proper. For being Three, and they all subsisting in the essence of one Deity; from the Father, by the Son, through the Spirit, all things are. That which the Son doth hear of the Father, and which the Spirit doth receive of the Father and the Son, the same we have at the hands of the Spirit, as being the last, and therefore the nearest unto us in order, although in power the same with the second and the first.[78]

The communal presence of the three divine persons therefore extends outward in their communal action toward creation. They are accessible together, but each in a way proper to himself. The implication is clear for Hooker, as it was for Aquinas: in the Spirit's gift of grace the perichoresis of the divine persons extends toward and over us.[79]

Reprising an 'ecumenical' Vision of God

Hooker's doctrine of God, then, draws sensitively upon the tradition of natural theology and the witness of Scripture as interpreted by the two great streams of Latin and Byzantine thought. In the former, Aquinas dominates as Hooker's preferred interpreter of the legacy of Augustine. That Dominican line of thought establishes some critical demarcations from the thought-world of Calvin and his successors. In the latter stream John of Damascus prevails as the source of Byzantine insights carrying forward the tradition of theology that built on the determinations of the councils of Nicaea, Chalcedon and Ephesus. In his use of those sources Hooker presents a doctrine of God and theology of the Trinity that is far more than the 'primitive fullness' which John Keble admired.[80]

It is clear in the progression of this chapter that Hooker's doctrine of God moves from theology to economy, from God in God's self to God's activity in creation as an expression of his goodness. The progression reflects the distinction between the first and second eternal laws in the early chapters of Book I and indeed the larger movement of the book as a whole. So, having surveyed Hooker's doctrine of God with our focus on the first eternal law of God's own being, we can now turn to Hooker's understanding of the second eternal law and its unfolding as an expression of God's work in creation.

---

78. I, ii, 2 [I, p. 201].
79. Emery, *Trinitarian Theology*, p. 310.
80. So Keble describes Hooker's account in the Editor's Preface to his edition of Hooker's *Works*, I, p. lxxxi.

Chapter 4
'To Shew Beneficence and Grace'
Creation

We easily forget that the doctrine of creation is one of the main distinctive marks of the Christian mind.[1] If an adequate doctrine is the distinctive test of its integrity, then it is important to understand Hooker's stance. Admittedly, his apologetic interest does not lie in cosmology, that is, in a coherent interpretation of the origin, order and destiny of the world in the light of reason and revelation. Yet his desire to rest his arguments in the *Laws* on deeply embedded moorings, and to do so with sensibilities shaped by the Christian tradition before him, mean that a theology of creation does indeed arise, chiefly from the pages of Books I and V. Some of this material was a commonplace in his age, but behind and around those commonplaces, under-girding, nuancing, developing them to theological purpose, lies a structure of thought which places Hooker in the deep flow of Christian orthodoxy. This chapter seeks briefly to present Hooker's understanding of that tradition.

We begin by describing how Hooker views creation as the Trinity's work, then. From there we turn to the creation itself with an eye on four categories of description which figure in the *Laws*. We can then explicate briefly the scheme of laws of which the laws of ecclesiastical polity are a part and to which the subsequent books of the *Laws*, as well as Hooker's later writings, will refer.

A Radical Difference

In his exposition of union and difference in the Incarnate Lord Hooker gently adds these words: 'All other things that are of God have God in them and he them in himself likewise. Yet because their substance and his wholly differeth, their coherence and communion either with him or amongst themselves is in no sort like unto the before-mentioned.'[2] Almost as an aside Hooker states the bedrock of the Christian doctrine of creation: every created thing is *essentially different* from the creator, and as such is strictly speaking unnecessary.[3] This goes hand-in-hand with the

---

1. So George Florovsky begins the important essay, 'The Idea of Creation': 53.
2. V, lvi, 5 [II, p. 247].
3. The difference, John of Damascus emphasises, is 'in nature', or, as Hooker says, 'substance' (*On the Orthodox Faith*), I, 13.

doctrine of creation 'out of nothing' (*ex nihilo*) by which dependence on God, that is, the *contingency of created beings*, is grounded. As possessing a 'substance' that 'wholly differeth' from that of their creator, created things are involved with the creator God on terms radically different from terms operative among the three divine persons themselves.

Creation, therefore, is in no sense an emanation of the divine nature. Instead, according to the Christian view, it is a wholly free act of the divine will. Hooker is clear on this. His interest in Trinitarian doctrine in the *Laws*, we have already said, is not so much in God's being *ad intra* but in 'operations' outward, *ad extra*, and those are freely willed by God apart from any compulsion of nature: they are operations, that is, which 'have their beginning and being by a *voluntary purpose*'. God's free eternal 'decree' has established when and how those operations should be.[4] The creative fiat, George Florovsky reminds us, is a free and ultimate act of God.[5]

The Second Eternal Law

We have already suggested that Hooker's unanticipated addition of the second eternal law to Aquinas' scheme of 'eternal law' indicates something like a '*contingent eternity* of the free acts of Divine grace'.[6] In any case, Hooker's second eternal law may best be understood as a composite term for all that forms God's timeless volitional thought.[7] The 'thought' is the benevolent predeterminations, images, patterns which taken together form the eternal 'counsel' of God.

It is easy to see why Hooker's exposition in Book I is described as an adaptation of a kind of *logos* theology.[8] Its source is more likely Byzantine in the stream of theology leading to John of Damascus' synthesis. However that may be, for Hooker, as for Aquinas, the eternal Word or *Logos* as the thought of the Father is at the same time the thought that forms creation, and what will be willed by God in time and become creation is the expression of the beauty of the wisdom possessed of God in eternity.[9] The creative work of God *ad extra* is 'unbegun' in the eternal counsel just as an object is in an artist's conception before it is ever made.[10] 'Therefore', he explains,

> Whatsoever we do now behold in this present world, it was enwrapped within the bowels of divine Mercy, written in the

---

4. I, ii, 2 [I, p. 200]; emphasis mine.
5. 'Idea of Creation': 56.
6. *Ibid*: 67. See the Second Eternal Law (p. 66).
7. *Ibid*: 63.
8. So Kirby in his essay 'Reason and Law', p. 252.
9. I, ii.5 [I, p. 203].
10. V, lvi, 5 [II, p. 248].

book of eternal Wisdom, and held in the hands of omnipotent Power, the first foundations of the world as yet unlaid.[11]

We will later consider the Spirit with respect to creation. For now, however, we simply underline that the creation is the result of the economic, or outward, life and work of the Trinity:

The Father as Goodness, the Son as Wisdom, the Holy Ghost as Power do all concur in every particular outwardly issuing from that one glorious Deity which they all are. For that which moveth God to work is Goodness, and that which ordereth his work is Wisdom, and that which perfecteth his work is Power.[12]

Four Characteristics of Creation

Our approach to the material in the *Laws* is not to pursue the order of argument that Hooker himself pursues, but to extract from his sequence the structural themes upon which he builds his presentation. On that basis we must consider creation as abundance, creation and causality, creation and providence, and 'fallen' creation.

Abundance

Because God, according to Hooker, is 'of infinite goodness by nature', all that flows as creative effects are an expression of God's 'mere goodness'.[13] God expresses his goodness in activity outside himself that is 'gracious, beneficial and bountiful'.[14] That truth, which Hooker expounds in Book I as apprehended in a tentative way in pagan philosophy, is ratified and confirmed by revelation's story of the creation with God's determination that all that he has made should be good.[15] Christian revelation is clear that God's goodness expressed in creation is bountiful, and creation's 'abundance' shows itself in 'variety' or, in Scripture's word, '*riches*'.[16] None of it is beneficial to God; rather, it manifests God's own beneficence and grace.[17]

---

11. V, lvi, 5 [II, p. 248].
12. *Ibid.*
13. *DF*, V, App. I [II, p. 565].
14. *Ibid.*
15. See I, ii, 3 [I, p. 202] where Hooker discusses the creation of woman. Ingalls argues that Hooker is following Boethius here ('Scriptures', p. 227); the latter was a source for Aquinas too, and it is to his treatment of *bonitas* to which Hooker more probably is looking in the first chapter of the *Laws*.
16. I, ii, 4 [I, p. 203]; pp. 44-5
17. Hooker's use of the word 'grace' should be noted here; it is unclear what exactly he means by it, and how it differs from saving grace such as will be taken up in chapter eight.

Hooker is emphatic, however, that the abundance and richness that shows creation's goodness is not random or chaotic but ordered. Like his Elizabethan contemporaries, Hooker inherited a cosmology in which order was a principal good, the observance, as Shakespeare put it, of 'degree priority and place . . . course proportion season form office and custom . . . in all line of order'.[18] Wisdom's 'measure, number, and weight' point up the characteristics of this abundance.

The order of creation's richness is part of a macro-movement of procession and return. Although the origins of that twofold movement are pre-Christian and neo-Platonic, the schema was embraced by theologians and Christianised. Aquinas' *Summa Theologiae*, building on Christian neo-Platonic sources like Dionysius, is structured according that very twofold movement. For Hooker, therefore, it is a commonplace. It is important here because it highlights two aspects of the created order that we should note: first, it's dynamic character, the element of movement; and second, the teleological aspect of creaturely existence. The first aspect is expressed in the second.

In drawing upon Aquinas Hooker was in touch with a tradition of thought in which God's reason, or counsel, gives a reason, or implanted directive, to everything that is made.[19] The reason, then, is the pattern of operation by which something moves toward its end, by which it fulfils its purpose. The pattern of procession from and return to God is the framework within which particular elements of creation operate toward their God-appointed end, or purpose. It is important to stress that the 'end' involved is not an end in the conventional temporal sense. While creation has a beginning with and in time, it has no temporal end.[20] The 'end' in question is the perfection or fulfilment of something according to the divine counsel and decree by which it was first thought and then willed into being. It is creation's dynamic movement toward perfection – goodness – beyond itself that accounts for *desire* within created things. 'Desire' is a curious word to apply to involuntary things, it is true; strictly, it applies to voluntary agents, including humankind. But we should understand the word to mean the impulse toward fulfilment, becoming itself, in everything that is. In so desiring its fulfilment, a creature desires Goodness itself from which it came; for divine goodness is the consummation of all created goodness. '[S]ince there can be no goodness desired', Hooker explains,

> which proceedeth not from God himself, as from the supreme
> cause of all things; and every effect doth after a sort contain,

18. From 'Troilus and Cressida', quoted by E. M. W. Tillyard, *The Elizabethan World Picture* (New York, n.d.), p. 9. See his chapter on 'Order' with its discussion of Hooker, pp. 13-14.
19. Byzantine theology had termed such a directive *logos*; Aquinas *ratio*.
20. See Florovsky, 'Idea of Creation': 56.

at leastwise resemble, the cause from which it proceedeth: all things in this world are said in some sort to seek the highest, to covet more or less the participation of God himself.[21]

Causality

God's goodness also takes the form of sharing his function as cause. Whereas the triune God is, as we have seen, the first cause, God endows his creation with the 'dignity' (Aquinas' word) of causality. The result is a web of secondary causes, a chief form of the rich variety in creation that God's abundant goodness has birthed. A number of important consequences flow from this endowment of secondary causality to created things.

First, secondary causes play an important part in the movement from potentiality, or potency, to act. We have already seen how God is exempt from that conception since God is wholly actualised as the expression of his perfection. The creation, by contrast, is at various points between potency and act. So, whereas God cannot be other than he fully and everlastingly is, 'all other things besides are somewhat *in possibility*, which as yet they art not *in act*'.[22]

Second, 'inferior' or secondary causes can be either necessary or contingent. Hooker does not dwell on this aspect of secondary causality in the *Laws* but he takes it up at length in the *Dublin Fragments*.[23] The nature of the cause is seen in the nature of its effects. If the effects are variable, the cause is contingent; if the effects are 'uniform and constant in operation' the causes are likewise, that is, necessary.[24]

Providence

The significance of Hooker's view, which in broad terms if not in every detail is that of Aquinas, pertains especially to God's providential engagement with creation.[25] We can build somewhat on the points made in the previous chapter. First, for John of Damascus, Aquinas and Hooker God's providence is the expression of his love and goodness toward creation.[26] This was, in fact, a commonplace derived from the Christian declaration of the goodness of creation itself. Goodness itself always wills the good.[27] Beyond that, providence is God's good and regular care for creation. From both John of Damascus and Aquinas Hooker had learned

---

21. I, v, 2 [I, p. 215].
22. I, v, 1 [I, p. 215]; emphasis mine. Paget describes this movement as 'progress' (pp. 66-7).
23. In the article 'touching predestination' [II, pp. 557-563].
24. *Ibid*, p. 557.
25. Aquinas treats providence in *ST*, Ia. 23.
26. Those two forebears built on insights of Nemesius of Edessa and Boethius respectively.
27. See, for instance, *On the Orthodox Faith*, I, 1 where John of Damascus affirms this.

in that regard that providence 'orders all things to their end'.[28] It is the divine 'counsel' (Ephesians 1.11) itself, says Aquinas, citing the very text that Hooker does when he asserts how reason informs the divine will.[29] Finally, for both Aquinas and Hooker God's eternal *providence* expresses itself in the temporal *governance* of secondary causes, both necessary and contingent, by which the divine plan and decrees are accomplished.

The streams of Byzantine and Latin thought upon which Hooker draws distinguished, as we have seen, between the divine 'antecedent' and 'consequent' wills. They made a further, important distinction which Hooker also uses, namely, between *approval* and *permission*.[30] Simply, the divine will approves, that is, actively supports, all that is good and works for good in creation; that same will only permits what is not good. However such a view may measure up to contemporary critical analysis, it was accepted by its originators as a way to maintain the goodness of God and the freedom of God's creation while recognising the fact of defection from nature's order and outright moral evil. Hooker accepts that distinction (and in so doing separated himself on a key point from Calvin and the Calvinist mainstream of his day). The distinction had an impact on understanding causes too: the first cause can only be a cause of what is good, whereas secondary causes, insofar as they are contingent, may be the cause of good *or evil*. Again, Hooker accepts that conceptual framework. This has important consequences for Hooker's anthropology, as we shall see.

Creation 'Spiritualised'

The direction of the exposition leads us to consider the place of the Holy Spirit in creation. We have already noted Hooker's portrayal of the Holy Spirit as the member of the triune community who is 'nearest' to creation, and whose mode of personal existence is 'power'. If the structures of creation which Hooker calls 'laws' are 'original draughts written in the bosom of God himself' associated with the Word, then their instantiation and operation are associated with the Spirit.

Hooker's vocabulary and manner of expression in this matter is not wholly clear, perhaps not even fully formulated in detail. Still, the broad view can be sketched. As a divine and infinite 'substance', God's presence is of the character of that substance: omnipresent. 'He filleth heaven and earth, although he take up no room in either,' says Hooker,

> because his substance is immaterial, pure, and of us in this
> world so incomprehensible, that albeit no part of us ever be

---

28. So Aquinas, *ST*, Ia. 23.1: 'The ordering of all things to their end, and especially to their final end, which is the divine goodness, is providence'.
29. See I, ii, 5 [I, p. 203], referenced in the previous chapter.
30. So John of Damascus in *On the Orthodox Faith*, II, 29; *ST*, Ia.19-26.

absent from him who is present whole unto every particular thing, yet his presence with us we no way discern farther than only that God is present, which partly by reason and more perfectly by faith we know to be firm and certain.[31]

Without denying the co-presence of the entire Trinity, Hooker also describes the Spirit as the 'executor' of God's providential care and purpose for creation as expressed in the laws that constitute the created *order*. The Spirit 'useth every particular nature, every mere natural agent'. If nature is 'nothing else but God's instrument', then the Spirit is truly the divine wind by which the instruments make their harmony.[32]

In acting thus, the Spirit executes God's providential plan for creation and works within created things to actualise the potential according to the laws of their being, leading all things to their 'end'. Insofar as those laws are implanted directives, the Spirit, in Hooker's account, energises them. But in so doing, the Spirit honours the necessary and contingent character of what it fills, uses and energises. We may add, in light of what has preceded in this section, that nature's seeking 'the highest' and coveting 'more or less the participation of God himself' – for providence orders things above all to their final end – is the Spirit's work as it empowers the creation to actualise its potential in its return to the Trinitarian source whence it first came.[33]

A Foundational Axiom

These comments on the Spirit's providential work in creation are the basis upon which Hooker retrieves and applies a foundational axiom which Aquinas had articulated so concisely: 'grace perfects nature and does not abolish it'.

Hooker works with that concept throughout the *Laws* and his other writings. Sometimes he even loosely translates it, as in Book III when, interpreting 1 Corinthians 2.14, he proposes that while 'nature hath need of grace', so 'grace hath use of nature'.[34] In proposing this, however, Hooker not only follows Aquinas but the whole scholastic tradition as it stands in the central stream of Christian theology both western and eastern. We need not dwell on the axiom here since it is everywhere in the chapters that follow and will be especially pertinent in our consideration of grace. For now we note how it epitomises in Hooker's theology of creation the careful balance of distinction with involvement, difference with 'being in' that marks his theology of the Trinity.

---

31. V, lv, 3 [II, p. 239].
32. I, iii, 4 [I, p. 210]. What can Hooker mean here by 'substance' insofar as uncreated and created substances are, as we have seen, radically different?
33. I, v, ii [I, p. 215].
34. III, viii, 6 [I, p. 367].

A Hierarchy of Laws

If Book I of the *Laws* is famous for anything it is for the hierarchy of laws which Hooker unfolds, beginning in chapter four. In these chapters Hooker reveals himself as a man of his time, imbued with a firm, vivid, inherited sense of reality as a great 'chain of being'.[35] The idea was by no means new to the Elizabethans. They inherited it from a long line of Christian and pagan thinkers.[36] As a Christian concept it flourished in the rich mixture of biblical and neo-Platonic ideas as presented, for instance, in the writing of Dionysius. There is Aquinas' source for his own hierarchical cosmology and array of laws as we find it in the *Summa Theologiae*.

For all of those pre-modern thinkers the Dionysian concept of hierarchy was one of connection and solidarity more than of division and distinction, though the concept includes both aspects. In the last book of the *Laws* Hooker is minded to recall that foundational principle of hierarchy:

> The whole world consisting of parts, so many, so different, is by this only thing upheld; he which framed it hath set them in order. Yea, the very Deity itself both keepeth and requireth for ever this to be kept as law, that wheresoever there is a coagmentation of the many, the lowest be knit to the highest by that which being interjacent may cause each to cleave unto other, and so all to continue one.[37]

Furthermore, hierarchy expresses the twofold movement of procession and return, of God's movement outward in creating, on the one hand, and the creation's return to the supreme Beauty, God, on the other.[38] It is in that sense, at least, that Hooker, following Dionysius and Aquinas, uses the idea as a description of reality.

At the same time the hierarchical universe, precisely as a form of divine *order*, gave everything not just a place but a *valued* place. The hierarchical chain of being accorded to each class or level, from the lowest to the highest, its own particularity.[39] Hooker knows and appreciates that aspect of hierarchy.[40] Here again we encounter the twin dynamics of distinction and solidarity, oneness (through connection) and multiplicity (through particularisation).

---

35. See chapter four on this very idea in Tillyard, *Elizabethan World*.
36. See Kirby 'Hooker's Generic Division of Law', pp. 251-71.
37. VIII, ii, 2 [III, p. 342].
38. So Louth describes the Dionysian view, *Denys*, p.52.
39. Tillyard, *Elizabethan World*, p. 29.
40. See I, vi, 1-2 [I, p. 217].

The Divisions of Laws

There are various ways to view the system of laws that Hooker describes through Book I. The laws of the system are not themselves the secondary causes of which we have spoken; if the secondary causes are the warp then the laws, precisely as 'directive rules unto goodness of operation', are the woof of the fabric of reality for which providence has care.

The system of laws which Hooker describes is an explication, so to speak, of his second eternal law and an expression of God's providential care for what he has made.[41] Kirby reminds us that from above, that is, from the divine point of view, the second eternal law is one, while from below it is expressed in rich diversity. It is that picture from below which Hooker paints on the canvass of Book I.

Broadly speaking Hooker's arrangement follows the *Summa*, but there are divergences to be noted.[42] It has been said, for instance, that whereas Hooker's general tendency is to simplify Aquinas' thought, in the case of his system of laws Hooker actually complicates the picture.[43] Specifically and as we have already seen, Hooker applies the notion of law to God's self. Hooker also adds a category of celestial law. It pertains to the immaterial, intellectual angels, and guides them in their 'high and admirable venture' of ceaseless adoration of God.[44] Hooker then stands on firmer ground with the laws of nature. But here too he distinguishes more than Aquinas does: the laws that guide involuntary agents Hooker describes as 'natural law', whereas the laws of voluntary agents, that is, humankind, Hooker calls the 'law of reason'.[45] So then, from the second eternal law flows a threefold categorisation: first, the law of natural agents; second, the law of angels, or the celestial law; and third, the law of men.

The Law of Men

As we can well suppose, Hooker has a special interest in the category of laws that relate to humankind. We will return to it in the following chapter and elsewhere. Here we need to note how this law itself is divisible into further subcategories. Francis Paget's at first somewhat alarming 'pedigree' of laws usefully and precisely maps these further distinctions as well as the overall system.[46]

The foundation of the 'law of men' is what Aquinas called natural law, but which Hooker prefers to title the 'law of reason'. Hooker wishes to

---

41. Thornton, *Hooker*, p. 104. See Paget's taxonomy (pp. 66-7).
42. On the general indebtedness see Munz, *Place of Hooker*, pp. 29-67, 177-93.
43. So Daniel Westberg, 'Thomistic Law and the Moral Theology of Richard Hooker', *American Catholic Philosophical Quarterly*, 68: supplement (1994): 206-7.
44. I, iv, 3 [I, p. 214].
45. Though, as we have noted elsewhere, Hooker is not consistent in his terminology.
46. *Introduction*, p. 99, reprinted below (pp. 66-7).

The First Eternal Law (iii. I).

That law which giveth life unto all the rest (i. 3). That order which GOD before all ages hath set down with Himself for Himself to do all things by (ii. 6. Cf. Sermon iii. pp. 624-626). The Being of God is a kind of Law to His Working; for that Perfection which GOD is, giveth Perfection to that He doth (ii. 2).

The Second Eternal Law

That order which with Himself GOD hath set down as expedient to be kept by all His Creatures, according to the several condition wherewith He hath endued them (iii. I).

The Law of Natural Agents, which keep the Law of their kind unwittingly (iii.2).

The Law which directeth them in the means whereby they tend to their own perfection (iii. 5).

The Law which toucheth them as they are sociable parts united into one body (iii. 5).

The Law of Angels

Considered each severally in himself: the Law whereby they (1) love, (2) adore, and (3) imitate GOD (iv. I).

Considered as associated: the Law which disposeth them as an army, one in order and degree above another (iv. 2)

Considered as having communion with us: the Law which bindeth them to works of ministerial employment (iv. 3).

The Law of Men, a Law of continual progress to that Perfection which is in GOD alone (v. I, 2).

The Law of Progress towards that Perfection which is most closely united to the creature that desire it: the goodness (1) of continuance in being, and (2) of constancy and excellency in its proper operations (v. 2, 3). [This Law being common to Man with all things in the world.]

The Law of Progress towards that goodness which grows externally (v. 3.)

The Law of Progress in the Exercise of Virtue: by the activity of the Will inclining to have or do that which is by the understanding made known to it as good and possible (vii. 4, 5), this knowledge being conveyed in Laws Natural, Human, or Supernatural.

The Law of Progress in the Knowledge of Truth: by the power of reason, emerging above sense, and then further advanced by the right helps of true art and learning (vi. 3).

Natural Laws* (Laws of reason, or of Nature.) The Mandates, which being imposed by the understanding faculty of the mind must be obeyed by the will of man (viii. 7). That which men, either by the direct discernment of clear and manifest principles, or by necessary inference from such principles so discerned, have, with the help of GOD (vii. 11), rightly found out themselves to be all for ever bound unto in their actions (viii. 8). Sentences either mandatory, permissive, or admonitory: but, properly, sentences mandatory (viii. 8). Discerned either (1) by the knowledge of the causes whereby goodness ismade such: or (2) by the observation of those signs and tokens which are annexed unto goodness (ix. 2). Enforced by that all-pervading Law of God which attaches welfare to the fulfilment of a creature's proper work and ruin to its abandonment (ix. 1). [Laws Natural do always bind: i.e. are all permanent (xv. 1).]

Human Laws or Laws Politic: Imposed by Societies of men; resting on the consent, express or implicit, of that Society: binding by virtue of that power which GOD, by Natural Law, has given to entire Societies (x. 8; cf. V. viii. 3), devised to preclude uncertainty or arbitrariness in the action of the rulers whom either the consent of the Society of the immediate apponginment of GOD has set to govern. These Laws are either Mixedly Human, i.e., Natural Laws affird and ratified by the authority of the Society: or Merely Human, i.e. enforcing something which reason doth but probably teach, and which therefore is not binding until so enforced. [Some Human Laws therefore are Natural, and so essentially Permanent: some are Positive, and so Permanent or Changeable according to their subject-matter (xv. 1).] Laws Human must be made according to the general Laws of Nature, and without contradiction unto any positive Law of Scripture (xvi. 5; cf. III, ix. 2) [Cf. also III. Viii. 18.]

Laws concerning a man's duty in relation to himself (viii. 6).

Laws concerning a man's duty in relation to men (viii. 7).

Laws concerning a man's duty in relation to GOD (viii. 7).

Laws concerning men linked with others in some form of politic society * [i.e. concerning each several state] (x. 12).

* Within each of these three kinds there is a distinction between Primary and Secondary Laws: the one grounded upon sincere, the other built upon depraved Nature (x. 13).

† The Church, being both a Society and a Society supernatural, has a twofold bond of association: being ordered (1) by Politic Laws, made by the Society, and (2) by Supernatural Laws revealed by GOD Himself concerning the substance of His Service (xv. 2; cf. III. Xi. 13, V. iv. 3)

Laws made by a Body Politic which is civilly united (x. 11).

The Law of Nations, touching all such bodies politic, so far forth as one of them hath public commerce with another * (x. 13).

Laws concerning severally the distinct Societies into which the Catholic Church is divided: Societies the place and limits whereof are certain: unto every of which the name of a Church is given, with addition betokening severally: as the Church of Rome, England, etc. (III. i. 14).

Laws of Spiritual Commerce between Christian Nations: Laws by virtue whereof all Churches may enjoy freely the use of those reverend, religious, and sacred consultations which are termed Councils General (x. 14).

Laws made by a Body Politic which is spiritually joined, and makes such a Body as we call the Church (x. 11).

As the Church is a Visible Society and Body Politic, Laws of Polity it cannot want (III. Xi. 14). Touching things which belong to discipline and outward polity, the Church hath authority to make canons, laws, and decrees, even as we read that in the Apostle's times it did † (III. X. 7). [Cf. V. viii, VIII. Vi. 1, 5).

Laws that concern men supernaturally as men, declaring duties which belong of necessity to all (xv.2).

Laws that concern men as parts of a supernatural society, which society we call the Church: Laws which GOD Himself hath revealed concerning that kind of worship which His people shall do unto Him (xv.2). Unto all Christian Churches a rule of the chiefest things † (x.14).

Supernatural Laws: Revealed by GOD to teach man how that which is desired naturally [viz. the absolute end, the infinite good, the perfect happiness of union with GOD (xi. 1-3)] may now [since guilt has disabled man from the means of attaining it, as the reward of good works (xi. 5)] supernaturally be attained (xii. 3, Sermon ii, § 23, Sermon iii. §15.) Laws concerning the supernatural way unto that end of life, the way of supernatural duty: the way of Faith, Hope, and Charity, through the Compassion of GOD, and the precious Death and Merit of our Saviour (xi. 6). Laws which, though for the most part they inculcate what is supernatural, yet sometimes incorporate and re-assert Natural Laws (xii. 1, 3). These Laws are contained in or may be deduced from Scripture: but (1) Scripture presupposes men to be already by other means (involving the use of understanding) persuaded of certain principles, of which one is the sacred authority of Scripture (xiv. 1); and (2) the sufficiency of Scripture does not exclude from authority rites and customs known to be Apostolical (xiv. 5). [Laws that concern supernatural duties are all positive: and therefore permanent or changeable according as the matter is concerning which they were first made (xv. 2, 1).]

anchor all other laws that relate to humankind – and they are numerous, as Paget's scheme shows – to the set of inner directives, discernible by reason, which guide human beings toward their perfection.

Supernatural Law

It is clear in Book I, however, that amid the array of laws ordering humankind toward its providential end supernatural law has a pre-eminent place. In that respect, Kirby is right to see in Hooker's system a threefold distinction between the second eternal law, on the one hand, and natural and supernatural law, on the other.[47] Paget's 'pedigree', for all its detail, easily obscures this. Indeed, given Hooker's polemical aims, the system of laws in Book I is not meant by any means to obscure or marginalise supernatural law. Rather, Hooker aims at a world-view that is more properly proportioned and balanced in accordance with reality than that of non-conformists. It means setting and seeing the particular, indeed unique, role of supernatural law in relation to the other laws by which humankind's place in the cosmos, and in the movement of procession and return, is structured and guided.

To What Purpose?

The cosmology arising in Book I was not merely an exercise in metaphysical speculation. However important and interesting it is as a component of a theological vision, it also has an argumentative edge. We can fittingly end this chapter by describing how that is so in three respects. First, the division of laws implies that guidance in any province of life should be sought in the laws relevant to that province. Second, while Hooker's interest is to 'distinguish and disentangle' what careless language readily does not, all laws are of God, all derived, says Paget in a brilliant phrase, 'from the same eternal law *reading itself out to the world*'.[48] Lastly, Hooker's system of laws underlines permanence and mutability in laws, and emphasises the importance of aptness or fitness for purpose in the laws which are mutable. In this Hooker never loses sight of the *telos* or end – the *finis* in Aquinas' language – toward which all laws are meant to steer those aspects of creation in which they are implanted or upon which they bear.[49]

What began deep in metaphysical concerns ends with a stance *vis-à-vis* contested issues of practical church polity. That, of course, reflects with accuracy the place of Book I and its concern with cosmology. We will see, however, how his 'model' of the universe, so 'drenched with Deity', moulds and shapes the various aspects of his theology as a whole.[50]

---

47. 'Reason and Law', p. 260.
48. *Fifth Book*, p. 100.
49. I am indebted to Paget for these three points of application (*ibid.* pp. 99-103).
50. Lewis, *English Literature*, p. 459.

Chapter 5
'The Noblest Creature in the World'
Humankind

Even a cursory reading of Book I might lead a reader to agree with C. S. Lewis' description of the *Laws* as a treatise *de dignitate hominis*, 'on the dignity of man'.[1] Insofar as that is so, it flows from the positive doctrine of creation of which in large measure the Christian understanding of humankind – its origin, constituent aspects and activities, its purposes and goal – is a part. It is true, as A. J. Joyce has observed, that Hooker nowhere provides a methodical and detailed theological anthropology such as we find in Aquinas' *Summa Theologiae*,[2] but it remains the case that the character of Hooker's apologetic situation, not just in the case of the *Laws*, but in fact throughout his writings, required attention to anthropological issues. Did not the author of *A Christian Letter* target a prime concern in that realm, namely the freedom of the will, when he charged Hooker with writing 'clean contrary' to the supposed teaching of the Church of England's formularies?[3] Hooker's response in the *Dublin Fragments* sought to settle the matter, but in fact Hooker's legacy in this sphere, as in so many others, has provoked divergent views.[4]

Our purpose in this chapter is to continue our line of description and analysis regarding analysis from creation generally to humankind, 'the noblest creature in the world'.[5] We will track the 'journey' of humankind from its first creation, through its fall and up to its point of need *in via*. Such an approach cannot ignore the saving economy since Hooker's own account presumes it as the operative key and lens. The economy of Son and Spirit will be considered in greater detail in following chapters.

This chapter will not exhaust issues of theological anthropology. We will return to specific aspects of it in the chapters on moral, spiritual and political theology. What we will explore here provides the ground upon which further insights into Hooker's anthropology and its implications

---

1. *English Literature*, p. 461.
2. *Richard Hooker & Anglican Moral Theology* (Oxford, 2012), p. 69; see *S. T.*, Ia.75-83, 90-102; moreover, he says, it 'coheres' with Aquinas' account (p. 86).
3. *ACL, FLE*, IV: 17; the author refers to Article 10, Of Free will.
4. See Joyce's helpful review of them, *Anglican Moral Theology*, pp. 70-3.
5. I, ix, 1 [I, p. 237].

can emerge. So here we will take up the stages in the human 'journey' from and to God with insights drawn chiefly from Book I of the *Laws*, the *Dublin Fragments*, and early sermons where pastoral concerns give some useful and constructive accents.

The Gift of Being Human

The metaphor of the journey is a good place to begin consideration of Hooker's anthropology. Torrance Kirby points out that the creation of humankind is the focal point of the movement of procession and return which, as we have seen in the previous chapter, characterises the creation as a whole.[6] Within that movement from and toward God three features distinguish the human journey: *imago Dei*, microcosm, and beatitude.

If humankind is the focal point of procession and return, and of the laws which make that possible, it is so because humankind is made 'in the likeness of his Maker' (Genesis 1.26). This 'resemblance', according to Hooker, shows itself 'in the manner of working' that distinguishes humankind from the rest of creation, namely, by reason and will. Of will more follows below. Here we highlight reason since that above all bears the honour of divine resemblance. In the *Dublin Fragments* Hooker reiterates his point in the *Laws* by saying that 'reasonable creatures' are 'the liveliest representations of his own perfection and glory'.[7] And with the Augustinian legacy by his side, this human rationality includes memory, understanding, and will.[8]

Most importantly regarding reason is its capacity to discern truth, and to grasp by understanding the final causes, or purposes, of things, and man himself above all. In Hooker's understanding, humankind's first parents were able to know and keep the laws of creation perfectly through the exercise of reason which rightly discerned nature's laws and humanity's purpose.

Precisely on account of such distinctiveness Hooker describes humankind as a 'microcosm', or 'a very world in himself'.[9] Here, as in the themes of order and the chain of being, Hooker articulates an idea current among the Elizabethans which had a long and noble theological ancestry. His contemporaries could see in the human being the summing up in itself of the variety of earthly phenomena.[10] There was, after all, a kind of hierarchy of composition within: soul above body at the centre, with the lesser appetitive part, on the one hand, and the higher, more divine part, namely, reason and will, on the other.[11] Precisely as an embodied

6. 'Reason and Law', p. 254; similarly, see his essay 'Grace and Hierarchy', p. 39.
7. V, App. I [II, p. 566]; the 'reasonable creatures' include angels.
8. Ingalls, 'Scriptures', p. 251. E.g. Paget's Law of Progress in the Knowledge of Truth (p. 66).
9. I, ix, 1 [I, p. 237].
10. Tillyard, *Elizabethan World*, p. 28.
11. Paul Surlis, 'Natural Law in Richard Hooker', *Irish Theological Quarterly*,

spirit sharing creation's insensate and sensate aspects, humankind was a concentrated expression of the cosmos. In its theological origins there was more, of which Hooker may have been aware: as a composite creature, humankind was seen to have a unique role in overcoming division, and in gathering all things together in the expectation of creation's final goal.[12]

Insofar as man shares his highest part, that is, his intelligence or rationality, with the angels, with them he also shares a desire for an infinite good. Infinite good alone can satisfy human nature; it is the end, or purpose, of his most defining inner directive.[13] Humankind's nature is such that it seeks beatitude, a supernatural happiness. For humankind happiness is the satisfaction of all desire. Hooker explains in the *Laws*:

> Happiness therefore is that estate whereby we attain, so far
> as possibly may be attained, the full possession of that which
> simply for itself is to be desired, and containeth in it after an
> eminent sort the contention of all our desires, the highest degree
> of all our perfections.[14] We are happy, Hooker concludes, 'when
> fully we enjoy God'.[15]

'The Ancient law of human freedom'

Whether or not Hooker had actually encountered that phrase from the third century church father Irenaeus of Lyons is less important than the fact that it highlights a key element in Hooker's anthropology, freedom, and more precisely, the freedom of the will.[16] It was a fiercely disputed topic in Reformation polemic, and it continued thus in the disputes between conformist and non-conformist Elizabethan churchmen. Hooker could hardly have avoided the issue, and nor did he. The challenge of *A Christian Letter* elicited a lengthy reply in which the issue of human freedom was central.

The basis of Hooker's argument in favour of the freedom of the will is the continuity of human nature from first creation through the fall to salvation and beatitude. If humankind is made in God's likeness, and if that resemblance includes will, which by definition includes the power to choose, then it follows that for humankind to be its natural self it must have freedom of choice.

To nuance his approach Hooker employs a distinction, draw from Augustine, between 'aptness' and 'ability'. At its first creation, Hooker

---

XXXV: 2 (1968): 183; see I, viii, 6 [I, p. 230].
12. On the patristic and Byzantine uses of the idea see Lars Thunberg, *The Vision of St Maximus the Confessor* (Crestwood, USA, 1985), p. 73; see also Louth, *John of Damascus*, p. 134.
13. Kirby, 'Reason and Law', p. 259.
14. I, xi, 3 [I, p. 255].
15. I, xi, 2 [I, p. 255].
16. Florovsky cites the phrase ('Idea of Creation': 75).

argues, humankind had both an *aptness* to make choices and an *ability* to make sound ones leading to beatitude according to right reason. That was possible by means of a general grace that made the exercise of freedom on behalf of God's appointed end possible but not inevitable.[17] The importance of this appears by means of a simple syllogism discernible in Hooker's description of the natural way to happiness; he explains,

> for presupposing that the will of God did determine to bestow eternal life in the nature of a reward, and that rewards grow from voluntary duties, and voluntary duties from free agents; it followeth that whose end was eternal life, their state must needs imply freedom and liberty of will.[18]

Most important in Hooker's discussion of freedom, as indeed of all the faculties that distinguish humankind, is that in their original intent and form, freedom and grace go hand in hand. 'What makes man truly man', a modern theologian has said, 'is the presence of this Spirit of God'.[19] Hooker agrees.

The Human Problem

While it would misrepresent Hooker to claim that the fall of humankind into sin is the determining feature of his anthropology, Hooker takes the issue of the fall of humankind very seriously as recorded in the first two chapters of Genesis and then developed in the New Testament. But taking it seriously can imply a variety of responses, and on this matter the author of *A Christian Letter* thought Hooker soft, charging him with failure to respect 'how in trueth we are by Adams fall perverted'.[20]

In fact Hooker calculates and quantifies the phenomenon of sin differently from his non-conformist critics.[21] For instance, he uses the phrase 'original sin' sparingly throughout his works; its concentrated use occurs during his last years in the *Dublin Fragments*. Given his focus there on grace and, by consequence, anthropology, we would expect that. Nevertheless, the idea, if not the exact phraseology, appears much earlier, as in his sermon *Of the Certainty and Perpetuity of Faith*. There Hooker describes how the minds of fallen humankind are 'darkened . . . with the foggie damp of original corruption', what years later in the *Dublin Fragments* he calls our 'native corruption'.[22] Reason is for Hooker the focal point of the fall; he likens it to intellectual sloth, a lazy preference for ignorance.[23] That corruption is a weakening disease as a result of

---

17. *DF*, V, App. I [II, p. 567].
18. *DF*, V, App. I [II, p. 567]; see also I, xi, 5 [I, p. 258].
19. John Meyendorff, *Living Tradition* (Crestwood, USA, 1978), p. 175.
20. *FLE* 4: 19; the context is a discussion of the capacities of fallen reason.
21. Gibbs makes this point 'Book I', *FLE*, VI, I: 105ff.
22. Further texts are cited by Egil Grislis in 'The Role of Sin in the Theology of Richard Hooker', *Anglican Theological Review*, LXXXIV: 4 (2002): 882.
23. I, vii, 7 [I, p. 224]; on this see, for instance, Egil Grislis, 'Richard Hooker's

which human nature by itself inclines only to evil. But Hooker chooses his words with care. Human nature remains good, albeit corrupted; natural capacities carry on, although seriously weakened, and so 'inclined' toward evil. In such a rendering of human depravity, or deprivation of its original powers, there is nothing the Catholic tradition did not insist on.[24]

The consequence is that the distinctly human powers of thought and will are henceforth debilitated in their exercise.[25] Insofar as reason's sight is obscured and will's choice of good is unreliable and unsupported, sin flows. Hooker employs the ideas for sin that Augustine prompted around his idea of disorder: it is 'irregular', 'exorbitant', 'out of course'.[26] But worst of all is this: the movement of procession and return in which humankind as *imago Dei* and microcosm is the centre, the crucial *vinculum* or link, has been de-railed; the cosmic order has been broken.[27]

A New Way Forward

In defence of his Reformed credentials against the criticisms levied against the *Laws* in *A Christian Letter,* Hooker says this about the laws and truths of nature and reason as they relate to fallen humankind:

> These truths and laws our first parents were created able perfectly both to have known and kept; which we can now neither fully attain without the grace of God assisting us in the search, nor at all observe availably to our salvation, except in the exercise thereof, both grace do aid, and mercy pardon our manifold imperfections.[28]

The particular kinds and means of grace by which God assists humankind for salvation are the subjects of later chapters. In describing Hooker's anthropology we need to take account of the economy of grace at least in relation to the frame within which the human journey to God takes place after the fall into original sin. How do the lines of assisting grace, mercy, and pardon, to name but some of the operative dynamics, intersect and interact as the frame within which the drama of salvation is performed? Here Hooker's anthropology must take account of his theology of providence, which we have already broached, and of predestination.

Image of Man', *Renaissance Papers* (Durham, USA, 1963), p. 75.

24. Ranall Ingalls puts that differently by saying that in Hooker's mature account of the fall and its results 'there is nothing with which Thomas Aquinas might not agree' ('Sin and Grace', p. 178).

25. See I, vii, 6 [I, pp. 222-4].

26. V, App. I [II, p. 572].

27. This angle on the fall and sin by Kirby is very insightful ('Grace and Hierarchy', p. 39).

28. *DF*, V, App. I [II, p. 543].

Debates About Predestination

As the growing literature on Hooker's views regarding predestination makes clear, Hooker expended considerable mental energy on the topic from the time of his first public pronouncements at St Paul's Cross in London to that of the writing of his final unpublished manuscripts penned quietly in Bishopsbourne. Roughly seventy percent of the *Dublin Fragments*, Neelands points out, concern grace and predestination; there Hooker made good an earlier determination to explicate his views on a subject which, in the *Laws* at least, plays little overt part.[29] The sketchy character of his early views make it difficult to assess with precision whether or how his views developed or changed, so we will use the mature and final exposition of the *Dublin Fragments* as our guide.[30] But even here we must tread with care. As an unfinished document – perhaps, in the form we have it, an assemblage of pieces written separately – it lacks the degree of clarity and terminological consistency that a reader would want about an issue which Hooker himself rightly describes as 'a gulf of bottomless depth'![31]

Debates about predestination had become vigorous by the mid-1590s, and Cambridge was the focal point, as divines fought for the doctrinal high ground of the authentic interpretation of the Church of England's formularies.[32] Hooker played no direct part but, if Loyer is right, he stood generally with those resisting the hegemony of a hard core Calvinist teaching of a double eternal decree of election and reprobation.[33]

It was – and is – a theological topic of considerable intricacy from which the modern reader is far removed conceptually and, perhaps more importantly, emotionally. Still, Hooker, like the Christian tradition before him, views predestination as a thoroughly biblical, and therefore unavoidable, topic of orthodox doctrine, so that we cannot accurately grasp his theology as a whole, let alone his anthropology, without wading into these waters.

Hooker seems to have two implicit interests in his exposition of predestination and its attendant ideas. The first is to be faithful to the scriptural testimony. That means taking account of various texts which describe God's relation with, and intention for, humankind both as creator,

---

29. 'Predestination', p. 190.
30. For an overview see Neelands, 'Richard Hooker and the Debates about Predestination', *RHER*, pp. 43-62.
31. *DF*, V, App. I [II, p. 556].
32. See the somewhat dated but still highly useful analysis of H. C. Porter, *Reformation and Reaction in Tudor Cambridge* (Cambridge, 1958), chapters XIII, XIV, XVI and XVII.
33. I, pp. 436-7. For a contemporary account of the doctrinal 'options' see Porter, *Reaction*, p. 387.

governor, and redeemer. Those texts varied. There was, for instance, God's primal declaration that what he had made was good and that humankind is made in his image. In the New Testament texts proclaimed God's desire that *all* should be saved. Some texts spoke of election, predestination and salvation, while still others spoken of a destiny of wrath.[34] Could the circle be squared for the sake of reasonable belief?

Hooker's second interest is to be faithful to the Christian tradition's interpretation of those scriptural variants. In so doing Hooker looks chiefly to Aquinas who, as we have seen already, modelled for Hooker a vision combining the dominant Augustinian stream of western thought with light from Byzantium, notably its great systematiser, John of Damascus. Fidelity here means that Hooker can make use of conceptual distinctions which Scripture alone does not offer but which are part of the received tradition of doctrine. As we have seen, Hooker brings into play Aquinas' teaching on causality, and the distinction between the two divine wills, antecedent and consequent, derived from the Damascene.[35]

In saying that Hooker's treatment of predestination closely follows Aquinas' account in the *Summa Theologiae* it must be admitted too that his treatment has none of the latter's expositional clarity of order and argument. Insights from the twenty-second and twenty-third Articles of the First Part are brought into play uncited, as and when they support Hooker's case.

Providence and Predestination

Hooker, with Aquinas, is clear that predestination is a part of providence. If providence embodies God's good purposes in returning his creation to himself in fulfilment, predestination embodies that same good purpose of God in returning humankind to himself in beatitude, 'the state of bliss, when our union with him is complete.'[36] Further, insofar as it is an axiom of providence that it guides all things 'according to the several condition and quality of their natures' – laws and causes, both necessary and contingent – so predestination works on those same terms. Hooker is clear that despite the obliquity of sin and its baleful consequences on the side of humankind and creation, God's good order of working persists; and so, he can affirm, '[p]redestination appointeth nothing but only that which proceedeth from God, as all goodness doth'.[37] This was not just a principle

---

34. E.g. Romans 8.29-30 is the key text in describing the order of foreknowledge, predestination, call, justification and glorification. Texts on wrath abound.

35. In fact, in the *Laws*, in his *Notes Toward a Fragment of Predestination, RHER,* and in the *Dublin Fragments*, Hooker's nomenclature varies; it deserves close study. To start, see Neelands, 'Debates', pp. 44-5.

36. I, xi, 3 [I, p. 255].

37. *DF*, V, App. I [II, p. 539].

inspired by Aquinas' own teaching, but an unequivocal rebuttal to hard-line Calvinists' view that humankind's sequence of sins, even original sin itself, resulted from an eternal decree fixed before creation. But sin, Hooker scribbled in his notes for the *Dublin Fragments*, while within the limits of God's foresight, is outside the 'limits' of predestination.[38] Sin is no seed of God's setting.[39]

There is another consequence of predestination's place under providence. Since nature's ways persist, human nature's freedom of will remains. It is one of the secondary causes that God continues to honour in his sharing of the dignity of causality with mortals; not even sin undercuts it. 'There is in the Will of man naturally that freedom, whereby it is apt to take or refuse any particular object whatsoever presented unto it.'[40] On that basis human beings, as voluntary agents, can still be viewed as 'lords and masters of that they do'.[41] And if lords and masters, then culpable when they choose against reason, against the law of reason, and against goodness both natural and supernatural.

There is a further aspect of providence in Hooker's discussion. The sinful state of humankind has released, as it were, a dimension of providence which was not hitherto in play, justice and punishment: 'Sin hath awakened justice, which otherwise might have slept.' 'The first rule therefore of providence now, is, that sin do not go altogether unpunished in any creature.'[42] The universal fact of death testifies that 'all have sinned and fallen short of the glory of God' (Romans 3.16). Still, with the good ordering of his providence in view, and with a desire that his purposes not be wholly frustrated, God extends his mercy; he seeks to mitigate the various degrees of punishment that various degrees and kinds of human sin deserve.

God's Consequent, Permissive Will: Obduration and Reprobation

Building on Scripture, the Christian tradition, as Hooker knows, recognised that saving grace could be resisted, if only for a time, and that it could be withheld either temporarily and partially, or consistently and finally. Here theology and theologians were up against a divine inscrutability before which even Hooker himself, despite all his claims for God's reason, order and goodness, had to submit. This is an aspect of the debate about predestination about which Hooker has rather a lot to

---

38. *NTFP*, *FLE*, IV, p. 88; that too follows Aquinas' teaching (*ST*, Ia. 23. 5). We can categorically reject Lake's view of predestination in Hooker as possibly 'from foreseen faith' (*ex praevisa fide*)(*Anglicans and Puritans?*, pp. 185, 195).

39. *DF*, V, App. I [II, p. 572].

40. I, vii, 6 [I, p. 222].

41. *DF*, App. I [II, p. 559].

42. *DF*, V, App. I [II, p. 570].

say in the *Dublin Fragments*, all of it with two chief aims, first, of saving God from responsibility for evil, and then, of preserving human freedom and locating responsibility for reprobation in human beings themselves. Several points deserve note here as, again, Hooker carries the insights of Aquinas into his Elizabethan debate.

Obduration

Hooker follows John of Damascus and Aquinas in support of a divine consequent permissive will. On the basis of that category of divine willing, neither Hooker nor his Byzantine or scholastic predecessors rule out the possibility of lapses in living the life of grace, or apparent 'abandonment'. John of Damascus, for instance, in the section on providence in *On the Orthodox Faith* with which Hooker seems to have been familiar, describes two kinds of abandonment: the 'abandonment of dispensation' and that 'of absolute rejection'. John's use of the distinction highlights the fact that the divine consequent permissive will sometimes withdraws or does not provide helping grace so that spiritual lessons can be learned on the way to eventual salvation. Such is the 'abandonment of dispensation'. By contrast, the 'abandonment of absolute rejection' is just that: a withholding of grace with the result that salvation is not attained.[43] In the case of the first abandonment the good purpose prevails although it is obscured by temporal ills or punishment. The second abandonment is good insofar as it is not unjust; but for him, as for Aquinas and Hooker centuries later, God only permits the abandonment of absolute rejection, and cannot be said positively to will it. Why? Divine providence is, they all accept, incomprehensible.[44]

While Hooker does not adopt John of Damascus' terminology, he seems to have something like the abandonment dispensation in mind with his own terms 'obduration' and 'final obduration'.[45] Such obduration, or 'hardening', says Hooker, describes how 'the malice of man's own heart doth harden him, *and nothing else*'. God's permissive will allows the lapses of obduration when, with the withdrawal or rejection of the Spirit's gracious influence, evil occurrences, even punishments, assault the person. But in the case of obduration the aim is that good might come.

Aquinas, like John of Damascus from whom he takes inspiration, proposes a permissive or, to use the term offensive to Hooker's non-conformist critics, 'consequent' will by which evil and punishment are allowed.[46] However, Aquinas, at least in his article on predestination, does not distinguish two kinds of abandonment or obduration. In that

43. II, 29 (*FC*, 37, pp. 261-3).
44. Louth, *John of Damascus*, pp. 141-2.
45. *DF*, V, App. I [II, pp. 588-91].
46. *ST*, Ia. 23. 3.

regard Hooker is more faithful to the Byzantine tradition. For all three theologians the action of such a permissive or consequent will, fully within the parameters of God's just freedom (for he owes his creatures nothing), is not an active deprivation but a non-provision of the strengthening and perfecting grace that would carry the recipient to beatitude. This is a subtle but perhaps not wholly satisfying distinction.

Reprobation

Hooker accepts the fact of rejection of grace and of God's proposed good and final goal, which the term 'reprobation' describes. The idea is in John of Damascus' notion of 'absolute abandonment'; Aquinas, for his part, uses the verb 'to reprobate' (*reprobare*) to signify God's permission that some people fall short of the goal of their supernatural calling. That falling short, for Aquinas, is not an active subtraction of anything from those reprobated; it is the allowance of their revolt or rebellion against the provision of grace.[47] The discussion in the *Summa* does not unravel the precise causes of that failure and falling short except to locate its cause in the acting person not in the good providence of God.

In the *Dublin Fragments* reprobation seems equivalent to 'final obduration'. Hooker describes that as 'eternal rejection', that is, the hardened disposition of 'lost children' continuing into eternity itself. Like John of Damascus and Aquinas, Hooker does not go far into the knotty whys and wherefores by which the action of grace is unproductive in a given human life. He remarks that a 'personal impediment' makes particular people 'incapable' of the good that grace affords.[48] To speak of punishment, as the Christian tradition does, is but to describe a life, extending through time into eternity, in which the path and aids toward the intended human destiny are rejected or fail. Physical death is a punishment that pertains to all of Adam's children as such; reprobation extends that legacy from the physical into the moral and spiritual spheres.[49]

God's Antecedent, Positive Will: Predestination

Within Hooker's assemblage of concepts, as within Aquinas', predestination has a specific meaning. Aquinas defines it as a 'sending forward' and uses the image of an arrow shot toward its target.[50] It has to do with

---

47. Aquinas' word, *deficere*, signifies desertion, rebellion, and so, falling short of providence's goal.
48. *DF*, V, App. I [II, p. 575]. The word 'incapable' is confirmed in the *FLE* text (IV, p. 141).
49. *Ibid*. p. 570.
50. *ST*, Ia. 23. 1. Aquinas corrects John of Damascus' rejection of the term 'predestination' for humankind.

being propelled toward an end; in the case of mankind that end is the vision of God (*divina visio*). So strictly speaking and as an expression of God's positive will predestination has *only* to do with God's provision to humankind of a way to reach its supernatural end, what Hooker calls the 'spiritual and divine' perfection, attainable only by supernatural means.[51] The economies of Son and Spirit are the way by which the Father provides those supernatural means. Now, though, we are considering the far side of those economies, recognising, as the Christian tradition always has in accordance with the New Testament, that some are indeed predestined, that is, they are the recipients of grace and use it fruitfully to reach their supernatural end, while others do not.

For Hooker, as for Aquinas, the fact of the predestination of some and the obduration and reprobation of others lay in the intersections of necessary and contingent secondary causes. In the *Dublin Fragments* Hooker devotes considerable space to this question and his exposition takes its inspiration largely from Aquinas and the application of his views of causality to predestination in article twenty-three of the *Summa Theologiae*. For Hooker what is at stake is not just a traditional biblical and Catholic doctrine of predestination, but a vindication of the traditional Christian doctrine of creation.[52] What is particularly at stake is the relative autonomy of secondary causes, both necessary and contingent.

Necessity, Contingency and Grace

Both Hooker and Aquinas grant that the cause of predestination is God. Predestination is empowerment and guidance toward goodness, and for humankind the form of that goodness is the supernatural goal of beatitude. As Goodness itself, God must be the ultimate cause of beatitude. At the same time, God works the 'carrying-forward' to perfection of humankind (which is what predestination is) by the secondary causes which God has providentially set in place. Some of those secondary causes are necessary, like those of human reason and will; most, though, are contingent or a mixture of necessary and contingent causes. In any case, for Aquinas humanity's freedom, which is, after all, a relative freedom and not an absolute freedom (for nothing is absolutely free but God), consists in the uninterrupted exercise of the laws of its being, that is, in the use of reason and will on behalf of what is good. God's provision of grace to heal and help the faculties of reason and will discern and choose the way to the goodness of beatitude is the

---

51. I, xi, 4 [I, p. 257]; on positive and permissive determinate will, see *DF*, V, App. I, [II, p. 564].

52. That point has eluded the analysts of Hooker's view of predestination to date.

effect of predestination in a way that does not compromise the freedom of human action. Neither sin *nor* predestinating grace 'translates' human beings 'out of the very number of voluntary agents'.[53]

It is equally important to note that the provision of grace works with and through secondary causes. We have already mentioned the necessary secondary causes of reason and will – necessary because they define human nature, being human – in addition, there are the contingent secondary causes constituting means by which God's predestinating will is accomplished.

Aquinas, for instance, argues that, while the prayers of the saints and good works do not strictly *cause* predestination (God's providential will alone causes it), predestination is nevertheless *effected* through them as means. God effects predestination, he insists, 'by intermediate causes'.[54] Interestingly, one flash-point of contention between Hooker and his critics on the issue of predestination was his defence of the Prayer Book's prayers for the salvation of all.[55] The 'saints' whose prayers for others Hooker is defending were not those canonised but all those baptised and gathered for public worship. But the material point is exactly the one for which Aquinas was arguing: God works his predestinating will by means of secondary, intermediate causes which, by the conveyance of cooperating grace, lend ability to the reason and will to make their free response. Hooker's *Dublin Fragments* ends with the pungent statement of that Thomistic point: 'God is no favourer of sloth; and therefore there can be no such absolute decree, touching man's salvation, as on our part includeth no necessity of care and travail'.[56] This has significant impact on Hooker's understanding of sacraments and the interpretation of 'faith working in love' (Galatians 5.6), as we shall see.

A modern commentator, using the word 'antecedents' to describe all the secondary causes amid which human decision-making and actions are set, explains how for Aquinas, 'the free act emerges from, and is conditioned by, created antecedents over which freedom has no control. It follows that it is possible for God to manipulate these antecedents and through such manipulation to exercise a control over free acts themselves'.[57] That attempt to describe the interaction between divine necessity and creaturely freedom accurately describes what both Aquinas and Hooker are aiming to say in their treatments of predestinating grace.

Like Aquinas, Hooker takes the view that God's predestinating grace

53. *DF*, V, App. I [II, p. 538].

54. *ST*, Ia. 23. 8

55. V, xlix, 3 [II, pp. 215-6]; it arises on the basis of 1 Tim. 2.4; Hooker employs here the terms 'general inclination' and 'occasional will', a terminological doublet inspired by John of Damascus and Aquinas, as we have already seen.

56. V, App. I [II, pp. 596-7].

57. *Grace and Freedom* (London, 1971), p. 115.

will finally prevail in those to whom it is really given. We could put it another way and say that the intermediate means which God orders to fulfil his decree of salvation for an individual will in the end be effectual. Hooker says as much in his summary statement at the end of the *Dublin Fragment*: 'to God's foreknown elect final continuance of grace is given'.[58]

Finally, Aquinas does not seek to assess or determine who is among the elect and who is among the reprobate. To know that would risk inducing either despair or pride. Hooker agrees. Indeed, his comprehensive church polity requires Christians to assume and hope for the best for one another; whatever the truth may be, no one has access to it here and now.

Hooker, then, has an asymmetrical doctrine of predestination. To quote again points in his summary in the *Dublin Fragments*: whereas no 'mere' human ability, freedom and power can reach salvation 'without grace', so 'it cannot be but their sins must condemn them, to whom the purpose of his [i.e. God's] saving mercy doth not extend'.[59] On the one hand, God's predestinating grace is the means to eternal life and beatitude and, precisely as predestinating grace, it will not finally fail. Insofar as that failure is the result of a human being's mysterious amalgam of the necessity and contingencies in their own freedom and choices, their reprobation is conditional; it is not predestined by God but only permitted. After the fall everyone has the capacity to reject God, but no one has the capacity to accept God by faith unless moved, because predestinated, by grace. To Hooker's overall conception of the relationship between God's purposes and human freedom we can aptly apply the description 'soft determinism', meaning a real but highly qualified assertion of the freedom of the will within a framework where God's will, whether positively through the gift of grace or permissively through its absence, prevails.[60]

God's Glory, Man's Good

For Hooker and the tradition of Christian thought which he reprises at significant points in his discussion of anthropology, God, as Goodness itself, is glorified when his creatures, and humankind above all, attain the good ends which his eternal counsel has proposed and to which his providence guides. Into the vexed issue of predestination which so beset theologians of his era Hooker introduces a wisdom which seeks to be faithful to Scripture and which draws upon the best of Christian thought before him. Whether or not the particular interplay of divine necessity and human freedom convinces a contemporary reader is less important than

---

58. *Ibid.* [II, p. 596]; see *ST*, Ia. 23. 6.
59. *Ibid.*
60. The phraseology is Anthony Kenny's *Aquinas on Mind* (London, 1993), pp. 77-8.

recognition of the fact that by the configuration of sources and insights which he brought to bear Hooker expanded the spectrum of options up for discussion and debate.[61]

None of the indeterminacies in Hooker's views on predestination, obduration and reprobation alter the target or end for which God has created humankind, the bliss which is the satisfaction of all desires, and union with the triune God. God stands at the door and knocks; all are called to open. Some do; some do not. That calculus is inaccessible to us, and so determination of others' spiritual status cannot be the basis for Christian association on any terms. Hooker's abiding ecclesiological concerns will reflect that conclusion.

In his 'resemblance' to God, the human being's realisation is precisely in surpassing himself through a power which is not his own but a gift with which he must work to actualise his calling.[62] In that care and travail the church, again, will have a decisive part. How can that happen? What way is open? What means are available? God's economy of creation looks to God's economy of salvation. To that saving economy the following chapters turn.

---

61. *Ibid.* p. 77; though Eppley makes nothing of the inspiration from Aquinas.
62. Florovsky, 'Idea of Creation': 76.

Chapter 6
'A Way Mystical and Supernatural'
Scripture

When Hooker moves from the largely philosophical considerations of Book I to a more focused response to contested points in Book II of the *Laws* he reckons that he is not only addressing 'the very main pillar' of the non-conformists' cause, but entering new theological territory.[1] The territory in question involves the non-conformists' 'root' desire 'to enlarge the necessary use of the Word of God' and by consequence to assert (as Hooker renders their position) 'that one law only, the Scripture, must be the rule to direct all things, even so far as the "taking up of a rush or straw"'.[2] That issue of Scripture's legitimate authoritative scope seems to Hooker new in that it had not been 'moved' in other churches; nor had the Admonition Controversy in England that had generated the troublesome non-conformist principles resolved it. Hooker alone realised as he sought to defend the church as established by law that a complete and consistent answer to non-conformist insistence on the 'universal jurisdiction'[3] of Scripture over and against all other laws was required. In so doing he set about to clarify an issue that the sixteenth-century Reformers had themselves left largely unexplored.[4] So in Book II Hooker explicitly takes up the challenge posed by this new question and then spins out the consequences of his answer in the books that follow. At one level, therefore, the entire *Laws of Ecclesiastical Polity* is an extended treatment of the proper authority, place and function of Scripture in Christian life.

This chapter surveys Hooker's doctrine of Scripture as it took shape in relation to his context and apologetic purposes. That involves identifying strands in the theological tradition that aided his response to the 'new question'; identifying key features in his understanding of Scripture's unique

---

1. Preface, vii, 3 [I, p. 172]; as Hooker quotes them there: 'That Scripture ought to be the only rule of our actions'.
2. II, i, 2 [I, p. 287]. The phrase "taking up . . . " had arisen in the volleys between Whitgift and Cartwright.
3. So Loyer, I, p. 132.
4. Haugaard, 'Introduction to Books II, III & IV', *FLE*, VI, I, p. 126; taking Haugaard's point further, Ranall Ingalls, '*Sola Scriptura*': 76. Ingalls' unpublished study 'Richard Hooker on the Scriptures' (henceforth cited as 'Scriptures' as distinct from the article just cited) argues that Hooker made a substantial contribution in clarifying the Reformer's principle of '*sola scriptura*'.

revelational role; placing Hooker's views in relation to its alternatives; and specifying aspects of Hooker's hermeneutics, that is, his principles for interpreting the Bible. In all of this Hooker sought to confirm the reformed credentials of the Church of England, to pick up the unfinished business with Thomas Cartwright and perhaps also with Walter Travers; but with uncharted terrain before him he was able to fashion a perspective with its own new and yet very traditional contours and priorities.[5] To those too we need to be alert.

<h2 style="text-align:center">Book II's Relation to Book I
'That unemptiable fountain of wisdom'</h2>

The contribution of Book II to Hooker's theology of Scripture cannot be separated from the argument and exposition of laws in Book I. By setting Scripture within a particular definition and a larger system of laws Hooker already laid the groundwork for his response in later books.[6] Hooker extends that point into Book II by turning one of Cartwright's own proof texts against him (a tactic Hooker often employs). For instance, the appeal to 'Wisdom' in Proverbs 2.9, Hooker argues, does not narrow the access to God's truth to scriptural revelation. Quite the reverse; it widens and extends it. Of course wisdom teaches 'every good way', admits Hooker, quoting Cartwright, but not every good way by '*one only way* of teaching'. Why? Because 'the bounds of wisdom are large'.[7]

This is a clever move on Hooker's part. His first rebuttal to the nonconformists in Book II uses their own proof-text from Scripture to support his appeal to natural theology in the first ten chapters of Book I. Nonconformists, Hooker contends, have failed to grasp the range and richness of Scripture's concept of wisdom; they have straightened the means and manner of divine self-expression, and so have claimed for Scripture alone more than it can rightly bear. In contrast, Hooker describes how from the 'unemptiable fountain of wisdom' which is God's own self a diverse impartation of truths flows 'unto the world'. He explains:

> As her [wisdom's] ways are of sundry kinds, so her manner of teaching is not merely one and the same. Some things she openeth by the sacred books of Scripture; some things by the glorious works of Nature: with some things she inspireth them from above by spiritual influence; in some things she leadeth and traineth them only by worldly experience and practice. We may not so in any one special kind admire her, that we disgrace her in any other; but let all her ways be according unto their place and degree adored.[8]

---

5. There is general agreement that the Admonitioners, especially Cartwright, are the objects of rebuttal in Books II and III.
6. Loyer, I, p. 130.
7. I, ii, 4 [I, p. 289].
8. *Ibid*. [I, p. 290].

A foundational aspect, then, of Hooker's response to the new question regarding Scripture's role and authority is an embrace of the patristic and medieval concept of the 'two books', or, as Hooker puts it in the passage above, 'the sacred books of Scripture' and 'the glorious works of Nature'.[9]

Augustine's *On Christian Teaching*

Ranall Ingalls argues that Hooker's reprisal of this idea owes much to the influence of Augustine's influential treatise *On Christian Teaching* (*De Doctrina Christiana*). From that quarry, chiefly its first book, Hooker extracted a view of the varied sources of truth that *together* could lead the Christians to their heavenly homeland.[10] The first ten chapters of Book I, as we have seen, reflect two key Augustinian views: first, that a limited but real and necessary knowledge of God is possible through creation; and second, that reason, however weakened through sin, retains a necessary place in the apprehension of God and of the 'way to the fatherland' (*via ad patriam*) in the sphere of both natural theology and of revealed truth. 'It sufficeth therefore', says Hooker, 'that Nature and Scripture do serve in such full sort, that they both jointly and not severally either of them be so complete, that unto everlasting felicity we need not the knowledge of any thing more than these two may easily furnish our minds with on all sides'. [11]

Both Augustine and Hooker are clear that the role of reason, so necessary with regard to the natural knowledge of God, must have a secure and honoured place with regard to the revealed knowledge of God too. They are equally clear that on account of 'the guiltiness of sin' and the condemnation it entailed God in his wisdom has revealed in Christ 'a way mystical and supernatural'.[12] In keeping with Augustine, what is important about this 'way mystical and supernatural' for Hooker's view of Scripture is this: it does not displace the way of nature, the truths it teaches, and the exercise of reason and will by which its truths are known and acted upon. Rather, it heals the workings of reason and will while it honours and builds upon the insights and truths quarried from nature; after all, 'her voice is but his instrument'.[13] Only by recognising the legitimate claims of nature and reason can Scripture be itself and offer its uniquely saving truth to humankind.

---

9. The idea of nature as a 'book' that complements Scripture goes back at least as far as St Basil's treatise on the creation story in Genesis, the *Hexaemeron*.

10. See Ingalls, 'Scriptures', pp. 146-169. Ingalls argues that while the Augustinian references are few, Hooker is drawing upon Augustinian commonplaces which all of his learned readers would recognise.

11. I, xiv, 5 [I, p. 271]. See Paget's Natural Laws and Human Laws (p. 66).

12. I, xi, 6 [I, p. 261]. See Paget's Supernatural Laws.

13. I, viii, 3 [I, p. 227].

That coordination of reason and revelation, of nature and grace, the book of nature and the books of Scripture, inspired by Augustine and then adopted and adapted by Aquinas and others, determines in large measure what Hooker says about Scripture. With this template in mind, therefore, we can turn to Hooker's understanding of various characteristics of Scripture as men and women assess its divine authority, and as Christians understand its role and depth of meaning as a 'doctrinal instrument' in their pilgrimage home to God and explore its depths of meaning.

Scripture and Law

The humanist phrase '*lex Christi*', or 'law of Christ', was not one that Hooker seems to have used but it accurately expresses his understanding of Scripture.[14] In contrast with Luther's basic hermeneutical principle dividing 'law' and 'gospel' not just as biblical testaments but, more importantly, as what we might call existential postures, Hooker, like Augustine and the tradition of western theology that he begat, holds them together.

Hooker's careful exposition of law in Book I asserted that creation is *lawful* in that it is ordered by the reason and goodness of God. In that basic sense Scripture also is lawful not because it contains particular laws and regulations, but because it too is ordered by the reason and goodness of God toward humankind's proper end, salvation. The laws of created things are the ways in which they participate in the reason and goodness of God. In the case of human beings in need of salvation Scripture teaches the ways by which humankind can participate in the offer of salvation, which is God's consummate expression of reason and goodness toward it. Scripture, uniquely comprising the 'way mystical and supernatural', is a divine law by which believers discover the necessary form and expression of fulfilment in their return to God.[15]

Scripture and Spirit

If Hooker differentiates himself from Luther in regard to Scripture and law, he takes issue with Calvin and his successors in regard to the relation between Scripture and the Spirit. Hooker, perhaps by temperament and certainly by conviction, opposes the illuminist tendencies in Calvin and Calvinism, that is, reliance on the interior illumination of the Spirit to convey and assure of revealed truth and scriptural interpretation.[16] Or perhaps more accurately,

---

14. Erasmus, for instance, who also took the view that the precepts of Christ did not abrogate the laws of nature; on both see Roland Bainton, *Erasmus of Christendom* (New York, 1969), p. 115.

15. See Ingalls, 'Scriptures', pp. 267-8.

16. Loyer, I, p. 145. I do not mean here simply to identify the views of Calvin in

he locates the Spirit's testimony elsewhere. After all, Hooker does not deny that faith and Christian understanding are gifts of the Spirit. He does, however, position and coordinate the Spirit's revelational economy rather differently than his non-conformist contemporaries.

In keeping with the coordinated witness of the two books described earlier, Hooker presents two means by which the Spirit guides humankind into saving truth, the one, 'that which we call by a special divine excellency Revelation, the other Reason'.[17] But those two means work together, 'both jointly and not severally either of them', as we have seen. Engagement with revelation, therefore, requires the use of reason. Right reasoning rather than ardour, with its abusive potential, is the basis of the surest convictions concerning things divine.[18]

Natural Knowledge Presupposed

Having established those two ways by which divine truth is accessible, Hooker is able to detail how reason is employed with regard to revelation. First, and in keeping with Augustinian and Thomist inspiration, Hooker recognises that knowledge of God through revelation, like knowledge of any subject, presupposes knowledge gained from elsewhere; in the case of revelation, the knowledge it presupposes is from the book of nature and the sphere of reason. 'Scripture teacheth us that saving truth which God hath discovered unto the world by revelation, and it presumeth us taught otherwise that itself is divine and sacred.'[19] Some have seen here Hooker's reliance on the scholastic concept of 'subalternate' knowledge, that is, the view that all knowledge presupposes principles learned from elsewhere and taken from other spheres of knowledge.[20] If so, it was but a scholastic specification of the basic approach of Augustine.

This is a key element in the position Hooker takes with regard to a chief point in Reformation polemic, namely, by what authority a Christian accepts Scripture as conveying the authoritative revelation of God. The

---

this regard with those of the English non-conformists of Hooker's day; there was, though, a line of theological connection. In any case, Nigel Atkinson's argument of parity between Calvin and Hooker in interpreting, say, the Old Testament is insupportable (*Richard Hooker and the Authority of Scripture, Tradition and Reason* [Carlisle, 1997], p. 120).

17. Preface, iii, 10 [I, p. 150].

18. Preface, *ibid.* [I, p. 151]; speaking of the Admonitioners, Hooker comments: 'It is not therefore the fervent earnestness of their persuasion, but the soundness of those reasons whereupon the same is built, which must declare their opinions in these things to have been by the Holy Ghost'.

19. III, viii, 13 [I, p. 376].

20. So D. H. Marot, 'Aux origines de la Théologie anglicane', *Irénikon*, XXXIII (1960): 333.

importance which Hooker credits to reason moves him to argue that
reason, rather than some illuminist impulse provides the motives for
accepting Scripture as Scripture. The argument assumes that the Spirit
is at work in rightly-ordered reason, and that the universal testimony of
believers, that is, the church, has Spirit-led, rational, evidential power in
forming an accurate understanding of Scripture. It also assumes that while
reason, together with the authority of the church's witness, provided the
initial motive, the truth inherent in Scripture would gain greater persuasive
power once a person has stepped into the scriptural world.[21] Still, Hooker's
approach to the acknowledgement of Scripture as Scripture is weighted in
the direction of reason, and by implication church, far more than that of
Calvin and his English non-conformist successors.[22] It was that which gave
the author of A Christian Letter pause, and prompted suspicions of 'the
underpropping of a popish principle' in Hooker's theology of Scripture.[23]

Reason's Role in Interpretation

Hooker's understanding of the relation between Scripture and reason does
not end there. In establishing reliably 'the sense of Holy Scripture' with
respect to the content of faith, reason is essential. As he explains in chapter
eight of Book III:

> Exclude the use of natural reasoning about the sense of Holy
> Scripture concerning the articles of our faith, and then that the
> Scripture doth concern the articles of our faith who can assure
> us? That, which by right exposition buildeth up Christian faith,
> being misconstrued breedeth error: between true and false
> construction, the difference reason must show.[24]

There we have, as applied to the interpretation of biblical texts, a
practical application of the primary epistemological issue in debate
between Hooker and the non-conformists:[25] the cooption of reason,
indeed its coordination, with revelation in the receipt and understanding
of divine truth.

---

21. See III, viii, 14 [I, p. 376].
22. So Calvin: 'Scripture exhibits fully as clear evidence its own truth'; 'we ought
to seek our conviction in a higher place than human reasons, judgments or
conjectures, that is, in the secret testimony of the Holy Spirit' (Institutes, Book II, 2
and 4 [LCC, vol. I, pp. 76-78]). Calvin gives here his view on Augustine's important
remark 'I would not believe the gospel except as moved by the authority of the
Catholic Church'; a view much debated in sixteenth- and seventeenth-century
theology.
23. The popish principle suspected was, the author stated, 'the Churches authoritie
above Holie Scripture' (I, p. 376, note 13).
24. III, viii, 16 [I, p. 378]; emphasis mine.
25. So Haugaard describes the theme of Book II ('Books II, III & IV', p. 129).

A Triad of Characteristics: Sufficiency, Perfection and Clarity

There is no cause to think that in his theology of Scripture Hooker wished to be anything but faithful to the established views of the Church of England as expressed, for example, in the Prayer Book and the Thirty-Nine Articles of Religion. Article Six, for instance, while it did not use the word 'sufficient', was clear that 'Holy Scripture containeth all things necessary to salvation'. For all the Reformation movements it was a point of self-definition against the Roman Catholic Church's insistence on the complementary role of tradition in matters 'of faith'.[26] In the Elizabethan context, however, the matter could not be left there. If that concise article had been regarded as wholly satisfactory to Reformers then the epistemological issue implied in the Elizabethan debates with non-conformity would never have arisen. Beyond that, with an eye toward drawing as many Roman Catholics as possible into the national religious settlement, how was the notion of sufficiency to be interpreted in light of the decrees of the Council of Trent and its affirmation of unwritten traditions necessarily supplementing the written scriptural record?[27] Insofar as he was advocating for the Elizabethan Settlement, Hooker had to bear both of these elements of the debate in mind.

Sufficiency and Perfection

In light of the coordination of reason and revelation that Hooker proposes in Book I, the notion of scriptural sufficiency must be suitably nuanced in terms of what Loyer calls Scripture's 'proper field of reference'.[28] Sufficiency can only be gauged within that appropriate 'field of reference'. We have already described much of that 'field'; we can specify it somewhat more in these terms.

First, Scripture contains natural as well as supernatural truths. In keeping with Aquinas' view, Scripture contains those natural truths, aspects of the moral law, for instance, for the sake of what we might call 'ease of access'.[29] Scripture's sufficiency in regard to saving doctrine does not really relate to those areas that are in principle discernible by rational enquiry. Second, positive law in Scripture is not necessarily supernatural law; within Scripture itself an array of diversely ordered laws, from various sources and so of different weight, can be found. Scripture's sufficiency

---

26. For descriptions of views leading to Trent see Tavard, *Holy Writ or Holy Church. The Crisis of the Protestant Reformation* (London, 1959), pp. 113-91.
27. Session IV, first decree (*'hanc veritatem et disciplinam contineri in libris scriptis et sino scripto traditionibus'*) (*DEC*, II, p. 663); see also Tavard, *Holy Writ*, pp. 195-209.
28. I, p. 131; my discussion here follows Loyer.
29. E.g. the Decalogue. On this Thomist influence on Hooker, see Grislis, 'Hermeneutical Problem', pp. 186-7.

only pertains to the supernatural sphere of Scripture's witness. So, third, Scripture is 'sufficient' with respect to 'all things necessary for salvation' (Article Six); however, not all that it contains is necessary for salvation. Sufficiency pertains to a specific field within the overall scriptural testimony. Fourth, therefore, Scripture is 'sufficient' with respect to matters necessary for salvation while at the same time containing a field of truths not strictly necessary, and a domain of matters that are, in the language of contemporary debate 'indifferent', that is, undetermined in Scripture and so determinable by other means and authorities.[30]

Finally, Hooker's teleological view of law expounded in Book I ties sufficiency closely to perfection, that is, to Scripture's end or purpose. We understand Scripture's sufficiency by answering the question: what is Scripture's 'principle intent'? For Hooker that answer is clear: 'to deliver the laws of duties supernatural'.[31] Speaking more specifically in terms of 'perfection' Hooker puts it like this: 'the absolute perfection of Scripture is seen by relation unto that end whereto it tendeth', namely, 'a full instruction in all things unto salvation necessary'.[32] In a stroke, then, Hooker has responded to the twin pillars of the current debates. Against non-conformists who wished to 'rack and stretch' Scripture's sufficiency and perfection to mean far more than they legitimately can, he has opened the field of relevant laws and freedoms beyond a narrow scripturalism; and against Tridentine Roman Catholic doctrine he has fastened 'all things necessary for salvation' to the written record of Scripture. 'Whatsoever to make up the doctrine's of man's salvation is added, as in supply of the Scripture's unsufficiency, we reject it'.[33]

Clarity

If Scripture is thought to be sufficient because it is perfect, and perfect insofar as it is sufficient with respect to 'all things necessary to salvation', are all things 'necessary' clear? There was an element of tension in the early Reformers' assertion of Scripture's clarity, and Hooker was sensitive to this in his reading of Article Six. With respect to Scripture containing

---

30. So-called 'adiaphora'; see chapter fifteen.
31. I, xiv, 1 [I, p. 267].
32. II, viii, 5 [I, pp. 333-4]. Having said that, because different parts of Scripture have different aims, for instance, some the aim of imparting natural knowledge, others supernatural knowledge, the quality of 'perfection' applies across all its areas: 'As therefore God created every part and particle of man exactly perfect, that is to say in all points sufficient *unto the use for which he appointed it*; so the Scripture, yea every sentence thereof, is perfect, and wanteth nothing *requisite unto that purpose for which God delivered the same*' (II, viii, 5 [I, p. 334]; emphasis mine).
33. II, viii, 5 [I, p. 334].

necessary articles of faith, what was the implication of the Article's claim that those articles had either to be 'read therein' or 'proved thereby'? The phrase 'read therein' suggests truth that is apparent and accessible; so Hooker describes 'the word of life' as a treasure 'though precious, yet easy, as well to attain, as to find; lest any man desirous of life should perish through the difficulty of the way'.[34]At the same time, the phrase 'proved thereby' could be read to suggest that even things necessary to be believed are not immediately clear, and that an exegetical process and tools – 'the industry of right discourse' and 'travail' – are required to extract and establish that content and its meaning.[35] So Hooker distinguishes what Scripture 'contains' from what it 'comprehends'.[36] On the one hand, according to Hooker, Scripture possesses an evangelical simplicity, an open exposure of its central, transcendent message; on the other hand, it requires both exegesis treating literal meanings and potential senses, and theology exposing implicit meanings by probable deductions. Out of that last aspect flows Hooker's appreciation of 'antiquity', or tradition, as an important element in expounding scriptural faith which we will consider later in relation to Hooker's practice of theology. [37]

Scripture's Christocentric Core

In keeping with its diversity of laws and their various ends or purposes there exists within Scripture a hierarchy of intent, a scriptural expression of Hooker's hierarchical principle. For Hooker the principal intent is its christocentrism, its unifying spiritual core.[38] Hooker is clear that the 'irreducible object of faith' and the 'specifically supernatural centre of Scripture' is Christ the Saviour: God manifested in the flesh and justified in the Spirit, that is, incarnate, crucified and risen.[39] Not only is that Scripture's centre; it is also, in accordance with Article Eight, Scripture's unifying theme.

It is noteworthy that the same tension inherent in Scripture between clarity, on the one hand, and depth on the other, pertains to Christology; and no wonder, since the person of Christ defines Scripture as core and content.

---

34. V, xxi, 3 [II, p. 85].
35. Loyer, I, pp. 149-50.; *ibid.* [II, p. 86].
36. I, xiv, 2 [I, pp. 268-9]; Hooker himself emphasises those words in the passage. Here he cites basic Christian tenets that are 'no where to be found by express literal mention' but can only be 'deduced' by 'collection'.
37. Marot, 'Aux origines': 331; Hooker was of course aware that Article Seven regarded the creeds as 'proved by most certain warrants of holy Scripture'. Tradition is taken up in chapter twelve.
38. Loyer, I, p. 157.
39. That phraseology is Loyer's, I, p. 133; so Hooker in his *LDJ* [III, p. 501].

Attention is sometimes drawn to Hooker's appeal to the ancient Chalcedonian Definition of the person of Christ to interpret this tension in Scripture. Far from supporting an unnuanced claim for Scripture's all-encompassing authority, Hooker sees in the Chalcedonian pattern a rationale for the diversity-in-unity in Scripture. This is really an argument for Scripture's unity, a unity that comprehends the diversity and variation in scripture's content, message, and importance arising over time, out of different settings, with varying aims. In employing the paradigm of Chalcedon, Ingalls explains, Hooker understands Scripture 'as a divinely-constituted unity in which what is human, historical, natural and what is divine and revealed are brought together "without confusion, without change, without division, without separation". As a result, 'temporal, natural and human things become the means of an eternal good by reason of their relationship to the Person of the Word of God'.[40] We are reminded of the Augustinian and Thomist insistence that the 'way of nature' is requisite for the 'way of grace'.

Outlines of an Interpretive Method

It is fair to say that Hooker does not offer a full-blown account of the interpretation of Scripture; what we would call today a hermeneutical theory. Still, his issues with the exegesis of those whose views he wants to counter indicate some favoured perspectives on his part. Further, the exegesis in the course of the arguments in the *Laws* and elsewhere reveals his own distinctive hermeneutical 'techniques'.[41] Five of them are worth noting.

Letter and Truth

In line with Reforming preferences, Hooker shows no sympathy with the traditional medieval fourfold allegorical method of interpretation; he is firm that where it will stand the literal meaning of a passage is to be preferred. Having said this, he recognises that Scripture comprehends within itself the dimensions of promise and fulfilment that broadly characterise the relation between the two Testaments.[42] Hooker's intent is to recover the approach and usage of 'the ancient Fathers' in whose writings the language, themes and usages of the age of promise continue under the new dispensation. '[T]he only difference', he explains, 'is, that

---

40. For instance, Ingalls, 'Scriptures', pp. 94-5.
41. Loyer, I, p. 151; on Hooker's own 'techniques' see Haugaard, 'Book II, III & IV', pp.154-7.
42. *Ibid.* I, p. 154; those dimensions can be variously expressed: law and grace, and shadow and reality, to name but two.

whereas before they had a literal, they now have a metaphorical use, and are as so many notes of remembrance unto us, that what they did signify in the letter is accomplished in the truth'.[43] Hooker's point is that when the letter, or literal meaning, acquires a metaphorical or symbolic meaning for Christians, the literal sense is not abrogated, as Calvin, Cartwright and others thought, but rather fulfilled.[44]

A Harmonic Hierarchy

The concepts of letter and truth, promise and fulfilment, point to the theme of *relation* informing the whole scriptural testimony. For that reason Hooker's interpretation acknowledges and seeks out the relation of all of its parts to the whole. Just as creation is a hierarchy of intersecting laws, so Scripture is a hierarchy of intersecting senses. They are unified in their relation to Christ the Word of God; beyond that, however, they form a rich and varied hierarchy of meaning, truth, and inspiration. As a result, Hooker can be remarkably nuanced in his approach to the issue of inspiration. This is a debated point in the interpretation of Hooker's view of Scripture, but it seems fair to say that Hooker sees how different scriptural truths can occupy different positions in relation to the promise of salvation.[45] That subtle discernment is the exegete's careful task. It requires sensitivity to the 'complex ensemble' that makes up Scripture. Indeed, the exegete's success depends on developing a trained ear that is attuned to Scripture's unique 'harmonics'.[46]

History

Hooker was not just a reformed theologian but a Renaissance theologian, so he took seriously a chief gift of Renaissance intellectual culture, namely, what William Haugaard calls 'historical contextualisation'.[47] The aim of

---

43. IV, xi, 10 [I, p. 460]; Hooker is responding to non-conformist criticisms of the use of the words 'altar', 'priest', and 'sacrifice'.

44. Loyer, I, p. 156; words like 'void' and 'abrogation' not fulfilment characterise Calvin's treatment of the relation of the Testaments in his *Institutes*; see Book II, ch. 10, secs. 7-10 [*LCC*, vol. I, pp. 454-60].

45. So Loyer, I, p. 158; he notes, for instance, that the natural moral law is not of the same inspired quality as, say, the Beatitudes. I see nothing here, if not pressed too far, contrary to the Augustinian notion of the two ways discussed earlier as the bedrock of Hooker's view of Scripture.

46. So Loyer describes this exegetical posture (I, p. 158).

47. In his 'Books II, III & IV', p. 157; I rely on many of his points in this section, as well his essay 'The Scriptural Hermeneutics of Richard Hooker', in D. Armentrout, ed., *This Sacred History: Anglican Reflections for John Booty* (Cambridge, USA, 1990), pp. 166-7.

the approach lay in judging the aptness of a text's example, meaning or direction in regard to an issue at hand, and it was a commonplace of the age to bring that contextualising approach to bear on matters of church history and historical interpretation generally. Hooker, however, was more vigorous and thorough in contextualising *biblical* texts in order to assess aptness in relation to considerations and debate over theology, praxis, and polity.[48]

The exegetical debates in which Hooker was implicated, and which the *Laws* address, were well-tilled soil among disputants who preceded Hooker in the establishment-non-conformist conflict. To these on-going debates Hooker made an important contribution by joining his teleological principle with thorough and acute historical perspective.[49] The perfection and absoluteness of God's words as recorded in Scripture, be they a moral law, a judicial law, or the record of an historical fact or precedent, are such only 'for the performance of that things whereunto they tend'. *Telos*, end or purpose, is key in determining the aptness of a scriptural text for contemporary needs. So, as Haugaard explains it, just as the identification of purpose within the particular human situation described in a historical text is an essential element of reasoned interpretation, so likewise in the exegesis of biblical texts. An important element in such an approach is the balanced operations of philosophical principles on the one hand, and historical analysis on the other. With his own alchemy Hooker unites philosophy and logical abstraction with a sharp historical sense in the exegetical task.[50]

Exegesis, Equity and Common Law

An inspiration parallel to that Renaissance historical sense was juridical science, and in particular the dynamic developments in legal theory associated with Hooker's contemporary Sir Edward Coke and the common lawyers of the Elizabethan period.[51] The ramifications of Hooker's exposure to that intellectual world during his years as Master of the Temple pervade his writings. As to the interpretation of Scripture, we need note first Hooker's understanding of the legal concept of 'equity'. It is a process by which laws that 'continually and universally should be of force' can be adjusted, extended, restrained and applied in particular

---

48. Ingalls fairly notes that this approach is legitimated by the principles of Augustine's *On Christian Teaching* too ('Scriptures', pp. 280-1).

49. In so doing, says Haugaard, Hooker introduces 'a seminal hermeneutical tool' into exegetical method ('Books II, III & IV', p. 159).

50. On the relation of scholastic and Renaissance concerns in this domain, see Loyer, I, p. 159-60.

51. Loyer, with special interest in law and legal theory, is insightful on this theme; for his discussion see I, pp. 167-75.

circumstances so as to practice 'general laws' 'according to their right meaning'.[52] All students of Aristotle's ethics had a grasp of this key aspect of the application of justice.[53] To the extent that Hooker understands Scripture as law, exegesis and interpretation must deal with this very issue: the elements of law within it must be correctly identified; the general character of the law must be discerned (is it, for instance, permanent or by intent limited?); judgment must be rendered as to how its general and permanent purpose can be suitably applied in a new and different context. As Hooker says: 'The end wherefore laws were made may be permanent, and those laws nevertheless require some alteration, if there be any unfitness in the means which they prescribe as tending unto that end and purpose'.[54]

The common law tradition was also important for Hooker. For in contrast to equity law's movement from the general to the particular, commonlaw moved from the particular, that is, from precedent to the general. In broad terms this meant working toward the identification of a legal rationale by the analysis of the concrete facts of a case. What was most important for the evolving tradition represented by Coke and then assimilated by Hooker is the close link between precedent law and the universals of reason and justice. The upshot is that precedents are not to be applied mechanically; from the precedents a principle or reason (Hooker would call it an end or purpose) needs to be identified. The reason arises from the concrete facts when they are accurately and judiciously analysed. In the practice of common law there is, therefore, a 'reciprocal interaction' between the principle and the facts. Finally, accurate and judicious analysis is required; in other words, the exercise of reason and discernment specific to the task acquired by intense study and experience. As we will see in a later chapter concerned with the practice of theology, those characteristics apply to exegetical and theological reasoning as well.

Example and Negative Argument

Two particulars flow from the interpretive values of history and law we have discussed so far: first, Hooker's use of examples cited in Scripture; and second, his evaluation of the so-called 'negative argument'.

The value of examples cited from Scripture in support of one's argument had been a contested point since Whitgift's volleys with the Admonitioners.

---

52. V, ix, 3 [II, p. 39]; in this section of Book V Hooker is discussing 'dispensations', or economies, in the life of the church.
53. See his discussion of equity as a corrective of legal justice in the *Nicomachean Ethics*, V, 10.
54. III, x, 3 [I, p. 387].

He had criticised Cartwright for repeatedly arguing 'from particulars', that is, from scriptural examples, 'to universals'.[55] It figured, given the omnicompetence accorded to Scripture by the non-conformists, that they would be disposed to see universal lessons in facts or deeds taken from the scriptural narratives or its rules.

For his part, Hooker was more open than Whitgift to the importance of scriptural example, and the influence of common law theory with its stress on precedent goes far to explain why. It is simply a fact of experience, says Hooker, that we live our lives 'partly guided by rules, and partly directed by examples'.[56] The chief issue, however, is not whether examples have an appropriate force to guide thought and actions, but whether whatever is invoked, however 'good', is 'fit' as an example. With respect to the evaluation of fitness the interpreter must bring the various tools already described; only in light of that critical scrutiny can the suitability of such citations from Scripture be made.

If the non-conformists seemed over-generous in their appeal to scriptural examples prescriptively to determine Christian attitudes and actions, they adopted a straightened approach in their commitment to the so-called 'negative argument'. This principle of interpretation, namely, that the absence of an express order to do something constitutes a negative order *not to do* something, accorded well with non-conformists' commitment to Scripture's 'universal jurisdiction' in ordering the life of the church. The trouble is, Hooker argues, if taken up without qualification, nuance or, indeed, reason, it is simply untenable. At one level Hooker's response exemplifies his reasoned analysis of historical evidence: could Tertullian's insistence that 'Scripture denies what it does not designate' be taken at face value? Then Hooker the logician comes to the fore in his dismissal of this approach to exegesis, for is it logical to suppose that Scripture denies the existence of Henry VIII because it does not mention him?[57]

In fact, Hooker is so little given to pedantry that he will not expend much energy in gainsaying this feature of non-conformist exegesis. It is noteworthy, however, in that it further signals Hooker's regard for Scripture as an open text whose rich history, complexity of content, and hierarchy of laws, makes simplistic approaches to its interpretation untenable.

The 'doctrinal instrument' of Salvation

In the fifth book of the *Laws*, amid a discussion of preaching by sermons, Hooker defines 'the word of God' as the 'heavenly truth touching matters of eternal life revealed and uttered unto men'. 'We therefore have', he adds,

---

55. '*ex solis particularibus*' or '*a facto ad ius*' (Loyer, I, p. 164).
56. V, lxv, 13 [II, pp. 328-9].
57. II, v, 5 [I, pp. 303-4].

'no *word of God* but the Scripture'.[58] With the end or purpose of that word of God in mind, Hooker declares that it is *to save*. Scripture is, by his reckoning, 'in the nature of a doctrinal instrument'.[59]

Each of the words of that phrase is important. Scripture is 'doctrinal' because 'they which live by the word must *know* it'. As we saw earlier, both the way of nature and the way of grace rely on the proper use of reason; reason, that is, ordered so that it might fully enjoy God as Truth. The 'way mystical and supernatural' that Scripture uniquely conveys involves what Hooker describes as 'an Apprehension of things divine in our understanding, and in the mind an Assent thereunto'.[60] Those 'things divine' – 'things above nature which our reason by itself could not reach unto'[61] – are the things 'necessarily required for the attainment of eternal life' and 'to procure our assent'.[62] It is that knowledge, and the commitment of the will that such knowledge directs, that Scripture conveys so that humankind might be "wise unto salvation". Scripture is the 'instrument', or means, that God has 'purposely framed' to that end.[63]

It would be wrong, though, to suppose that Hooker's intellectualism has got the better of him in so defining Scripture. Ranall Ingalls reminds us that for Hooker the word of God in Scripture must always be understood in relation to the Word of God incarnate. Scripture is only an effective doctrinal instrument when it is the means by which Christ is received by reason and will, and by those faculties indwells a believer. Hooker's *Discourse on Justification* describes the role of the doctrinal instrument like this:

> The cause of spiritual life in us, is Christ, not carnally or corporally inhabiting, but dwelling in the soul of man as a thing which (when the mind apprehendeth it) is said to inhabit and possess the mind. The mind conceiveth Christ by hearing the doctrine of Christianity . . . [O]ur life is Christ, by hearing of the Gospel apprehended as a Saviour, and assented unto by the power of the Holy Ghost.[64]

As a doctrinal instrument, therefore, Scripture's purpose is spiritual; indeed, it is nothing less than the union of the believer with God through Christ by the Spirit.

---

58. V, xxi, 2 [II, p. 85]; the emphasis is Hooker's.

59. V, xxi, 3 [II, p. 85].

60. *Ibid.*

61. III, viii, 12 [I, p. 374-5].

62. V, xxi, 3 [II, pp. 85-6]. On the meaning and relation of 'apprehension' and 'assent' in Hooker see chapter ten below.

63. Cranmer had used the word 'instrument' of Scripture years before in his first homily 'A Fruitful Exhortation to the Reading of Holy Scripture' in Book I of the *Homilies*.

64. *LDJ*, 26 [III, p. 516].

Scripture: A Reasonable and Reverent Approach

When the author of *A Christian Letter* accused him of esteeming Scripture no more than Aristotle and the schoolmen, Hooker bristled: 'I think of the scripture of God as reverently as the best of the purified crew in the world . . . in which mind I hope by the grace of God that I shall both live and die'.[65] However honest the protestation, Hooker's exploration of Scripture's authority, especially in relation to reason and law, developed new insights and opened up wider horizons than English theologians had so far grasped. By synthesising insights from Augustine, Aquinas and the scholastic tradition, from Renaissance learning and from the legal theorists of the day, Hooker is rightly said to have entered fields that had been largely untouched by theologians in England and on the continent.[66]

The approach Hooker takes with respect to the themes of subsequent chapters is in large measure the fruit of those creative steps on Hooker's part to re-formulate the 'general grounds and foundations'[67] of a genuinely reformed yet Catholic Christian doctrine of Scripture as the basis for the understanding and exposition of Christian truth.

---

65. *FLE*, IV, p. 68.
66. So Haugaard, 'Scriptural Hermeneutics', p. 166.
67. Preface, VII, 5 [I, p. 172].

Chapter 7
'Life and Light Eternal'
Jesus Christ

It may reasonably be asked why consideration of Jesus Christ comes only now in the exposition of Richard Hooker's theology. The simple answer is: because this is where Hooker himself takes up the theme. A reader of the *Laws* is surely surprised by a kind of fundamental theology set within a treatise largely concerned with matters of polity and worship.[1] That placement itself helps readers position Hooker's doctrine of Christ within the overall terrain of theology. While Hooker's treatment of Christ appears here and there throughout his writings, there is no doubt of the determinative significance of what Hooker has to say in chapters fifty through fifty-six of Book V of the *Laws*.

To begin with, Hooker's placement tells us important things about Christology itself. The study of who Jesus Christ is, and why he is significant for believers, might be pursued as a self-contained topic. Hooker, however, is not so tempted. The study of Christ rises from the desire to understand how the soul's union with God – 'our life supernatural' – can happen. So, '[f]orasmuch as there is no union of God with man without that mean between both which is both, it seemeth requisite that we first consider how God is in Christ, then how Christ is in us'.[2] The fact that Hooker's chief exposition prefaces his discussion of sacraments in particular, yet in relation to the return of the human soul to God in general, places Christology itself in what John Meyendorff calls a 'universal perspective'. He means that Christology can no longer be separated from Christian anthropology or the doctrine of creation, nor from the theology of the Holy Spirit. It becomes, indeed, the 'key' for understanding the Gospel as a whole.[3] This is Hooker's approach also. So the centrality of Hooker's Christological 'treatise' in the middle of the fifth book – the 'central tower'[4] of the *Laws* – suits Hooker's aim to re-balance the word-centred piety of so many of his contemporaries. But it does far more.[5] It is itself a kind of programmatic statement for the place of Christology within the church's theological and doctrinal universe.

Insofar as that is so, we can justly coopt a modern phrase to describe

---

1. Loyer, I, p. 476.
2. V, l, 1 [II, p. 220].
3. From 'The Christological Issue' in *Byzantine Theology* (New York, 1979), p. 32.
4. Thornton, *Hooker*, p. 54.
5. Loyer, I, p. 476.

the place of Jesus Christ in Hooker's theological vision: 'Christ the Centre'.[6] But what kind of centre? Hooker himself uses two words in the course of his Christological chapters, and around them we can shape an answer to that question. The two words are 'mean' and 'mediator'.[7] So by means of those two words this chapter will describe Hooker's Christology by describing his understanding of the person and work of Christ. We will try to discern how Hooker understands and uses the resources of the Christian tradition before him, and indicate how his interpretation relates to and serves his overall theological vision. The fifth book of the *Laws* is the central pillar of such discussion, but sermons and tractates offer important evidence too. In all of this we see Hooker connecting creatively with the Christian traditions of east and west by means of a line which links him with Anselm and Aquinas too.

'Institution' and 'Restitution'

Hooker's exposition of the person of Christ begins with a reprisal of orthodox Trinitarian belief. That in itself is noteworthy. In a fashion that tracks the progress of the patristic conciliar debates over God's triune identity, Hooker places his Christological interests in the framework of the concepts of and relations between 'nature' and 'person' which gained clarity in the post-Nicaean period. To this Hooker brings his Thomistic gloss. What we must note about that legacy as Hooker understands it with the aid of John of Damascus and Aquinas is the dynamic perichoresis, or 'being in', by which three persons share one substance by means of their distinguishing subsistent relations. But under the Damascene's influence this means for Hooker that Incarnation 'may neither be granted to any person but only one, nor yet denied to that nature which is common to all three'.[8] The 'incomprehensible' yet 'convenient'[9] mystery of the Incarnation begins, therefore, with the eternal generation of the Son and Word. Sonship and Word-ness are the natural and eternal gifts of the Father.[10] For Hooker both identities, Word and Son, are important in a balanced Christology. The Son as 'Word' is also 'wisdom'. Hooker is aware of Cyril of Alexandria's insistence that the Son as Word was indeed God's eternal wisdom, and not a wisdom created by God before all things.[11] That very divine Word and wisdom is active in the Incarnation.

But why should the divine wisdom and Word alone become incarnate? The answer is a strong and direct line between creation and recreation in the

---

6. A title given to Dietrich Bonhoeffer's 1933 lectures on Christology in English translation, *Christ the Center* (San Francisco, 1978).

7. V, l, 3 [II, p. 220]; V, li, 3 [II, p. 222].

8. V, li, 2 [II, p. 221]; referring to *On the Orthodox Faith*, III, 6.

9. V, li, 3 [II, p. 221].

10. V, liv, 2 [II, pp. 232-3].

11. V, liii, 4 [II, p. 226].

operation of the eternal and incarnate Word. Hooker does not use those exact words; he uses a turn of phrase translating Aquinas' *'convenire'* ('it is seemly', 'appropriate'): 'It *became* therefore him [*sc.* the Son] by whom all things are to be the way of salvation to all, that the institution and restitution of the world might be wrought by one hand'.[12] We are taken back to Book I's description of the second person of the Trinity as eternal 'counsel' and 'order' according to which the divine creative will then enacted in time its eternal thought. We can see as well why, in Hooker's scheme, the way of salvation works with and perfects nature. The 'one hand' of the incarnate Word holds them together.

Jesus Christ: the 'Mean'

To speak of Christ as the 'centre' elicits in Hooker's case the ideas of connection, coherence, balanced distinction and proportion. Hooker's word 'mean' carries those significations. In fact, the word takes Hooker to the heart of Christology in as much as the possibility of 'the union of God with man' requires that 'mean between both which is both'.[13] Christology generously defined deals with the person and with the work of Christ. In this explication of Christ as the 'mean' we will look more closely at Hooker's rendering of the patristic heritage *vis-à-vis* the person of Christ. But before doing so we should note an obvious question that can be easily overlooked: does the person of Christ interpret his work? Or does the work of Christ interpret the person?[14] For the patristic tradition with which Hooker is working the answer is clear: the person interprets the work. There are two ways in which that is so for Hooker.

A Wary 'Middle Course'

Hooker's focus in patristic Christology is the phase following the Council of Ephesus in A.D. 431. and extending through the Council of Chalcedon's famous definition of the person of Christ in A.D. 451 Those fifth-century debates addressed matters left open by earlier conciliar and theological disputes; gradually they formulated Cyril of Alexandria's insistence on the unity of the divine and human in Jesus Christ into viable conceptual terms. Those terms were derived, on the one hand, from the Cappadocian Fathers' distinction in Trinitarian theology between 'person' and 'nature', and from western Christology's terminological distinction between 'nature' and 'hypostasis'.[15] Hooker's interest in Cyril's contribution and its consequences is apparent in his discussion in Book V.

---

12. V, li, 3 [II, p. 222]; emphasis mine.
13. V, l, 3 [II, p. 220].
14. The question is considered by Bonhoeffer, taking inspiration from Luther (*Center*, p. 37).
15. I follow the discussion 'Christology in the Fifth Century' in Meyendorff, *Christ*, pp. 13-28.

'four words'

The importance of the Council of Chalcedon regarding the relationship between the divine and human natures in Christ is focused for Hooker in four key words in the conciliar definition. 'In four words', says Hooker, the shape of orthodox Christology is drawn: *'alēthōs, teleōs, adiairetōs, asungkutōs, truly, perfectly, indivisibly, distinctly*; the first applied to his being God, the second to his being as Man, the third to his being of both One, and the fourth to his still continuing in that one Both'.[16] Within that matrix of terms, and of the relationship between the divine and created natures which they describe, Hooker recognises how Jesus Christ can be both human and divine.

Of course the integrity of those four words as saying something meaningful about Christ is wholly dependent on the clarification of the idea and terminology of 'person'. What the Cappadocian Fathers and others had accomplished regarding the triune God was applied to the mysterious union of divine and human in Christ. While Cyril himself had never attained thorough going clarity with his terms, the so-called neo-Chalcedonians after the council did. Cyril's contribution lay in his insistence that the Word and Son was the sole personal subject of all that the two natures did or experienced. While Cyril was clear that the two natures are never confused and, as we might say, amalgamated, it remains true that their respective activities are truly those of the one person who is their subject. On the one hand, Hooker insists as a necessary 'rule' and 'principle' concerning the two natures of Christ that 'of both natures there is a *cooperation* often, an *association* always, but never any mutual *participation*, whereby the properties of the one are infused into the other'.[17] His word 'association' seems to be an attempt to render the term perichoresis. So, while the divine and the human can (but need not) act together toward a shared effect; and while the two natures are interwoven like strands of different substances; yet those substances are never confused in 'participation', that is, in an exchange of natural properties.

On the other hand there is what Hooker calls 'a kind of mutual commutation' 'whereby those concrete names, God and Man, when we speak of Christ, do take interchangeably one another's room'. The consequence, he explains, is that

> [F]or truth of speech it skilleth not whether we say that the Son of God hath created the world, and the Son of Man by death hath saved it, or else that the Son of Man did create it, and the Son of God die to save the world. Howbeit, as oft as we attribute to God what the manhood of Christ claimeth, or to man what

---

16. V, liv, 10 [II, p. 238].
17. V, liii, 3 [II, p. 230].

his deity hath right unto, we understand by the name of God and the name of Man neither the one nor the other nature, but the whole Person of Christ, in whom both natures are.[18]

Thus Hooker affirms the principle in Cyril's 'theopaschite' insistence, namely, that it was both possible and necessary to say, for instance, that in Christ "God suffered in the flesh". From that insistence, vindicated by the Chalcedonian formula, Christians could speak of a 'communication of attributes' by which attributes of either the divine or the human natures could be posited of one and the same divine Son and Word, Hooker's 'whole Person of Christ'. In all of this 'conjunction' and 'distinction' not 'distraction' and 'confusion' prevail.[19]

Three Gifts to the Son

With the framework of the divine-human relationship established on Chalcedonian terms chiefly in chapters fifty-one through fifty-three, Hooker uses chapter-fifty four to describe in more detail the way the two natures relate. It will give him an opportunity to enrich the set of terms associated with that subtle and mysterious relationship of grace in the Incarnate Word. He does this with regard to what the Son in his unique relationship receives from the Father. Taken together these gifts encompass the whole mystery of Christ.

As if to keep the divine, uncreated moorings of all that unfolds *ad extra* in view, Hooker describes the first 'gift' to the Son *ad intra*, the gift of eternal generation. 'For every beginning is a *Father* unto that which cometh of it; and *every offspring is a Son* unto that out of which it growth.'[20] We have discussed this previously. More relevant to his purpose at this point in the *Laws* is Hooker's description of two other gifts from Father to Son that pertain to God's operations *ad extra* in the economy of salvation. Complementing the gift of eternal generation, then, is, first, the 'gift of union', and second the 'gift of unction'.[21] Hooker speaks of these gifts as received of Christ 'by grace'.

The Gift of Union

This gift refers to the Father's bestowal to the Son of full participation in human nature. It is, in other words, the gift of the Incarnation which we have described already; and as we have seen, Hooker's interest in describing this gift is to promote the Chalcedonian tradition's respect for the integrity of natures. Nevertheless:

---

18. V, liii, 4 [II, p. 230].
19. V, liii, 4 [II, p. 226]; 'theopaschism' asserts that God in Christ suffers.
20. V, liv, 2 [II, p. 232].
21. For Hooker's discussion, see V, liv, 3-10 [II, pp. 233-8].

The union therefore of the flesh with Deity is *to that flesh* a gift
of principal grace and favour. For by virtue of this grace, man
is really made God, a creature is exalted above the dignity of all
creatures, and hath all creatures else under it.[22]

Whereas the 'admirable union' of the Incarnation causes no substantial
'alteration', no change in essence, to the assuming Deity (for God by
definition is not subject to substantial change), yet it does change the
person of the Word, to whom Hooker refers when he speaks here of
'the manner of subsistence'. This is a subtle but highly significant point
that indicates Hooker's grasp of the implication of post-Chalcedonian
Christology as it continued to develop in the Byzantine East.[23]

This hint of dynamism in the divine-human union in the single person
of the Incarnate Word grows when Hooker considers the effect of deity's
union with humanity. If the eternal Word is in some sense changed in the
manner of his subsistence, then humanity is potentially changeable in the
capacity of its reach. He puts it in the form of a question: 'But may it rightly
be said concerning the Incarnation of Jesus Christ, that as our nature hath in
no respect changed his, so from his to ours as little alteration hath ensued?'
By no means. The very purpose of the Incarnation, says Hooker, was to
'change' human nature, 'to better the quality', 'to advance the condition
thereof', to 'add perfection to the weaker nature', while all the while
honouring the proper limits of both natures.[24] There are 'many glorious
effects' that issue from the near 'copulation with Deity' in the Incarnate
Word.[25] Through this grace of union God hath 'deified our nature'.[26]

The Grace of Unction

If the grace of union is unique to Christ, as the Incarnate Word, the grace
of unction extends beyond the human nature of Christ alone; it can flow to
believers as well. This rich Augustinian theme includes what Christ brings
to human nature apart from his own unique salvific role.[27] So it refers to
that which humankind can potentially enjoy through the saving economy
of Son and Spirit. It is the category of gift in which Hooker reprises the
patristic doctrine of deification.[28] One key to understanding the grace

22. V, liv, 3 [II, p. 233].
23. Specifically, the possibilities of divine personhood as distinct from divine
nature in relation to the creation, and especially humankind.
24. V, liv, 4-5 [II, p. 234].
25. V, liv, 5 [II, p. 235].
26. *Ibid.*
27. I find Loyer's discussion of these graces very helpful (I, pp. 476-83). See also
Émilien Lamirande, *Études sur l'Ecclésiologie de saint Augustin* (Ottawa, 1969),
pp. 52-4.
28. Loyer, I, p. 479.

of unction first in Christ's human nature and then in ours is the word 'apt', which we have encountered in discussion about human nature. In the context of chapter fifty-four of Book V aptness is not complemented with ability as it was in Book I.[29] Here aptness seems to imply that human nature itself is open to expansion, as if *the nature itself*, quite apart from the abilities that are natural to it, is somehow capable of enlargement without ceasing to be *human* nature. We might think of them as capabilities possible for human nature but never yet actualised. In Christ, the new Adam, both the aptness and abilities of human nature are maximised. As Austin Farrer has said in a different context, the perfect manhood of Jesus gave him pre-eminence in the capacity for 'spiritual enlargement'.[30] That dynamic is the force of the simile Hooker uses under patristic inspiration: the heated sword not only cuts with its normal nature, but, insofar as it is made fiery, it burns as well as cuts. The nature enjoys perfections which it is 'apt to receive'. Grace perfects nature and does not destroy it.

The point of the grace of unction, however, is that some measure of that capacity for spiritual enlargement is available to believers. Thus the Incarnation is the basis for the spiritual transformation which is the Spirit's special operation. We see that Chalcedonian and neo-Chalcedonian Christology has for Hooker a direct impact on the potential of fallen human nature. On that account his Christology has a determining role in his understanding of what salvation means for humankind, and how it happens.

His 'infinite worth': Anselm's Legacy

In keeping with that last remark, the patristic debates, despite their highly conceptual aspects, were thought to impinge directly on the possibility and character of salvation.[31] The affirmation of Jesus' shared divine nature with the Father and Spirit, and then the cooperation and association of the human and divine natures in the person of the Son and Word, credited and preserved in Jesus of Nazareth an 'infinite worth'. In a sense this was the orthodox fathers' way of asserting salvation by grace; there could be no value, no efficacy in anything that Christ did or suffered as a mere man, but only as the eternal Son whose eternal generation and grace of union gave to his human nature and to his natural human experience infinite force and value.[32] We are in a position, therefore, to appreciate why for the fathers as for Hooker the person of Christ informs the work; indeed, the work is (using Grislis' apt word) 'imbedded' in the doctrine of the Incarnation.[33]

---

29. See pp. 71-2
30. *The Triple Victory* (London, 1965), p. 32.
31. Meyendorff, *Christ*, p. 14.
32. V, liii, 3 [II, p. 226].
33. 'Continuity and Creativity': 7.

What of the work of Christ, that is, his atoning, sacrificial death on the cross? Here we enter a line of consideration that the *Laws* assumes but does not at length explicate. Other texts, mainly sermonic, complement the *Laws*' exposition of the person with exposition of the work; in the *Laws* Hooker himself tells us why in thoroughly evangelical terms: the knowledge of the cross is 'the only subject of all our preaching'.[34]

Jesus Christ: the 'Mediator'

In understanding the full mystery of Christ, that is, how Christ's person informed his work, no western theologian was more influential than Anselm. His writings, most classically in the *Cur Deus Homo* (*Why the God-Man*), presented an integrated view of Christ's person and work, seamlessly uniting them through fidelity to the conceptual apparatus of the Chalcedonian definition of the person of Christ. The argument of the *Cur Deus Homo* developed a soteriological syllogism: humankind's sin against God is as infinite and eternal as God is; since sinful humankind itself cannot pay the debt incurred by its sin, a man who shares the attributes of God must do so; Christ, the Word made flesh, is the man who as man can offer a satisfaction equal to the dignity of God. Building his interpretation on the two divine attributes of justice and love, Anselm's theory sought to acknowledge God's unspeakable love out of which God the Father receives from sinful humankind in the person of the Incarnate Son a satisfaction rather than a punishment.

In light of the concentration of historic interest in Hooker's patristic Christology, it is important to recognise the place of Anselm's atonement theory in Hooker's understanding of Christ's work.[35] To see this enables us to appreciate better how Hooker works with two streams of thought in his Christology. The presence and influence of the Anselmic stream should not surprise us. The passion of Christ was central in sixteenth-century liturgy and devotion generally, and of the Communion service of the *Book of Common Prayer* in particular.[36]

In line with the spirit of both public and private devotion and with the dominant strain in late-medieval western theology, Hooker uses conventional atonement language as found in the New Testament and developed in the Christian tradition. In his *Learned Discourse of Justification* Hooker employs an array of terms and phrases highlighting Christ's work of atonement developed on thoroughly Anselmic lines.

---

34. V, xxii, 9 [II, p. 97].

35. John McIntyre first noted Hooker's 'completely Anselmic soteriology' in *St. Anselm and His Critics* (Edinburgh, 1954), p. 127.

36. See John Booty, 'The Judicious Mr. Hooker and Authority in the Elizabethan Church', in Stephen Sykes, ed., *Authority in the Anglican Communion* (Toronto, 1987), p. 105.

'Satisfaction is a work which justice requireth to be done for contentment of persons injured', he explains in Book VI, 'neither is it in the eye of justice a sufficient satisfaction, unless if fully equal the injury for which we satisfy'. 'Seeing then', he goes on,

> that sin against God eternal and infinite must needs be an infinite wrong; justice in regard thereof doth necessarily exact an infinite recompense, or else inflict upon the offender infinite punishment.[37]

In that concise and sensitive rendering Hooker – distinguishing himself from Calvin's distortions of Anselm's atonement theory – reprises Anselm's own doctrine in which *either* satisfaction *or* punishment may be exacted for an injustice like sin. In Christ's bearing the cross, Hooker argues, a punishment has not been exacted so much as a satisfaction been offered and accepted.[38] Although as measured by God's infinite being the measure of sin against God is infinite too, yet through 'love and mercy' the 'extremity and rigour of justice' are remitted.[39] Because Christ has paid the ransom, 'because he hath offered himself as a sacrifice for sin', believers are liberated from the 'bands of corruption'. In this Christ is for believers 'justice' and so curbs the law of punishment following upon the fact of original sin.[40] It remains a consistent component of Hooker's view of the importance of the work of grace: Christ's shedding of blood in his death upon the cross will silence the outcry of any sinful deeds.[41] In keeping with the uniqueness of Christ's gracious mediation flowing from the union of natures in the person of Christ, Hooker insists (surely with a sense of the double meaning of his terms) that the meritorious sacrifice is Christ's 'bare and naked work'.[42]

We see, then, how through the work of Christ the wrath and justice of God are ameliorated by love and mercy.[43] On account of Christ's sacrifice of infinite worth, the Father has condescended to 'favourable conditions' for humankind.[44] In that the Incarnation implies an 'amiable course', 'framed', as Hooker puts it, 'ever according to the very state wherein we are'.[45] That Christ's sacrifice is efficacious for all accords with God's 'principal will' (here Hooker invokes John of Damascus again).[46]

---

37. VI, v, 2 [III, p. 56].

38. On Hooker's return to a pure Anselmic doctrine see Neelands, 'Crime, Guilt, and the Punishment of Christ: Traveling another Way with Anselm of Canterbury and Richard Hooker', *Anglican Theological Review*, 88: 2 (2006): 209, 211-13.

39. *DF*, V, App. I [II, pp. 570-1].

40. *LDJ*, 2 [III, p. 485].

41. *NTFP*, FLE: IV, p. 86.

42. *LDJ*, 32 [III, p. 531].

43. 'Wrath' is not an emotive word in Hooker's usage; it has nothing to do with anger since God is by definition passionless.

44. *DF*, V, App. I [II, p. 571].

45. *Ibid*.

46. *DF*, V, App. I [II, p. 573].

Retributive or Restorative Justice?

Commentators on Anselm have legitimately asked whether the justice connected with Christ's atoning death is simply retributive, as the payment of a debt, or whether it is restorative too?[47] Simply put, does the atonement leave humankind where it was before, or does the ransom paid release humankind for a different kind of future? Whatever the case may be in Anselm's own theory, Hooker's Christology implies a restorative justice. How else could there be a real link between the person of Christ, the work of Christ in his meritorious, debt-satisfying death, and the prospect of humankind's gracious transformation after the pattern of Christ's own deifying of human nature? In that Hooker fashions a theology of Christ's person and work into a unity that is far more like his ancient and medieval sources than it is like the current Reformed orthodoxy of his day.

Three Christological Themes: Exemplar, Sonship, the 'whole Christ'

Exemplar

Although the witness of Aquinas has been largely silent in Hooker's doctrine of Christ, there is an area where it discretely appears. For Hooker, as for Aquinas, Christ is an 'exemplar' of predestination. Hooker does not use the word 'exemplar', but he insists in a way consistent with Aquinas yet distinct from double eternal decree Calvinists that believers are predestined 'in Christ'. Aquinas takes the matter up in article twenty four of the Third Part of the *Summa* on the predestination of Christ. We will be familiar with the parameters of his discussion and its conclusion on the basis of earlier remarks on providence and predestination. Precisely as ordered to a particular supernatural end by the graces of union and unction, the Incarnate Son, possessing his grace-filled human nature, is regarded by Aquinas as predestined by the Father toward his supernatural glory.[48] In that predestinating decision Christ is *not* our exemplar. However, he is the exemplar in the working of grace upon human nature so that it might attain its supernatural end.[49]

For Hooker the predestined are 'of one stamp of character, which is

---

47. On this see Dániel Deme, *The Christology of Anselm of Canterbury* (Aldershot, 2003), pp. 87ff.

48. Aquinas distinguishes the eternal decision which is unrelated to Christ's assumed humanity from the 'manner' ('*modus*') 'in the order of time' ('*ordo quod est complendum ex tempore*') of the predestinating, which is wholly determined by the human nature assumed (*ST*, IIIa. 24. 4).

49. He is exemplar, that is, in regard to predestination's '*terminus*' and '*effectus*', and by the manner of bestowal, that is, by grace (*ST*, IIIa. 24. 3).

the image of his [the Father's] own Son', so that in Christ the predestined 'are said to be chosen'.[50] We have seen that for Hooker, as for his patristic sources, there are both differences and similarities in the workings of grace upon the assumed nature of the Incarnate Son and upon the rest of humankind. Likewise for Aquinas, Christ's role as exemplar, while it posits important areas of likeness, displays areas of real difference.[51] Among the areas of likeness, three are noteworthy.

Sonship

For one thing, according to Aquinas, Christ exemplifies predestination wholly apart from 'preceding merit'.[52] Hooker, as we have seen, fully supports that under-cutting of any predestination on the basis of foreseen merit.

Also important for Aquinas and Hooker is the example of Sonship, what Aquinas calls *'filiatio'* or 'filiation'. It is, of course, a thoroughly biblical term and concept deeply rooted in Paul's soteriology (e.g. Romans 8.14-15). From that source the theological tradition taught that the Word became incarnate precisely so that humankind, insofar as it is chosen and called, might appropriate by grace the Sonship that Christ enjoys by nature. What the Son enjoys through eternal begetting, the Christian enjoys through new birth by grace. For Hooker, Christ's role as 'mediator' is closely linked to his Sonship, and the possibility of humanity's return to the Father as adopted sons. So that 'if some cause be likewise required why rather to this end and purpose the Son than the Father or the Holy Ghost should be made man, could we which are born the children of wrath be *adopted the sons of God through grace*, any other than the natural Son of God being Mediator between God and us?'[53]

The 'whole Christ'

Finally, we should recall Hooker's phrase 'the whole Person of Christ'. The source of the phrase in Hooker is not clear.[54] Certainly it pertains to the *encompassing role* of the person with respect to both natures in the Incarnate Son, and for that reason it may derive from the Greek writers who fashioned the Chalcedonian synthesis.[55] At the same time, it echoes

---

50. *DF*, V, App. I [II, p. 595].
51. Subsequent articles in Part Three detail those.
52. *'nullis suis praecedentibus meritis'*.
53. V, liii, 3 [II, p. 222].
54. Neelands assures us that it derives from Aquinas' *'suppositum'*; see 'Christology and the sacraments', *CRH*, pp. 372-3. The term is largely equivalent to *hypostasis* (*ST*, IIIa. 2. 3).
55. The terminology generally of Hooker's Christological chapters in the *Laws*

Augustine's phrase 'the whole Christ, Head and Body'.[56] For Augustine it
signalled the inextricable gracious bond between Christ as Son, Lord and
Saviour, and the members of his body the church by grace and baptism.
Certainly as we review Hooker's Christology, and especially Christ's
role as predestinated exemplar, and as the 'first-born of many brethren'
(Romans 8.29), we can see how the notion of 'the whole Christ' implies
participation in his body, the church, by those who are being conformed
to Christ's example. And that is, in fact, what we find. As we will see in
the discussion of sacraments and faith and works, eternal election must
be actualised by what Hooker calls 'external vocation'. The Christ whose
predestination and filiation are exemplary is not disconnected from his
body, the visible sacramental community of grace, nor from 'faith working
in love' (Galatians 5.6). In that configuration Christology, predestination,
sacraments, and ecclesiology are interwoven as the person of Christ
exercises his effects in the economy of salvation.

An 'Open' Christology

As our discussion of Christology ends, we must anticipate a thought that
will re-emerge at the end of this study, namely, how theology is as much
about emphasis and proportion as it is about content. Hooker's magisterial
review of patristic Christological developments easily obscures the
emphases and proportioning which he brings to his presentation of the
orthodox, ecumenical tradition regarding the person and work of Christ.
So we must allow his own accents to sound.

First, we should note Hooker's attraction to the line of Christological
thinking associated with Cyril of Alexandria, with the Chalcedonian
definition, and those who continued that Cyrillian trajectory through
the fifth century and beyond. A number of important points follow.
First, for that stream of patristic thought, as later for Aquinas, salvation
focuses around participation in divine life; that is, humankind is most
authentically itself when it shares in the life of God. The perfection of
Christ's human nature by its association with divine nature assumes as
much. As a consequence, the human nature of Christ is thought to be
open. This Christological insight converges with what we have already
seen in Hooker's anthropology – and we will return to this in later chapters
– namely, that human nature is not closed in on itself in an 'illusory
independence' but is teleological, it is open to an end (*telos*, or *finis*) that is
beyond itself; it is a 'supernatural' end that fulfils human nature.[57] Although

---

needs much closer attention by scholars.
56. '*Totus Christus, caput et corpus*'. The theme is discussed thoroughly by Antonio
Piolanti, 'Il mistero del "Cristo totale" in S. Agostino', *Augustinus Magister*
[Congrés International Augustinien] (Paris, 1954), II, pp. 453-69.
57. Meyendorff, *Christ*, p. 211.

our sequence of chapters has inverted the logical order, it ought to be clear that Hooker's anthropology in general arises out of the patristic sources with which we are dealing here, and which in fundamental ways the subsequent Byzantine and scholastic theologians adopted and developed.

The openness of human nature, however, is only possible on account of an even more radical assertion fashioned over decades and with great care by those who honoured Cyril of Alexandria's basic instinct and insight: that the union of natures is in the one person, or hypostasis of the eternal Son and Word.[58] Hooker's phrase 'the whole Person of Christ' highlights what is key in this stream of Christology: *the comprehending capacity of God's personal or hypostatic life*. The divine person, by its very assumption of and participation in human nature in the act of Incarnation, reveals itself as *open*. That, explains one of the great twentieth-century interpreters of this patristic Christology,

> presupposes that God is not only an immutable and imparticiple essence but also a living and acting person. By assuming humanity hypostatically, the Logos "becomes" what he was not before and even "suffers in the flesh". This "openness" of a hypostatic or personal God to the creature, and especially man…"modifies" God's personal existence.[59]

Hooker, as we have seen, suggests as much. The implications for theology properly speaking are enormous insofar as it complements God's immutability with a dynamic principle. They are significant for economy too, that is, for the operations of God *ad extra* especially in the work of salvation.[60] And that, as we have repeatedly said, is Hooker's focus. In Hooker's case it relates to his use of the Christological concept of person. For him, as for Cyril and his Chalcedonian and Byzantine successors, the person is able dynamically to comprehend natures other than its own in the accomplishment of the saving work. As for Hooker, this is the key to the Incarnation of the Son and Word, so it is the key to his elusive theology of sacramental participation. In that respect, as in others, Hooker's Christological personalism is rich in implications.[61]

---

58. Key to the development of this Christological school of thought was the gradual convergence of the Latin term *persona* (which we translate as 'person') with the hitherto ambiguous Greek term *hypostasis*. That link in its doctrinal context was famously proposed by Pope Leo the Great; see Meyendorff, *ibid*. pp. 24-8.

59. *Ibid*. p. 210.

60. *Ibid*. p.213

61. See, for instance, Rowan Williams fascinating exploration of Hooker's view of Christ's person in his lecture 'Christology and Inter Religious Dialogue' at http://www.archbishopofcanterbury.org/articles.php/2279/the-future-of-interfaith-dialogue-archbishop-speaks-at-presence-of-faith-conference.

Chapter 8
'Generative Force and Virtue'
The Holy Spirit and Grace

In contrast to his treatment of Christ in the midst of Book V, which acts as a keystone not for that book alone but for the *Laws* in its entirety, Hooker's treatment of the Holy Spirit in the *Laws* and in other writings receives no equivalent attention. To an extent we may credit this to the fact that Hooker, as a man of his times, carried on the general christocentrism of the medieval western tradition.[1] But if the person and work of Christ stand as a 'central tower' of his theology as a whole, the wide fields around it are occupied by the Spirit and its work in a way that is diffuse but real.

Doubtless the Calvinist revolution *vis-à-vis* the concept of sanctification accounts for this in part. Its renewed emphasis on the Spirit's gracious work within redeemed humanity gave rise to numerous trajectories of doctrine and practical theology which formed a large part of the Elizabethan period's dynamic, vying theological market place. Hooker seems to find there a refreshing latitude within which to consider the role of Spirit and grace.

As in so much of Hooker's thought, here we face an eclectic and independent thinker pushing the boundaries of received orthodoxies. In his theology of grace we find the legacies of the magisterial Reformation both embraced and challenged. This is acknowledged in recent studies of Hooker's thought even as it was in Hooker's lifetime.[2] If Hooker's biographer Walton is to be believed, as early as his St Paul's Cross sermon of 1581 Hooker was already identified with a 'movement of resistance' to some of the implications of the then regnant English Calvinism.[3] How much of that resistance affected his theology of grace in those early years is debated by specialists.[4] There is no doubt, however, that 'resistance' showed itself in his doctrine of grace in notable ways. In this department of theology Hooker's mind was on the move.

---

1. That is, a focus on Christ's person and work, minimising salvation as a Trinitarian action.
2. Loyer, Neelands and Voak, for instance, all recognise both continuity and discontinuity with the views of magisterial reformers, although admittedly they disagree on the extent and location of it.
3. Neelands, 'Grace', p. 136.
4. As we have seen, as early as 1585, during the Temple years, Walter Travers attributed to Hooker the dubious view that predestination, *vis-à-*the divine will, was not absolute but conditional – dubious in Travers' view.

The purpose of this chapter is to introduce the main contours and content of Hooker's theology of grace in relation to the much controverted Reformation-era issues of justification, sanctification and glorification. We will, of course, connect those ideas with themes already encountered and then position ourselves for the topics that then naturally follow. Since, as Olivier Loyer reminds us, Hooker resists all attempt to reify, substantialise or give grace any autonomous status as a 'thing', [5] we need before all else to position the concept of grace within Hooker's doctrine of God and, in particular, of the Holy Spirit.

The Spirit in the Trinitarian 'Order'

Hooker's various discussions of grace need to be read against the backdrop of his doctrine of the Trinity. We have already seen how for Hooker God's working with his creation is always Trinitarian. 'Whatsoever God doth work', he says, 'the hands of all three persons are jointly and equally in it according to the order of that connexion whereby they each depend upon other'. While being of one essence and therefore of one efficacy, in their 'order' the Spirit is last. That is by no means a diminution of the Spirit's work; in both the work of creation and of redemption the Spirit is 'consequently nearest unto every effect which growth from all three'.[6] We have here a view of Trinitarian life *ad extra* in creation where the Father acts towards his creation through the Son whose work is effected and fructified by the Spirit.[7] While the Son, or Wisdom, 'ordereth' the work of the Father, the Spirit, or Power, 'perfecteth' that work. A little later Hooker applies that view in more salvific terms. 'Life as all other gifts and benefits', he says, 'growth originally from the Father, and cometh not to us but by the Son, nor by the Son to any of us in particular but through the Spirit'.[8] The Trinitarian work of salvation reverses the order insofar as the Spirit draws humankind into the Son, in whom we are presented to the Father. In both trajectories the Spirit is 'nearest unto every effect'. Such a pattern Hooker could deduce from a careful reading of Scripture and its patristic commentators both eastern and western.

Therefore the Spirit functions as the divine person who extends the divine life of the Son, whose source is the Father, to humankind. The Spirit does this by joining human beings to Christ who, because he joins in a perfect personal union human nature with divine life, shares the grace of unction with those who are in him.

The Abiding Spirit

How does the Spirit join human beings to Christ? It is important to note that

---

5. Loyer, I, p. 494.
6. V, lvi. 5 [II, pp. 247-8].
7. *Ibid.*
8. V, lvi. 7 [II, p. 249].

from his early sermons onward Hooker prefers the language of 'in-dwelling' to describe the Spirit's near presence in believers, a usage reminiscent of Aquinas' language of 'being in' (*essein*). In conformity with that language Hooker also prefers the Pauline image of the believer as the 'temple of the Holy Spirit', and the Petrine image of God's 'habitation' by the Spirit.[9] In that it is the abiding *Spirit*, Hooker does not use the scholastic terminology of 'uncreated' and 'created' grace, revealing a sensibility unhappy with certain inherited scholastic distinctions. Still, the force of his preferred terms, imagery, and usage is to emphasise as the start and end of all further discussions that believers are the recipients of God's self-communication.

The Anthropological Context

We must remind ourselves also of Hooker's understanding of humankind's destiny to which the work of the Spirit is ordered: we seek 'a triple perfection', he explains in Book I of the *Laws*, sensual, intellectual and spiritual. The third and final perfection, 'spiritual and divine', consists, he says, 'in those things whereunto we tend by supernatural means here, but cannot here attain unto them.'[10] He comments further that even when the first two perfections are in some sense fulfilled, there remains in man a lurking discontent. 'For man doth not seem to rest satisfied', he observes,

> either with fruition of that wherewith his life is preserved, or with performance of such actions as advance him most deservedly in estimation; but doth further covet . . . that which cannot stand him in any stead for vital use; that which exceedeth the reach of sense; yea somewhat above capacity of reason, somewhat divine and heavenly, which with hidden exultation it rather surmiseth than conceiveth; somewhat it seeketh, and what that is directly it knoweth not, yet very intentive desire thereof doth so incite it, that all other known delights and pleasures are laid aside, that give place to the search of this but only suspected desire.[11]

In that remarkable passage Hooker seems to ascribe to humankind what modern theologians, interpreting the legacy of Aquinas, have called an 'openness of being'. That is, dependent human nature is naturally orientated toward a supernatural calling and fulfilment.[12]

Hooker's understanding of grace is both underpinned and consummated by that view, and his sensitivity to that accounts for the

---

9. *Second Sermon on Jude* [III, p. 688].

10. I, xi. 4 [I, p. 257].

11. I, ix, 4 [I, pp. 257-8].

12. The phrase is that of E. L. Mascall, *The Openness of Being: Natural Theology Today* (Philadelphia, 1971). Mascall remarks: 'By their very dependence on God, finite beings are inherently open to him' (p. 146).

distinctive way he describes the 'way of grace'. So, behind all the nuances of Hooker's doctrine of grace lie these two elemental assertions: first, that God's Trinitarian self is accessible by the Spirit's gracious action; and second, that humankind is naturally orientated toward the receipt of that divine presence and power in this sense at least, that its receipt, presence, and effect do no violence to, but rather perfect, the God-given integrity of human nature.

Grace: Hooker's 'Revolution'

A survey of Hooker's works quickly reveals how little space he gives overtly to the discussion of grace, and, where he does, how much ambiguity he leaves us with.[13] He himself seems to have thought this intrinsic to the subject. 'In grace there is nothing of so great difficulty as to define after what manner and measure it worketh.'[14] One dense part in Hooker's answer to *A Christian Letter* gives definitions of grace; otherwise, no single sermon, no chapter of the *Laws*, is devoted to it.[15] Still, overtly both in the early and late sermons and treatises, and then more diffusely throughout the *Laws*, a rich and creative theology of grace comes into view.

Hooker was a grateful beneficiary of aspects of the Reformers' revolution regarding the theology of grace. At the same time, he introduced his own revolution on the subject within the evolving English tradition. That 'revolution', as David Neelands calls it, refers to Hooker's provision of a careful account of the basic relationship between nature and grace – an account that owes little to the dominant reforming theologies of the time and everything to the pattern of nature and grace expounded by Thomas Aquinas and other theologians of the High Middle Ages.[16] We have already noted the guiding Thomistic pattern of procession and return (*exitus* and *reditus*) for God's relationship to his creation.[17] Two other, more specific aspects of the scholastic vision inform Hooker's evolving treatment of grace.

First – and this too we have already mentioned – Hooker insists with Aquinas that grace does not destroy nature but perfects it.[18] As A. M. Allchin once put it: he holds together the glory of God and the true dignity of man.[19] Or, to put it a little more technically by a modern interpreter of Aquinas:

---

13. Those points are made by Loyer (I, p. 490).

14. *DF*, V, App. I [II, p. 548].

15. *Ibid*. [II, pp. 548-50].

16. Neelands, 'Grace', pp. 65-6; there is, of course, a strong Augustinian backdrop.

17. See chapter 4.

18. *ST*, Ia. 2. 2; *fides praesupposit cogitationem naturalem sicut gratia naturam et ut perfectio perfectibile*.

19. *Participation in God* (London, 1988), p. 7.

'nature is the very material in which grace works and for whose ultimate perfection grace itself exists.'[20] So Hooker has no interest in denigrating human capacity unnecessarily on behalf of the working of grace.

As applied to the doctrine of grace Hooker confirms this perspective by means of the twofold distinction between 'healing grace' (*gratia sanans*) and 'elevating grace' (*gratia elevans*). Behind that distinction lies a continuity between creation, redemption and consummation which is key to Hooker, and which supports his view that grace is given not just to rectify human 'obliquity' (as he sometimes calls it)[21] but to bring humankind to the beatitude for which it was created in the first place, and for which it is naturally inclined. Any reasonable account of Hooker's thought needs to assume his interest in the insights of the scholastic tradition. By the time he wrote his responses to *A Christian Letter*, Hooker's use of scholastic categories seems to have expanded. So, in the *Dublin Fragments* Hooker makes use of a third feature of Aquinas' theology of grace: the twofold distinction between 'sufficient grace' and 'efficacious grace'. Hooker describes them as 'grace which abideth not' and '*grace that abideth*'.[22] They are important conceptual distinctions as Hooker tries to understand the issue of perseverance in Christian faith and works.

These are the scholastic tools with which Hooker repairs and tightens the understanding of grace that he inherited both from his English predecessors and from their continental teachers. While they exercise influence variously throughout the numerous topics and themes of Hooker's works, they are especially pertinent to his view of the gracious process by which, through Christ and the Spirit, humankind is transformed by grace.

The Threefold Pattern of Salvific Return

The Reformers' radical readjustment in understanding grace, begun by Luther, took place within the most basic soteriological concern: how can a fallen human being enter into a right relationship with a holy God?[23] The answer to that question gave rise, first, to Luther's new understanding of justification by grace through faith alone, and, second, to Calvin's concept of sanctification as a next stage in what came to be known by Calvinist divines as the 'order of salvation' (*ordo salutis*).[24]

---

20. Mascall, *Openness*, p. 153.
21. Used by Hooker as an almost technical term to refer to the two ways in which human beings need grace (Neelands, 'Grace', pp. 83-4).
22. V, App. 1 [III, 594]; Hooker's emphasis; cf. *ST*, Ia, IIae. 109. 9; I owe this reference to Neelands, 'Grace', p. 183.
23. So Alistair McGrath, *Reformation Thought: An Introduction* (Oxford, 1993), p. 90; but see his treatment generally, pp. 87-119.
24. The 'order' actually begins with the eternal decrees of God, but justification and

Certainly Hooker embraces this terminology as he seeks to relate God's grace to the human situation. However, given the way in which Hooker positions the work of grace within the trajectory of humankind's spiritual destiny, it is helpful to describe it in terms of a threefold pattern of salvific return. That description emphasises two distinctive aspects of Hooker's treatment of the received Reformation doctrines: first, Hooker's sensitivity to the role of saving grace in the larger frame-work of the return of all things to God (*reditus*) as medieval schoolmen (and Augustine before them) understood it; and second, the integral relation not just between justification and sanctification, but between those first two elements and the third element, which Hooker terms 'glorification'. Although Hooker speaks in a sermon of 'justifying righteousness' and 'sanctifying righteousness', etc., we can, *mutatis mutandis*, speak of justifying grace, sanctifying grace and glorifying grace.

Lee Gibbs speaks of Hooker's 'via media' doctrine of justification, and in so doing highlights areas where Hooker nuances the received Reformation teaching.[25] There is debate about his interpretation.[26] At the very least, though, his proposal encourages us to expect from Hooker a creative angle on this important aspect of the theology of grace.

The sequence is expounded by Hooker in his sermon *A Learned Discourse of Justification* preached at the Temple in the first year of Mastership. In his desire to declare 'how Christ is made the righteousness of men'[27] Hooker offers this explanation of the 'grand question' between the Church of England and the Council of Trent:

> There is a glorifying righteousness of men in the world to come: and there is a justifying and a sanctifying righteousness here. The righteousness, wherewith we shall be clothed in the world to come, is both perfect and inherent. The righteousness, whereby here we are justified is perfect, but not inherent. That whereby we are sanctified, inherent, but not perfect.[28]

Here we can see clearly Hooker's threefold pattern of salvific return and the way grace effects it. Let us turn to each stage of the process to grasp its nuances, novelties and ambiguities.

---

sanctification form its most important stages for a believer within the temporal sequence. For a useful discussion of the idea of the '*ordo salutis*' and how it was used in Elizabethan theology, see Bryan Spinks, *Two Faces of Anglican Elizabethan Theology* (Lanham, PA, 1999), pp. 39-67, and 109-34; his discussion is oriented toward sacraments.

25. First argued in 'Richard Hooker's *Via Media* Doctrine of Justification, *Harvard Theological Review*, 74: 2 (1981): 212.

26. See, for instance, Corneliu C. Simuţ, *Richard Hooker and His Early Doctrine of Justification* (Aldershot, 2005); he rejects any suggestion of a 'via media' view (p. 151); and Ingalls, 'Sin and Grace', pp. 168-76.

27. *LDJ*, 2 [III, pp. 485-6].

28. *Ibid.* 3 [III, pp. 485-6].

'God's gracious eye': Justification

The atoning work of Christ, his infinite 'worth' as a ransom to God the Father, and as a satisfaction for humankind's sins, is the basis of the favour which comes upon a believer by the Spirit's 'power' and gift of faith. Such divine favour – Hooker's first and principal definition of 'grace' – is wholly and without qualification an unmerited act of divine mercy. So much so, in fact, that in his *Second Sermon on Jude* (perhaps Hooker's earliest extant text) Hooker compares the act of justification to creation 'out of nothing'.[29] The upshot of such a reference highlights the unmerited and imputed character of such justifying grace and the righteousness it brings. This 'imputation of righteousness', Hooker explains, 'hath covered the sins of every soul which believeth; God by pardoning our sin hath taken it away . . . we are as free and as clear as if there were not one spot or stain of uncleanness in us.'[30]

Hooker describes the reformed doctrine of justification in his own words like this in his *Learned Discourse of Justification*:

> the righteousness wherein we must be found, if we will be justified, is not our own; therefore we cannot be justified by any inherent quality. Christ hath merited righteousness for as many as are found in him. In him God findeth us, if we be faithful; for by faith we are incorporated into Him. Then, although in ourselves we be altogether sinful and unrighteous, yet even the man which in himself is impious, full of iniquity, full of sin; him being found in Christ through faith, and having his sin in hatred through repentance him God beholdeth with a gracious eye, putteth away his sin by not imputing it, taketh quite away the punishment due thereunto, by pardoning it; and accepteth him in Jesus Christ as perfectly righteous, as if he had fulfilled all that is commanded him in the law.[31]

The righteousness conveyed by this grace-as-God's-favour is, Hooker explains in the same *Discourse*, perfect but not inherent (i.e. not 'our own', not within us). So the believer's status as righteous and thus accepted by God is based on the notional transfer of the merit of Christ to the believer.[32] We are fully adopted by God before we are to any degree inherently changed. Thus far in Hooker's exposition there is nothing novel or ambiguous.

---

29. *SSJ*, 28 (III, p. 694). Neelands points out that this scriptural simile had a long pedigree through English divines back to Aquinas (p. 34).
30. *Ibid.* 25 [III, pp. 693-4].
31. *LDJ*, 6 [III, p. 490].
32. Voak, *Reformed Theology*, p. 173.

'Baptism with heavenly fire': Sanctification

Though impossible without justification, for they rise upon it, sanctification and the effort it involves are also, Hooker teaches, necessary for salvation.[33] Sanctifying grace brings a righteousness that differs from that of justification. It differs chiefly in that whereas the grace of justification is imputed, the grace of sanctification is imparted.[34] Later, in the *Laws*, he writes: 'We participate Christ partly by *imputation*, as when those things which he did and suffered for us are imputed to us for righteousness; partly by *habitual* and *real infusion*, as when grace is inwardly bestowed while we are on earth.'[35]

The righteousness that is imparted to the still-sinful believer by sanctifying grace, cannot be perfect. Sanctifying grace is a grace that coopts the capacities of the still-sinful believer and enables him to live into the 'way of grace'. At this point we find Hooker's treatment takes a somewhat scholastic turn insofar as this phase of humankind's salvific return requires both the healing of the effects of the fall that have wounded man's aptitude, and the laborious transformation of man's ability as he grows towards the triple perfections, and especially the spiritual perfection, for which he was made. Thus, both healing grace and elevating grace are forms of sanctifying grace and over time construct within the believer the righteousness of sanctification. This edifice consists chiefly in the so-called theological virtues of faith, hope and love.

Even in his early *Learned Discourse of Justification* Hooker applies another scholastic distinction, that of 'habitual' and 'actual', to his understanding of sanctifying grace.[36] Through the habitual grace of sanctification the 'infused virtues proper and particular unto saints' are lodged within a person. Although Hooker does not name them, he seems to have in mind at least the theological virtues of faith, hope and love.[37] Those, then, are the chief forms of sanctifying grace, the principal gifts which the Holy Spirit brings when it begins its abiding within the believer.

But Hooker knows that in the phase of sanctification, that is, through the whole temporal life of the believer, there is work to be done. 'Now concerning the righteousness of sanctification . . . we grant, that unless we work, we have it not.'[38] Sanctifying grace is therefore also 'actual', and that refers to the *effects* of habitual sanctifying grace. In his own words:

33. Neelands, 'Grace', p. 39.
34. *LDJ*, 7 [III, p. 491].
35. V, lvi, 11 [II, p. 254].
36. *Ibid*. 21 [III, p. 507].
37. At the very least this gives Hooker a way of placing the virtue of faith within a person to be the means by which justification by grace 'through faith' can occur; this issue will be taken up in a discussion of faith in chapter eleven.
38. *LDJ*, 7 [III, 491].

Habitual, that holiness, wherewith our souls are inwardly indued, the same instant when we first begin to be the temples of the Holy Ghost; actual, that holiness which afterward beautifieth all the parts and actions of our life.[39]

Clearly Hooker's understanding of sanctifying grace and the emphasis he places upon it, places works front and centre.[40] That is a theme to which we will return. Here, it is important to note several consequences of his understanding.

Dynamics in the Experience of Sanctification

First, although Hooker stresses works as an expression of sanctifying grace within a Christian, he does not attribute a meritorious quality to such works in the sense of their possessing any intrinsic meritorious worth which God is then obliged to honour.[41]

Second, Hooker admits that lapses are possible, and if sin is great enough, they jeopardise a Christian's justified status. As a result, the actual sanctifying grace would need to facilitate a 'second justification' through repentance. Part of Hooker's aim in so teaching is to guard against the view that works are irrelevant for the salvation of those who are justified. In a striking step 'alien' to the Calvinist mainstream, Hooker maintains that those who fall from grace through serious sin will only be saved by repentance and the renewal of their first justification.[42] All of this serves to underline the importance of a thorough use of the means of sanctifying grace as intermediate causes to accomplish God's gracious will.

Third, Hooker's view of sanctification influences his evaluation of human reason and will. In his study of Hooker's understanding of these two key human faculties Nigel Voak argues that sanctifying grace has a decisive transforming impact. The consequence is that 'mere natural reason' and 'mere natural will' become, under the influence of sanctifying grace, 'divinely enhanced reason' and 'divinely enhanced will'.[43] Voak's interest in the concepts pertains specifically to Hooker's theory of human action and belief formation, but they have a wider significance in helping us understand how believers can grasp what is true and good, and 'do the works of Abraham'[44] – a necessary capacity for a Christian operating within Hooker's understanding of the good works and growth in holiness enabled by sanctifying grace.

39. *Ibid.* 21 [III, p. 507].
40. Grislis argues that sanctification more than justification is Hooker's interest ('Continuity and Creativity': 7ff.).
41. *Ibid.* 7 [III, p. 494]; 'as if we had him [*viz.* God] in our debt-books'; chapter eleven will nuance this.
42. Voak, *Reformed Theology*, pp. 182-3.
43. *Ibid.* p. 97, and his chapter 4.
44. *LDJ*, 7 [III, p. 491]

'Associates of Deity': Glorification

The partial participation in Christ by 'habitual and real infusion' 'inwardly bestowed while we are on earth', Hooker teaches, becomes fully, and finally complete, when our souls and bodies are 'made like unto his in glory'.[45] Hooker speaks here of the third, glorifying righteousness, that characterises a Christian 'in the world to come'. The grace that effects our glorification shares characteristics of the graces that precede and lead to it. Like the grace that justifies, glorifying grace is 'perfect'; like the graces that sanctify, glorifying grace is 'inherent' as well as perfect.

Were we left only with Hooker's exposition in his *Learned Discourse of Justification*, the study of this third phase in the threefold pattern of salvific return might end here. In fact, most discussions of grace in Hooker's thought, orientated as they usually are to its relation to the areas of public polemic whether in England or further afield, say little about this third phase.[46] However, Books I and V of the *Laws* compel us to consider this grace and goal at more length since those sources add depth and breadth to what the *Discourse* itself only hints at; they enhance an appreciation of the full scope of Hooker's understanding of the Spirit's working through grace and its effects.

Much of Hooker's perspective on this third phase of 'the way of grace' is informed by Augustine and his medieval disciple Aquinas. From both Hooker implicitly grasps that grace in this life is the beginning of glory hereafter.[47] As Hooker works with the notions of glory and 'glorifying righteousness' in the *Laws* he embraces another, complementary set of terms to explain the Christian hope. Equally, the *Laws* makes it possible for us to see how Hooker's understanding of glorifying grace and the hope it consummates are linked to anthropology and Christology. Therefore, we need to revisit briefly those two areas of concern.

Man and his desire for the Good

In the eleventh chapter of Book I of the *Laws* Hooker describes man's openness to a supernatural end centred on the role of desire in relation to it.[48] As a nature that seeks perfection, humankind, in Hooker's account, desires various goods. We have already recalled the idea of humankind's 'triple perfection' to which the graces of humankind's salvific return respond. Just as various goods to be

45. V, lvi, 11 [II, p. 254]. On deification as a truth in nature see I, v, 3 [I, p. 216].
46. E.g. Simuţ's study cited in note 26.
47. E.L Mascall, *Grace and Glory* (New York, 1961), p. 20. He seems to be quoting Augustine.
48. On the importance of desire, an interesting perspective is advanced by Patrick Peterson, 'Hooker's Apprentice: God, Entelechy, Beauty and Desire in Book One of Richard Hooker's *Lawes of Ecclesiasticall Politie*', *Anglican Theological Review*, LXXXIV: 4 (2002): 982-5.

desired honour natural and intellectual perfections, so there is a 'Sovereign Good' or 'Blessedness' 'wherein the highest degree of all our perfection consisteth, that which, being once attained unto there can rest nothing further to be desired.'[49] That 'Sovereign Good' is God, the fulfilment of man's infinite desire for good, and so the goal of humankind's spiritual perfection: 'with it our souls are fully content and satisfied . . . and thirst for no more.'[50]

Having established God as the end of all human desire for good, Hooker then adds a small yet important bundle of ideas: 'union', 'participation', and 'conjunction'. Those are the words that describe the possession of the Good. In his perfection man is able to possess God (the Good), to be united or conjoined to, and participate in, God. Our natural desire for the Good, namely God, is implanted in us by God with the intent that it be fulfilled so that, as he explains, 'although we be men, yet by being unto God united we live as it were the life of God.'[51] We should note Hooker's qualifying phrase 'as it were' lest a wrong literal sense be attributed to his affirmation of divine-human union; still, he clearly understands human destiny to be *in* and *with* God.

The 'grace of unction' in Christ

Humankind's destiny to participate in God is answered by the Incarnation: by the union of divine and human natures in the personal Word. Hooker's exposition of the doctrines of the Trinity and the Incarnation in Book V collect and take forward both the theme and terminology of Book I.[52]

In the previous chapter's discussions of Christology we noted Hooker's concepts of the 'grace of union' and the 'grace of unction' to describe different aspects and effects of the union of two natures in the Son. It is in relation to the incarnate Son alone that Hooker clearly employs the language of 'deification' or *theosis*.[53] 'The union therefore of flesh with Deity is to *that flesh* a gift of principal grace and favour.' 'For by virtue of this grace', he continues, 'man is really made God, a creature is exalted above the dignity of all creatures, and hath all creatures else under it.'[54]

While Hooker has emphasised the singular character of that personal union of natures in Christ ('by grace') by which God 'hath deified our nature', he nevertheless makes clear that the 'deification' of Christ's human nature has real consequences for the human nature of those who are in Christ by gracious adoption:

---

49. I, xi. 1 [I, p. 253].
50. *Ibid.*
51. I, xi.3 [I, p. 295].
52. In particular in chapters 54-6 of Book V.
53. William Harrison uses this idea as a key to interpreting Hooker; see for instance his essay 'The Church', *CRH*, p. 305. It is key also for Allchin, *Participation*, pp. 8-14.
54. V, liv.3 [II, p. 233]; emphasis mine.

The very cause of his taking upon him our nature was to *change* it, to *better* the quality, and to *advance the condition* thereof, although in no sort to abolish the substance which he took, nor to infuse into it the natural forces and properties of his Deity.[55]

Hooker is trying to clarify what can legitimately be said of humanity under the influence of sanctifying and glorifying grace while maintaining the distinction of natures, which his philosophical framework requires.[56] 'We have right to the same inheritance with Christ, but not the same right which he hath, his being such as we cannot reach, and ours such as he cannot stoop unto.'[57] He is unwilling to say that we are 'deified' as Christ is, yet he insists that a real enhancement of 'quality' and an 'advance' in human nature's conditions are possible by our gracious adoption as God's children and his fellow-heirs, and by our being 'temples of the Holy Spirit'. For whereas 'the natural properties of Deity be not communicable to man's nature, the supernatural gifts, graces and effects thereof are'.[58] Hooker seems to have in mind here the effects of what he terms the 'grace of unction'. While Hooker is unclear as to what those effects precisely are both in Christ and in us, he is clear that, as temples of the Holy Spirit, we can by grace share in some of the transformed characteristics of Christ's now deified human nature as the grace of unction has adorned it.

In arguing thus Hooker seems to reprise the concept of 'aptness' that features in his anthropology. We have seen how it refers to latent potentialities within human nature, to an aspect of humankind's transcendent openness to grace implanted in his nature from the beginning, to that area of human being where grace can effectively *elevate* the believer. Hooker invokes a vivid patristic image to convey how human nature's latent potentialities are actualised by grace in the incarnate Son:

> Surely as the sword which is made fiery doth not only cut by reason of the sharpness which simply it hath, but also burn by means of that heat which is hath from fire, so there is no doubt but the Deity of Christ hath *enabled* that nature which it took of man to do more than man in this world hath the power to comprehend; forasmuch as (the bare essential properties of Deity excepted) he hath imparted unto it all things, he hath replenished it with all such perfections as the same is in any way *apt* to receive.[59]

---

55. V, liv.5 [II, p. 234]; emphasis mine.
56. We will see that same view operating in his view of eucharistic presence, see chapter 10 below. In this Hooker is faithful to his sources John of Damascus and Aquinas both of whose theologies of deification are within a philosophical account that maintains the integrity of uncreated and created natures.
57. V, lvi.5 [II, p. 235].
58. *Ibid.*
59. V, liv.6 [II, p. 236].

That very imagery was furnished by Origen and then adopted by Cyril in advocacy of the meaning of the Incarnation and, by consequence, believers' deification.[60]

Enough has been said to indicate how the Incarnation, building upon man's primal vocation from God, takes humankind forward to its glorious destiny; and how, in the participation with God that it enables, the glorifying grace of the Holy Spirit perfects the inner transformation of the human person according to the full stature of humanity renewed in Christ. 'For this reason', Hooker explains as he considers that Trinitarian way of salvation, 'the Apostle wisheth to the Church of Corinth "The grace of our Lord Jesus Christ, and the love of God, and the fellowship of the Holy Ghost." Which three St. Peter comprehendeth in one, "The participation of divine Nature."'[61]

Capax Dei: the Content of Our Participation in God

Complementing Hooker's language of desire, possession, union and participation is another assemblage of ideas: knowledge, love, happiness, enjoyment and delight. They all describe what we might call the content of humankind's union with God, and are directly derived from the western development of the goal of grace extending from Augustine through Aquinas and beyond to his scholastic successors. Both of those great expositors stand directly behind Hooker in this regard.

In keeping with the view advanced in Book I of the *Laws* that grace perfects nature and does not ignore or destroy it, Hooker eloquently affirms that 'complete union' with God 'must be according unto every power and faculty of our minds apt to receive so glorious an object'.[62] Humankind's primordial orientation toward truth and goodness, its irrepressible desire for them through life and rekindled by grace, is perfected by the glorifying grace of union. Hooker insists, building upon the previous quotation:

> Capable we are of God, both by understanding and will: by understanding, as He is that sovereign Truth which comprehendeth the rich treasures of all wisdom; by will, as He is that sea of Goodness whereof whoso tasteth shall thirst no more. As the will doth now work upon that object by desire, which is as it were a motion towards the end as of yet unobtained; so likewise upon the same hereafter received it shall work by love. *"Appetitus inhiantis fit amor fruentis,"* saith St Augustine: "The longing disposition of them that thirst is changed into the sweet affection of them that taste and are replenished."[63]

60. I owe this to Metropolitan Kallistos of Diokleia; see, for instance, Origen, *On First Principles*, II, vi, 5-6.

61. V, lvi.7 [II, p. 249].

62. I, xi.3 [I, p. 255].

63. I, xi.3 [I, pp. 255-6]; we see here Hooker's talent as a translator.

The longing is perfected in love to the extent that it is shorn of self-regard and is in rapt attention Godward. 'Whereas we now love the thing that is good, but good especially in respect of benefit unto us; we shall then love the thing that is good, only or principally for the goodness of beauty in itself.' 'The soul being in this sort, as it is active, perfected by love of that infinite good, shall,' he goes on, 'as it is receptive, be also perfected with those supernatural passions of joy, peace, and delight. All this endless and everlasting'.[64] In that rapturous loving regard the human being experiences delight and happiness, what Christian tradition calls 'beatitude'. We are made, says Hooker, to attain just that 'felicity and bliss', and it is God's gift to those who continue in Christ by faith, through the gift of the Holy Spirit.[65]

Standing with the Great Tradition

It is important, finally, to highlight two aspects of the theology of participation in the wider theological tradition to which Hooker seeks to be accountable. First, deifying union with God is seen as the norm of Christian growth into God. It is not understood as an experience or goal reserved for a mystical elite. Everything in Hooker's account of grace and participation in God accords with that. Second, the language of 'union' and 'participation' notwithstanding, great care is also taken to guard the 'ontological divide' between Creator and creature, between God and man. Hooker, as we have seen, is highly sensitive to this, as were his patristic, Byzantine and medieval predecessors. Still, by comparison with them readers may find Hooker's language ambiguous, perhaps even unresolved. However that may be, an accurate reading of Hooker must take account of his insistence on careful distinctions in any and all language about 'union' in Christian theology.

In his study of Hooker's theology of grace Neelands argues that in his language of participation and deification Hooker invests Elizabethan Christianity with a significant new element.[66] This reprisal of the theology of deification places Hooker within the theological patrimony of his predecessors Augustine and Aquinas for whom the deification of the believer is the goal of the way of grace.[67] Behind Aquinas especially stand the towering figures of the eastern Christian tradition, Cyril of Alexandria

---

64. V, xl.3 [II, p. 256].

65. God, says Hooker in the *Dublin Fragments*, appointed the gifts of grace 'to accomplish our happiness' (V, App. I [II, p. 572]).

66. 'Grace', pp. 48-52.

67. On this aspect of Augustine's thought see Norman Russell, *The Doctrine of Deification in the Greek Patristic Tradition* (Oxford: OUP, 2004), pp, 325-442 where the Augustinian perspective is discussed; and on Aquinas' views, A. N. Williams, *The Ground of Union: Deification in Aquinas and Palamas* (New York: OUP, 1999), pp. 34-101; and her conclusion, pp. 157-165.

and John of Damascus, who through him extend an oblique but weighty influence upon Hooker's theological vision.[68] In all those expositors this view of humanity's goal forms a continuous theological line with the doctrines of the Trinity and the Incarnation. It is a noteworthy measure of his grasp of the contours of the patristic tradition that this is so for Hooker too.[69] In this he played a significant part in regulating the English Reformed vision of God and man, and its understanding of God's gracious dealings, to the patristic patrimony of the undivided church.[70]

In a tidy summary of his taxonomy of grace near the end of his life Hooker wrote this in response to his critics:

> By grace we always understand, as the word of God teacheth, first, his favour and undeserved mercy towards us: secondly, the bestowing of his Spirit which inwardly worketh: thirdly, the effects of that Spirit whatsoever but especially saving virtues, such as are *faith*, *charity* and *hope*; lastly, the free and full remission of our sins. This is the grace which *Sacraments* yield, and whereby we are all justified.[71]

But by grace believers are more than justified; they are sanctified toward glorification too.[72]

To understand believers' access to those sanctifying and glorifying graces, then, we must turn to Hooker's understanding of worship, and then, more especially, to its centre, the sacraments themselves.

---

68. But the influence is not only oblique, at significant points Hooker quotes them directly.

69. This important point about the coherence of these three aspects of theology is made by Allchin, *Participation*, p. 5.

70. He was not alone, though, as studies of his exact contemporary Lancelot Andrewes show, not least in regard to the theology of grace and deification. On Andrewes' theology of *theosis*, see, for instance, E. C. Miller, *Toward A Fuller Vision* (Wilton, CT, 1984), pp. 25-44.

71. *DF*, V, App. I (II, p. 552).

72. This is not to say that the content of the goal of deification, beatitude, is conceived identically in the traditions of the Latin west and Byzantine east; Hooker's view is western; on the matter generally, see Myrrha Lot-Borodine, *La Déification de l'Homme* (Paris, 1970), pp. 239-78.

PART THREE

PARTICIPATION

Chapter 9
'The Sovereign Observances of God's Grace'
Worship and Sacraments

Despite variety and debate in the interpretation of Hooker's *Laws* there is unanimity in the recognition of the importance of Book V. In this keystone of the *Laws*' architectonic shape Hooker tackles issues of worship and sacraments. It has been said that this book constitutes the first commentary on the *Book of Common Prayer*, and we can agree with this as long as we do not take the term 'commentary' in too strict a sense.[1] As we have seen, the publishing history of this book reminds us that it emerged within the welter of pressing Parliamentary political challenges, so that we cannot expect it to be a disinterested treatise of liturgical theology. Still, it is worth remembering that Hooker represents a generation whose experience of worship and sacraments within the Church of England was wholly and exclusively formed by the 1559 revision of the *Book of Common Prayer*. In the case of Hooker – as distinct from non-conformists with whose views he takes issue in Book V – the Prayer Book was a well from which he drank deeply and with satisfaction. The fifth book of the *Laws*, then, embodies an incisive and theologically deep rebuttal to the complaints and criticisms that had by the 1590s become a staple of Elizabethan non-conformity.[2]

At the same time, as we saw in Hooker's treatment of Scripture, something more is going on. However much Hooker may have been defending an ecclesiastical *status quo*, his probing nature took opportunities to delve deeply and look widely, so that in this chapter and the next we find Hooker urging the Reformed tradition to which he was committed toward areas of thought and experience with which it had lost touch or with which it still needed to grapple. Olivier Loyer speaks of Hooker giving back the Reformation tradition's 'true centre'.[3]

However this may be, there is no doubt of the extent to which this book has drawn the interest of generations of Hooker readers, especially through the first half of the last century.[4] Therefore we are entering territory where

---

1. McAdoo, 'Richard Hooker', p. 118.
2. James Turrell discusses the background in 'Uniformity and Common Prayer', *CRH*, pp. 339-47.
3. Loyer, I, p. 476; his point is made specifically with regard to Hooker's exposition of the Trinity and the Incarnation in his discussion of sacraments; but his point holds more widely in my view.
4. McAdoo, recalling his theological training in the 1930s, noted that the *Laws*'

the soil has been well ploughed and where opinions and assessments abound. So the focus of this chapter, coupled with the next, is what we might call Hooker's liturgical theology, drawing its broad contours in Book V but aware of the accumulating insights from Books I and IV.

Law and True Worship

Lest it be supposed that the concerns of Book V stand isolated from the earlier books of the *Laws*, it is important to note how Hooker himself relates the themes and topics of Book V to the principle of law. At first glance this approach may appear to reiterate conformists' conventional appeals to obedience to established laws and, by implication, to the godly prince.[5] But Hooker's appeal to law goes deeper.

To clarify the area of discussion Hooker begins his treatment of worship by distinguishing 'inward reasonable' worship from 'solemn outward serviceable worship'. Inward worship encompasses 'all manner virtuous duties that each man in reason and conscience to Godward oweth', whereas outward solemn worship, including the public rites and ceremonies of the church as embodied in the Prayer Book and the Ordinal, refers to 'whatsoever belongeth to the Church or public society of God by way of external adoration'.[6]

That second kind of worship is the subject of Book V and it is to that sphere of worship that Hooker applies his taxonomy of law as we encountered it in Hooker's hierarchy of laws.[7] In regard to principal matters the church orders its worship 'by none but precepts divine only'; with respect to 'things of inferior regard', by contrast, the church relies on 'ordinances as well human as divine'[8] since, in keeping with the inter-connected laws described in Book I, 'the word of God leaveth the Church free to make choice of her own ordinances'.[9] Hooker faces a non-conformist criticism of the *Book of Common Prayer* whose presumption, as he understands it, is 'that our laws have not ordered those inferior things as behoveth, and that our customs are either superstitious, or otherwise amiss.'[10] Therefore his task throughout Book V is to legitimate the forms of worship of the Church of England as in accord with divine precept and human reason, as sanctioned by law, and as established by ecclesiastical custom.[11]

---

fifth book was a set text for study; see his essay 'Hooker', *ibid*.

5. See Lake, *Anglicans and Puritans?*, p. 164.

6. V, iv, 3 [II, p. 27].

7. See Paget's Laws that concern men as parts of a supernatural society (p. 67).

8. *Ibid*.

9. *Laws*, V, x, 1 [II, p. 41].

10. V, iv, 3 [II, p. 27].

11. On the use of reason in devising forms of worship see V, vi, 1 [II, p. 28].

Though many of the concerns of Book V are 'things of inferior regard', Hooker does not on that account minimise their importance within the overall experience of religious life. Far from it, for 'touching the nature of religious services, and the manner of their due performance,' he insists,

> thus much generally we know to be most clear; that whereas the greatness and dignity of all manner actions is measured by the worthiness of the subject from which they proceed, and of the object whereabout they are conversant, we must of necessity in both respects acknowledge, that this present world affordeth not anything comparable unto the public duties of religion.[12]

In his explanation and defence of the established church's worship Hooker takes his first stand on the importance of 'public devotion' and the set of forms they require. Such properly liturgical, that is, public, corporate, and ordered prayer carries a unique 'virtue, force, and efficacy' commensurate with its 'reverend solemnity'. Why is that appropriate? Because, he claims, it stirs 'affection of heart' and it releases 'the power of our souls'.[13] With that as his starting point, Hooker highlights three aspects which set his liturgical theology at odds with non-conformist critics, and which widen the conformists' justification of the worship of the *Book of Common Prayer*: imitation, iteration and sensation.

Three Aspects of Worship

Imitation

In keeping with his hierarchical cosmology Hooker repeatedly emphasises the 'correspondence' between the earthly and the heavenly.[14] As we saw in an earlier chapter, Hooker understands hierarchy as a unifying, connecting principle within the overall cosmic order. It is not surprising, then, that within the ecclesial sphere of awareness and experience earthly and heavenly worship are linked. (We can, for instance, account for Hooker's interest in angelology in part by his belief that angels are the chief means of connection between heaven and earth.) One form of that link is how the church's 'solemn outward worship' is so ordered so as to correspond to what Christians believe about heavenly worship and realities, that is, when the external form of religion 'concurs' with 'celestial impressions in the minds of men'.[15] Byzantine liturgical sensibility inspires

---

12. V, vi, 1 [II, p. 29].

13. V, xxv, 1 [II, p. 118].

14. Ramie Targoff uses the phrase 'mimetic correspondence' of the relation between the heavenly and the earthly church as Hooker describes it, in 'Performing Prayer in Hooker's *Laws*: The Efficacy of Set Forms', *RHCCC*, p. 278.

15. V, vi, 2 [II, p. 30]; see Lake, *Anglicans and Puritans?*, p. 167.

Hooker's line of thought as he translates from Dionysius the Areopagite's *Ecclesiastical Hierarchy*: 'The sensible things which religion hath hallowed, are resemblances framed according to things spiritually understood, whereunto they serve as a hand to lead, and a way to direct'.[16]

For that reason, and in contrast to both non-conformist critics and most conformist defenders of the established church, Hooker accords to the 'scenic apparatus' of worship a positive, even vital edifying role.[17] 'Yea then are the public duties of religion best ordered,' explains Hooker, 'when the militant Church doth resemble by sensible means . . . that hidden dignity and glory wherewith the Church triumphant in heaven is beautified.'[18] Both ritual and ceremony prompt the imagination and so mediate awareness and contemplation of heavenly realities to worshippers.[19] Liturgical music too is justified on the same basis of correspondence, by which the aural experience engenders a spiritual awareness in 'that very part of man which is most divine.' For music has an 'admirable facility', Hooker explains with piercing insight,

> to express and represent to the mind, more inwardly than any sensible mean, the very standing, rising, and falling, the very steps and inflections every way, the turns and varieties of all passions whereunto the mind is subject.[20]

So it has a unique power to fire affection for things divine.[21]

Iteration

In rebuttal to non-conformist criticisms of 'common prayer' in favour of sermon-dominated worship and extempore prayers (or, as he describes them, 'endless and senseless effusions of undigested prayers'),[22] Hooker advocates the use of fixed forms. While from a polemical point of view Hooker's preference for the fixed forms of 'common prayer' according to Prayer Book norms works to curtail the dominance of sermons and a preaching-oriented ministry, a more fundamental preference is advanced. In keeping with his commitment to the *edifying* value of worship, Hooker esteems the repetitive character of public services. The engagement of the imagination over time and the resultant incitement of affections are sound means to build up worshippers in the apprehension of religious truths and in the practice of Christian virtues.

---

16. IV, 1, 3 [I, p. 420].
17. See Lake's excellent discussion in *Anglicans and Puritans?*, pp. 164-9.
18. V, vi, 2 [II, pp. 29-30]. See Paget's Law of Angels (p. 66).
19. On the importance of imagination see V, lxv.7 [II, p. 323-4].
20. V, xxxviii, 1 [II, pp. 159-60].
21. See, V, xxxix, 1 [II, p. 169].
22. V, xxv, 5 [II, p. 121].

Hooker's appreciation of the importance of what we are calling the principle of iteration is also seen in his conservative attitude to change with respect to ecclesiastical rites and ceremonies generally. Long-approved ancient ordinances, rites and customs (many of which Hooker defends through Book V) have by their very continuance among generations of believers proved their effectiveness as media through which divine truth is accessible to worshippers.

In this, at least, Hooker advocates forcefully for the mass of unlettered worshippers for whom the rhetorically focused, highly conceptual religion of Puritan preachers was both alien and inaccessible. Instead Hooker posits a liturgical culture that aids apprehension for the average worshipper through its repetitive habits and long-established customs.

Sensation

In keeping with the central place Hooker accords to the Incarnation within his theology as a whole, his liturgical theology acknowledges the importance of the senses.

The bodily character of worship is asserted by Hooker in contrast to a disembodied spirituality. We have already noted public worship's 'resemblance' to the celestial church 'by *sensible* means'. So, for instance, Hooker defends the Prayer Book's rubrical directions about kneeling at Communion, and at other points he affirms the appropriateness of actions which express an interior spiritual attitude.[23] Public prayer and worship, says Hooker, ought to be far more about 'knees and hands' than about 'ears and tongues'.[24]

At the same time, ceremonies can possess positive power as much by their cooption of the body into the act of worship as by the overt way in which they convey the correspondence between things earthly and heavenly.[25]

Likewise, the church buildings that house the worshipping community are sacred spaces that invite positive spiritual encounter. A church, in Hooker's view, is it not simply an auditorium in which the worshipper listens to a sermon but a sensorium in which all the faculties and senses join in the act of prayer and praise. He is eloquent about the importance of such sacred spaces; in varied, complementary ways they convey the spiritual correspondence between heaven and earth by wide appeal to the senses of worshippers.[26] 'As therefore we every where exhort all men to worship God', he acknowledges, yet

> [e]ven so for performance of this service by the people of
> God assembled, we think not any place so good as the church,

23. V, lxviii, 3 [II, pp. 365 –6].
24. See V, lxxxi, 10 [II, p. 524].
25. See V, lxv, 3, 5-6 [II, pp. 320-22].
26. See Lake's references to the *Laws*, *Anglicans and Puritans?*, p. 167.

neither any exhortation so fit as that of David,
"O worship the Lord in the beauty of holiness".[27]

As to particular senses, reference has already been made to the importance Hooker ascribes to the aural experience of music. Sight is a sense of primary importance in worship. It is 'the liveliest of all other', and so the use of 'visible signs' a 'deep' and 'strong impression' of the profound truths and insights conveyed by the rhetoric of worship.[28] Hooker's awareness of spiritual sight as a chief component of the soul's perfection leads him to estimate the worship of this world as an anticipation of the soul's receipt of the beatific vision. On that account Hooker is clear that public worship ought to captivate the eyes of worshippers by its solemnity and by the beauty of its ceremony and setting.

The Sacramental Centre

Hooker's treatment of the sacraments builds naturally upon the foundations laid in his discussion of worship. In the sacraments above all worship is materialised, bodily, and is in the strict meaning of the word, *sensational*: 'for it pleaseth Almighty God to communicate by sensible means those blessings which are incomprehensible'.[29] Here we penetrate far below matters of 'inferior regard' into the rich soil of Hooker's theological vision. To start we need to lay out the general features of Hooker's sacramental theology in preparation for discussions of baptism and the Eucharist in the following chapter.

If Book V as a whole is the *Laws'* conceptual centre then Hooker's treatment of the sacraments within Book V is the keystone.[30] Again, a quick glance at the expansive contents of Book V can easily obscure the importance of what we may call the 'sacramental centre' chiefly in chapters Fifty through Fifty-Seven. Brevity, however, is no measure of importance. Besides, there are other sources for Hooker's sacramental theology beyond the *Laws*, and we will have reason to cite them.

The Source of the Sacramental Principle: Trinity and Incarnation

If, as Olivier Loyer declares, the theology of the sacraments is the 'crown' of Hooker's theology, that is so because it is tightly moored to the doctrines of the Trinity and the Incarnation.[31] The preface to Hooker's discussion of the sacraments in Book V is nothing short of a treatise on fundamental theology whose content *vis-à-vis* God and Christ we have already explored.

---

27. V, xvi, 2 [II, pp. 57-8].
28. IV, i, 3 [I, p. 418].
29. V, lix, 3 [II, p. 257].
30. So William Gregg argues in 'Sacramental Theology in Hooker's *Laws*: A Structural Perspective', *Anglican Theological Review*, LXXIII, 2 (1995): 155.
31. Loyer, I, p. 475.

We can bring those considerations onto the stage now by means of Hooker's theme of participation, and by identifying four chief forms of participation implied in the doctrines of the Trinity and the Incarnation. First, we have seen how the doctrine of the Trinity teaches an eternal circumincession, or perichoresis, of the three divine persons. That is the basis of all other forms of participation. Second, we have seen how the doctrine of the Incarnation reveals the participation between the Father and the Son through the grace of union. Third, we have seen in Book I Hooker's concept of participation between divine and created being by means of God's active and permanent causality.[32] Finally, as we have seen in the chapter on grace and the Holy Spirit, God and humankind participate in one another most fulfillingly by grace. Hooker's theology of the sacraments builds upon that rich array of participations. No wonder sacraments have been described in Hooker's theology as a 'constitutive part of the eternal economy of salvation.'[33]

What are 'the Sacraments'?

Without prejudging Hooker's 'Reformed', 'Roman Catholic' or 'Anglican' credentials, we can safely agree with W. C. Dugmore that Hooker builds his sacramental edifice within the parameters of Article Twenty-five of the Thirty-Nine Articles of Religion.[34] That is, Hooker restricts the term 'sacrament' to the two 'Gospel sacraments' of direct dominical institution, baptism and the Eucharist; they, therefore, are the subject of Book V's discussion of sacraments.[35] His reference to sacraments in the *Dublin Fragments* confirms this. It is required of a sacrament, he explains, that, first,

> it be a perpetual duty in religion; and of a *Christian Sacrament*, that it be proper to Christian religion: Secondly, that Christ be author thereof: Thirdly, that all men be bound to receive it: Fourthly, that it have a promise from God for the effect of some saving grace to be thereby wrought in the person of the receiver: Fifthly, that there be in it a visible sign, both betokening the grace wrought, and the death of our Saviour Christ, to us the fountain of all grace: Lastly, that all these things concerning it be apparent in holy Scripture, because they are supernatural truths which cannot otherwise be demonstrated.

---

32. In expounding Hooker's understanding of this idea, Loyer speaks of a 'double principle of inclusion' by which first, every being is in some way in what derives from it; and second, every being is in some way in that from which it derives (I, p. 485).

33. Gregg, 'Sacramental Theology': 165.

34. *Eucharistic Doctrine in England from Hooker to Waterland* (London, 1942), p. 15.

35. Loyer speaks of Hooker's fidelity to Article Twenty-five's 'spirit of moderation' in so restricting the number of the sacraments (I, p. 505).

'Wherefore', he can deduce,

> because in *Baptism* and in the *Eucharist* only, as much as hath
> been declared is most manifest, what should forbid us to make
> the name of a *Sacrament*, as St. Augustine doth, by way of
> special excellency proper and peculiar to these two.[36]

Although Hooker attributes a grace-giving function analogous to that of the 'sacraments' to other rites, like confirmation and ordination, they do not figure in Hooker's key exposition at this point in the *Laws*.[37]

Building on a conceptual foundation first developed by Augustine in his symbolic-realist doctrine of sacraments, Hooker affirms that every sacrament has a visible part subject to the senses and an invisible part, a supernatural grace that accompanies the visible sign.[38] Thus far, anyhow, Hooker's approach conforms to the traditional definition to which he himself refers: sacraments are 'visible signs of invisible grace'.[39]

However, as we have seen, Hooker is not a straightforward thinker in that he ingeniously tries to build coherence from diverse sources. Using Article Twenty-five as a parameter and the traditional notion of a sacrament quoted above as a spring-board, Hooker tries to hold various current theories of sacraments together in a constructive tension.

Sacramental Causality

The degree to which Hooker is thought to have integrated such differences effectively is the measure by which his sacramental theology has been evaluated. Here above all assessments diverge. Such divergence has its source in regard to Hooker's understanding of sacramental causality, or how the sacraments are means of grace. Whatever ambiguities Hooker's sacramental theology may contain, he is clear that the sacraments are no mere spiritual illustrations, moral prompts, or reminders of benefits received. Rather, explains Olivier Loyer: 'They are necessary means which God requires of us so as to impart his grace; they are effectual means by which God puts us in possession of the grace by which we may attain eternal life.'[40] Why does Loyer say that?

Hooker rejects any concept of sacraments according to which they are the only tokens or memorials of grace previously or otherwise received. Instead, argues Hooker, the sacraments objectively bear the grace to which they symbolically point: they are 'means', 'instruments' or 'causes'

---

36. *DF*, V, App. I [II, p. 551].

37. Thornton, *Hooker*, p. 79; see IV, i, 4 regarding quasi-sacraments.

38. Dugmore sees Hooker building upon a revival of Augustine's sacramental doctrine in a line of English divines beginning with John Frith (*The Mass and the English Reformers*, [London, 1958], p. 102).

39. V, I, 3 [II, p. 219].

40. Loyer, I, p. 496.

of grace. (We remember the importance of secondary causes in Hooker's theology of creation.) The import of those three words colours his entire discussion of the sacraments; each of them sheds its own light on Hooker's understanding of sacramental causality.

The sacraments are 'means' of grace. They, like the Word, have 'generative force and virtue', and are accompanied by 'grace which worketh Salvation'. [41] That is, their grace-bearing force is objectively tied both to the sacramental action as a whole and to the sacrament's outward and visible form (water, bread, wine). Hooker is happy to use the language of 'representation' – the symbol represents the invisible grace – as long as representation is taken in its proper sense, that is, to re-present or to render present. In Hooker's treatment we feel ourselves within the gravitational force of Augustine's realist-symbolist perspective. According to such a view, although the sacramental sign and the grace it signifies are distinct, the sign is no mere 'figure' but the way by which grace is communicated to the believer.[42] As a 'means' of grace, then, the sacraments possess what they signify; in a sense they are what they signify.[43]

Sacraments are also 'causes' of grace. Hooker uses this stronger term and by doing so seems to want to tighten the link between the sacramental sign and the thing signified. It underlines the role of the sacraments as (to use Loyer's phrase) 'the ordinary requisite condition for the acquisition of grace.'[44]

Having said that, Hooker is very careful, even guarded, in both his understanding and his use of the word 'cause'. Above all he wants to tread a path that adheres to the great Christian sacramental sense, on the one hand, and yet avoids dubious scholastic concepts of causality, on the other. As we saw in the previous discussion of grace, Hooker's main criticism of at least one strand of scholastic sacramental theology is its attribution of causality to the sacramental sign or indeed to any created thing apart from its divine source.[45] To avoid this error Hooker qualifies the casual role of the sacraments by describing them as 'causes instrumental'.[46] By means of that crucial adjective 'instrumental' Hooker makes the point that sacraments are efficacious not because of an autonomous inherent quality,

---

41. V, l, 3 [II, 220].

42. As Dugmore describes the Augustinian sacramental tradition: 'The res is distinct from the signum, but it is offered to the faithful by, or together with the signum, which is "no figure"' (Eucharistic Doctrine, p. 229).

43. Loyer, I, pp. 497; see his discussion of the Augustinian tradition in I, pp. 520-1.

44. Loyer, I., p. 497.

45. Here is one area where Hooker clearly diverges from Thomas Aquinas whose sacramental theology attributed a 'supernatural inherent virtue' to the sacramental matter (Loyer, I, p. 498).

46. V, lxvii, 5 [II, p. 352].

but because God is always present and active when they are celebrated.[47] The 'assistance', 'concurrence' and 'conjunction' of the Holy Spirit makes sacraments effectual, and by the Spirit they really 'exhibit' the grace they bestow.[48]

Sacramental 'Substance'

Another important element in Hooker's sacramental universe is the distinction between 'form' and 'matter'. Together 'form' and 'matter' constitute what traditional medieval theology came to call the 'substance' of the sacrament. Actually, while Hooker accepts the received notion of sacramental substance, he shapes it in his own way. The conceptualisation which he inherited from western medieval scholastic thought differentiated the 'form' of a sacrament, that is, the form of words by which a sacrament is ritually identified, from the 'matter' of a sacrament, that is, its material substance – the 'outward visible sign' – such as water, bread or wine by which a sacrament is visually identified and sensibly experienced.

For his part, Hooker reworks the concept of substance. Instead of a twofold distinction between 'form' and 'matter', Hooker identifies 'exterior substance', on the one hand, and 'true essential form', on the other. The 'exterior substance' of the sacrament refers to both the 'form' and the 'matter' of the traditional definition. The 'true essential form' refers to the grace which is conveyed.

Why does Hooker rework the traditional understanding of sacramental 'substance'? Simply, it seems, because he thinks his reworking better preserves the source of sacramental efficacy in divine action rather than in the sacramental matter itself.[49]

Sacramental Efficacy

Lionel Thornton insightfully remarks that Hooker's incarnational theology makes much of the relation between person and things.[50] That interactive relationship is woven into Hooker's understanding of sacramental efficacy. By 'efficacy' is meant the factors by which a sacrament successfully conveys grace. Hooker's interest is to affirm the grace-bearing force of a sacrament without disconnecting the sacrament from God, who is the source of grace, or from those who minister it.[51]

47. Neelands points up Hooker's suggestive use of the word 'shadow' in regard to sacraments (V, lviii, 2 [II, p. 260]) giving a possible Platonic cast to his view of sacramental participation ('Grace', p. 333).
48. *Ibid.* Hooker's word 'exhibit' is part of Greek patristic liturgical vocabulary. In the liturgy of St Basil, for instance, it is the operative word of the epiclesis; see Gregory Dix's discussion 'The Origins of the Epiclesis', *Theology*, 28: 165 (1934): 136-7.
49. Loyer, I, p. 502.
50. *Hooker*, p. 82.
51. The issue became overt in criticisms against him in *A Christian Letter*. On the

In his discussion of baptism in Book V Hooker distinguishes three forms of the 'perfection' of a sacramental act by means of which a sacrament has integrity and conveyance of sacramental grace is assured. He speaks there of a threefold perfection: moral, ecclesial and mystical.[52] The moral perfection refers to the minister of the sacrament, and the minister's intention to act out the church's intention in the performance of the rite. The ecclesial perfection refers to the conduct of the rite according to the terms and forms of service required by ecclesiastical authority and canons. The mystical perfection depends on the use of the 'exterior substance' of the sacrament as dominically ordained.

According to Hooker, then, a sacramental act so 'perfected' is the assured instrumental means by which a believer graciously participates in God through Christ.

The 'moral instrument' of Salvation

We have seen that Hooker describes Scripture as the 'doctrinal instrument' of salvation.[53] To that biblical 'instrument' Hooker couples the sacraments as, collectively, the 'moral instrument of salvation'.[54] His use of the word 'moral' may seem strange to a contemporary reader. In Hooker's usage the '*moral* instrument' complements the doctrinal instrument as being and acting complements knowing. So the sacraments communicate the active energy by which Christians 'work out their salvation in fear and trembling' (Phil. 2.12). It is important to note the parallelism in Hooker's usage. By using it he highlights the mutually supporting roles of Scripture and sacraments, intellectual apprehension of saving truth, on the one hand, and the power by which we actually share in God's life by grace, on the other. It is not that Hooker prefers a sacramental religion to a religion of the Word;[55] rather, he advocates a better balanced, more wholesome relation between the two.

There are, however, two further aspects of Hooker's sacramental theology which tend to sharpen the distinction between his perspective and that of non-conformists. The first is the relation between 'eternal' and 'actual' in what theologians of Hooker's day called the 'order of salvation'.[56] In a marked departure from the Calvinist mainstream,

---

distinction between *opus operantis* and *opus operatum*, see V, lxii, 15 [II, p. 295].

52. V, xliii, 15 [II, pp. 294-5].

53. See chapter 5 above.

54. V, lvii, 4 [II, p. 257].

55. Lake, *Anglican and Puritan?*, p. 177.

56. Discussion of the '*ordo salutis*' was almost an obsessional topic in the Calvinist theologies of the later Elizabethan and Stuart periods. It relates to the interaction between divine election, the gracious gift of faith, and perseverance; see, for instance, R. T. Kendall's exposition in *Calvin and English Calvinism to 1649*

Hooker insists that whatever eternal decree of election may favour some in the eyes of God, there is no spiritual benefit, no living into such a decree, apart from actual receipt of grace through the sacraments. Hooker's theology of election does not undercut but rather underlines the necessity of sacraments in the life of grace. Eternal decrees must be earthed in actual receipt of grace through the instrumentality of the sacraments as secondary causes. The sacraments, therefore, have an inalienable place in soteriology for Hooker.

Finally, Hooker's perspective makes sacraments key means of growth in the life of grace. In the discussion of his theology of grace we noted what we called Hooker's gradualism. We see now that the sacraments are key not simply for first access to the life of grace to which a Christian has been called, but they are the regular means by which Christians grow more and more into the divine fellowship for which they have been created. In that sense, sacraments have a 'constitutive place' in Hooker's overall ecclesiological vision.[57]

A Revolution in Worship

In his exposition of Hooker's understanding of sacraments Lionel Thornton wrote of Hooker that 'for him sacramental rites are the outward means through which human personality is regenerated, cleansed, blessed, nourished and consecrated that it may share in the life and activity of God.'[58] To varying degrees we can apply those words to Hooker's theology of worship altogether since, as we have seen, the sacraments are the centre of a coherent constellation of outward and visible means by which believers, as embodied spirits, gain access to saving truth and divine power. In this Peter Lake rightly identifies a revolution in the quality and the content of apologetic on behalf of the *Book of Common Prayer* and the patterns of worship within the established church. In crediting worship and its scenic apparatus with the importance that he does, in connecting traditions of rites and ceremonies with a deep and nuanced sense of how divine truth and power are apprehended and interiorised by worshippers, Hooker sets a new standard for both apologetic and positive theology. There was no going back. At the centre of that constellation of experiences and actions, and as the chief external media by which divine life is communicated to humankind, stand the sacraments of baptism and the Eucharist. To them we now turn to complete the picture of Hooker's theology of sacraments and worship.

(Oxford, 1979). See also the analysis by Spinks, *Two Faces*, pp. 109-33.
57. See Gregg, 'Sacramental Theology': 160; he is referring to McGrade's analysis in his essay 'Coherence'.
58. *Hooker*, p. 78.

Chapter 10
'The Signs of God's Love'
Baptism and the Eucharist

In unequivocal words which end Hooker's discussion of sacraments in general and serve as a preface to his detailed considerations of baptism and the Eucharist, Hooker insists upon the vital force of sacraments in the receipt of saving grace. 'For', he explains on behalf of his establishment co-religionists,

> we take not baptism nor the eucharist for bare *resemblances* or memorials of things absent, neither for *naked signs* and testimonies assuring us of grace received before, but (as they are indeed and in verity) for means effectual whereby God when we take the sacraments delivereth into our hands that grace available unto eternal life, which grace the sacraments represent or signify.[1]

From that premise Hooker then insists on the unity of baptism and the Eucharist for Christians' gracious participation in Christ. If, to use a modern phrase, Christ himself is *the* sacrament of God, Christians are joined to and then grow into his divine life by means of the dominically instituted sacraments.[2] So, the discussion of the sacraments draws together important lines from Hooker's understanding of grace as well as from themes in his theology of worship.

Unlike many treatments of baptism and the Eucharist, though, where consistent sacramental terminology and analytic categories pertain, Hooker's discussion does not provide them. While there are deep substructural connections and continuities, at surface level his treatment is uneven and in some ways disappointing. Much ink has been spilt over Hooker's understanding of the Eucharist not because he has said so much but because he said relatively little; likewise with baptism. Therefore as we turn to each of them we cannot present a parallel analysis; rather, we must follow the contours thrown up by Hooker's argumentative context, and underline the broad and distinctive brush-strokes in his exposition of each.

---

1. V, lvii, 5 [II, p. 258]; Hooker's emphasis.
2. For the idea of Christ as the 'primordial sacrament' see Edward Schillebeeckx, *Christ the Sacrament of encounter with God* (London, 1963), p. 16; pp. 13-17.

Baptism: 'the seed of God'

The Necessity of Baptism

Hooker's argument for the necessity of baptism is, more precisely, an argument about the necessity of what he calls 'external baptism' or, according to Hooker's terminology, the *sacrament* of baptism. The argumentative context of his discussion (taken up in chapters fifty-eight and fifty-nine of Book V) was the non-conformists' claim that in the key proof-text for 'outward baptism' (John 3.5), 'water' is just a metaphor for the Holy Spirit. From that point of view, no necessity could be ascribed to the sacrament of baptism (the rite with water) for the receipt of saving grace. Hooker firmly disagrees. 'Water', he insists, should be taken literally not metaphorically; of all that the outward ceremony of baptism involves, water is 'principal'.[3]

In terms that are consistent with Hooker's general discussion of sacraments, 'external baptism' is the 'instrument' by which grace is received while the water of baptism is no cause in itself but is an outward, instrumental cause, and as such 'a duty required on our parts'. The presence of work of the Holy Spirit is annexed as the 'gift which God bestoweth'.[4] The Spirit as a 'necessary inward cause' is tied to the water of baptism as 'a necessary outward mean to our regeneration'.[5]

Does this mean that saving grace is always and exclusively attached to the sacrament of baptism? No, he says. Hooker admits that 'life by virtue of inward baptism' is possible, but only as an economy, and never as an alternative to the dominical institution of 'external baptism'.[6] The liturgically ordered sacrament of baptism is normatively necessary for entrance into the kingdom of God.[7]

Baptismal Grace

Hooker is clear that to each sacrament there is a particular grace, a specific description of the Spirit's work. Each such grace enhances the participation between the believer and Christ which sacraments are to effect. The close relation between baptism and the Eucharist to which reference has already been made depends on just this complementarity of graces offered and received. There are three ways to describe the grace of baptism as Hooker understands it: the grace of external vocation, the grace of incorporation, and the grace of imputed and imparted righteousness.

---

3. See V, lviii, 4 [II, p. 262].
4. V, lix, 4 [II, p. 264].
5. V, lx, 2 [II, p. 265].
6. V, lix, 5 [II, p. 269].
7. V, lx, 4 [II, p. 266].

As we have seen in a previous chapter on grace, Hooker distinguishes himself from thorough going Calvinist contemporaries within the established church by distinguishing the grace of eternal election from that of external vocation. In his focus on external vocation the real time, conscious engagement of the soul with its Saviour through the sacraments are key. They are not, as Hooker's contemporary William Perkins insisted, seals or mere signs of a saved status already in hand and unaffected by contingent causes; they are instead the 'means effectual' by which justifying and sanctifying grace are in fact given to the believer.[8] Baptism is the necessary door by which a believer enters into the domain of the grace of external vocation.

That difference in theological focus accounts for Hooker's insistence (in keeping with the rubrics and rites of the *Book of Common Prayer*) on the legitimacy of infant baptism. His view of the ordinary necessity of the sacrament, combined with solid roots in primitive and on-going Christian practice, leads Hooker to view baptism as the occasion of the first receipt of the grace of external vocation even though the conscious embrace of the vocation by the believer would come later.[9] So whether baptism took place in private or was tied to 'public assemblies' was a lesser issue in comparison to the greater issue of obedience to the dominical command to baptise.[10]

A second aspect of the grace of baptism is incorporation. 'Baptism is a sacrament which God hath instituted in his Church,' he explains, 'to the end that they which receive the same might thereby be incorporated into Christ'.[11] Hooker asserts this in various ways throughout his chapters on baptism; for instance, he says that baptismal grace makes people 'partakers of that grace whereby he [Christ] inhabiteth whom he saveth'.[12] Baptism is the beginning of Christ's mystical indwelling of believers, and of believers being 'very members incorporate' in Christ's mystical body.[13]

Closely linked to incorporation is the idea of filiation. Whereas incorporation highlights membership in Christ's mystical body, the church, filiation highlights the privilege of believers as co-heirs with Christ in the status of sonship.[14] This is the foundational status of those baptised and the point of irrevocable spiritual solidarity and equality between them: 'none any more a son than another'.[15]

---

8. See Spinks, *Two Faces*, p. 144; V, lvii, 5 [II, p. 258].

9. In this, as John Stafford notes, Hooker's sacramental theology reflects theological principle ('Practical Divinity', *CRH*, pp. 540-1).

10. See V, lxii, 5 [II, p.280].

11. V, lx, 2 [II, p. 265].

12. V, lvi, 10 [II, p. 253].

13. The phrase is from the post-Communion prayer of the Communion service of the *Book of Common Prayer*. Says Hooker: 'It pleaseth him in mercy to account himself incomplete and maimed without us' (*ibid.*).

14. It is a Pauline term and idea; see, for instance, Romans 8.15 and Galatians 4.5.

15. V, lvi, 12 [II, p. 255].

Hooker's point about filiation occurs as part of a discussion of a third aspect of the grace of baptism: the grace of imputed and imparted righteousness. Kenneth Stevenson observes how Hooker's doctrine of the sacraments draws his readers into the complex controversies over grace which were part and parcel of Reformation and post-Reformation polemic.[16] They relate to Hooker's understanding insofar as baptism is the occasion when both imputed and imparted, or infused, grace begins to work within the believer.

We must recall Hooker's differentiation of those two kinds of righteousness. '[W]e participate Christ partly by imputation', he explains, 'as when those things which he did and suffered for us are imputed to us for righteousness; partly by habitual and real infusion, as when grace is inwardly bestowed while we are on earth, and afterwards more fully both our souls and bodies made like unto his glory.' The richness of baptismal grace, as Hooker presents it, includes both imputed and infused grace.

Imputed grace is undifferentiated, whole, complete; it does not admit of degrees.[17] It has two chief benefits. First, by imputed grace those baptised are 'cleared from all sin'. Flowing from Christ's redemptive work once for all, imputed baptismal grace is the 'wellspring of new birth wherein original sin is purged',[18] so that the grace of baptism restores innocence in the sight of God. Its second benefit is filiation or sonship, to which reference has already been made.

Yet baptismal grace is, according to Hooker, infused as well. Complementing the purification and innocence effected by imputed grace, infused grace establishes traction within those baptised, and so is the foundation for the process in which 'by steps and degrees' the recipients of baptismal grace, whether infants or adults, 'receive the complete measure of all such divine grace, as doth sanctify and save throughout, till the day of their final exaltation to a state of fellowship in glory, with him whose partakers they are now in those things that tend to glory.'[19] That is so not least because those baptised, as 'very members incorporate' of the church, begin to live and grow within the context of its grace-giving corporate life.

A Covenant of Grace

Issues such as the necessity of outward baptism and the use of 'interrogatories', or questions and answers, within the baptism service of

---

16. Stevenson, *The Covenant of Grace Renewed* (London, 1994), p. 27; see also his *The Mystery of Baptism in the Anglican Tradition* (Norwich, 1998), pp. 44-53.
17. 'they which have it by imputation must have it such as it is whole' (V, lvi, 12 [II, p. 254]).
18. V, lxiv, 3 [II, p. 312].
19. V, lvi, 13 [II, p. 255]. Hooker is clear that the idea of degrees of grace applies only to imparted grace and not to imputed grace (see V, lvi, 12 [II, p. 254]); that is a principal insight for his moral and ascetical theologies.

the *Book of Common Prayer*, gave Hooker the opportunity to discuss the covenantal aspect of baptism. One chief gap between Hooker's theology and that of the regnant Calvinism of the non-conformists is found in the use of covenant or 'federal' theology. For English Calvinists in Hooker's day such federal theology was becoming the conceptual keystone of their whole theological system. It used the biblical idea of 'covenant' (in Latin *foedus*; whence 'federal') to map the relationship of God with humankind from eternal election to salvation. Calvinist double predestinarians tended toward a unilateral covenant scheme in which God's irrevocable eternal decree determined the fate of a person.

The covenant theme itself was, of course, thoroughly biblical as well as one that had a long-standing place within the church's liturgical tradition through the rites of baptism. Hooker knew this. He was primed, therefore, both by his own context and by his sources to take account of the covenant character of baptism and, indeed, of the whole Christian life. Given what we know of Hooker's view of predestination, and more especially of the importance of the grace of external vocation, it is no surprise that Hooker sees in baptism a bilateral covenant scheme. This is not to say that the terms of relationship between God and a believer are the subject of mutual negotiation. God alone sets the terms, the 'laws', and they are conveyed both by reason and revelation. Baptism embodies and expresses a bilateral covenant in that it expresses a believer's free decision and establishes mutual obligations by which God aids a believer's journey from life, through grace, to glory.

Hooker, however, is not interested in plotting the shape and content of the covenant of grace according to its eternal origin and end. In this part of Book V, at least, he reminds his readers that it is through Christ's 'compact' with the church that baptism gives the grace of new life and remission of sin.[20] When he discusses the 'interrogatories' of the baptismal service, where vows and promises are made either by or for the person to be baptised, he describes baptism as 'a covenant or league between God and man'.[21] He then draws out the covenantal aspect by describing the respective commitments:

> [a]s God doth bestow presently remission of sins and the Holy Ghost, binding also himself to add in process of time what grace soever shall be farther necessary for the attainment of everlasting life; so every baptised soul receiving the same grace at the hands of God tieth likewise itself for ever to the observation of his law, no less than the Jews by circumcision bound themselves to the law of Moses.[22]

---

20. V, lxii, 15 [II, p. 295]; 'compact' is one of the numerous English words to render the Latin term *foedus*.

21. The covenant is, according to Hooker, 'implied' not overtly stated.

22. V, lxiv, 4 [II, p. 312]; on this covenantal aspect see Paget, *Fifth Book*, p. 169.

The covenant of baptism is really a covenantal commitment to live according to the law of God, by the grace of the Spirit, and following the example of Christ.

The 'Sacrament of Faith'

Hooker affirms categorically that the sacraments and the posture of faith go hand in hand.[23] It is important to note that for Hooker both infant and adult baptisms are acts of faith.

In the case of an adult or 'elder sort', God's covenant requires 'Faith and Baptism'. Because the sacraments are built upon faith it is fitting that the sacramental 'door' of baptism includes a profession of faith. As Hooker describes it, the baptismal profession consists not so much in knowledge as in 'acknowledgement': 'the highest point of our wisdom', he says, 'is *believe*'; the baptismal profession is above all an acknowledgement of 'all things that heavenly wisdom revealeth'.[24] The profession is fuelled less by the discursive comprehension of mind and more by what Hooker calls 'affection of faith'. Insofar as sacraments are signs of God's love, a believer engages them best when they are a part of his profession of love for God.[25] In the case of the baptism of adults the 'actual habit of faith' is needed. Hooker means by that the power to apprehend the principles, or elemental aspects, of revealed truth. For 'belief consisteth', he explains,

> not so much in knowledge as in acknowledgement of all things that heavenly wisdom revealeth; the affection of faith is above her [knowledge's] reach, her love to God-ward above the comprehension which she hath of God.[26]

Love and knowledge *in that order* constitute the 'apprehension' of faith's gracious content.

Since love and 'acknowledgement' go hand in hand in the apprehension of faith, 'an evil moral disposition' will obscure and even extinguish affection for God and God's revealed truth. Therefore, explains Hooker, baptism includes two covenants: one, the profession of faithful obedience to Christ, the other, 'relinquishment of Satan'.[27]

In distinction from what is required of adults, in the case of children 'the sacrament of Baptism alone' is required, says Hooker. The bilateral covenant still applies since the godparents make the vows on the child's behalf.[28] The child is purified and joined to Christ through imputed grace;

23. V, lx, 4 [II, p. 267].
24. V, lxiii, 2 [II, p. 305].
25. V, lxiii, 1 [II, p. 305].
26. V, lxiii, 1 [II, p. 305].
27. V, lxiii, 3 [II, p. 306]. Hooker is quoting from Isidore of Seville's *De Ecclesiasticis Officiis*.
28. 'That infants may contract and covenant with God, the law is plain'; Hooker refers to Genesis 17.14 (V, lxiv, 4 [II, p. 313]).

the godparents' covenantal role is to see that the child then enjoys the benefits of infused grace as it grows within the life of the church, the Christian family, and society. While a child does not possess an 'actual habit of faith', the sacrament of baptism establishes its 'first foundation'. Hooker describes sympathetically how baptism, 'the sacrament of faith', becomes over time 'the faith of the sacrament'.[29] He insists on the continuity of grace within the '*believer*'[30] as the 'first foundation' of the habit of faith becomes the actual habit itself. 'For that which there we professed without any understanding, when we afterwards actually come to acknowledge, do we anything else but only bring unto ripeness the very seed that was sown before?'[31]

Confirmation

Within Hooker's covenantal scheme, and in accord with ancient Christian practice, confirmation holds an important place. God's covenantal commitment 'to add what grace so ever shall be farther necessary for the attainment of everlasting life' finds expression in the Prayer Book's provision for confirmation by the bishop. In keeping with the actual pastoral practice of the Prayer Book, in which confirmation preceded reception of Communion, chapter sixty-six acts as a ligature between Hooker's discussion of baptism and the Eucharist. The issue of confirmation also evoked sharp criticisms from non-conformists. Hooker's discussion reflects the contours of that debate and this accounts for the considerable patristic evidence with which Hooker justifies both its practice and its theology. We can extract from his argument useful points to set confirmation within the framework of grace and sacraments that we are mapping here.

While Hooker does not consider confirmation as a 'sacrament' by strict definition he accepts it as a 'sacramental complement'.[32] There is no doubt, however, that confirmation is grace-giving. Its justification within Hooker's sacramental universe is tied to a principal of Christian experience, namely the *process of growth*. Confirmation imparts, or infuses, grace for growth. Hooker's terminology about this varies, as does that of his ancient sources: it 'confirms', 'perfects', 'arguments' the grace begun in baptism.[33]

In keeping with his sources, Hooker qualifies the grace of confirmation rather more. Although it is not a grace that makes people Christians, it

---

29. V, lxiv, 2 [II, p. 310].
30. His use of the term 'believer' (his emphasis) here is important, emphasising that from baptism onward a person can be justly so described, even though faith has not yet been 'owned'.
31. V, lxiv, 2 [II, p. 310].
32. V, lxvi, 7 [II, p. 344].
33. V, lxvi, *passim*.

is grace which 'assisteth us in all virtue, armeth us against temptation and sin'.[34] The grace of confirmation, then, supports in particular the developing spiritual posture of renunciation of evil owned at baptism. The kingly, royal ascriptions to the grace of confirmation reveal its aim to empower dominion over 'the whole band of that roaming and spoiling adversary'; to aid, that is, in forsaking 'the devil and all his works', 'the covetous desires' of the world, and 'the carnal desires of the flesh', as the service of baptism put it.

In conveying gracious assistance for growth in conformity to God's laws, confirmation recalls baptism, and looks forward to the table of the Eucharist, which, in the practice of Hooker's own day at least, was the canonical means of entry into the active life of the church.

The Eucharist – 'real participation of Christ'

In his subtle and elucidating discussion, Olivier Loyer alerts readers to a sense of apprehension which attends the exposition of Hooker's theology of the Eucharist.[35] There are numerous reasons for this and no consensus has emerged as to the most satisfactory interpretive key with which to bring Hooker's views to the clarity we might wish. Hooker himself seems content to leave large areas of debate and controversy in shadow, or even darkness, and it is important to realise this as we step into an area where we might wish to find much light. [36]

It is important to recognise that Hooker was the inheritor of considerable ambiguities in the realm of eucharistic theology. After all, one chief source, the order for 'Communion' in the *Book of Common Prayer* of 1559, was the product of Archbishop Cranmer's vacillations, and those were only intensified in the few but important textual emendations in the revisions of 1552 and 1559.[37] Add to this the European context of Lutherans, Roman Catholics, Calvinist and Zwinglians (to name the chief), whose views furnished Hooker's intellectual world, and we can see why it was so hard for Hooker to construct a coherent and convincing eucharistic doctrine.

It is clear that in this key area of Christian practice and experience Hooker lamented the opposition of theologies, and sought to reconcile them. '[W]hy do we vainly trouble ourselves', he wonders, 'with so fierce contentions whether by consubstantiation, or else by transubstantiation the sacrament

---

34. V, lxvi, 4 [II, p. 340].
35. Loyer, I, p. 509.
36. One area of darkness is the question of eucharistic sacrifice (Stevenson, *Covenant of Grace*, p. 34).
37. On the issue of Hooker's sources, and the possible influence of the *Book of Common Prayer*, see John Booty's essay 'Hooker's Understanding of the Presence of Christ in the Eucharist', in John Booty, ed., *The Divine Drama in History and Liturgy* (Allison Park, PA, 1985), pp. 131 – 148.

itself be first possessed with Christ, or no?'[38] In England such a course was in line with political policy which sought to secure 'general tranquillity' in all spheres of the commonwealth.[39] In pursuit of resolution of contention Hooker takes as the frame of his doctrine four points of reference.

First, Hooker instinctively wants to be guided by the witness of the early Christian fathers.[40] His summary of agreed Christian teaching about Christ's presence in the Eucharist takes direct guidance from them.[41]

Second, Hooker wants to distil agreement from the various contemporary theologies. When he gathers 'that wherein all agree', he identifies the following features of eucharistic teaching. First, the sacrament is 'a true and mystical participation of Christ' as head of the body of which the communicant is a member. Second, the sacrament conveys the sanctifying Spirit to communicants. Third, the sacrament gives to communicants 'what *merit, force or virtue soever there is in his* [Christ's] *sacrificed body and blood . . . '*. Fourth, a '*real transmutation*' of the soul and body of the communicant is effected by sacramental sharing. And fifth, the ability of the bread and cup to be the sacrament and to have its effect is solely by '*the strength of his* [God's] *glorious power*'.[42]

Third, and more obliquely, Hooker's discussion applies two aspects of his basic conceptual tool kit: the Aristotelian idea of distinction and limitation, and the Platonic idea of participation.[43] These notions are attached, respectively, to two concepts that are prevalent in Hooker's treatment of eucharistic presence: substance and person.

Fourthly, a strand of three ideas forms the positive conceptual core of Hooker's understanding: participation, presence and person.

The Eucharistic Triad

Participation

In chapter sixty-seven of Book V, which is the core of his theology of the Eucharist, Hooker emphasises believers' 'participation' in Christ. In that relatively short chapter Hooker uses the word ten times.[44] Indeed, the '*real participation* of Christ' is, according to Hooker, the point of 'general agreement' among the various and vying doctrines of the Eucharist.[45]

---

38. V, lxvii, 6 [II, p. 353].
39. See the Elizabethan text quoted by Dugmore, *Eucharistic Doctrine*, p. 20.
40. Stevenson, *Covenant of Grace*, p. 33.
41. That, anyway, is what Hooker himself thought; on his mistake of sources see Booty, 'Presence of Christ', pp. 135-6.
42. V, lxvii, 7 [II, pp. 354-5].
43. See chapter seven above.
44. Stevenson, *Covenant of Grace*, p. 28.
45. V, lxvii, 2 [II, p. 349].

Hooker's theme of participation arises from the testimony of Jesus' words in John 6.35, a foundational passage for Hooker's eucharistic theology: 'I am the bread of life. Whoever comes to me will never be hungry, and whoever believes in me will never be thirsty'.[46] The 'participation of Christ', then, is also the participation 'of life in his body and blood by means of the sacrament'.[47] He explains:

> Whereas therefore in our infancy we are incorporated into Christ and by Baptism receive the grace of his Spirit without any sense or feeling of the gift which God bestoweth, in the Eucharist we so receive the gift of God, that we know by grace what the grace is which God giveth us . . . we understand that the strength of our life begun in Christ *is Christ*.[48]

On that basis Hooker presents the complementary grace of the Eucharist as nourishment and food 'prescribed for the *continuance of life*'.[49] That 'real participation' is also a 'mystical participation'.[50]

Presence

The participation in Christ's body and blood 'by means of the sacrament' presumes the sacramental presence of Christ. How is that presence to be described and understood? Hooker consistently refuses to describe Christ's presence as a 'substantial' presence. He rejects both the Lutheran notion of consubstantiation and the Thomist, Roman Catholic one of transubstantiation on the grounds that both views dissolve the integrity of created 'substance'.[51] In so doing they violate the paradigm provided by the Chalcedonian doctrine of the union of different substances within the single person of God the Word.

In Hooker's view, Christ's human nature, the 'substance' of his humanity, cannot assume the attribute of omnipresence required of sacramental presence without over-stepping the fixed limit of created substance. On that basis it is incontrovertible to Hooker that, as the Prayer Book rubric asserted, Christ's corporeal (this is, human substantial) presence is in heaven and ever remains so. That is why Hooker rejects the idea of a

---

46. A point rightly noted by Thornton, *Hooker*, p. 83.

47. *Ibid.*

48. *Ibid.*; my emphasis.

49. V, lxvii, 1 [II, p. 348]

50. V, lxvii, 9 [II, p. 355].

51. The Lutheran view by ascribing the divine attribute of omnipresence to the substance of bread and wine, the Thomist view by abolishing the substance of bread and wine altogether so as to 'make room' for the substance of Christ's body and blood. See V, lxvii, 2 [II, p. 349]. See Loyer, (I, p. 498) where he claims Hooker's agreement with at least one important strand of the Tridentine sacramental view. Booty insists that, despite the paucity of overt citations, the influences of Aquinas' *Summa Theologiae* prevails throughout Book V ('Introduction to Book V', *FLE*, VI, I, p. 218.

substantial change in the sacramental elements of bread and wine as well as language that suggests that the sacramental elements contain Christ's body and blood.

At the same time, Hooker is forthright in his use of the word 'real' in relation to both the participation and the presence of Christ. 'Real' and 'really' are, Loyer reminds us, abundantly used throughout Hooker's discussion of the Eucharist.[52] Hooker therefore rejects the language of 'substantial presence' while he affirms that of 'real presence' and 'real participation'.[53]

Person

So, believers participate in Christ 'really' and 'mystically', but not substantially. Or we can say, using another distinction from Hooker's tool kit of words, that Christ is present not corporeally but *personally*. Loyer says, accurately, I think, that Hooker has a 'personalist theology of presence'.[54] In fact, Hooker's use of the patristic theology of person is essential for grasping his understanding of eucharistic presence.

Hooker uses the theological notion of 'person'[55] in two complementary ways.

First, he views the person as the reality which encompasses or contains the human nature, or substance. As a result, the person of the Word, insofar as it contains, or embraces, the human nature of Christ, gives access to that limited human nature. That line of thought is clearest when Hooker speaks of sacramental efficacy. Since there is no inherent and autonomous power in the sacramental elements themselves, it can only be through the medium of the divine personal Word, the person of the Word, that the human nature of Christ gains an unlimited efficacy which otherwise, because of the intrinsic limitations of human nature, it could not have. This is how Hooker understands the patristic sources: they teach

> that Christ *personally* there present, yea present whole, albeit a part of Christ be *corporally* absent from thence; that Christ assisting this heavenly banquet with his personal and true presence doth by his own divine power add to the natural substance thereof supernatural efficacy, which addition to the nature of those consecrated elements changeth them and maketh them that unto us which otherwise they could not be.[56]

---

52. I, p. 529.
53. *Ibid.*
54. I, p. 485.
55. This is the patristic Greek theological term 'hypostasis'.
56. V, lxvii, 11 [II, p. 357].

Hooker means – to coin an ungainly term – that Christ the eternal Word *en-personalises* the sacramental elements within himself.[57]

Second, Hooker speaks of the sacramental elements as the instrumental means by which the communicant participates in Christ's personal presence. In his summary of agreed points about the Eucharist Hooker lays down first and foremost 'that this sacrament is a true and real participation of Christ, who thereby imparteth himself even his whole entire Person'.[58] Again, against 'sacramentarian' views, Hooker insists that the eucharistic elements instrumentally 'impart unto us even in true and real though mystical manner the very Person of our Lord himself, whole, perfect, and entire'.[59]

It can be said, then, that the communicant participates in the Person of Christ through the sacramental elements. Further, through such participation in Christ present personally the communicant has access to the efficacy of Christ's sacrificed body and blood, even though his body and blood are not locally and substantially present *in* the elements themselves.

Sacramental Encounter, Change and Presence

So, Christ's personal presence creates a change in the sacramental elements as the passages cited demonstrate. But the idea of 'personal presence' has further significance.

Modern theology sometimes speaks of sacraments as necessarily involving encounter between persons.[60] Hooker would not, of course, use language quite like that; but he would recognise and affirm the theological insight to which our use of 'encounter' points, namely, that religious life involves *relation with God in virtue of grace*.[61] His view of 'real presence' makes much of the persons enacting and receiving the sacramental elements. On that account Hooker's teaching on the Eucharist is

---

57. Hooker is implicitly working toward a concept that was explicated in Byzantine theology, namely, 'enhypostasisation'. Leontius of Byzantium is credited with introducing a 'new notion' into Christological discourse: existence within something. In Christology it means that the person (hypostasis) of Christ can embrace or contain multiple natures (i.e. divine and human); see Meyendorff, *Christ*, pp. 47-68. Is Hooker tending toward that idea as applied to the natural sacramental elements of bread and wine?

58. V, lxvii, 7 [II, p. 354].

59. V, lxvii, 8 [II, p. 355].

60. See, for instance, the discussion of Dumitru Staniloae's view about the personal dimension of sacraments in Charles Miller, *The Gift of the World* (Edinburgh, 2000), pp. 87-8.

61. So Schillebeeckx describes what lies behind 'encounter' (*Christ the Sacrament*, p. xvii, note 1).

sometimes called 'receptionist'.[62] We have seen in our discussion of grace how Hooker studiously avoids all attempts to make grace a 'thing' in itself, to detach it from its sole source, God.[63] As a result, Hooker speaks of a 'real presence' but insists that it is spiritually received. He tries to maintain a fragile equilibrium in asserting that Christ's presence in the Eucharist is apprehended by faith but not dependent on faith, or created by the faith of the believer. The sacramental presence of the person of Christ is grasped and realised in the soul by the personal, faith-filled act of the communicant. After all, since the presence is *for* us, it must also be *in* us. That is why Hooker insists that '[t]he real presence of Christ's most blessed body and blood is not therefore to be sought for in the sacrament, but in the worthy receiver of the sacrament.'[64]

In that regard Hooker uses some of his most creative expressions. So, whereas Hooker avoids the language of substantial change in regard to the sacramental elements, he applies such language when describing the effect of those same elements upon the communicants who faithfully receive them, declaring that

> to us they [*viz.* the elements] are thereby made such instruments as mystically yet truly, invisibly yet really work our communion or fellowship with the person of Jesus Christ as well in that he is man as God, our participation also in the fruit, grace and efficacy of his body and blood, whereupon there ensueth *a kind of transubstantiation in us*, a true change both of soul and body, an alteration from death to life.[65]

So, the presence is not to be thought of simply with*in* the sacramental elements but *in* the sacramental action and with*in* those acting. Those who find this view less than 'Catholic' insofar as it seems to undercut any notion of an 'objective presence' outside the believer may helpfully consider Loyer's point: Hooker's theology of eucharistic presence intentionally unites the mystery of the presence of Christ's sacramental body with his mystical body.[66] What Kenneth Stevenson calls 'the two essential foci' of Hooker's eucharistic theology are the individual's faith, on the one hand, and Christ's dynamic self-gift on the other, finely balanced in relation to one another.[67]

---

62. So, for instance, J. R. Parris, 'Hooker's Doctrine of the Eucharist', *Scottish Journal of Theology*, 16 (1963): 153. Hooker, he argues, takes a 'non-substantialist' approach; true, but is he therefore a 'receptionist'?

63. See chapter seven above; as Loyer puts it, grace for Hooker is not an 'autonomous reality' (I, p. 494).

64. V, lxvii, 6 [II, p. 352].

65. V, lxvii, 11 [II, p. 358]; emphasis mine.

66. I, p. 521; he regards this as 'the most significant point of all' in Hooker's eucharistic theology as a whole.

67. *Covenant of Grace*, pp. 33-4.

Hooker's Legacy

The rich, suggestive theological combinations that characterise Hooker's eucharistic theology account, no doubt, for the difficulty in placing him in relation to contemporary views. There are voices that confidently place Hooker on the Reformed side of that theological divide, or that see in his views the 'incipient "central" churchmanship' of later 'Anglicanism'.[68] His theories influenced those of subsequent Anglican divines, chiefly in the area of accountability to the paradigm of the Chalcedonian Definition, and in the intent to honour the relation between the two natures within the personal Word. Whether Hooker himself found the right balance between maintaining the natural limits of created 'substance' while also arguing for a change of the elements into that 'which otherwise they could not be' is an open question, and key to the assessment of Hooker's eucharistic theology. His language sometimes suggests that he erred on the side of limitation.[69]

Still, just because his was less doctrinaire than other contemporary views, and consensual in its sources and aims, Hooker's eucharistic theology can be seen, as Stevenson suggests, to 'loosen' up the eucharistic legacy of his day.[70] He gave English divinity a Christological paradigm through which to explore and articulate the eucharistic mystery further. In addition, he tied baptism and the Eucharist together in a way that provided a solid and necessary basis for growth in the life of grace. 'Christ, as fully human, inaugurated a new humanity and it is that grace-transformed humanity which we enter in baptism and grow in to perfection through the Eucharist'.[71]

There is another way in which Hooker 'loosened up' the sacramental sensibilities of his day. The *Laws'* structural centre in Book V, with its irradiating theme of participation especially points to it. Booty observes that Hooker's overall advocacy of religion in the commonwealth is rooted in the concept of participation in Christ which centres principally in the sacraments of incorporation and participation.[72] If the perimeter of the Church is the nation as a whole, then its centre is the Church's sacramental life. For Hooker, precisely because they are the public and, as he would say, 'solemn' actions of the whole community assembled, the sacraments gather

---

68. Respectively, Spinks, *Two Faces*, p. 158; and Dugmore, *Eucharistic Doctrine*, p. 17.

69. It is worth noting that John of Damascus, whom Hooker often cites, is clear that substances cannot be mixed in and between themselves; see his *On the Orthodox Faith*, I, 14, III, 8 and 16, where he explains the union with natural distinction preserved in Christology.

70. Stevenson, p. 34.

71. Booty, 'Presence of Christ', p. 133.

72. 'Introduction to Book V', pp. 193-7.

the many into one. Recalling his understanding of law in which the inner impulse directs forward to an end but also outward to other people, so the sacramental principle or law fosters both individual spiritual participation in Christ and spiritual solidarity with one's neighbours in faith and, above all, love. Through worship and the sacraments as approved and ordered in the *Book of Common Prayer*, the praying kingdom is led through its natural end, the life well-lived, toward its supernatural perfection, God's Kingdom.[73]

This chapter began with reference to a twentieth-century theologian's description of Christ as the sacrament of encounter with God. We can fruitfully return to that idea with all that this chapter has considered about baptism and the Eucharist. For in understanding Christ as the sacrament of divine-human encounter 'the sacraments themselves can be seen as inseparable from the whole economy of revelation in word and reality, a revelation of God in Trinity, of Incarnation, grace, the Church and indeed of man and his destiny, for it is within this economy of sacramental encounter that we as men achieve the fullness of our personal being'.[74]

With this wide field now opened, we can profitably turn to the workings of God's grace in the experience of individuals and the Christian community.

---

73. Booty, *Reflections*, p. 160.
74. Cornelius Ernst in his 'Foreword' to Schillebeeckx, *Christ the Sacrament*, p. xvii.

PART FOUR

APPROPRIATION

Chapter 11
'A Holy Rule of Doing Well'
Faith and Works

The traditions of Christian thought upon which Hooker built his theological edifice wrestled with two key features of Christian life: faith and works. The long-standing Catholic tradition of the church, and then the reforming movements of Hooker's own century, were opposed regarding the meaning of and relationship between faith and works. All could admit that they were corollaries of the doctrine of grace, but how so?[1] The English theological ethos out of which Hooker's particular vision grew had seen significant change in the understanding of faith and works, which reflected evolution within the streams of thought of the magisterial Reformation itself. In addition, there were different, vying trends in post-Tridentine Roman Catholicism of which Hooker seems to have been aware, and which may have discretely influenced him.[2]

As regards Hooker's own theology, consideration of faith, with its corollary works, does not hold the central and foundational place that it does in the theology of Luther or Calvin. The Reformation's incendiary issue, the problematic of faith, is hardly touched on in the *Laws* where, in sharp contrast to the Reformers' agenda, Hooker defends an institution and its laws, and advocates for its liturgy, sacraments and order.[3] Still, as a son of the Reformation, Hooker acknowledged the importance of accurate views on faith and works in themselves and in relation to one another, and he took the opportunities of contemporary discussion and debate to expound them. Beyond that which we can glean from the *Laws*, two early sermons, *On the Certainty and Perpetuity of Faith in the Elect* and *A Learned Discourse of Justification*, together with comments on the *Christian Letter* in the *Dublin Fragments*, help to construct an understanding of faith and works in Hooker's thought. So this chapter forms a hinge between Hooker's theology of the Spirit's economy of grace and its mediation through Word and Sacraments to the sphere of experience where grace is active and felt.

---

1. As witnessed, for instance, by Augustine's early fifth-century treatise *On Faith and Works.*
2. This is conjecture; but Voak argues that, as regards justification at least, Hooker's mature views are patient of an interpretation akin to the late Franciscan school (*Reformed Theology*, p. 192).
3. Loyer draws attention to such different starting points (I, p. 395).

Faith

Gift and Virtue

Hooker's understanding of faith is firmly set within his theology of justification and sanctification. Each of those two phases of the salvific process sheds light on the character of faith as both gift and virtue, and as something both imputed and imparted.

'[T]he true reason wherefore Christ doth love believers,' Hooker affirms in Book V of the *Laws,* 'is because their belief is the gift of God'.[4] With simply clarity Hooker expresses the heart of Reformation doctrine, namely, faith as God's free, gracious gift to an undeserving person. Unlike his non-conformist contemporaries though, who, inspired by Calvin, made the gift of faith to the believer perfect and adamantine, impregnable vanquisher of the old Adam, Hooker prefers (as we have seen) to describe the 'First Grace' which brings the gift of faith as 'the *seed* of God'.[5] It not only begins very small, but it does much of its growth hidden from view.

Faith as divine gift is complemented by an equal insistence that faith is a virtue. The kind of virtue it is will be explored later in the chapter. Now it is important to draw attention to two key features of faith's status as a virtue. First, while faith begins as a wholly extrinsic gift from its divine source, it becomes intrinsic to the believer as an interior habit or disposition.[6] We recall the theme of participation which runs like a thread through Hooker's theological cloth; the human partakes of the divine life because the divine condescendingly and graciously shares it with the human. Whereas faith begins as a gift passively received, it takes root and grows as the virtuous 'place' of active cooperation between the believer and God, between nature and grace. Second, faith, a virtue nestled in the dynamics of humanity, grows and develops like every virtue. Faith's divine source does not nullify the natural growth in virtue (theological or otherwise) that occurs in human beings.[7]

In both those regards Hooker sets a distinct trajectory when dealing with the phenomenon of faith. His starting point is an insistence on faith as a divine gift given in the very act of justification, and he complements this with traditional Christian insights regarding faith as an imparted, theological virtue growing and changing under the influence of the grace of sanctification.

---

4. V, lxiii, 1 [II, p. 305].

5. *CPFE* [III, p. 473].

6. A virtue, generally speaking, is a habit of acting well, that is, in pursuit of natural or, in the case of faith, supernatural good. The issue of virtue is taken up in chapter thirteen.

7. Faith is one of the three 'theological virtues' mentioned in 1 Cor. 13; see also 1 Thess. 1.3, Gal. 5.5, and Col. 1.4f.

The 'Foundation of Faith'

In the sermon preached in the first year of his Mastership of the Temple, *A Learned Discourse of Justification, Works, and How the Foundation of Faith is Overthrown*, Hooker deals extensively with the 'foundation of faith'. His treatment concerns both the object of faith as that *in which* we believe, and the form of faith *by which* we believe.[8] In each case we find Hooker taking his theology beyond the confines of both the English and the continental legacies present around him.

We see this, for instance, in his understanding of the very word 'faith'. Although the English Church earlier in the century was influenced by Luther's view of faith as *fiducia*, or trust and assurance, Hooker understands 'faith' more expansively.[9] We see this when we consider the object or the foundation of faith and its expression in the act of believing that characterises Christians. Hooker defines the 'Foundation' of faith in his sermon on *Justification* as 'the principal thing which is believed', and provides a synopsis of relevant scriptural texts: "'God manifested in the flesh, justified in the Spirit," &c.: that of Nathaniel, "Thou art the Son of the living God; thou art the king of Israel:" that of the inhabitants of Samaria, "This is Christ the Saviour of the world"'.[10] We find there the affirmations which the creedal tradition formulated in the twin doctrines of the Trinity and the Incarnation, the latter implying not just the taking flesh but also the redemptive work of the cross. Here is the 'principle in Christianity', and 'the foundation of our faith'.[11] While Scripture witnesses to that 'foundation', the 'foundation' and object of faith is the Good News itself: the promise of salvation in Christ.[12]

The Act of Believing

When we turn to the act of believing, Hooker's advance in thinking beyond his Lutheran-inspired predecessors and his non-conformist contemporaries is evident. Hooker, does not reject the notion of faith as trust and assurance (*fiducia*) – what Loyer has described as 'the inter-subjective rapport between saviour and saved'.[13] However, Hooker

8. A traditional bi-partitite discussion of '*fides quae*' ('faith which') and '*fides qua*' ('faith by which').
9. Neelands,'Grace', pp. 35-6.
10. *LDJ*, 16 [III, p. 501].
11. *Ibid.* 23 [III, p. 513]; the redemptive work of the cross is highlighted by Hooker in a brief consideration of the object of faith in *Laws*, V, xxii, 9 [II, p. 97].
12. That is the *kerygma*, as distinct from the act of proclamation itself, the *kēruksis* – a distinction Hooker makes to counter non-conformists' conflation of the Gospel itself and the ministry of preaching; See Loyer, I, pp. 406-7.
13. I, p. 403; the notion, Loyer tells us, 'abounds' in Hooker's writings (I, p. 404).

expands the act of believing to include a traditional element of which the Reformation traditions had grown suspicious, namely, an intellectual habit of the mind that includes the intellect's assent to truth.[14] Hooker's reprise of scholasticism's 'virtue of faith' significantly reorders the way faith figures within the edifice of theology, and how theology accounts for the phenomenon of faith. Whereas for Luther and the Reformed tradition God was visible only in our trust in him and in his mercy toward our sinfulness and impotence, for Hooker, as in the Catholic tradition, that experience – legitimate as far as it went – does not exhaust the concept or the experience of faith. Faith manifests itself also in good works, dogma and doctrine. Intellectual assent means assent to the idea that God became man, with its implications for the being of God, for humankind within the wide scope of salvation history, and for the world as the object of divine love and providential care. Within Hooker's view of faith, 'inter-subjective rapport' in the form of assurance and trust (*fiducia*) goes hand-in-hand with dogmatic and doctrinal affirmations and commitment.[15]

Apprehension and Assent

The act of faith, whether as assurance or as intellectual habit, involves a process of 'apprehension' and 'assent'.[16] Apprehension is the process by which the intellect grasps, or is persuaded, that what is revealed is true. Such apprehension is the first step in the act of faith; it could even be called 'faith' in a limited sense. Devils and 'the most ungodly' can be said to have 'faith' like that.[17] But apprehension of revealed truth by the intellect only becomes 'the faith, which indeed doth justify' when the intellect apprehends what is true as also *good*. 'It is the spirit of adoption which worketh faith in us . . . the things which we believe, are by us apprehended, not only as true, but also as good, and that to us.'[18] Apprehension of the *goodness* of divine truth is what leads a person not just to believe but to 'cleave' and 'stick' to God through Christ. Grace thus provokes the will as well as enlightens the intellect and in so doing moves the believer from apprehension of the object of faith to assent and adherence to it.[19]

---

14. Hooker follows, for instance, Aquinas' view that some virtues are intellectual virtues, and as such involve an intellectual *habitus*, habit or disposition, according to which we move toward perfection. In the case of faith that perfection toward which it disposes us is union with God, or beatitude; see Davies, *Aquinas*, pp. 240-1.

15. More on those topics in chapter twelve.

16. Voak identifies what he regards as inconsistency in Hooker's vocabulary in this discussion; see *Reformed Theology*, pp. 30-2. Whether or not that is so, it seems to me that the broad shape of Hooker's view is clear and consistent.

17. *LDJ*, 26 [III, p. 515].

18. *Ibid.*

19. *CPFE*, III, p. 471.

Faith so conceived is clearly a faith that is not given from the start in full, final form. Like the growth of a seed, the acts of apprehension and assent, the enlightening of the intellect and the captivating of the will, grow. How Hooker describes the Christian life generally is wholly applicable to the act of faith itself: 'by steps and degrees they [*viz.* believers] receive the complete measure of all such divine grace, as doth sanctify and save throughout.'[20] His use of the word 'sanctify' should be noted. When we recall Hooker's view of sanctifying grace as imperfect in this life, we realise that the gift and virtue of faith too cannot be anything other than imperfect through the course of a believer's life. Like every other aspect of Christian life, the grace and virtue of faith is in a process of continual growth towards perfection in the life hereafter.[21]

Faith and Certainty

Hooker is interested in what we call belief formation, that is, the mental process by which beliefs are accepted as true. This interest accounts for one of his early public tangles with non-conformists;[22] it had to do with the certainty that is credited to the object of faith specifically, and to matters of belief generally. Hooker explores this issue in a sermon on a text from the prophet Habbakkuk (1.4). The question is this: 'whether the Prophet Habbakkuk, by admitting this cogitation into his mind, "The law doth fail," did thereby show himself an unbeliever.'[23] It was a provocative theme to explore in the face of non-conformists' view that faith, because it is a divine gift, could not allow for variance or shadow of change; one believed either perfectly or not at all. In the course of the sermon Hooker expounds his most important points about the nature of faith and the experience of believing. In doing so he establishes a trajectory of thought that takes him outside non-conformist orthodoxy regarding the certainty that characterises what we believe.

Because faith involves intellectual assent, it stands within the framework of Hooker's theory of certainty. Hooker's theory correlates various kinds of intellectual assent to varying degrees of certainty. What kind of certainty, then, can be ascribed to matters of faith?

The chief insight gained from Hooker's discussion in the sermon on *Certainty* is the distinction he draws between 'certainty of evidence', on

---

20. V, lvi, 13 [II, p. 255].
21. That is the key reason why Hooker rejects the non-conformist doctrine of faith; see Loyer, I, pp. 415-19.
22. Voak explores this interesting area of Hooker's thought in the chapter 'Philosophy of Action: Defective Action and Belief Formation' in *Reformed Theology*, pp. 68-91.
23. *CPFE*, III, p. 470.

the one hand, and 'certainty of adherence', on the other.[24] The distinction accords with Hooker's foundational view of nature and grace, reason and revelation, insofar as nature and reason, and revelation and grace relate to different kinds of certainty. The 'certainty of evidence' is wholly rational; it involves varying degrees of certainty based upon the kind and persuasive force of evidence that is presented to the reasoning subject. On that basis something may, for instance, be assessed as infallibly certain or merely probably. The 'certainty of adherence', by contrast, while it involves a rational recognition of truth, is more than a rational exercise. Hooker describes it as a persuasion of 'the heart', or, as we might put it, of the whole person. As such it involves the will, so that, as we said earlier, the apprehending subject desires to adhere – to 'cleave' and 'stick' as Hooker puts it – to what is presented to it for belief not only as true but also as good: 'the faith of a Christian doth apprehend the words of the law, the promises of God, not only as true, but also as good.'[25] Knowledge *and love* promote the certainty of adherence.[26] In fact, the certainty of adherence is promoted by more than a confluence of rational and volitional powers. Hooker is well aware of the powers of the imagination and other senses, as we saw in his discussion of worship, so we can fairly surmise that the 'certainty of adherence' is the result of a subtle, wide-ranging confluence of forces within the believing subject. Of course the 'adherence of certainty' as described in the sermon on *Certainty* is another name for the 'adherence of faith' insofar as the chief object of such adherence are the truths revealed in the scriptures and both apprehended and adhered to by the working of grace.

Paradoxically, the 'certainty of adherence' is in many respects disproportionate to the rational evidence for what is believed. Hooker explains it like this:

> That which we see by the light of grace, though it be indeed more certain; yet is it not to us so evidently certain, as that which sense or the light of nature will not suffer a man to doubt of . . . I conclude therefore that we have less certainty of evidence concerning things believed, than concerning sensible or naturally perceived.[27]

---

24. *Ibid.*

25. *Ibid.* p. 471.

26. Although the apprehension of the object of faith is analogous to the apprehension of rationally-known objects, Hooker distinguishes knowledge from faith. The latter consists 'not so much in knowledge as in acknowledgement of all things that heavenly wisdom revealeth' (V, lxiii, 1 [II, p. 305]).

27. *CPFE*, pp. 470-1. Loyer comments on this distinction: 'the certainty is in the thing itself, the evidence is in us' (I, p. 407). We are dealing therefore with a tension inherent in the exchange between the divine and the human, between grace and nature.

While the truths of faith are less *evidentially* certain than other things, they are more *intrinsically* certain than everything else. That was the point that caused such concern to Hooker's critics. Hooker is clear, though, that the 'certainty of adherence' is greater in us than any certainty of evidence.

> The reason is this: the faith of a Christian doth apprehend the words of the law, the promises of God, not only as true, but also as good; and therefore even then when the evidence which he hath of the truth is so small that it grieveth him to feel his weakness in assenting thereto, yet is there in him such a sure adherence unto that which he doth but faintly and fearfully believe, that his spirit having once truly tasted the heavenly sweetness thereof, all the world is not able quite and clean to remove him from it; but he striveth with himself to hope against all reason of believing, being settled with Job upon this unmovable resolution, "Though God kill me, I will not give over trusting in him." For why? this lesson remaineth for ever imprinted in him 'It is good for me to cleave unto God."[28]

The 'Perpetuity' of Faith and the Fact of Doubt

Could a Christian fall from the adherence of faith? Hooker's sermon on the certainty of faith is also a sermon on the perpetuity of faith. Here too Hooker found himself at odds with the non-conformist interpretation of the experience of belief. Candid reflection on the actual experience of believers convinced him that the non-conformists' view of the perpetuity of faith was too simplistic, too all-or-nothing. Did the prophet Habbakkuk's doubt about the law reveal him to have lost his faith? In exploring that question Hooker does not, in fact, reject the notion of the perseverance of faith in the elect. From his early sermons onward Hooker is clear that 'the faith whereby ye are sanctified cannot fail'.[29]

Having said that, however, Hooker is more interested in how faith really functions in the experience and perceptions of the believing subject. Precisely because it is both divine gift and inherent virtue, faith and the certainty of adherence which it entails are caught up in the imperfections that characterise the creaturely limitations of the believer. On that account, therefore, there is a legitimate doubt of 'infirmity' when faith is not absent but weak.[30] Also, as we have already noted, the

---

28. *Ibid*. p. 471.
29. *Ibid*. p. 473. Whether Hooker affirmed that so categorically in his last writings is questionable. For the truly predestinated, *final* perseverance is assured.
30. *Ibid*. p. 472; this is distinguished from the doubt of 'Infidelity' which does not stand with 'true faith'.

inherent grace of faith in the believer in the process of sanctification is unavoidably imperfect.[31] We should not expect or require 'supposed perfection in certainty touching matters of our faith'.[32]

Hooker's sermon is really an exercise in pastoral theology in which he sets out a theological principle and then applies it to Christian experience. In this case Hooker explores the place of doubt in the life of faith. In the face of non-conformity's dogmatic expulsion of doubt from faith, Hooker insists that it is a part of the normal experience of believers. Why? One factor is the evidential paradox that we have just discussed. Another is the 'foggy damp of original corruption' which skews the knowledge and love of saving truth and which grace does not immediately and finally disperse. Beyond that is 'the incomprehensible wisdom of God which doth limit the effect of his power to such a measure as seemeth best unto himself' so that a believer can be providentially afflicted with doubt – a form of 'obduration', we may suppose. Hooker reveals sharp insight into the experience of spiritual aridity, perhaps even desolation, when the imperfection of faith is felt as a wholesale deprivation: 'they think imperfection to be plain deprivation, weakness to be utter want of faith'.[33] 'Happier a great deal,' he explains,

> is that man's case, whose soul by inward desolation is humbled, than he whose heart is through abundance of spiritual delight lifted up and exalted above measure. Better is it sometimes to go down into the pit with him, who, beholding darkness, and bewailing the loss of inward joy and consolation, crieth from the bottom of the lowest hell, "My God, my God, why hast thou forsaken me?" than continually to walk arm in arm with angels, to sit as it were in Abraham's bosom, and to have no thought, no cogitation, but "I thank my God it is not with me as it is with other men." No, God will have them that shall walk in light to feel now and then what it is to sit in the shadow of death. A grieved spirit therefore is no argument of a faithless mind.[34]

So doubt and fear as well as other forms of disconsolation characterise the life of faith.

Lively Faith

Whenever Hooker speaks of 'faith' and insists that it is faith alone that 'tieth us to him [*viz*. Christ]'[35] he means what the Roman Catholic tradition understood as '*fides formata*', 'formed faith', and what reformed theologies

---

31. *Ibid*. p. 471.
32. *Ibid*. p. 472.
33. *Ibid*. p. 474.
34. *Ibid*. pp. 474-5. The experience is consistent with what John of Damascus means by 'abandonment'.
35. *FSJ* [III, p. 670].

described as 'lively faith.'[36] The divine gift of faith that justifies, sanctifies and glorifies is just such a 'lively faith.'[37] To grasp the full content of 'lively faith' it helps to recall that such faith is also a virtue. In Book VI of the *Laws*, where Hooker discusses spiritual jurisdiction and repentance, he notes in passing that 'the whole train of virtues, which are implied in the name of grace' are infused in the believer 'at one instant.'[38] In other words, with the gift of the virtue of faith come the other two theological virtues of hope and love. For Hooker, therefore, faith in its full sense necessarily includes love.

At the end of his sermon on *Certainty* Hooker reminds his hearers that however sure the persevering faith of true believers may be by the grace of Christ, '[H]is prayer must not exclude our labour.'[39] 'Surely if we look to stand in the faith of the sons of God, we must hourly, continually, be providing and setting ourselves to strive . . . . To our own safety, our own sedulity is required.'[40] However freely given the gift of faith may be in the divine act of justification, in the divine act of sanctification, leading to glorification, faith must be enacted in love, as Paul himself argued in his Letter to the Galatians (5.6).

Works

The conclusion of Hooker's sermon on *Certainty* prepares us to turn to his *Learned Discourse of Justification* in order to explore further the relationship between faith and works. The sermon is concerned with that relationship as its full title testifies: *A Learned Discourse of Justification, Works, and How the Foundation of Faith is Overthrown*.[41] We have already encountered the sermon in considering Hooker's doctrine of grace since it includes Hooker's first, defining discussion of the issues of grace and righteousness which divided the Church of England from the Roman Catholic Church. At this point, however, we need to attend to Hooker's treatment of the relationship between justification, sanctification and glorification, on the one hand, and works, on the other.

Abraham, Paul and James

In differentiating the Church of England's understanding of grace, faith and works from that of the Church of Rome, Hooker invokes the example of the patriarch Abraham as he is cited by Paul and James in

---

36. As distinct from *fides informis* or 'unformed' faith.
37. Neelands describes it in Hooker's thought as 'the recognition of God as the object of natural desire' ('Grace', p. 38, note 17).
38. VI, iii, 2 [III, p. 7].
39. *CPFE*, [III, p. 480].
40. *Ibid.* pp. 480-1.
41. The sermon was preached at the beginning of March 1586.

their letters (Romans 4 and James 2). Each of them highlights a distinct yet complementary aspect of the righteousness of grace and its relation to works. Hooker speaks clearly for himself at this point in the sermon:

> Now concerning the righteousness of sanctification, we deny it not to be inherent; we grant, that unless we work, we have it not; only we distinguish it as a thing in nature different from the righteousness of justification: we are righteous the one way, by the faith of Abraham; the other way, except we do the works of Abraham, we are not righteous. Of the one St Paul, "To him that worketh not, but believeth, faith is counted for righteousness." Of the other, St John, "Qui facit justitiam, justus est: – He is righteous which worketh righteousness." Of the one, St Paul doth prove by Abraham's example, that we have it of faith without works. Of the other, St James by Abraham's example, that by works we have it, and not only by faith.[42]

The twofold example of Abraham illustrates the two kinds of righteousness: one that is extrinsic, imputed, unrelated to works; the other in us, 'which consisteth of faith, hope and charity', to which works are necessarily annexed as the form of 'faith working in love', as the 'fruit' of God's 'working Christian righteousness in us'.[43] Works figure as the fruit of the 'actual influence of grace', as Hooker puts it, an influence 'whereby the life which we live according to godliness is his [*viz.* Christ's], and from him we receive those perfections wherein our eternal happiness consisteth'.[44] Hooker's location of works as an intrinsic part of sanctifying righteousness challenged the sole sufficiency of Christ's imputed grace, and in doing so distanced Hooker from both his Lutheran precursors and Calvinist contemporaries.[45]

St Augustine

'Grace is not given us to abandon labour, but labour required lest our sluggishness should make the grace of God unprofitable.'[46] For that assertion of the necessity of works in the *Dublin Fragments* Hooker could look to reliable and esteemed patristic support. Had not Augustine argued similarly in his treatise *On Faith and Works*? Augustine was responding to a view of the requirements for baptism that so construed faith and profession as to exclude any necessary consequences for manner of life

---

42. *LDJ*, 6 [III, p. 491].
43. *Ibid.* 21 [III, p. 507].
44. V, lvi, 10 [II, p. 253].
45. That is, from the practitioners of 'experimental divinity' like Hooker's highly-regarded contemporary William Perkins. On the similarities and differences between them see Spinks, *Two Faces* generally and, more specifically, Neelands, 'Grace' p. 46.
46. *DF* [III, p. 549].

and morals. Hooker does not indicate whether he had Augustine's treatise in mind in his sermon on *Justification*; however, like Hooker after him, Augustine had invoked the respective witness of Paul and James, and cited Paul's key text Galatians 5.6 where the apostle says clearly that 'that faith is good and in conformity with the teaching of the gospel which results in works of love: and *faith*, he says, *that worketh by charity*'.[47]

Years later Hooker explicitly cited that treatise in the *Dublin Fragments*,[48] and when we consider some of the other developments in Hooker's theology in that last phase of writing we might reasonably suppose that the influence of Augustine's treatise *On Faith and Works* had grown.[49]

'Second Justification'

Whereas Hooker had been critical of the Roman Catholic concept of a second justification in his sermon on *Justification*, by the time he penned the *Dublin Fragments* he had adopted the terminology and adapted its sense according to his evolving theology of justification and sanctification.[50] In the *Fragments* the term describes sanctification. Between the first justification and future glory Christians need to be 'qualified with the righteousness of a *second justification* consisting in good works, therefore as St *Paul* doth dispute for faith without works in the first [i.e. justifying righteousness], so St James to the second justification [i.e. sanctifying righteousness] is urgent for works with faith.'[51]

Yet there may be more to it. There is a reason to think that Hooker's notion of a second justification relates to the need to reclaim the first justification that may have become compromised by sin.[52] The importance of repentance for Hooker points that way. When, for instance, he describes the purpose of spiritual jurisdiction in Book VI, it is 'to heal men's consciences, to cure their sins, to reclaim offenders from iniquities, and *to make them by repentance just*'.[53] For Hooker, the process of second justification (sanctification) relies on works done by the intertwined virtues of faith and love – of 'faith working in love' – and on the work and virtue of repentance in the face of sin.[54]

47. Ch. 14, sec. 21 (*ACW*, vol. 48, p. 29).
48. See Hooker's *Autograph Notes on A Christian Letter*, sec. 6, *FLE*, IV, p. 19.
49. And the testimony of the *Summa* too, with Aquinas' emphasis on secondary causes (e.g. prayer, works) in the receipt and workings of grace.
50. He was, says Neelands, unique among contemporaries in adopting this terminology ('Grace, p. 47, note 32).
51. *DF*, V, App. I [II, p. 533]; emphasis mine.
52. This is in part related to Hooker's mature view that the first justification remits all past sin but does not remit present and future sins.
53. Gibbs, 'Richard Hooker's *Via Media* Doctrine of Repentance', *Harvard Theological Review*, 84:1 (1991): 67-8 [he cites *Laws* VI, iv, 1 (III, p. 13)]; emphasis mine.
54. On Hooker's doctrine of repentance and the elements of virtue and work it

Reward and Merit

The close interrelation of faith and works is not understandable apart from the consummation of both in glorifying righteousness. That glorifying righteousness, namely, Christians' inheritance as 'partakers of divine Nature', (2 Peter 1.4) involves, according to Hooker, 'reward'.[55] Hooker's understanding of that progression from the free gift of justifying grace through the grace of sanctification, or second justification, to the 'reward' of glorifying righteousness distances him from the sensibilities of his Reformation predecessors as, indeed, from most of his conforming and non-conforming contemporaries.

The roots of Hooker's views on reward lie in the foundational relationship between nature and grace, and in the threefold perfection for which humankind has been made and which Hooker had advanced in Book I of the *Laws*. It is later, though, in the seasoned theology of the *Dublin Fragments*, and especially in discussion of grace, freewill and sin, that Hooker gives those foundations a sharper theological edge. He reminds readers of this 'presupposition': that God had first determined to bestow eternal life 'in the nature of a reward'.[56] The effects of sin had rendered any natural attainment of that reward impossible. So what could not, on account of sin, be attained by natural powers could only be achieved with the help of grace. But such gracious help for the attainment of the reward did not overthrow, as Hooker insists, the 'voluntary duties' out of which rewards grow, that is, the good works that express lively faith.[57] God, he explains,

> bestoweth now eternal life as his own free and undeserved gift;
> together also with that general inheritance and lot of eternal
> life, great varieties of rewards proportioned to the very degrees
> of those labours, which to perform he himself by his grace
> enableth.[58]

So, in his mature theology Hooker describes the goal of spiritual perfection as a mixture of gift and reward given by God; as gift on the basis of election and the first grace of justification; as reward on the basis of the effects of gracious virtues enabling and accomplishing the duties of a free, believing subject.

If the reward is given by God in response to the duties practiced by a 'lively faith', and if in crowning the believer God crowns his own work of

entails, see Gibbs' article cited above: 65-9.

55. *DF*, V, App. I [II, p. 571].
56. *Ibid.* p. 567.
57. The point is made in the course of an argument about human freedom, and, specifically, that the help of grace in attaining the reward does not curtail the freedom of the agents performing their 'voluntary duties'.
58. *DF*, V, App. I [III, p. 571]; emphasis mine.

grace (as Augustine once put it)[59], can any merit be ascribed to the works of those so rewarded? This is a somewhat ambiguous area in Hooker's theology about which commentators disagree. Hooker's reformed pedigree is felt to hang upon the question, and we can appreciate why: the meritorious quality of all human effort, or works, was high among the presenting issues that separated Roman Catholics from dissidents. Article Eleven, 'Of the Justification of Man', among the Thirty-Nine Articles clearly located merit only in Jesus Christ and ties its application to believers by faith 'and not from our own worth or deservings'.

Hooker affirms the primacy of Christ's meritorious work; he declares in his sermon on *Justification*, 'Christ hath merited righteousness for as many as are found in him'.[60] But as his thought matures, Hooker pursues the matter. While it is true that he is careful, even wary, of the language of merit, Hooker recognises its presence in the theological tradition to which he is accountable. In his treatise *On Faith and Works* which, we have seen, Hooker cites to justify his own views on that subject, Augustine had written that 'the works of the law are meritorious not before but after justification'.[61] In Book V of the *Laws* Hooker admits how Ambrose and Augustine ascribed a meritorious value to acts of penitential piety such as 'weeping and fasting'.[62] Although Hooker does not laud their view, neither does he condemn it, and Voak may well be right when he suggests that Hooker himself has moved a significant way toward them in his view of merit.[63]

That same part of the *Dublin Fragments* is important also because it helps us grasp with greater clarity the nature of such meritorious works. Speaking of specifically penitential acts, Hooker explains that, according to Ambrose and Augustine, they are 'means whereby through God's unspeakable and undeserved mercy we obtain or procure to ourselves pardon'.[64] That merit seems to approximate what scholastic theology called 'congruous merit'. Scholastics meant by that a qualified merit by which an act, though intrinsically unworthy of reward, is accepted by God as rewardable through compassion and mercy gained by Christ.[65] Discussion of satisfaction in the threefold process of repentance in Book VI of the *Laws* suggests that Hooker had by then embraced something like a theology of congruous merit, at least in relation to repentance:

---

59. Neelands, 'Grace', p. 64.

60. *LDJ*, 6 [III, p. 490].

61. *Op. cit.*, 14.21 (p. 29).

62. V, lxxii, 9 [II, pp. 416-17].

63. Voak, *Reformed Theology*, p. 185.

64. V, lxxii, 9 [II, p. 417].

65. Voak offers a helpful discussion of 'congruous merit' and 'condign merit'. In the case of condign merit an act is rewardable by God on account of its intrinsic worth (*Reformed Theology*, pp. 183-5). In the case of such merit God is in some sense obliged. Hooker never uses merit in that sense.

our repentance and the works thereof are therefore termed
satisfactory, not for that so much is thereby done as the
justice of God can expect, but because such actions of grief
and humility in man after sin are *illices misericordiae divinae*
(as Tertullian speaketh of them) they draw the pity of God
towards us, wherein he is for Christ's sake contented upon our
submission to pardon our rebellion against him; and when that
little which his law appointeth is faithfully executed, it pleaseth
him in tender compassion and mercy to require no more.[66]

Congruous merit is, for Hooker, a way of asserting the real value and
necessity of works as an expression of lively faith. Equally, it is a way to
acknowledge the atoning work of Christ as the only basis that leads God
the Father to extend to believers' works a meritorious value in aid of
acceptance and final reward.

So it seems unlikely that we can accept the view that Hooker wholly
rejects merit in human action.[67] Instead, at least in the mature theology at
the end of his life, Hooker reprises a more rounded Augustinian account
of the relationship between faith and works on the basis of his Thomistic
coordination of nature and grace. Within that framework he is able to
link in a careful, coherent chain the gratuity of faith, the necessity of
works as a component of lively faith, that is, 'faith working in love', and the
congruously meritorious character of those works, especially the work of
repentance, in receiving the reward of glory;all generously allowed by God
the Father through the merits of his Son's atoning sacrifice.

The sphere of faith and works is as wide as the Christian life itself. On
the conceptual basis we have laid, we are in a position to consider other
areas of that sphere. From one angle worship and sacraments are, of course,
part of it. But so too are other aspects of the Christian life as traditionally
conceived and practiced. The following chapters consider these other
aspects. We have noted, for instance, the importance of formed or 'lively'
faith for Hooker; and while he does not identify this with intellectual assent
pure and simple, he knows how important a correct and reasonable belief
is both for the individual Christian and for the believing community. We
can now profitably turn to the ways believers think through and explain
their faith by means of theology and doctrine.

---

66. VI, v, 2 [III, p. 57].
67. As Neelands, for instance, argues ('Grace', p. 51).

Chapter 12
'The Science of Things Divine'
Theology and Doctrine

Hooker, it has been said, is an 'heir of the ages'.[1] In no respect is that more true than in his role as a theologian. Preceding chapters have given ample evidence of this in both the wide sweep of Hooker's perspective and in the richness of his sources. This diversity accounts in large measure for the difficulty in placing Hooker on the theological 'map'. As I mentioned at the start of this study, Hooker is claimed as a representative of diverse, sometimes opposed perspectives intellectually, politically, ecclesiastically and theologically.[2] We are not going to negotiate this minefield, but turn to Hooker's understanding of theology with a view to building up a picture of how believers can meaningfully and responsibly talk about God and the faith. To that end we will look at how Hooker himself does so, chiefly in the *Laws* but with occasional reference to his other writings.

We will not attempt to place Hooker on the field of theological traditions and doctrinal options, though there will naturally be reason to consider different perspectives within the traditions of thought, theology and intellectual culture which preceded and surrounded Hooker as he set about the work of theology. The presumption with which we began this study, that Hooker is an independent, eclectic thinker, means that we will resist attempts to align Hooker with established perspectives, customary churchmanships or preferred movements, and doctrinal 'orthodoxies'. In this way we can better focus on the way Hooker understands, executes and models the work of theology, and appreciate his particular 'voice' as a theologian

Context and Style

Having said that, theology always has a context because theologians do. Our examination of Hooker's life indicated what analysts of his theological contribution emphasise: the controversy between the established church and its non-conformist critics was key in shaping Hooker's theology.[3] But so too were non-polemical factors; intellectual streams both general and

---

1. John Marshall, *Hooker*, p. 66.
2. On that variety see Grislis, 'Hermeneutical Problem', pp. 159-62.
3. McAdoo, *Spirit*, p. 3; his point is aimed at the specific issues of theological method (p. 4) which will be considered in this chapter.

specific had an impact. For instance, Hooker was influenced by what John Booty calls an 'orthodox Protestant scholasticism', which was current in the English universities.[4] Hooker's college was a pioneer in advancing the Erasmian Christian humanist project with its especial appreciation for Aristotle's philosophy, logic and rhetoric. Then too there was an additional strain of contemporary 'neo-Thomism', exemplified by the humanist Spaniard Cardinal Cajetan with whose writings Hooker seems to have been well acquainted.[5] That context, together with the alchemical influence of his own intellectual and spiritual worlds, gives to Hooker his distinctive theological style.[6]

'Style' is not a sharp descriptive term, to be sure. Here it points to a sensibility, to an intellectual disposition or tendency, which in turn influences theological approaches and positions. The intellectualism of Hooker's theological style has already been identified. Beyond this, Richard Church highlights the characteristics of 'concurrence' and 'cooperation' in Hooker's thought. He means by this an approach that 'presupposes' other factors, and implies that Hooker sees theological issues *in relation*.[7]

In keeping with that is the rhetorical factor in Hooker's style. In both the *Laws* and in the sermons the influence of the classical rhetorical tradition is seen in the architectonic character of Hooker's prose. But it is not just a literary feature. It reflects the convergence of thought and expression.[8] Division, relation and balance at once characterise his style of thought and his mode of literary expression. In spite of Hooker's indebtedness to the scholastic tradition, we are far removed from the dialectical '*sic et non*' form of theological discourse that characterised 'school divinity'.

Despite the formal difference between the scholastics and Hooker, his critics still accused him of a 'metaphysical and cryptical method' that brought his readers into a 'maze'.[9] Those were the objections of non-conformists about Hooker's ungarnished style. It is true, though, that his rhetoric was concept rather than image or feeling-oriented – in that way 'scholastic', perhaps - and that distinguished it from the preferred Puritan style of thought and expression.[10] A thoroughgoing biblical

---

4. 'Hooker and Anglicanism', *SRH*, p. 213.
5. I put the term neo-Thomism in inverted commas since that phrase is chiefly used of the French Thomist revival of the twentieth century; but the sixteenth century had its own revival of Aquinas' philosophy and theology. On Hooker's acquaintance with Cajetan, see Marshall, *Hooker*, pp. 56-62.
6. Neelands says 'it is not misleading to see Hooker as a self-defined "Protestant," although he appears not to find the word itself useful' ('Grace', p. 32, note 3).
7. *Introduction*, p. xvii.
8. Gibbs makes this point in his essay 'Theology, Logic, and Rhetoric': 178.
9. So the author of *A Christian Letter*, quoted by Gibbs, *ibid.*: 179.
10. A point made by George Knapp and cited by Gibbs (*ibid.*). On the Calvinist preference from Ramist logic and its rhetorical counter-part, see Gibbs, *ibid.*: 181-2.

theology was bound to be less concept-laden. Still, there is a profound, 'hellenic' beauty to Hooker's literary style. It testifies to Hooker's awareness that the medium and the message ought to correlate: 'God-talk' ought, insofar as possible, to reflect the transcendental character of God as *the* Beautiful.

The Theological Milieu

With these characteristics of theological 'style' in mind, we can begin to sketch numerous concentric circles whose content, like multiple lenses, enable us to bring Hooker's understanding of theology into clearer focus. In turning first to the *milieu* of Hooker's theological thought we want to identify the larger conceptual frame within which Hooker's theological 'sight' operates. We have encountered it often in preceding chapters as we have described Hooker's take on particular issues, namely the coordination of nature and grace. Here above all we see Hooker setting his own corrective trajectory in relation to the inherited Lutheran and Calvinist, and then contemporaneous, non-conformist theologies in which the medieval synthesis of nature and grace was suspected or demoted, if not wholly dismissed.[11]

However we might describe the relation between the two – concurrence, cooperation, coworking, balance – such a corrective approach was not of Hooker's own making. He discovered it in the sources with which he worked as his theological vision took shape. It was there *in nuce* in the writings of Augustine whose wide perspectives he sought to bring into theological play.[12] It was also very evident in the legacy of Aquinas' philosophical and theological vision as he repulsed the idea of two truths, of two separate spheres of what is *known*, on the one hand, and what is *believed*, on the other. It became foundational for Aquinas that, as one interpreter has put it, 'faith presupposes and therefore needs natural knowledge of the world'.[13] Unlike his establishment predecessors as well as his non-conformist interlocutors, Hooker views the spheres of nature and grace, of reason and revelation, as inter-penetrating and mutually supportive. So both spheres, both approaches and means, could work together as one activity of the Spirit.[14] Says Hooker,

---

11. I say this in spite of a body of recent interpretive literature which presents Hooker as *both* a *bona fide* exponent of 'magisterial' Reformation doctrine *and* the early Christian and Thomistic nature-grace synthesis; see, for instance, Kirby's works cited throughout. I am unconvinced by that angle.

12. At best the sixteenth century inherited a modified Augustinianism that owed much to the moderating effect of scholasticism with its appreciation of the value of the natural order and its positive anthropology.

13. Joseph Piper, *Scholasticism* (New York, 1964), p. 121; echoing *STh*, Ia. 2. 2.

14. So Luomo puts it, 'Who Owns the Fathers?': 59.

It sufficeth therefore that Nature and Scripture do serve in such full sort that they both jointly and not severally either of them be so complete, that unto everlasting felicity we need not the knowledge of any thing more than these two may easily furnish our minds with on all sides.[15]

Insofar as Hooker is said to have given 'direction'[16] to subsequent Anglican theology, such direction lies chiefly in attempting to reconcile nature and grace, revelation and reason. That is the *milieu* of Hooker's theology, both the mould within which it is constructed, and the principle guiding the relation of the parts within it.

The Posture of the Theologian

What of the theologian? Often we talk of theology as if it could be separated from the human subjects who practice it. But clearly that is not the case. So, if the theologian breathes, so to speak, by means of the twin lungs of nature and grace, what is the theologian's interior 'posture'? Hooker embodies a posture which can be described in terms of three adjectives: ascetical, ecclesial and pastoral.

Ascetical

Students of Hooker have not, I think, appreciated sufficiently Hooker's ascetical posture as a condition of his theology.[17] Various strands are at work here. First, we have to take account of the trajectory of Hooker's life and ministry. Simply, it was a process of withdrawal. From the welter of a highly public ministry aflame with controversy in the metropolis, Hooker retreated further and further into a kind of self-imposed seclusion, in fact a 'private kind of solitary living'.[18] It was, of course, a retreat as a clergyman with pastoral responsibilities; but Hooker was clear that he wanted space for reflection and meditation amid the dutiful pastoral round of a parish, and formed by the ascetical pattern of the *Book of Common Prayer*, of which he was such a stout defender. Walton's description of Hooker's final days, his formal repentance, his contemplation of the heavenly hierarchies, point to a soul persevering in personal devotion shaped by canonical order.[19]

Two characteristics of a theologian flow from those spiritual habits. First, we can discern an eirenicism borne of charity. We have no reason

15. I, xiv.5 [I, p. 271].
16. McAdoo, *Spirit*, p. 6.
17. But among modern interpreters both Grislis and Booty appreciate this aspect.
18. I, x, 12 [I, p. 250]. Porter insightfully applies this to Hooker ('Tudor Constitution', p. 112).
19. Walton's *Life*, pp. 224-5.

to doubt Hooker's seriousness when he describes humility as 'the crown and glory of a Christianly disposed mind'. That charity and humility reflect the 'meekness of Jesus Christ'.[20] Second, judiciousness, a word that Hooker frequently applies to theology itself but which equally applies to the practitioner of theology. Judiciousness is the centre of a cadre of adjectives – 'learned', 'polite', 'wise', 'sagacious' – which underline a posture of studied, habituated detachment.[21] The spiritual ethos of Hooker's day had largely jettisoned the ascetical language of detachment and *apatheia*, but it returns in Hooker himself and is expressed in another guise, as what was described in an earlier chapter as a 'spirituality of truth'.[22]

Building on those strands, we need to recall Hooker's sensitivity to the apophatic aspect of theology. While due acknowledgement has been given to Hooker's rhetorical skill and to the power of his theological prose, he nevertheless appreciates that all human words, all positive theological constructs, are built upon silence and speechlessness before God; theology must have an element of wonder and 'learned ignorance'.[23] We can profitably recall words from the start of the *Laws* which we have already quoted:

> Dangerous it were for the feeble brain of man to wade far into the doings of the Most High; whom although to know be life, and joy to make mention of his name; yet our soundest knowledge is to know that we know him not *as indeed he is*, *neither can know him*: and our safest eloquence concerning him is our silence, when we confess without confession that his glory is inexplicable, his greatness above our capacity and reach. He is above, and we upon earth; therefore it behoveth our words to be wary and few.[24]

Hooker subscribes to the Dionysian distinction between cataphatic theology, the way of affirmations, words and concepts, and the more fitting way of apophatic theology, recognition that we cannot know God 'as he is', 'that light which none can approach unto'.[25] Theology – and this Hooker

20. Preface, I, iii [I, p. 127].

21. On this see Gibbs, 'Hermeneutical Problem': 174; Gibbs, however, does not make this ascetical application.

22. This is not to suppose Hooker was a saintly figure as contemporary sketches and later biographies might suggest; see Brydon, *Evolving Reputation*, chapters 1 and 2; nor does it compel us to ignore or minimise the irony and sarcasm which Hooker brings to his arguments in both the *Laws* and in his annotations in the *Dublin Fragments*. Whatever Hooker's spiritual stature, he remained a man well versed in the argumentative scope and use of rhetoric, as Brian Vickers ably shows: 'Hooker's Prose Style' in A.S. McGrade and Brian Vickers, ed., *Of the Laws of Ecclesiastical Polity: An Abridged Edition* (London, 1975), pp. 41-59.

23. *DF*, V, App. I [II, p. 563].

24. I, ii, 2 [I, p. 201]; italics mine.

25. III, viii, 9 [I, p. 370]. On this distinction and the way of 'the divine darkness' see Vladimir Lossky, *The Mystical Theology of the Eastern Church* (Crestwood,

shows throughout – is necessarily an intellectually humble and humbling enterprise; negations and silence are more eloquent than concepts and words. That awareness and discipline of mind go hand in hand with an interior spiritual posture.

We can make two final points about the ascetical posture of the theologian. First, and in general, there can be no saving knowledge without the illumination of sanctifying grace. Second, and in particular, Hooker's approach posits what Egil Grislis calls the 'purification of reason' by grace as a necessary condition for sound theological reflection and discourse.[26]

Ecclesial

Theology, as Hooker understands it, takes place within and on behalf of the life of the church. The church is an obvious reference point in the *Laws* insofar as its eight books defend a particular institution and form of ecclesial life. But for Hooker there is a more profound meaning to theology's ecclesial character.

First, his whole approach assumes that the offerings of an individual theologian are qualified by the corporate mind of the church. Hooker is highly critical of the "*methinketh*" approach to theology which, in his view, exalts individual and subjective insights and interests above those of the community of faith.[27] We will have cause to return to this point through the chapter.

Second, the theologian's contribution is made from a posture of active participation in ecclesial life. The root form of that participation is the canonical round of public prayer and praise, offices and sacraments, and the ordering of one's life according to the church's canonical vision, all of which convey and nurture the fruits of sanctifying grace. Hooker, as we know, moved from context to context, yet those features were constant. Out of the pattern of corporate Christian life authentic theology takes shape. To build upon the first point: authentic theology, and the purification of mind and heart required for it, need the common life of the church.

Pastoral

Following from that ecclesial stance, Hooker understands that the theologian has a pastoral responsibility. That is not meant to compromise a theologian's intellectual rigor. Hooker himself, at least, could never be accused of intellectual laxity. A pastorally responsible theologian will,

---

USA, 1975), pp. 23-5.
26. On those two points see respectively Voak, *Grace*, p. 304; and Grislis, 'Hermeneutical Problem', p. 195.
27. IV, iv, 2 [I, p. 430].

however, take care that theology contributes practically and healthily to the attainment of Christians' spiritual perfection. Hooker's sermons evidence this responsibility.

For instance, Hooker sees the moral-spiritual hindrances of a theology which abrogates the link between nature and grace. If God speaks to humankind only through the scriptures and without any use of reason, then the scriptures themselves become, says Hooker, 'a snare and a torment to weak consciences, filling them with infinite perplexities, scrupulosities, doubts insoluble, and extreme despairs.'[28] As an omni-competent guide to life, the scriptures by themselves fail. A pastorally responsible theology will be on guard against such a theology of Scripture and its baleful consequences.

The Sources of Theology

Having assumed this posture, Hooker draws upon three foundational sources which provide the material out of which his theology is formed: Scripture, reason and tradition. That set of terms, usually identified as the constituents of a distinctively Anglican theological 'method', has become a common-place in understanding the 'direction' which Hooker is credited with giving the Church of England.[29] However, Hooker offers no simple, articulated doctrine of such a methodology.[30] On reflection it is easy to see why: use of those sources was a long-standing feature of the Christian theological tradition which Hooker could hardly be said to have invented. He simply adopted and adapted it to his own situation.

Surely Hooker's thorough reading of Aquinas – 'the greatest among the school divines'[31] – would have inclined him toward such sources since they are the angelic doctor's too. 'Sacred doctrine', as Aquinas understood it, is a product of the confluence of Scripture, tradition and philosophy. By philosophy Aquinas meant the grasp of rational principles and arguments necessary for intelligible discourse.[32] Hooker prefers the term 'reason' to identify this strand in his sources; but the sources are identical.

Hooker, of course, approaches those sources with the perspective of a Renaissance theologian shaped by the intellectual temper of Erasmian humanism; so how does he understand and relate the three sources that he inherited from the great Christian tradition?

---

28. II, viii.6 [I, p. 335].
29. The main exposition of that view is McAdoo in *Spirit*, pp. 1-12; but its origin lies in Paget's *Introduction* to Book Five.
30. The eighth chapter of Book III is key in identifying that Anglican 'tripod'.
31. III, ix, 2 [I, p. 381].
32. On the relation of philosophy and theology in Aquinas I follow Mark Jordan in his essay 'Theology and Philosophy' in N. Kretzman and E. Stump, ed., *The Cambridge Companion to Aquinas* (Cambridge, 1993), p. 234.

Scripture

In Book III of the *Laws* where Hooker attends to non-conformist views of Scripture, he asks rhetorically: 'The whole drift of the Scripture of God, what is it but only to teach Theology?'[33] With an eye on Scripture's role as a source for theology and its methods, five points deserve mention on the basis of that text.

First, and above all else, Scripture is considered by Hooker as the sole means of revelation, understanding that term to refer to saving truth. To the contemporary eye, Hooker's Protestantism is clear in his rejection of any additional source.[34] This stance does not, as we already realise, mean that revelation provides theology's only data; it means 'though' that where 'any revealed law of God' is sought Scripture is primary in the hierarchy of sources.[35]

Second, theology is an exegetical project and exegesis is a theological one. While not a full-blown commentator in his own right, Hooker's training fitted him extremely well for the task of the new learning's 'literal interpretation'. Likewise, the influence of patristic and scholastic theology encouraged theological exegesis, that is, interpretation, informed by and directed toward ecclesial faith.[36]

Third, recalling a point made in chapter five, Hooker's theological approach to Scripture puts Christology at its centre. 'The main drift of the whole New Testament', says Hooker,

> is that which St John setteth down as the purpose of his own history; "These things are written, that ye might believe that Jesus is Christ the Son of God, and that in believing ye might have life through his name."[37]

Fourth, because of the interplay of nature and grace within the sacred text itself (as we have seen in a previous chapter, Scripture contains much besides unchanging revelation), revelation has a Christological core, surrounded by peripheral matter. This allows Hooker to develop a nuanced kind of theological exegesis that avoids interpretation as mere restatement passage by passage; instead, he favours the reasoned analysis of a selection of pertinent texts and words.[38]

Both of the preceding points mean that finally a widely-sourced

---

33. III, viii, 11 [I, p. 374].

34. Regarding the Council of Trent and the Church of England respectively, see Tavard, *Holy Writ*, pp. 195-209 and 210-43; on Hooker, pp, 240-3.

35. See I, xiii, 2 [I, p. 265].

36. See Hooker's description of the 'matter contained' at the head of Books II and III to illustrate this.

37. I, xiv, 4 [I, p. 270].

38. See Grislis, 'Hermeneutical Problem', p. 191; but this is not necessarily to accept his assertion of 'an implicit distinction between uninspired and inspired Scripture'.

doctrinal exposition can arise out of Scripture. With Christology at its core, Scripture becomes the mine out of which the riches of both nature and grace can be quarried. Grislis argues that the strength of Hooker's exegesis and hermeneutic is that he can 'build a systematic theology that is truly overarching and encompasses all wisdom available to man'.[39]

Reason

Hooker is bitingly clear that the way to be 'ripe in faith' is not to be 'raw in wit and judgment'.[40] In other words, reasoned reflection in essential. There may be variety in the order of importance attributed to Scripture, reason and tradition in establishment theology after Hooker, but in the case of Hooker himself it is clear that reason should be considered second. At the same time, we must avoid the view that reason's place in theology as Hooker understands it can be carefully circumscribed. Just as earlier we presented the relation of grace and nature as a *milieu* in order to avoid mechanically circumscribing their respective presence and influence, so the same must be said here: Hooker's particular theological *milieu* is one in which reason and revelation, Scripture and reason, intersect and interact. Reason, therefore, suffuses the primary source of Scripture even as a revealed truth has a supremacy in the theological project which reason cannot possibly challenge or equal.

In holding that ground Hooker may have distanced himself from Reformed theology, but in so doing he stood within a long-established line of Roman Catholic theology. With due acknowledgement of the unknowability of God in God's self, there remains the possibility of knowledge of, and reflection upon, God's words and ways which constitute the sphere of positive theology. The Christian tradition affirmed this. In that cataphatic domain reasoned reflection and exposition have a necessary place. Aquinas thought of this component more precisely in terms of philosophy; the methodological point, though, was the same: critical perception and analysis of reality, both experienced and spoken, are essential parts of any responsible God-talk.

Hooker stands in that theological stream. Neelands reminds us that Hooker nowhere presents a full exposition of philosophical theology, but that it stands as a background, appears throughout Hooker's writings, and shapes his grasp of principles of procedures for intelligible discourse without reality.[41] We have already noted the neo-Platonic structure of 'exit' and 'return' which guides the whole theological project; onto that base Hooker – echoing Aquinas – co-opts Aristotle as a primary exemplar and guide. So when Hooker speaks of 'reason' he implies the battery of philosophical tools available to the thinking person and community.

---

39. *Ibid.* A useful point, the caveat about 'systematic' notwithstanding.
40. III, viii, 4 [I, p. 366].
41. 'Grace', p. 330. See Paget's Law of Progress in the Knowledge of Truth (p. 66).

Reason, then, is a necessary ingredient in theology both in relation to the chief source, Scripture, and in relation to the project of theological construction as a whole. We have already pointed out the place and influence of reason in Hooker's expositions, not least in the chapter on Scripture. Now we need to look more closely at reason's role in the whole theological enterprise. This means going beyond the broad coordination of reason with revelation to discover three things: the *kind* of reason with which theology works; its implications for practitioners of theological 'science'; and the specific tools of reasoning which, in Hooker's view, are indispensable to credible theological thought.

The Restoration of Reason

At numerous points in this study we have encountered Hooker's view of the need for the reason of fallen humanity to be healed and helped. There are two ways in which Hooker understands the restoration of reason, and those ways roughly correspond to the categories of nature and grace.

First, Hooker shares the Renaissance concept and concern for 'right reason' (*ratio recta*).[42] This is not chiefly a theological concept; perhaps it is best described as a philosophical concept. It involves the awareness that the human power of reasoning is one that needs instruction and training if it is to function well and so lead an individual to his intellectual perfection. The fact that all human beings by nature are endowed with reason does not mean that all human beings can or do reason *well*. 'Right reason', then, refers to the qualitative exercise of a human being's rational powers; it signifies reasoning well. Appreciation for Aristotle, for example, across the theological spectrum in Hooker's day was in large measure because he was thought to have consistently practiced a high degree of right reasoning.

Second, and beyond the natural sphere, Hooker affirms that of course the apprehension and assent of faith are the result of grace.[43] Of course the very apprehension and assent implicit in faith is the result of grace. Beyond that, right reasoning must be further attuned by the continuance of assisting grace that influences the theologian by means of ecclesial life and the ascetical patterns it proposes and encourages. It is but a conceptualisation of the psalmist's declaration, "In thy light we see light" (Psalm 36.9).For fallen human reason becomes 'right reason' by experience, by education and by philosophic training; and 'right reason' needs to become engraced by the gift of grace and by growth in grace within the life of the Spirit-filled mystical body, the church.[44]

---

42. For Aquinas too *ratio recta* is central not just for theology but for right living generally.

43. We leave aside here the issue of so-called 'common grace' in the theology of Hooker; it is a debated point.

44. Hooker never illegitimises infused knowledge by a special grace; but his concern is with norms.

Practitioners of Theological 'Science'

Hooker does not use the phrase 'theological science' but the import
of our previous discussion makes it appropriate. The intellectual and
ascetical rigor required of theological practitioners takes theology out of
the domain of common knowledge and puts it squarely in the hands of
specialists, those who 'spend their whole time principally in the study of
things divine'.[45] However, Hooker does not mean that all knowledge of
God is esoteric and beyond the conceptual reach of the average believer.
In an important passage in the Preface to the *Laws* Hooker recognises
that while core belief is 'plainly set down in Scripture; so that 'he that
heareth or readeth may without any great difficulty understand', there
is still much of importance that is obscure and requires that the trained
understanding of some 'might be a light to direct others'.[46] It simply stands
to reason.

> If the understanding power or faculty of the soul be (saith the
> grand physician) like unto bodily sight, not of equal sharpness
> to all, what can be more convenient than that, even as the dark-
> sighted man is directed by the clear about things visible; so
> likewise in matters of deeper discourse the wise in heart do
> shew the simple where his way lieth?[47]

As in all spheres of natural life, so in the supernatural life of grace,
reason does not level all voices in theological discourse simply because
all men have a reasoning power. Far from it. Because that reasoning
power needs training and enlightenment, only those skilfully trained are
apt to apply it to illuminate 'things divine'. [48] Although it runs counter
to our egalitarian and democratic sensibilities, it is accurate to describe
Hooker's view of reason in theology as an élite rather than a simply
democratic principle.[49]

Four Tools in Theological Reasoning

How does reason function in theological discourse for Hooker? We
can point to four ways in which reason offers heuristic tools in the

45. Preface, III, ii [I, p. 143].
46. *Ibid.*
47. *Ibid.* pp. 143-4.
48. *Ibid.* p. 143.
49. 'Whatever its concessions to the "simpler sort," explains Debora Shuger, 'the
whole point of the *Laws* . . . is that philological training, extensive familiarity
with sacred and profane learning, and a solid grounding in logic are requisite for
framing and judging ecclesiastical polities'. The *Laws*, in other words, assumes
an élitist humanism ('Society supernatural': the imagine community of Hooker's
Laws, in C. McEachern and D. Shuger, ed., *Religion and Culture in Renaissance
England* [Cambridge, 1997], p. 125).

construction of theological system which supports his claim that theology is a matter of 'demonstrative principles' and 'demonstrable conclusions'.[50]

Analogical Language

Hooker recognises the importance of analogical language in theological discourse.[51] Through such language he can use words and concepts that carry a similar *but not exact* meaning when applied from creaturely beings to the divine Being.[52] Its basis lies in the relation between cause and effects and the concepts of participation and hierarchy by which all created things relate to their creator. Hooker explicitly explains, as we know, that all things participate in God as effects participate in their cause. As a consequence, there is an analogy of being (*analogia entis*) which links creatures to the creator, and from that primary analogous relationship flows the analogical language related to the characteristics of creaturely and uncreated being.[53] While the Platonic principle of participation under-girds the concept, Aristotelian distinction gives it concrete shape. This gives Hooker, as it gave Aquinas, a way to describe God intelligibly while preserving the otherness of God in the face of human conceptualisations.[54] When combined with Hooker's sense of apophasis, we have a double way to overcome the limits of our language: the way of negation and the way of analogy.[55]

Inference

Hooker, like Aquinas, uses a method of inference to build theological understanding. By means of its two operations, analysis and synthesis, a theological system can arise from the twin sources of revelation and reason.[56] We see this operating in Book V. The scriptural narrative of the

50. V, lxiii, 1 [II, p. 304].

51. Aristotle had posited a twofold way of speaking, i.e., univocal (where a word's meaning remains the same) and equivocal (where a word can have two different meanings when applied differently). Aquinas expanded that conceptualisation by the addition of a median kind of speech, analogous; but Aquinas did not state a theory of analogy.

52. On analogy as a specific feature of God-talk, see Davies, *Aquinas*, pp. 70-9.

53. Hooker speaks in a passage about 'proportionality', thus revealing awareness of the systematisation of Aquinas' analogical thinking by later Thomist commentators like Cajetan; see Marshall, *Hooker*, p. 68.

54. Those who developed Aquinas' analogical approach introduced distinctions such as analogy of intrinsic attribution and of proportionality; Hooker's seems to work with such distinctions though he does not feel the need to explain them to his readers.

55. So Florovksy, describing of theology proper this double way of *negationis* and *eminentiae*' ('Idea of Creation': 69).

56. 'Synthesis' and 'analysis' are technical terms in Aristotelian inference.

Incarnation is analysed so as to yield a general doctrine of the relationship between nature and grace; that universal principle is then synthesised in Hooker's particular doctrine on eucharistic presence.[57]

Degrees of Certainty

Hooker takes the view that human knowing recognises that truth claims possess various *degrees of certainty*. The consequence is a simple axiom: 'such as the evidence is which the truth hath either in itself or through proof, such is the heart's assent thereunto'.[58] So reason has a key part in correlating degrees of certainty with what we know. Throughout his writings we can discern a fourfold scale of certainty.

We have already encountered this idea in our discussion of Hooker's understanding of faith. There we saw that in the sphere of what is believed as 'principle points' of faith the certainty of assent is infallible; it admits of no doubt. We saw too, though, that such certainty is out of proportion to what the evidence for such points of faith rationally yields. So, for instance, while the Christian believes the doctrine of the Trinity is intrinsically certain, he recognizes that it is not found in scripture by 'express literal mention', and that the doctrine as explicated is the result of a process of rational deduction.[59]

Most things Christians believe or think, however, do not possess the 'intrinsic certainty' of the principal points of faith; they possess a degree of rational certainty matched by the kind and quality of evidence for them. In this wide sphere Hooker describes three further degrees of certainty.

The next level of certainty is that of 'plain aspect and intuitive beholding'.[60] 'Plain aspect' refers to what is known by sense perception. 'Intuitive beholding' refers to self-evident truths that require no proof, logically necessary statements such as 'the whole is greater than its parts'. Moving down the scale of certainty, then, is what Hooker calls 'strong and invincible demonstration'. This includes logical deductions necessarily deduced from principles. Last, Hooker speaks of evidence that elicits the 'greatest possibility'. In this sphere of reasoning assent is not strictly necessary. It refers to the most certain element in a vast range of probable truths. In this range of information reason must move freely and work hard to weigh up and decide where the truth of a matter most *probably* lies.

Objectivity

The fourth and final tool in theological analysis and discourse is

---

57. As Marshall explains this feature of Aristotle's *Posterior Analytics* in the hands of Aquinas: 'analysis' infers the universal from the particular; and 'synthesis' infers the particular from the universal (*Hooker*, p. 68).
58. II, vii, 5 [I, p, 323].
59. I, xiv, 2 [I, p. 269].
60. II, vii, 5 [I, p. 322-3].

objectivity. Beginning in its Preface and then throughout the *Laws* as well as his other writings Hooker is determined to keep theology out of the realm of the subjective and in the realm of the objective. There is no simple formula to assure this, but Hooker takes the view that if theologians are properly trained and prepared, and if they assiduously and judiciously pursue their task in the ecclesial context, then the resultant insights and conclusions will be as far removed from idiosyncrasy and self-interest as possible. His concern about the non-conformist approach, as the Preface and subsequent arguments in Book II and III make clear, is that it functions as a self-referential circle in which the subjective '*methinketh*' dominates to the exclusion of any critical and objective counter-point. In Hooker's view that is a disaster for theology.

The four tools of reason, then, offer a necessary alternative both in the construction of a reliable theological language and logic, and in promoting a self-critical and accountable habit of theological reasoning. Of course its practitioners are liable to error, but when all is said and done theirs is the safer, because the more reasonable, course.

Tradition

The third and final element among Hooker's triad of sources, tradition, takes its place in relation to Scripture and reason in various ways. We have already noted that it was a firmly established source for theological reflection in the tradition of, for example, scholastic theology in which Hooker took keen interest. However, the Reformation reaction had to different degrees challenged the long-standing authority ascribed to tradition, and on that basis Hooker faced a non-conformist mentality in which only the scriptural testimony carried authority. A benign 'primitivism' widely current in English theology became more and more circumscribed in the hands of non-conformist practitioners. Their revolt against philosophy and its habits of reasoning was echoed in a similar rejection of the testimonies of Christian history. If Scripture was omni-competent then what need could there be for the witness of the intervening Christian centuries and the documented experience and perspectives of the church? In contrast, the *milieu* of nature and grace, and the hierarchy of laws which provides the inner structure, so to speak, of that relationship, mean that for Hooker the testimony of the church through history is an important, even necessary ingredient in sound theological reflection.

We can appreciate why and how that is so by looking at tradition in relation to Scripture and reason. First, however, we need to gain a clearer sense of the word 'tradition' as Hooker understands it.

Tradition and 'Traditions'

It is fair to say that Hooker shares the general Reformers' mistrust of 'tradition'.[61] Its negative associations derive from Roman Catholic claims that unwritten traditions supplement saving truths revealed through Scripture.[62] Hooker rejects such a view, as he explains early in the *Laws*:

> When therefore the question is whether we be now to seek for any revealed law of God other than only in the sacred Scripture; whether we do now stand bound in the sight of God to yield to traditions urged by the Church of Rome the same obedience and reverence we do to his written law, honouring equally and adoring both as divine: our answer is, No.[63]

On the other hand, once 'traditions' are taken out of the sphere of 'revealed law' and are positioned in the sphere of apostolic and ecclesiastical ordinances,[64] Hooker's evaluation shifts. In the face of stiff non-conformist objection to 'traditions ecclesiastical' like the sign of the cross in baptism, Hooker explains that, lest 'the name of tradition' be 'offensive' to any, he means by the term

> ordinances made in the prime of Christian religion, established with that authority which Christ hath left to his Church for matters indifferent, and in that consideration requisite to be observed, till like authority see just and reasonable cause to alter them.[65]

So Hooker clears a path for 'traditions' that avoids either according them a status equal to Scripture or dismissing them altogether.

Hooker's positive evaluation, on the other hand, equates 'traditions' with 'ordinances', that is, with aspects of ecclesiastical discipline or custom distinct from doctrine. With an interest in theology to the fore, can we identify 'tradition' as a legitimate theological source in the thinking of Hooker? Can we, in other words, detect in Hooker's theology an appreciation for 'tradition' that embraces Christian thought and so influences the shape and content of theology and doctrine? To do so we need to invoke a set of ideas and terms with which Hooker works but which are not given a simple and consistent vocabulary in his writings.

---

61. Loyer, I, pp. 136-7.

62. The so-called two-source theory of revelation; see note 34.

63. I, xiii, 2 [I, p. 265]. Sea also I, xiii, 2 [I, p. 265]; xiv, 5 [I, p. 271]; II, v, 7 [I, pp. 308-9]; III, viii, 14 [I, pp. 376-7]; *LDJ*, 11 [III, p. 497].

64. Hooker dislikes the difference between 'apostolic' and 'ecclesiastical' ordinances made in Roman Catholic theology; for Hooker all traditions are ecclesiastical; see Loyer, I, p. 136.

65. V, lxv, 2 [II, p. 318]; on the point of 'matters indifferent' see chapter fourteen.

Primitive and Patristic

While we have just seen Hooker credit church ordinances made 'in the *prime* of the Christian religion' we must also note that for Hooker 'prime' is not an easily limitable term. Whereas conformists' also invoked primitive church life, they meant by that the apostolic witness of doctrine and discipline detectable (or so they thought) in the pages of the New Testament. Hooker, in marked contrast, is not so formulaic.

We can account for Hooker's appeal to a wider view of 'prime' in part by remembering how Hooker works with a keen sense of historical development growing out of his Renaissance sensibility. The majority of Hooker's quotations from church fathers and other sources span the first six centuries of the Christian era (thus embracing the main period of conciliar dogma, doctrine and discipline).[66] It is noteworthy that when he responds to a raft of criticisms by the author of *A Christian Letter* Hooker replies not on the basis of sixteenth-century authorities but on the basis of patristic texts.[67] Certainly that era of 'undifferentiated catholicism' was a kind of lode star for Hooker, a benchmark to determine the essential theological and doctrinal patrimony of the Christian tradition.[68]

Having said that, Hooker is not mechanical in deference to the 'prime' of the Christian religion as chronologically conceived. One feels that in Hooker's hands 'prime' is as much a qualitative notion as a chronological one. We have seen throughout this study the breadth of Hooker's appeal to sources which are non-apostolic and which in fact supersede the first six centuries, as the scholastic component in Hooker's theological tool kit illustrates. In his analysis of the patristic appeal in Hooker's theology, therefore, John Luoma has pertinently concluded that Hooker's theology makes room for patristic and, by implication, other influences as part of 'the continuing activity of the Spirit'.[69]

Consensus

Consensus is the key word in Hooker's appeal to the church fathers.[70] Of course the patristic period saw the emergence of the church's conciliar habits, and through its corporate search for truth came the crystallisation of key dogmatic and theological insights. So there was plain historical evidence of a consensus-seeking model in the discernment and determination of contested issues in the church of which Hooker was aware.

The relation of this concept to Hooker's appeal to reason as a theological

---

66. For a useful view of the patristic appeal see Luoma, 'Who owns the Fathers?'.
67. Neelands makes this point ('Grace', pp. 298).
68. McAdoo speaks of the church of the first five centuries thus, and describes it as a 'pivotal point' for Anglican theology in the hands of Hooker and others (*Spirit*, p. v).
69. Luoma, 'Who owns the Fathers?', 59.
70. *Ibid.*: 53.

source is important too. From the start of the *Laws* Hooker emphasizes that the law of reason is most readily discernible through the 'general and perpetual voice of men'.[71] Given his view that '[n]ature as much as possible inclineth unto validities and preservations',[72] Hooker is almost bound to give weight to habits and views that extend through time and space – the weight of long experience.[73]

Remembering too that Hooker's concept of reason looks not to majority opinions but to the sagacious insights of those who labour with the methods, sources and issues at stake, Hooker's appeal to consensus looks to those called and equipped to labour in the field of 'matters divine'. Such consensus might take the form of a solemn conciliar decision; more likely, it will be discerned by careful searching and analysis of the history of the church and its wise and godly witnesses. 'The bare consent of the whole Church', he argues against non-conformist critics of church authority, 'should itself in these things stop the mouths, who living under it, dare presume to bark against it.'[74]

By means of consensus above all subjectivity is kept at bay and objective truth is more assuredly grasped. Equally, within the realm of rational consideration the individual's faulty use of reason is checked and corrected. In that respect, at least, the sources of reason and tradition are interactive and mutually supportive.

The consensus which Hooker invokes, then, is an assemblage of learned and holy insights compacted into a discernible unity of opinion and extending through time. For Hooker the rational component in the act of belief, as well as justification for matters of lesser importance regarding doctrine and discipline (where assent is strictly tied to the degree of rational certainty), find their strongest basis where consensus reigns. In that Hooker gives momentum to a concern for historical evidence so as to test the existence of consensus and to assess the degree of rational certainty creditable to a particular theological opinion or ecclesiastical ordinance.

Hooker himself sums up his use of the sources of Scripture, reason and tradition early in Book V of the *Laws* when he explains that

> what Scripture doth plainly deliver, to that the first place of credit and obedience is due; the next whereunto is whatsoever any man can necessarily conclude by force of reason; after these the voice of the Church succeedeth.[75]

There, in a clear and succinct formulation, Hooker declares the threefold appeal which gives distinctive 'tone' and 'method' to Anglican theology.[76] While it is important to note the three component sources as the constituents

71. I, viii, 3 [I, p. 227].
72. V, lxii, 13 [II, p. 292].
73. V, viii, 3 [V, II, pp. 33-5].
74. V, viii, 3 [V, II, pp. 34-5].
75. V, viii, 2 [II, p. 34].
76. Neelands highlights the uniqueness of this text in Hooker's works as part of his critique of some expositions of this threefold appeal in Anglicanism ('Grace', pp. 90-1).

of what Egil Grislis has called – rather too doxologically perhaps – a 'holy triangle',[77] we must also note their order in the discernment of Christian faith and the evaluation of the church's practices.

Hooker's Theological Contribution: 'A turning point'

Henry McAdoo once claimed that Anglicanism produced theologians far more than theologians produced Anglicanism.[78] It is certain that the Church of England's reformation arose from a tangle of motives, largely from the top down, and that no single theologian sparked or dominated the founding project. At the same time, since McAdoo's words the study of Hooker has advanced so that it is now possible to place him and assess his contribution in a more nuanced way.

Whereas an older generation saw Hooker as the next stage in an already fully operative 'Anglicanism' so that he can only be credited with altering its 'tone' and 'direction', the results of subsequent study regard Hooker as a far more important force in the evolution of Anglicanism. John Booty, though focused on 'method' and the diffuse idea of 'attitude', has rightly described Hooker's contribution as a 'turning point'.[79]

Proceeding like a gradually sharpening spiral, we have plotted far more than an attitude or tone. We have progressed in our study from the foundational relationship between nature and grace, to the proper theological posture of the theologian, to a detailed examination of Hooker's dynamic interplay of sources. This examination contained key points about exegetical method, tools of theological reasoning, and principles for assessing the historical data of the Christian movement in history. We have not just the direction, but the defining content of a particular theological style. Beyond that, and with the aid of the insights of previous chapters, we find a theological vision whose basis is the patristic doctrines of Trinity, Incarnation and deification, or *theosis*, by grace, and whose operations are legitimated by their coordination with that doctrinal core.[80] Those are structural details of what John Marshall has rightly called 'a coherent theology'.[81] Hooker dug his foundations deep enough that his theology has continued to attract, teach and inspire not only theologians but others concerned with the application of doctrine to discipline, theology to life. Hooker himself was fully aware of theology's long 'reach', so to some of its implications and consequences we should now turn.

77. In his essay 'Jesus Christ – The Centre of Theology in Richard Hooker's *Of the Laws of Ecclesiastical Polity*, Book V', *Journal of Anglican Studies*, 5:2 (2007): 234.
78. McAdoo, *Spirit*, p. 321.
79. 'Hooker and Anglicanism', p. 231.
80. See A. M. Allchin's 'Trinity and Incarnation in Anglican Tradition' in *The Kingdom of Love and Knowledge* (London, 1979), pp. 93-112; and his study *Participation in God* cited elsewhere in this study.
81. *Hooker*, p. 66.

Moral Theology

Hooker was well aware that Christianity requires deeds to be done as well as articles to be believed. His views on faith and works, rooted in long-standing Christian perspectives, presupposed as much. The very link between faith and action, central to the Letter of James that Hooker had invoked years before he penned the *Laws* as he clarified his views on justification, was the starting point for what the Christian tradition later came to call moral theology.[1] If ethics is chiefly concerned with thought about action, then Christian ethics, or what Hooker from his theocentric stand point might have termed moral theology, is thinking about right action, understood in light of God's self-revelation in Jesus Christ and the grace of the Spirit.[2]

For Hooker and his contemporaries theology was a comprehensive science so faith's expression in behaviour was a presumptive commonplace. English Calvinist divinity, Hooker's intellectual context, was obsessed with so-called 'practical divinity'.[3] That made it inevitable that moral theological concerns would surface in the pages of the *Laws* as well as in Hooker's other writings. Another factor was Hooker's abiding interest in metaphysics. This inclination, evidenced time and again in his study of root principles and assumptions, meant that even within the particular controversial parameters of the *Laws* Hooker was motivated to take up issues pertaining to moral theology.

Indeed, the justification of the established church's laws of polity raised, as we have already seen, crucial epistemological issues with implications concerning the sources and authority of laws guiding individuals and communities. With this came the issue of objectivity and subjectivity in

---

1. Refer to chapter eight's discussion of Hooker's views on justification. While the proposal of a Christian scheme of ethics began with St Ambrose's *De Officiis*, it was common at least from the time of Peter Lombard to commit significant parts of systematic theological treatises to moral theology (Kenneth E. Kirk, *Some Principles of Moral Theology* [London, 1920], p. 2).

2. Those broad definitions follow Holmgren, *Ethics After Easter* (Cambridge, MA, 2000), pp. 22-3.

3. Egil Grislis reminds us, though, of the issues raised by the ambient Roman Catholic tradition, of which Hooker remained ever aware; see 'The Role of Sin in the Thought of Richard Hooker', *Anglican Theological Review*, LXXXIV, 4 (2002): 885-89.

the apprehension of truths, and so Hooker's desire to clarify how a human being discovers and commits to what is true and good. We have seen how Hooker eschewed notions of winning or meriting salvation; even so, he retained, as Peter Lake has reminds us, a strong sense that our fate in the next world depends upon our conduct in this,[4] as the discussions of justification, sanctification and glorification have shown. So, although we do not find in the *Laws* anything like a manual of moral theology or a treatise on what his seventeenth-century successors called 'casuistical divinity',[5] Hooker gives us enough material to construct a rudimentary map of this department of theology. Also, around the *Laws*, Hooker's sermons provide ample evidence of his concern to give practical moral-spiritual application to theological principles.[6]

What is 'Moral Theology'?

However traditional moral theology may have been, by Hooker's day it was variously construed, so it is important to understand Hooker's approach. How did Hooker understand moral theology?

In contrast to an approach focusing on the regulation of behaviour according to a legal moral code – 'the interpretation and application of law' – Hooker takes a reformed view.[7] That is, moral theology's concern is with the whole movement of human beings, both as individuals and as members of communities, toward their fulfilment both naturally and supernaturally.[8] Plainly an understanding like that ties the moral theological project to deep moorings both in metaphysics and in Christian doctrine, a posture amply evidenced in Books I and II of the *Laws*.[9] Further, while Hooker has much to say about the duties and obligations that pertain to Christians and citizens, he is also vividly aware that those find their justification and much of their purpose in the form of virtues and excellences which adorn the character of the moral agent, setting him on a course toward the vision of God.[10]

---

4. *Anglican and Puritan?*, p. 185.
5. See, for instance, H. R. McAdoo, *The Structure of Caroline Moral Theology* (London, 1949) and Thomas Wood, *English Casuistical Divinity During the Seventeenth Century* (London, 1952).
6. Kenneth Stafford explores this in relation to Hooker's *Sermon on Pride* in 'Practical Divinity', pp. 535-61. In the course of concluding this study J.A. Joyce's study appeared; it is cited later.
7. So McAdoo describes the Tridentine era Roman Catholic approach (*Structure*, p. 15). The adjective 'reformed' here does not refer to the Reformed tradition of Calvin and his successors.
8. As McAdoo puts it: 'The subject matter of moral theology is man' (*Structure*, p. 6).
9. For the metaphysical link in Hooker see Surlis, 'Natural Law': 179.
10. On these two emphases, see Kirk, *Principles*, p. 10. Kirk notes that 'the thought of the *vision of God* as the goal of human life and the determinant, therefore, of

In situating himself in this manner, Hooker stands in the stream of thought dominant in the west beginning with the Greek ethical theories of Aristotle, and then given their Christian orientation, extended, and developed by Augustine and Aquinas. Having said that, Hooker cannot simply be identified with any one or all of those predecessors; his moral theologising, as in his metaphysics and theology, has its distinct context, and Hooker feels free to adopt and adapt from a wide range of sources and authorities. One thing is clear, however: Hooker regards the pure ethical dimension of moral theology, precisely because of its metaphysical and revelational moorings, as an objective science not unlike the scientific study of nature itself.[11]

Moral Theology's Twofold Basis

In keeping with the Augustinian-Thomistic commitment to nature and grace as coordinated means for human fulfilment, Hooker locates the foundations of moral theology in the 'books' of nature and Scripture. Together they form its two basic 'reference points'.[12] Just as the 'Book of Nature' refers to the reasoned or philosophical reflection on the created world and creaturely experience within it, so the 'Book of Scripture' is conceived as including the doctrinal tradition embodying the church's reasonable and gracious reflection on those sacred texts. In this we see the application to this sphere of the relationship between nature and grace that Augustine had plotted in his *On Christian Teaching* and that Aquinas had developed further.[13] Augustine, for his part, had argued that attaining humankind's spiritual homeland necessitated honouring the laws of nature as well as of grace, and that the books of nature and of Scripture were both laws to orientate and guide the journey. Aquinas' *Summa Theologiae* tells the same story.

Moral Law

This starting point for Hooker invites us to consider his idea of law in understanding the moral life. The first point we must recall from an earlier chapter is Hooker's understanding of law in relation to creation and its creator. We saw there how Hooker expands the received conception of law (and so makes it his principal paradigm for understanding the workings of created reality) to mean before all else a 'pattern of characteristic behaviour',[14] a directive of behaviour not imposed from without but

human conduct, came rapidly to its own', noting Matthew 5.8 and St Irenaeus of Lyons (*The Vision of God* [Cambridge, 1932], p. 1).

11. So Voak, *Reformed Theology*, pp. 31-2.

12. The phrase is Holmgren, *Ethics*, p. 33.

13. See chapter six.

14. McAdoo, *Structure*, p. 16; see chapter four.

implanted *within* a being. For Hooker, therefore, moral theology is very much about law and laws, so long as we understand that its concern is with them first and foremost as energies and directives that enable and guide creatures toward their God-appointed end or fulfilment. This is a structuring relationship between means and end(s), in fact, Aquinas' 'rule and measure of actions'.[15] Only in subordination to this view of law and laws does Hooker treat and evaluate specific positive laws as they pertain to communities and individuals.

Second, Hooker's expanded concept of law means that law and laws must always be considered with three interactive elements in mind: the agent; the principle or rule of action, what we have described as an implanted directive; and the action or operation itself.[16] With that triad in mind Hooker's moral theology can use law in a dynamic and purposive way which does not disconnect means from ends, nor principle from persons.

Third, an important aspect of law for Hooker relates to his reliance on Aquinas' discussion in the *Summa Theologiae*. Law is something discernible by reason. Not only does this imply that reason must apply itself to divine law, as we saw in our discussion of doctrine and theology, but it means also that reason is the necessary tool for decoding nature and for discerning its moral-ethical implications.[17] In short, the content of the moral law is the judgement of reason applied to the goodness of human actions.

Finally, because all law is hierarchically ordered, moral laws have their ultimate source *via* the second eternal law in 'that eternal law which God hath made to himself'. For Hooker law is not chiefly the relationship of a governor to that which he governs. Instead it is a relationship between the beauty and wisdom of God and their expression in the workings of God's creation. Law is nothing less than the wisdom of which Proverbs 8.22 speaks and whose face is a 'most perfect beauty'.[18] We will see later how that connects with Hooker's sense of moral goodness.

The Book of Nature

In chapter eight of Book I, Augustine's influence is explicit in establishing the discernment of binding moral norms from the book of nature. Hooker interprets him as 'touching the Law of Reason', that is, those laws that reason can discern within the natural order and human experience, so that

---

15. *ST*, Ia IIae. 90.1: 'Any law is a rule or measure of actions according to which something is lead to do something, or not'.
16. So Kirby, 'Generic Division': 55.
17. Law is '*aliquid rationis*' in the phraseology of the *Summa* (see Surlis, 'Natural Law': 182).
18. I, ii, 5 [I, p. 203].

there are in it some things which stand as principles universally agreed upon; and that out of those principles, which are in themselves evident, the greatest moral duties we owe towards God or man may without any great difficulty be concluded.[19]

Hooker understands those 'greatest moral duties' to include the duties to worship God, and to love our neighbours as ourselves.[20] Hooker is neither surprised nor disturbed that a coherent natural moral law can extend from Plato and Aristotle, through Moses, to Christ himself.[21]

However, even the book of nature cannot be construed, according to Hooker, as a mere directory of 'grand mandates'.[22] The law of reason operates within the parameters of nature and human experience in a twofold way. First, by the law of reason 'general principles' for directing human actions are 'comprehended'; and second, 'conclusions' are derived from them.[23] We see, then, that both the content and the reasoned reflection of moral theology are inextricably tied to nature, human experience, and disciplined deductive and analytic processes in pursuit of the laws of natural and humane fulfilment.

The Book of Scripture

That high estimation of nature and reason notwithstanding, Hooker is clear that 'the light of nature is never able to find out any way of obtaining the reward of bliss, but by performing exactly then duties and works of righteousness'; and that to achieve that bliss, a mystical and supernatural way is needed.[24] Two points characterise the relationship of the book of Scripture to the book of nature as Hooker understands it. We might describe them as the *voice* of Scripture, on the one hand, and the *silence* of Scripture, on the other.

Scripture's Voice

As we have seen, it is axiomatic for Hooker, as for the stream of Christian thought in which he stood, that 'nature hath need of grace'. Like Augustine

19. I, viii, 10 [I, p. 235].

20. Faulkner has rightly drawn attention to Hooker's qualification of Aristotle's ethics for whom moral obligation extends more restrictedly to one's fellow citizen ('Reason and Revelation in Hooker's Ethics', *American Political Science Review*, LIX, 3 [1965]: 684); his article generally describes Hooker's debt to and differences from Aristotle in his *Politics* and *Nicomachean Ethics*. On religion and virtue as reasonable, see also Neelands, 'Grace', pp. 100ff.

21. See I, viii, 6-8 [I, pp. 230-4] with special attention to Hooker's citations of pagan and scriptural sources. See Paget's Natural Laws 'of reason' and 'of Nature' (p. 66).

22. I, viii, 7 [I, p. 230].

23. II, viii, 6 [I, p. 334]; in this passage Hooker uses the phrase 'law of nature' to mean the law of reason; his usage is not consistent throughout the *Laws*.

24. I, xi, 5-6 [I, pp. 260-1]. 'See Paget's Law 'that concerns men supernaturally' (p. 67)

and Aquinas in affirming that Scripture includes and ratifies great moral principles and mandates taught by nature,[25] Hooker also agrees with them in that Scripture teaches a unique, salvific law by which humankind's spiritual fulfilment is possible. As he himself says: 'the principal intent of Scripture is to deliver the laws of duties supernatural'.[26] This is the revelational and Christological core that we have described.[27] However doctrinal it may be, that revelational centre has a direct bearing on behaviour—'the duties and works of righteousness'. Two examples of Scripture's unique moral law will illustrate this.

First, and briefly, Hooker points to evangelical precepts that bind all Christians in their practice of the faith. In addition, and surprisingly, he defends the so-called 'counsels of perfection' that constitute moral goals for those striving toward a higher spiritual ideal.[28]

Second, Hooker consistently emphasises the importance of the three so-called theological virtues for the Christian: faith, hope and love (1 Corinthians 13). Despite his commitment to justification by grace through faith, Hooker, in keeping with Scripture itself and long-standing Christian interpretation of it, refuses to isolate faith from and exalt faith over hope and love. In chapter eleven of Book I, where he is considering 'supernatural duties' in light of St John's description of the 'work of God', namely, 'that ye believe in whom he hath sent', Hooker explains:

> Not that God doth require nothing unto happiness at the hands
> of men saving only a naked belief (for hope and charity we may
> never exclude); but that without belief all other virtues are as
> nothing, and it the ground of those other divine virtues.[29]

The voice of Scripture complements, with its precepts, counsels and theological virtues, the natural moral virtues taught through the book of nature by the law and light of reason.

Scripture's Silence

Bearing in mind the particular salvific end by which Scripture's perfection is measured, and allowing for the laws of nature and reason to contribute to the discernment of truth and to the saving return to God, Hooker can accept that in many aspects of Christian living Scripture is silent. That was important to affirm in the controversial context where much of Hooker's argument was aimed at justifying a basis for authority and action beyond the explicit commands of the Bible.

---

25. So, for instance, as regards Aristotle's view that happiness is humankind's proper end, Hooker cites 1 Timothy 6.8 (I, x, 2 [I, p. 240]).

26. I, xiv, 1 [I, p. 267].

27. See chapters six and eleven.

28. On 'precepts' and 'counsels' see Kirk, *Vision*, pp. 103-10.

29. I, xi, 6 [I, p. 261].

A credible and intelligent approach to Scripture means for Hooker 'that Scripture in many things doth neither command nor forbid, but use silence'.[30] In relation to those silences, 'to allege reason serveth as well as to cite Scripture'.[31]

This has important implications for moral theology. It means, for instance, that individuals and communities must take full advantage of the law and light of reason to 'fill in the blanks' left by the silences of Scripture. The law of reason, 'the force of natural wit',[32] as both a corporate and an individual tool, must be used to draw out from even supernatural principles and mandates their specific implications and applications. There we see the prudential aspect of moral reflection which is such an important feature of the exercise of right reason.

The Moral Agent

Thomas Wood reminds us how much the English writers in the field of moral theology adopted and adapted the general principles, terminology, categories and distinctions of their medieval predecessors.[33] That is surely true of Hooker in his understanding of the moral agent. In the seventh chapter of Book I, where Hooker takes up the workings of practical reason, that medieval conceptual assemblage is brought into play. That is not to say that Hooker simply receives from those predecessors; as we find so often throughout his writings, he works creatively, and as a man of his times he shows at points a freedom to adjust or innovate. This both distances him in some respects from his scholastic sources and also distinguishes him from the Reformed habits of mind dominant in his theological *milieu*.

In considering Hooker's views of moral agency we will look chiefly at the workings of and relation between reason and will, and then at the notion of conscience and how Hooker views the application of principles to situations.[34]

Reason: 'the eye of the understanding'

'Goodness', Hooker insists, 'is seen with the eye of the understanding. And the light of that eye is reason'.[35] In keeping with the conceptual trajectory begun by Aristotle and continued by Augustine and medieval schoolmen

---

30. II, v, 7 [I, p. 308].

31. *Ibid.* Hooker is interpreting an argument adduced by Cartwright from Tertullian's *de Corona*.

32. I, viii, 10 [I, p. 234].

33. *Casuistical Divinity*, p. 57.

34. In this regard we have the benefit of Voak's substantial analysis of Hooker's philosophy of mind and action in *Reformed Theology*, pp. 25-91.

35. I, vii, 2 [I, p. 220].

like Aquinas, reason is the foundational faculty of every moral agent. Its 'seeing' is metaphorical, of course, and as we saw in the discussion of Hooker's anthropology, the light or eye of reason distinguishes humankind from the rest of God's sentient creatures. We are capable of awareness and of creating meanings beyond sense experience: reason is 'the ability of reaching higher than unto sensible things'.[36]

In appreciating reason's role within the moral agent four important aspects arise in Hooker's discussions, and above all in chapters seven and eight of Book I of the *Laws*.

First, in keeping with Aristotle's treatment in the *Nicomachean Ethics*, and in line with what Loyer calls Hooker's 'intellectualist' strain, Hooker views reason as the highest power of the mind. As such the *reasoning* mind, 'requireth general obedience at the hands of all the rest [i.e. other mental faculties and bodily powers] concurring unto action'.[37] A moral agent can only act well, therefore, when the highest power within the agent directs all the rest.[38] As that insight suggests, Hooker accepts a philosophy of mind inherited from scholasticism which divided the mind into various 'faculties', or independent centres of power and motivation, such as reason, will, emotions, etc. For our part, we view the moral agent more holistically; we suspect too separable a distinction between, say, the thinking, the feeling, and the desiring aspects of decision-making.[39]

Second, Hooker does not separate reason from experience or experience from reason. At times, it is true, he can use the words distinctly; but in the actual operation of reason, and in appeal to the law or light of reason, experience is implied.[40] Given Hooker's Thomistic epistemic axiom from Aristotle that nothing is in the mind which is not first in the senses, how could it be otherwise?[41]

Third, the reasoning moral agent seeks a discernible end, goal, or perfection. We remember the close connection for Hooker between reason and law. If for Hooker all law is rational, then humans' moral reasoning,

36. I, vi, 3 [I, p. 217].

37. I, viii, 6 [I, p. 230].

38. 'seeing that all these concur in producing human actions, it cannot be well unless the chiefest do command and direct the rest' (I, viii, 6 [I, p. 230]).

39. See Kirk, *Principles*, pp. 38-9; see his note 1 (p. 38) for references to Aquinas' discussion.

40. So says the ethicist Philip Turner. Seeing experience separated from reason is, he claims, a product of the Romantic Movement. 'Experience as something independent of these other sources of moral and religious knowledge, is a category Hooker would have had trouble even recognizing' ('Episcopal Authority', in Ephraim Radner and Philip Turner, ed., *The Fate of Communion* [Grand Rapids, MI, 2006], p. 156).

41. '*Nihil in intellectu quod non prius in sensu.*' This axiom, derived from Aquinas' reading of Aristotle, is distinct from Plato's notion of pre-existent ideas and knowledge as a participation in them.

if it is successful, is law-full in the sense that it recognises and honours an implanted law or directive of being; and if reason is law-full in that sense, then it aims at a perfection of some sort by which human purpose in being is genuinely fulfilled.[42] In the case of humankind as a reasoning agent, truth and goodness – or at least the supposition of them – will be a law in the rational decision-making process, '[f]or', Hooker explains, 'the Laws of well-doing are the dictates of right Reason'.[43] In addition, reason will direct toward what is possible, since for Hooker and the tradition in which he stands it is axiomatic that nature's laws cannot remain frustrated. It would, therefore, be unreasonable for reason to propose as a sought-for end something that is in fact unattainable.[44] Hooker's reference to 'right Reason' in the quotation above reminds us that while fallen reason maintains its gubernatorial role in moral discernment, its effectual performance of that role requires both the honing of its natural power according to humane wisdom and the influence of grace.

The fourth and final point reveals again Hooker's debt to the Aristotelian and Thomistic philosophies of mind. According to that schema, reason directs the will in the sense that reason proposes to the will what is good in a manner that assures reason of its directive role in the moral agent. At the same time, it prompts us to consider in more detail the will's relation to reason as well as the larger question of freedom that so vexed theologies in Hooker's era.

The Will: The 'root' of All Man's Actions

Hooker's philosophical and theological starting points couple reason and will. His theology of divine agency, as we saw earlier, links reason and will, [45] something his anthropology echoes: humankind has a capacity for God 'both by understanding and will'.[46] It follows, then, that in human agency, insofar as humankind honours the divine image after which it has been made, reason and will are at work. How is this so?

In his doctrine at the start of the *Laws*, Hooker argues that in God's actions there is always 'a proper and certain reason'; indeed, he stresses that God works not simply according to his will but, as the Letter to the Ephesians puts it, according to '"the Counsel of his own will"', that is, with a will guided by reason.' We could render that 'with a will guided by reason'.

---

42. I disagree with Westberg's assessment that in making law the primary mode to describe agency Hooker displaces attraction to the true and the good by 'an exterior code' ('Thomistic Law': 211).

43. I, vii, 4 [I, p. 222].

44. Surlis, 'Natural Law': 181.

45. See chapter three.

46. I, xi, 3 [I, p. 255]; this may be by inspiration from Augustine's *On the Trinity* (see Ingalls, 'Scriptures', p. 80).

That is the correlation between reason and will that Hooker proposes in his exposition of moral agency in chapters seven and eight of Book I, and we have considered it somewhat in our discussion of reason.

Several further points help us qualify Hooker's understanding of the link between reason and will. We have already said that, according to Hooker, the chief function of reason in moral agency is the discernment of what is good. The will, for its part, instinctively wants what is good. This is a key limitation upon the will about which other theologians, despite differences in other respects, agreed.[47] Furthermore, reason and will interact in that reason presents to the will what is good, where the true good lies, and how it can be attained.[48] In broad terms that view accords with Aquinas' philosophy of mind.

Is the will, however, wholly determined by the dictates of reason vis-à-vis the good? In other words, does the will have any power of choice in and of itself to follow the dictates of reason or not? Here there were divisions in the scholastic tradition.[49] For his part, Hooker seems to prefer the Scotist view. In this view, the will is an active intellectual faculty; it has a 'liberty of indifference' by which it may actively accept *or reject* what reason proposes to it. 'There is in the Will of man naturally that freedom, whereby it is apt to take or refuse any particular object whatsoever being presented unto it'. Hooker speaks too of the will's 'pursuit *and refusal*', 'the one the affirmation, the other *the negation of goodness*, which the understanding apprehendeth'. In line with Scotist teaching, the will, according to Hooker, can choose to reject the good that has been apprehended and presented by reason since it may have 'some difficulty or unpleasant quality annexed to it'.[50] Moreover, that same active power to choose between objects presented to it by reason is what Scotus called 'freedom of the will'.[51]

Human Freedom

We must assume that partly on this ground Hooker can assert that 'whatsoever we work as men, the same we do work wittingly and freely'.[52] On the basis of passages like these some contemporaries of Hooker detected divergence from the Reformation's doctrine of the bondage of the will. That knotty debate is not one that Hooker was eager to engage with, though the phraseology and sentiments expressed in his *Laws* prompted

---

47. Voak names, for instance, Aquinas and Calvin (*Reformed Theology*, p. 55); see also Joyce, *Anglican Moral Theology*, p. 161.
48. Thornton, *Hooker*, p. 37.
49. Between Aquinas, on the one hand, and Scotus, on the other.
50. I, vii, 6 [I, pp. 222-3].
51. *Liberum arbitrium* (Voak, *Reformed Theology*, pp. 38-9).
52. I, vii, 2 [I, p. 220].

suspicions among self-appointed inquisitors of the reformed Church of England. 'You to our understanding', wrote the author of *A Christian Letter*, 'write . . . *there is in the will of man naturallie that freedom, whereby it is apt to take or refuse anie particular object, whatsoever being presented unto it*.'[53] A serious charge that challenged Hooker's loyalty to the article 'Of Free Will' of the Thirty-Nine Articles.[54]

Hooker did indeed challenge that article; or, at least, he thought that important qualifications and distinctions were required in the conceptual field that lay behind the article in particular, and in the debate on the freedom of the will generally. Hooker's broad posture has already been described in the chapters on his doctrine of God and anthropology. In the latter we saw how in creating God had endowed humankind (along with angels) with 'liberty' suitable to a reasonable creature so that freedom was part of humankind's 'very nature'.[55] Here we need to draw attention to a kind of syllogism that relates that posture to the concerns of his moral theology.

The presupposition for free will and choice takes the form of a threefold line of assertions by Hooker. First, God's bestowal of eternal life is in the nature of a reward; second, rewards grow from what Hooker calls 'voluntary duties'; third, voluntary duties are only such if they are performed by free agents. 'It followeth', Hooker argues in his response to *A Christian Letter*, that whose end was eternal life, their state must needs imply freedom and liberty of will.'[56]

Taking up the critical distinction between 'aptness' and 'ability', Hooker argues that aptness, as of the very essence of our creaturehood, remains intact; consequently the inherent aptness of the will to choose remains intact.[57] At the same time, he acknowledges the ill effects of the fall on humankind's ability to exercise the will's natural aptness effectively. Hooker is equally firm, therefore, on the need for grace so that reason might perceive and that the will might indeed choose the good. 'Freedom of operation we have by nature', he explains, 'but the *ability* of virtuous operation by grace'.[58] He describes grace's action in this regard as 'amiable' precisely because what God holds out for a believer he holds out as a reward; in the act of human willing God's grace does not compel the will by making its object, namely goodness, irresistibly

---

53. *FLE*, IV, pp. 17-8.
54. Article Ten: 'we have no power to do good works pleasant and acceptable to God, without the grace of Christ preventing us, that we may have a good will, and working with us, when we have that good will'.
55. *DF*, V, App. I (II, p. 567).
56. *Ibid.*
57. Hooker explains that although man's will is fallen, it is still 'framable' to good things (*DF*, V, App. I [II, p. 539]).
58. *Ibid.* 539; emphasis mine.

apparent.[59] That relationship of respect between God and humankind made in the image of the divine freedom led Lionel Thornton to speak of this circle of divine-human interaction as a 'kingdom of free-will'.[60]

Conscience

As Hooker makes clear in the Preface of his *Laws*, the issue of true and reliable discernment of truth *vis-à-vis* polity and, by implication, the goodness of particular duties and practices which the laws of polity enjoined, were issues that raised the question of conscience. As we noted earlier, there is reason to interpret the *Laws* as a sustained attempt to inform and sway the consciences of those who stood aloof from the established church. It is not a little frustrating, therefore, that what Hooker says about the act of judging good from bad, true and false, right and wrong, is sparse, and not always clear.[61]

We should expect, given the importance of the light and law of reason in his anthropology, that Hooker would posit an innate power to make moral judgments by the guidance of that law. He speaks in the Preface of the 'force' of humankind's natural 'discretion' as the first means by which we judge good from evil.[62] Such a power to judge good from evil accords, in at least a rudimentary way, with a traditional definition of conscience.[63] In Book II, where Hooker is coordinating the law of Scripture with the law of nature (by which he means the law of reason), he speaks of an 'infallible knowledge imprinted in the minds of all the children of men, whereby both general principles for directing human actions are comprehended, and conclusions derived from them'. Upon those principles and conclusions, he continues, 'groweth in particularity the choice of good and evil in the daily affairs of life'.[64] The 'imprinting' of which Hooker speaks seems to refer to the acquisition of knowledge through the exercise of speculative reason rather than by means of something like Aquinas' practical reason drawing upon an innate *habitus* of moral principles.[65]

Whatever nature may teach, though, provides only a basic capacity

---

59. *Ibid.* pp. 541; 'amiable' appearing again from Wisdom 8.1.
60. *Hooker*, p. 32.
61. Harrison, 'Prudence', *CRH*, p. 900, note 15: 'the meaning of conscience is the *Lawes* is unclear, since Hooker rarely employs the term and does not define it'.
62. Preface, III, 1 [I, p. 143].
63. Kirk defines conscience as 'an innate power both of perceiving what is good and right, and of aspiring to it' (*Principles*, p. 9).
64. II, viii, 6 [I, pp. 334-5].
65. What the scholastic tradition termed *synderesis*; on this whole issue in Hooker see Faulkner, 'Reason and Revelation': 685-6; for the term's origins see Charles E. Curran, 'Conscience in the Light of the Catholic Moral Tradition', in Curran, ed., *Conscience* (New York, 2004), pp. 3-24.

for judging truth and error, good and evil. Education, by which Hooker means learning by experience and instruction, that is, learning by taught precept, are needed if the faculty of reason is better to make judgments.[66] The exercise of conscience, in other words, involves a prudential power in which people are able to grow and develop.[67]

That explains why for Hooker the discoveries of right reason concerning goodness and right action can happen in two ways. The preeminent and most reliable way is to discern goodness 'in its causes', that is, to grasp the nature or essence of goodness. But that is an onerous task for which few are equipped. Another way, less reliable but easier and therefore common among men, is by examination of the 'signs' connected to goodness: what do most people reckon goodness to look like in practice? By such a means we find ourselves once again in the realm of universal consent and the probable persuasions that it supports. But whether by a grasp of its 'causes' or through practical testimony to its actual expressions within the human community, 'conscience' is 'bound' by goodness.[68]

Moral Action

In discussion of the moral agent we have inevitably stepped into the territory of moral action; it is impossible to talk about the one without reference to the other. Now, therefore, we turn to a brief discussion of the content of moral actions by describing Hooker's views of virtue and moral goodness.

Moral Good

In a rich passage highly significant for our consideration of moral theology Hooker writes this:

> Goodness in action is like unto straightness; wherefore that which is done well we term *right*. For as the straight way is most acceptable to him that travelleth, because by it he cometh soonest to his journey's end; so in action, that which doth lie the evenest between us and the end we desire must needs be the fittest for our use. Besides which fitness for use, there is also in rectitude, beauty; as contrariwise in obliquity, deformity. And that which is good in the actions of men, both not only delight as profitable, but as amiable also. In which consideration the Grecians most divinely have given to the active perfection of men a name expressing both beauty and goodness, because

---

66. I, vi, 5 [I, p. 219].
67. Westberg, however, thinks that Hooker neglects any prudential factor ('Thomistic Law': 210).
68. I, x, 10 [I, p. 249]. See Paget's Natural Laws (p. 66).

goodness in ordinary speech is for the most part applied only
to that which is beneficial. But we in the name of goodness do
here imply both.[69]

That single passage, so dense in terms relating to the moral life, and rich in
resonances from the philosophical and theological traditions, gives us scope
to grasp three main elements in Hooker's interpretation of moral good.

Goodness, Desire and Perfection

While the passage does not neatly connect goodness, desire and perfection,
those three concepts run, as we have seen, through the whole of Book I
and beyond like a silver thread. As a function of the will, desire is a motion
toward an end that is as yet unattained.[70] As guided by reason, desire aims
at ends that are good, that is, which conform to the law of our being
and thereby bring us to satisfaction and perfection.[71] Hooker explains,
'whatsoever such perfection there is which our nature may acquire, the
same we properly term our Good'.[72] This is a wide understanding of the
good and of the variety of desires and perfections that partake of human
goodness; equally, it supports the generous definition of the subject matter
of moral theology as we defined it at the start of this chapter. 'The nature
which himself [*viz.* God] hath given to work by he cannot but be delighted
with, when we exercise the same any way without commandment of his
to the contrary.'[73]

'The sundry degrees of goodness'

In the same way that there are different kinds of human perfection, Hooker
also identifies three degrees of goodness. Like the sensual, intellectual
and spiritual perfections, these three kinds of goodness are related; a full-
bodied moral life engages with them all to some extent or other. We can
describe them simply as forms of goodness that are, first, allowed, then
required, and finally 'of great dignity'.

The forms of goodness that are allowed and not disapproved by God
are those that human beings can discern by the 'light of Nature'. This is a
low degree of goodness, according to Hooker, a kind of moral 'bottom-
line' such as doing good to those who do good to you (Matthew 5.46) –
'the very publicans themselves do as much'.[74]

---

69. I, viii, 1 [I, pp. 225-6].

70. I, xi, 3 [I, p. 256].

71. Marshall, *Hooker*, pp. 80-1. For examples of what man desires as good see V,
lxxvi, 2-4 [II, pp. 445-8].

72. I, xi, 1 [I, p. 253].

73. II, iv, 5 [I, p. 298]. Those words relate to discretion in matters 'indifferent' but
the principle applies to human endeavours more widely.

74. II, viii, 2 [I, p. 331-2].

Above what is allowed are forms of goodness that are 'required as necessary to salvation'. Without performance of such forms of goodness a person cannot expect salvation. With an eye on economy, Hooker is quick to qualify this requirement by adding 'by ordinary course'; equally, with an eye on the pastoral need for assurance, he adds 'nor by any means be excluded from life observing them'. In knowing those forms of goodness 'our chiefest direction is from Scripture, for nature is no sufficient teacher what we should do that we may attain life everlasting'.[75]

Lastly, there are forms of goodness that are above and beyond what is required by the normal testimony either of reason or revelation, though this third degree of goodness flows from their testimonies as an appropriate consequence. If left undone, therefore, they do not exclude from salvation, but because they are they are of 'so great dignity and acceptation with God' this high degree of goodness receives 'accessory augmentation' of bliss. This 'highest perfection of man by way of service towards God' is the measure by which 'the state of saints in glory' is distinguished from that of ordinary Christians.[76] To this degree the counsels of perfection, for instance, pertain.

Benefit and Beauty: *Kalokagathia*

Those 'degrees of goodness', and an implicit scale in the idea of goodness, provide a framework for Hooker to introduce a further diversification in his understanding of moral good. In the passage on goodness quoted earlier Hooker refers the classical Greek concept of 'active perfection' 'expressing both beauty and goodness'. Hooker is referring to *kalokagathia*, a substantive elision of the adjectives 'beautiful' (*kalos*) and 'good' (*agathos*). In Aristotle's ethical treatises, whence Hooker surely derived it, the word originally meant something like 'the perfect gentleman', a man adorned with both normal and the higher virtues.[77] However, its application expanded to include the perfect character of anything, its admirable or splendid qualities. Thus was forged a link between goodness and beauty which later found its way into the stream of Christian reflection on God, not least in expositors like Augustine (particularly sensitive to aesthetic matters) and Aquinas.[78]

As we have seen from the quotation from chapter eight of Book I, Hooker prefers this expansive concept of moral goodness and makes clear

---

75. Hooker seems to mean spiritual life now and eternal life hereafter; but it is not wholly clear.

76. II, viii, 4 [I, p. 332]. Needless to say, this discussion by Hooker points back to his views on reward; see chapter eleven.

77. For instance in the *Nicomachean Ethics*, the *Politics* and the *Magna Moralia*.

78. See the discussion by Patrick Sherry, *Spirit and Beauty* (Oxford, 1992), pp. 8-11.

that when he uses the word 'goodness' he means something that is both beneficial and beautiful. By 'beneficial' he means something, according to the root derivation of the English word, that is, 'well done', a 'right' action, 'like unto straightness'. We have returned, have we not, to action 'in most decent and comely sort' (Wisdom 8.11)?

In what sense, though, is an action beautiful? For Hooker there are three ways in which moral goodness is beautiful. First, picking up the link between goodness, desire and perfection, we can say that a person's law-full actions are beautiful actions insofar as those actions tend toward ends that fulfil legitimate desires and God-given purposes. Second, it follows that the formation and use of reason and will according to the laws of nature and reason beautifies the moral agent insofar as those higher powers converge in right reasoning and right desiring. In such rectitude reason and will reflect the integrity and harmony of purpose and action that Aquinas, for instance, predicated of beauty.[79] This is in keeping with Augustine's teaching that temporal and physical beauty is a step by which we climb to the apprehension of a higher immaterial beauty, and finally to God who is the 'Beauty of all things beautiful'.[80] Third, on the basis of his theme of participation, Hooker understands the beauty of human moral goodness as a created expression, perhaps even the chief expression, of the divine beauty and goodness, 'the goodness of beauty in itself'.[81]

At the same time the life of faith calls believers to the goodness of holiness in which the Spirit 'beautifieth all the parts and actions of our life'. The sanctifying Spirit 'irradiates' them with the beauty of God manifested in the ways of both nature and grace.[82]

'That sea of Goodness': The Moral Goal

As an example of the concurrence of reason and revelation, Book I of the *Laws* advances the view that human happiness is the end or purpose of the moral life. Although the text of 1 Timothy 6.8 does not use the word *eudaimonia*, Hooker interprets the author's reference to 'contentment' as signifying the very thing that the Greek philosophical tradition meant by 'happiness'.[83] In the *Nicomachean Ethics*, for instance, Aristotle had

79. See *ST*, Ia. 29. 8; his terms are *integritas/perfectio* and *debita proportio/ consonantia*. Aquinas' treatment of the beauty of God was indebted to that in Dionysius' *The Divine Names*, on which Aquinas wrote a commentary.
80. See Sherry, *ibid*. pp. 10-11, 9 (from his *Confessions*, iii.6).
81. I, xi, 3 [I, p. 256].
82. Richard Harries' vivid word in *Art and the Beauty of God* (London, 1993) p. 137.
83. 1 Timothy 6.8 employs the word *arkeō*; its sense of sufficiency can carry the connotations of contentment and goodness too.

proposed that all human desires aim to one end: human happiness, or *eudaimonia*. In addition, Aristotle argued that all such desires for happiness must have an end, and that end must not only be good but be the chief good and fulfilment of all desiring.[84]

Hooker adopts the eudaimonic principle that Aristotle had made a cornerstone of ethics. Beyond that he, like Aquinas before him, interposes God the holy Trinity as the 'object and accomplishment of our desires'.[85] In chapter eleven of Book I Hooker describes the 'happiness' very specifically as 'that estate whereby we attain, so far as possibly may be attained, the full possession of that which simply for itself is to be desired', adding 1 Timothy's language in the background, and 'containeth in it after an eminent sort the contention of our desires, the highest degree of all our perfection'.[86]

Hooker's insistence on humankind's capacity for God by understanding and will means that the final 'contention of our desires' in God is by the perfecting of those human powers according to both nature and grace.[87] Since Hooker accepts Aristotle's view that happiness is above all an activity of the soul in accordance with virtue, he can argue, as he does in his mature theology, that the 'state of greatest happiness' for a person is acquired by 'actions of most dignity, proceeding from the highest degree of excellency, that any created nature was to receive from him [*viz.* God]'. If the attainment of this happiness or 'felicity' is by the mysterious cooperation of nature and grace, the continuance of such happiness is by no necessity. The understanding's happiness in forever beholding God as 'sovereign Truth' and the will's in perpetual enjoyment of God as 'our sovereign Good or Blessedness' is simply by the will of God 'which doth both freely perfect our nature in so high a degree, and continue it so perfected'.[88]

A Fulcrum for Development

We see how Hooker's moral theology rises as a consistent strand from his vision of God. More especially it is woven with the themes of order and beauty, the integration of nature and grace, reason and revelation, and a richness of laws tending to perfection. Hooker's moral theology accords well with the importance he gives to sanctification in the Christian life, and in this, we should recognise, he stands closer to Calvin than to Luther

---

84. *Nicomachean Ethics*, I, 2 (Ross, ed., p. 1).

85. I, viii, 1 [I, p. 225].

86. I, xi, 3 [I, p. 255]. See Paget's Law of Men progressing 'to that Perfection which is in God alone' (p. 66).

87. Hooker, like Aquinas and others before him, has more precision in defining Aristotle's *eudaimonia* than we can have; there is no ready modern equivalent, as David Brown reminds us (*Choices* [Oxford, 1983], p. 22).

88. I, xi, 1, 3 [I, pp. 255-6].

in the tradition of the continental Reform. The light shed by Aristotle and Aquinas is bright, and to that extent Hooker's conceptual basis for 'practical divinity' was therefore significantly different from Calvin for whom, when all is said and done, divine command dominates.

In the case of Hooker, the insights of Augustine as modified by Aquinas ground the ethical life in nature even as it is transformed by grace, and the focus is not on externally imposed dictates so much as on moral life as an expression of implanted directives (laws in Hooker's sense) leading the moral agent to beatitude.[89] To that extent Hooker acted as a fulcrum in the progression and development of the western Roman Catholic moral tradition into a distinctive reformed English form. In that respect Hooker gave to his successors more than he gave to his contemporaries; seventeenth century casuistic divinity, with its profound reliance on the second part of Aquinas' *Summa Theologiae*, built upon the legacy bequeathed by the *Laws* and moved the English moral compass much further from the continental influences of the Elizabethan period.

In his discussion of the scope of moral theology, Kenneth Kirk includes the means by which God enables a soul to progress towards it ideal.[90] In that view Kirk was by no means original. It is the common testimony of the Christian tradition that growth toward human perfection, insofar as it is a spiritual task, requires specifically spiritual tools. Hooker assumed that. So we must now complement our exploration of his moral theology with an examination of his views on the form of, and tools used for, the progression of the soul's ascent to God.

89. Brown, *Choices*, p. 23.
90. *Principles*, pp. xi and 8.

Chapter 14
'Our Desire to Behold God'
Spiritual Theology

It is a measure of the depth and breadth of Hooker's theology that it leads seamlessly into the sphere of what today we call spiritual theology.[1] That modern term, wide and sometimes rather diffuse, is best thought of as comprehending what previous eras termed 'ascetical' and 'mystical theology'. The first has typically been concerned with the theological explication and description of the preliminary and general aspects of spiritual life relevant to all Christians journeying toward beatitude; the latter has focused on the less common gifts and experiences of infused grace.[2] These are categorisations that a contemporary reader may find rather contrived, but they remained current and influential in Hooker's era. Followers of Reformed Christianity still found aspects of Roman Catholic spiritual literature compelling, with the result that the Roman Catholic and scholastic-era language and concepts endured at least as a subliminal backdrop to the new spiritualities that were taking shape.[3]

Hooker was formed spiritually during the period when those dynamic currents of interest and influence were being fashioned into something distinctively English. It is clear when we read the *Laws* and other pertinent writings that Hooker's spiritual theology does not venture into the rarefied domain of mystical experience; rather, it deals generally with the expressions and characteristics of spiritual life applicable to all Christians, laity and clergy alike.[4] The nature and purpose of Hooker's advocacy surely account for that: the *Laws* concerns the public performance of religious duties that are incumbent on everyone. Book V's focus on liturgical matters and, by implication, liturgical spirituality, reflects both an assumption of the age *vis-à-vis* the primacy of liturgical prayer, and a key reference-point for Hooker's considerations of spiritual theology.[5]

---

1. So, for instance, Allen in his *Spiritual Theology* (Cambridge, USA, 1997), pp. 7-20.
2. By 'infused' meaning received as the gift(s) of the Holy Spirit apart from normal human effort and practices.
3. The widespread interest in the Spaniard Juan Luis Vives' writings is but one example.
4. Egil Grislis is rash in describing Hooker as a 'mystic' ('Creativity and Continuity': 12.
5. On the assumption in Hooker's era that liturgical prayer was the basis of all private prayer, see Stranks, *Anglican Devotion* (London, 1961), p. 17. His chapter, 'The Reformation and Personal Religion' is useful for the background to Hooker

The concerns of this chapter follow closely on those of the preceding one since, as we noted there, Hooker's moral theological scope is wide. The traditional concerns of spiritual theology must be seen in relation to moral theology's own end, namely, human perfection, happiness or, to use a distinctly theological word, beatitude. In this Henry McAdoo reminds us that Hooker set the stage for rich developments in the following century.[6] As in the preceding chapter, discussion of Hooker's spiritual theology builds upon the considerations of grace already explored by clothing the theology of grace and the Spirit with actual forms and expressions in the process of ascent toward humankind's spiritual 'homeland'.[7]

Hooker the Asceticist

In describing Hooker as an 'asceticist' in the manner of Augustine and Aquinas, Martin Thornton explains that ascetical theology in its basic sense is not just tied to the theology of grace; rather, it applies the dogmatic and theological vision of God in creation and salvation to believers' actual experience of sanctification and glorification.[8] Hooker is an ascetical theologian in that wide sense. A further qualification is in order: whereas Hooker writes ascetical theology in that wide and foundational sense, he does not provide what may be more narrowly defined guidance on specific regimens of personal piety, or a precise description of the regulated and graduated means of spiritual ascent from beginning to what Aquinas calls 'proficiency'.[9]

We can account for this lack by remembering both the shape and the purpose of Hooker's *Laws*. In defending England's established ecclesiastical polity, Hooker lays out in Book I the philosophical and theological basis of his defence. In Book IV he begins what amounts to a commentary on the *Book of Common Prayer*, leading into Book V where liturgical principles and practices, and above all the sacraments with their theological foundations, are explored in expansive detail. We can expect, then, that Hooker's concern for the *Book of Common Prayer* will both guide and focus his ascetical concerns.

This chapter will explore Hooker's spiritual theology with regard to the evolving 'English School' of spirituality, and then highlight key themes and elements of Christian spirituality in the salvific journey towards God.

---

and his thinking on this subject (pp. 13-34).

6. McAdoo, *Structure*, p. 15.

7. Augustine's '*via ad patriam*', as we have seen in the chapter six.

8. We have seen, though, how Hooker proposes a justification-sanctification-glorification/deification continuum; see chapter eight. On 'ascetics' see Thornton, *English Spirituality* (Cambridge, USA, 1986), p. 232.

9. Thornton, *Christian Proficiency* (London, 1959), pp. 1-4.

Hooker and the 'English School'

If Hooker can be credited with reinventing the ethos of the English Church's worship, as we have seen in chapter nine, he can just as readily take credit for setting the tone of English spirituality as it settled into a 'new synthesis' during the so-called Caroline period.[10] In his analysis of that second phase in the development of the 'English School' Thornton identifies Hooker as the chief embodiment of continuity of the spiritual tradition while expressing it in a distinctive 'idiom' appropriate to his age.[11]

'Inward reasonable worship': Prayer

Early in Book V Hooker sets out a twofold division between 'solemn serviceable worship' and 'inward reasonable worship'. They are divisible as taking different forms and being ordered by law in different ways. They are not, however, meant to be separable in Christian experience; or rather, outward forms are meant to be inhabited by an authentic spirit of worship interior to each believer. Thus the field of 'inward reasonable worship' is wide: 'all manner various duties that each man in reason and conscience to God oweth'.[12]

In chapter twenty three of Book V Hooker begins a lengthy consideration of prayer. The subsequent nine chapters nuance the discussion by taking up serially various contentious points about the *Book of Common Prayer*. At the start, though, Hooker lays out his views on prayer itself both in relation to the ministry of teaching that he has just considered, and as the basis for further discussion of prayer in the Prayer Book. Hooker begins that chapter by recalling the theme of connection between the heavenly and the earthly that we saw was so central to his theology of worship in general.

> Between the throne of God in heaven and his Church upon earth here militant, if it be so that Angels have their continual intercourse, where should we find the same more verified than in those two ghostly exercises, the one Doctrine, and the other Prayer? For what is the assembling of the Church to learn, but the receiving of Angels descended from above? What to pray, but the sending of Angels upward? His heavenly inspirations and our holy desires are as so many Angels of intercourse and

---

10. The 'Caroline' period is not strictly limited to the reigns of Charles I and II (1626-88) but, from the angle of spirituality at least, extended from the time of the publication of Hooker's *Laws* in 1594 to that of William Law's *A Serious Call to a Devout and Holy Life* in 1729; see Thornton, *English Spirituality*, p. 230. For an in-depth treatment of this and related nomenclature of the period see Julian Davies, *The Caroline Captivity of the Church* (Oxford, 1992), pp. 5-45.

11. For a description of the components of this 'English School' see *English Spirituality*, p. 232.

12. V, iv, 3 [II, p. 27]. Hooker's use of 'reasonable' is taken from Romans 12.1.

commerce between God and us. As teaching bringeth us to
know that God as our supreme truth; so prayer testifieth that
we acknowledge him our sovereign good.[13]

It is important to note the balance between knowledge and desire, truth
and goodness, expressed in the twofold spiritual enterprise of teaching and
prayer, doctrine and devotion. In the Prayer Book, Hooker recognises, they
are interwoven, and in that interweaving of reason and will, so central to
Hooker's anthropology and moral theology, is what Martin Thornton has
called an 'affective-speculative synthesis'.[14] We should also notice Hooker's
keen sense of the inter-connection between celestial and earthly realities.
In fact, he quickly underlines that link by reminding his readers that while
we know little of heaven, '[n]otwithstanding thus much we know even of
Saints in heaven, that they pray'.[15]

So prayer is a work common to the church militant and the church
triumphant together, a work common to men and angels together. Prayer
itself is born of and points to the unity of the church. In that insistence
both here and at many points in the *Laws* Hooker reveals one of the
characteristics of the English School as it had emerged over the centuries,
its vivid sense of the unity of the church.[16] We immediately see also the
'double motion' of prayer, of messages sent from above and then returned
by worshippers from below, a spiritual form of the dynamic of procession
and return which shapes all creaturely experience.[17]

The 'Christian Framework'

There is more to be said about prayer, of course. But before returning to the
subject we need to lay out a wider map upon which we can locate prayer
in its various forms and in relation to the broader terrain of spiritual life.

From his early writings onward Hooker is clear that the 'cause' of spiritual
life within believers is Christ. Of spirituality's Christological basis there was
no doubt. This does not mean that spiritual life for Hooker is to be understood
or defined by the boundaries of scripture alone. As in the whole Christian
enterprise, Scripture's principal place is not an exclusive one so Hooker, in
conceiving of the 'life spiritual', can draw upon the *Book of Common Prayer*
and the rich diversity of spiritual practices that it enshrines and draws upon.[18]

---

13. V, xxiii [II, p. 115].
14. *English Spirituality*, pp. 48-9.
15. V, xxiii [II, p. 116]. He cites Revelation 6.9.
16. Thornton, *English Spirituality*, pp. 49-50.
17. On this 'dialectical motion' see Kirby's essay 'Angels descending and ascending:
Hooker's discourse on the "double motion" of Common Prayer', *RHER*, p. 114 and
passim.
18. For Hooker's clear christocentrism regarding the spiritual life see, for instance,
his *LDJ*, 26 [III, pp. 515-17].

The Prayer Book was, it is claimed, a contemporary and indigenous expression of a 'Christian Framework' that had taken shape in the early centuries and had become the irreducible skeleton of the western spiritual tradition. Broadly, that framework had come to embody three forms and contexts of prayer: the Mass, or the Holy Communion service, the daily 'offices' of Morning and Evening Prayer, and private prayer, interrelated and practiced as 'one whole balanced organic *life*'.[19] Beginning with chapter twenty-three of Book Five, Hooker unfolds a vision of the praying Christian that encompasses just that foundational structure of prayer.

'This holy and religious duty of service towards God concerneth us one way in that we are men, and another way in that we are joined as parts of that visible mystical body which is his Church.'[20] With that Aristotelian distinction between man as an individual and as a member of a community, Hooker affirms the distinct but related elements of spiritual life and worship: it is both private and public.

Of course, it serves Hooker's apologetic needs to honour the consistent witness of the spiritual tradition of the church in giving primacy of place to public, liturgical prayer.[21] The liturgy, or service, 'which we do as members of a pubic body, is public, and for that cause must needs be accounted by so much worthier than the other [i.e. private prayer] as a whole society of such condition exceedeth the worth of any one'.[22]

Hooker's advocacy of corporate worship lies in its qualitative difference precisely as a corporate and public action. Its 'force and efficacy' arise from the 'very form' and 'due solemnity' of common prayer that is 'duly ordered'. What Hooker has in mind clearly is not just group prayer but ordered, solemn, *liturgical* prayer as embodied chiefly, but not exclusively, in the Prayer Book's orders for Holy Communion, Matins and Evensong.

As we have already seen, however, the public, outward and visible, and the hidden, personal and interior inform one another in Hooker's ideal of the praying Christian. We should never interpret Hooker's advocacy of the *Book of Common Prayer* and its public rites as a reversion to formalism. To avoid this, private prayer is key. The Prayer Book does not displace it, but presumes, supports and nourishes it.[23] As we would expect of someone so

---

19. Thornton, *Christian Proficiency*, p. 18; for an account of its ascetical importance see pp. 17-24; emphasis his. Thornton refers to Augustine and Benedict as the well-springs of this spiritual tradition.

20. V, xxiii, 1 [II, pp. 116-7].

21. Scripture (2 Corinthians 1.2) and tradition (St Basil of Caesarea) supported it; *ibid.*

22. V, xxiv, 1 [II, p. 117].

23. Hooker was surely aware of resources like *The Primer, or Book of Private Prayer*, published in the reign of Edward VI in 1553, which laid out a day-by-day regimen of prayer.

rooted in Scripture and the literature of the Christian tradition, Hooker affirms the established divisions of prayer, *viz.*, adoration, thanksgiving, petition, intercession and penitence.[24]

Aware of the rich field of ascetical materials and habits, Hooker affirms the freedom that characterises this element of the framework. 'As men, we are at our own choice, both for time, and place, and form, according to the exigence of our own occasion in private.'[25] To that freedom of time, place and form Hooker adds breadth to his conception of prayer. Those three parameters are dissolvable as prayer's circumference widens to include the whole warp and woof of daily life. 'Is not the name of prayer usual to signify even all the service that ever we do unto God?'[26] But even deeper than 'service' (however Hooker construes that) is the simple yearning of the soul. 'Every good and holy desire', Hooker explains, 'though it lack the form, hath notwithstanding in itself the substance, and with him the force of a prayer, who regardeth the very moanings, groans, and sighs of the heart of man'.[27]

The Spirit of the Framework: Recollection

The diffuse nature of prayer points to recollection as a goal of spiritual practice. 'Recollection' here means the periodic remembrance of God that leads, when practiced assiduously, to a constant awareness of the divine presence known as habitual recollection – what Evelyn Underhill once described as 'confident, unbroken interior communion with God'.[28] Its structural supports are the forms of liturgical life referred to already; but those very supports, when fully in play, nurture the experience of recollection that is wholly interior and even wordless.

It is striking how often in his defence of the religious duties and customs enshrined in the *Book of Common Prayer* Hooker commends them in part because of their recollective power. Hooker's advocacy of 'festival days', for instance, relies heavily on their recollective force. He does not use the word 'recollection' but speaks of them as 'memorials' and 'tokens' prompting memory and thought – all forms of recollective practice.[29] 'Generally therefore', he says, 'touching feasts in the Church

---

24. See Booty, *Reflections*, pp. 100-1.

25. V, xxiv [II, p. 117].

26. V, xxiii, 1 [II, p. 115].

27. V, xlviii, 2 [II, p. 201]. Booty suggests that Hooker is inspired by Aquinas, *ST*, IIa.IIae. 83.1 (*Reflections*, p. 101)

28. In her essay 'Life as Prayer', in Menzies, *Collected Papers* (London, 1946), p. 72. That experience of communion implied in the notion of habitual recollection with God is applied to Hooker's understanding of prayer by Booty, *Reflections*, p. 101.

29. V, lxx, 1 [II, p. 384].

of Christ, they have that profitable use whereof St. Augustine speaketh, "By festival solemnities and set days we dedicate and sanctify unto God the memory of his benefits, lest unthankfulness thereof should creep upon us in course of time".[30] Sunday itself has recollective force in two complementary ways:

> [t]heir [*viz.* the Jews] Sabbath the Church hath changed into our Lord's day, that as the one did continually bring to mind the former world finished by creation, so the other might keep us in perpetual remembrance of a far better world begun by him which came to restore all things, to make both heaven and earth new.[31]

His spiritual theology advocates the traditional Christian framework, and from this Hooker advocates the chief structural elements of his ascetic: liturgy and recollection. Together they hold the corporate and the personal, the community and the individual, in a nourishing, mutually supporting and necessary relation.

Spiritual Warfare

As we move from a consideration of the spiritual life at what we might call the horizontal level, or the level of human experience that 'formats' God's approach to believers and their exposure to God, to the vertical concerns of gracious transformation under the pressure of the Spirit's work, it is important to bear in mind some words in a letter of uncertain date to his Oxford mentor and friend John Rainolds. Notwithstanding God's intention that we partake of his good will toward believers, 'we see', Hooker wrote, 'that our life must be lived as a ceaseless warfare, as warfare with the allurements of the world, with the disordered affections of the heart, with timidity of spirit, with the flesh and the Devil, with temptations so various, so hostile and so strong that there is constant danger that devouring powers will act against us and that we will be swallowed up like a lump of lead in roiling waters'. The weaponry of defence, says Hooker, is prayer 'by means of which God arms us with his Spirit who alone is able to make us stand firm'.[32]

Whatever may be said of Hooker's sense of balance, of moderation, of resistance to stridency, that description of the spiritual life suggests anything but an easy-going laxity. However affirmative his theology may be, he is not insensitive to the threats constantly posed to believers' spiritual welfare, and, by implication, to the urgency of Christians' reliance on God and the need for grace. His language is wholly consistent with that

---

30. V, lxx, 8 [II, p. 388].
31. *Ibid*, [II, pp. 388-9].
32. 'A Latin Letter', in *FLE*, V, p. 427; translation my own; 'the exact date and occasion are a puzzle' say the editors (p. 422).

of a hugely influential Roman Catholic spiritual classic published abroad during his life-time in which among the author's foundational spiritual principles was this weapon: 'Distrust of yourself'.[33]

Can we say more, though, about the strategies of the spiritual combat and of the soul's confrontation with and triumph over the allurements, disorders and temptations that constantly assail?

The Threefold Way

Relevant to that question is another threefold pattern that is discernible in Hooker's spiritual theology. The pattern expresses growth in spiritual life and stages in the experience of justification, sanctification and glorification. It complements the framework of sacraments, public prayer and private devotion, and, like the framework, links Hooker's spiritual theology to the patristic and medieval sources that inform his vision of God.

The threefold way is described variously in the Christian tradition, and there is no single terminology or description of its content. One terminology, common in the west but derived from Dionysius the Areopagite, names the three components of the way: purgation, illumination, and union.[34] Hooker does not, in fact, employ any overt terminology for the threefold way with the result that, on the face of it, we might suppose it has no part in his spiritual theology. But that would be a mistaken supposition. A close reading of his description of spiritual life reveals a sensitivity to the experiences to which the threefold way points. In that regard it is useful to bear in mind the Greek Christian nomenclature of the three aspects of this threefold way with their different nuances, that is, '*praktikē*', '*physikē*', and '*theoria*'.[35]

The approach to this domain of spiritual theology requires us to appreciate how for Hooker, as in the Christian tradition generally, there is no formal division between dogmatic or doctrinal and spiritual concerns. The firm integration of devotion and reason that has been claimed as a distinction feature of the English school of spirituality is found also in patristic and later Christian literature, and Hooker shares it both from his own English context as well as from his sources.[36]

---

33. In chapter two of Lorenzo Scupoli's, *The Spiritual Combat* (London, 1890), p. 8. The Italian treatise, a classic spiritual writing of the Counter-Reformation, was first published in 1589.
34. See F. P. Harton, *The Elements of the Spiritual Life* (London, 1932), pp. 305-32.
35. Allen, *Spiritual Theology*, pp. 10-14.
36. On this aspect of the patristic witness see Andrew Louth, *The Origins of the Christian Mystical Tradition* (Oxford, 1981), p. xii; on its place in English spirituality see Thornton, *English Spirituality*, pp. 48-9.

Elements of the Threefold Way

Purgation

The first aspect of the threefold way is often known as the purgative way. During this first phase, practical exercises and disciplines are begun as the starting point of intentional spiritual life. Its alternative designation in Greek, *praktikē*, highlights the practical steps or actions taken to redirect one's course more steadily Godward and to uproot sinful habits and replace them with virtuous ones. As we have already noted, Hooker does not use those terms, but he affirms practices that typically characterise this stage of spiritual endeavour. Remarks throughout Book V reveal Hooker's support for practices engendering preliminary orientation and discipline. Prayer and worship according to a 'set and standing order' and the seasonal round of 'festival days', for instance, are part of that regime.

More pointedly, relevant to the purgative or 'practical' way are the use of nightly vigils, or 'watching', and 'fastings', two well-established means to deepen conversion in the early stages and to fight temptation and sin.[37] Hooker does not expand on the practice of vigils; but chapter seventy-two of Book V is an insightful exposition of fasting from the perspective of its scriptural basis, ecclesiastical practices, and its spiritual import.[38] It contributes positively 'in sign of devotion and reverence toward God' to the attainment of spiritual discernment and intensification of prayer, and negatively 'in token of penitency, humiliation, grief and sorrow'.[39]

An aspect of that last point is taken up by Hooker in Book VI of the *Laws* where, in the context of a discussion of ministerial authority, he speaks of the practice of repentance and of auricular confession and lays out his view of the 'virtue of repentance'. As Loyer points out in a careful discussion of this topic, Hooker stands within the so-called contritionist school of medieval theology regarding the virtue of repentance. That theology emphasised the 'inward secret repentance of the heart' as the essence of the spiritual act by which God through Christ forgives sins.[40] The importance of this is its link with the biblical idea of personal *metanoia*, or conversion, and its emphasis on interior compunction in the purgative experience of spiritual growth.[41] In Hooker's contritionist

---

37. Neelands draws general attention to the importance of watchfulness as a function of Hooker's understanding of the need for intentional and careful effort in the cultivation of the good works of sanctification ('Grace', p. 203).

38. V, lxxii, 6-7 [II, p. 413]. Both private and communal fasting are affirmed.

39. V. lxxii, 7 [II, p. 413].

40. Loyer, II, pp. 614-18.

41. On repentance and contrition in Hooker see John Booty's essay 'Contrition in Anglican Spirituality: Hooker, Donne and Herbert' in William Wolf, ed., *Anglican Spirituality* (Wilton, CT, 1982), pp. 26-30.

account the personal penitence of a believer suffices to gain forgiveness of sins; however, he is sensitive to, and supportive of, the Prayer Book's few but noteworthy references to the 'quieting of conscience' through 'ghostly counsel, advice, and comfort' and the making of a 'special confession' when a conscience is 'troubled by any weighty matter'.[42]

Sin

What, then, of sin? We might have taken up the subject in the previous chapter, but insofar as its confronting and uprooting is a major part of purgative endeavour, we can profitably turn to it now.

Sin, as we saw in the chapter on Hooker's anthropology, is 'no plant of God's setting'; it arises out of human choice, itself a function of the freedom that was part of God's general and good will for humankind in the act of creation. The threefold way, and especially its purgative aspect, is the gracious means by which the obliquity of sin in all its forms is identified and insofar as possible healed.

In Hooker's account, chiefly in the first book of the *Laws* but also in parts of his *Dublin Fragments*, sin is always voluntary. It is either a positive function of the will that, as we saw, has the power to choose regardless of reason's dictates; or, it is the result of reason's sloth or 'sluggishness', its lack of concentration, by which reason discerns badly.[43] In Book I Hooker explains that sin always involves the wilful choice of a lesser good in preference to a greater good; so, it disrupts the divine order which dictates that choice should always be in accordance with the good purpose of the thing chosen, the best meriting acceptance.[44] Both reason and will cannot, according to Hooker's traditional reckoning, desire evil for itself, but they can mistake evil for good. In either case, sin is also disordered. In the *Dublin Fragments* the echoes of Augustine's language are strong, as we have seen: sin within us is 'a thing irregular, exorbitant, and altogether out of course'.[45]

At the same time, there are gradations to sin, and, if Voak is right, it is possible to piece together from Hooker's disparate remarks something like a traditional Roman Catholic distinction between venial sins, on the one hand, and mortal sins, on the other. In interpreting various New Testament passages the western tradition had erected a twofold categorisation of sins according to which great, or mortal sins, exclude from salvation unless repented of, whereas lesser, or venial sins, do not.[46] In the *Dublin Fragments*

42. VI, ii-v [III, pp. 3-73]; phrases from the Prayer Book's 'Exhortation to Communion' and the rite of 'Visitation of the Sick' respectively.
43. *DF*, V, App. I (II, p. 544).
44. See I, vii, 7 [I, pp. 224-5].
45. *DF*, V, App. I [II, p. 572].
46. Relevant texts include 1 Cor. 6.9-10, Gal. 5.19-21, Eph. 5.5, and James 3.2, 1 John 1.8; 5, 16-18.

Hooker interprets 1 John 1.8 as referring to *peccata*, or venial sins, as distinct from *crimina*, or mortal sins.[47] In Book III of the *Laws* Hooker already employed the distinction; he speaks of 'errors' and 'faults' which do not exclude from salvation when committed, on the one hand, and heresies and crimes which, when not repented of and forsaken, 'exclude quite and clean from that salvation which belongeth unto the mystical body of Christ', on the other.[48]

The purgative path, however, aims at all levels and degrees of sin. That reminds us that it is wrong to speak of the purgative aspect of the spiritual way as a 'stage', as if it were ever out-grown. Nowhere does Hooker suggest that, and in this respect his view accords with the best understanding of the Christian spiritual tradition. What may well be outgrown are those very 'heinous' sins that obstruct the flow of grace and put a Christian's salvation at risk; however, the range of venial sins persist as the substance of a Christian's spiritual warfare. Therefore, the Christian stands in perpetual need of the grace of repentance.

Illumination

The second stage of the threefold way is when, on the basis of positive disciplines established and initial obstacles overcome, insight into oneself, the world and God develops. This phase does not leave behind the aspect of purgation, but compensations begin to emerge, and overt and intentional deprivation gives way to acquisition. The believer's positive practice of the virtues gains traction together with the deepening gifted expression of the theological virtues of faith, hope and love. Some writers refer to this stage as '*physikē*', a phase when meditation and contemplation on the ways and being of God become possible. The term derives from the Greek word for nature, so the illumination gained derives from the contemplation of God through nature – all created existence – as well as through Scripture. Those two sources in fact become interactive and mutually enlightening.

In previous chapters we have discussed Hooker's coordinated view of the 'two books' of nature and Scripture, and we have seen how his wide concept of law links them as a kind of double source for the apprehension of God's truth. Here we see that same dynamic applied to his spiritual theology. We recall the Augustinian paradigm of the two ways that Hooker employs. Its importance here is the place it accords to nature as a 'voice' to be heard as part of the spiritual journey to God: 'Her voice', Hooker insists, 'is but his instrument'.[49] Nature, in other

---

47. Voak, *Reformed Theology*, p. 206; and generally, pp. 204-9.
48. III, i, 13 [I, p. 350].
49. I, viii, 3 [I, p. 227].

words, has a declarative, evidential force *vis-à-vis* the ways and beings of God; in it the traces, or *vestigia* (to use Augustine's word), can be discovered by the enlightened mind. In this Hooker keeps company with the patristic and medieval spiritual tradition. With the aid of engraced reason and the gift of faith it is possible to discern God's presence and activity throughout the created world, and so to grow closer to God.[50] The more we understand the universe, the more we understand God.[51]

The book of Scripture, as we have seen, complements the book of nature with revealed, saving knowledge of 'the laws and duties supernatural'. Insights from the book of nature clarify saving knowledge; insights from the book of Scripture illumine the meaning and purpose of the natural world and human experience. Certainly Hooker makes much of such cross-referencing in his theological 'method' especially in Book V. We have there, in fact, a solid theological foundation for the experience of illumination when both the natural and the spiritual worlds come alive with a deepened and deepening sense of the divine presence, identity and purpose.

Virtue

If the first stage of spiritual life concentrates on clearing the path and uprooting sinful obstacles, the stage of illumination emphasises the cultivation of the natural and theological virtues.[52] Hooker provides no distinct and extended treatment of the virtues, but, as in the case of sin, we find throughout his writings an understanding shaped by the patristic and scholastic streams of western Christian thought.

Virtue, as Hooker understands the term, is a kind of power of action. We have already encountered Hooker's occasional use of the scholastic term 'habit', so that Hooker's concept of virtue seems to accord with Aquinas' understanding of virtue as a habit that inclines us toward our perfection.[53] That suits Hooker's overall conceptual universe well since, as we know, his understanding of law is chiefly of an inherent tendency toward an end which is good and, for that reason, perfecting. On that basis, a virtue is an interior power enabling a human being to fulfil the law of its being. Surlis has described virtue in relation to Hooker's

---

50. An example is Hooker's treatment of natural cycles, say, of seasons; they have a recollective force in themselves and also support the spiritual value of the liturgical calendar.

51. So Kirk with reference to the Thomistic method of analogical predication; but the point is pertinent to this phase of spiritual experience too (*Vision*, p. 156).

52. The 'natural' virtues referred to here include the so-called cardinal virtues of pagan moral philosophy: justice, temperance, fortitude and prudence.

53. *ST*, Ia. IIae. 55.1; see Voak, *Reformed Theology*, p. 194.

thought as proportion and order in human action, and that accords well with the aspects of beauty that we identified in Hooker's account of moral goodness.[54]

According to this account, the life of virtue is not merely the successive performance of good or upright actions. Those are but expressions of a mind that knows the law of its own being, and cultivates the powers or virtues by which the energies of will, appetite and desire can be rightly ordered so that perfection can be attained. Hooker's concept of virtue, therefore, distances him from a simplistic divine command theory of moral action.[55] Its pull is more in the direction of formation of character so that right or virtuous actions express the law of one's being as it moves from potentiality to actuality or perfection.

It should be clear, then, that the virtues are not cultivated for their own sake; they serve an end beyond themselves. In pursuance of that end, the virtues play a key role by distinguishing between use and enjoyment in the course of human affairs. In that Hooker relies upon Augustine's teaching and its legacy. For Augustine the journey Godward involved the ordered use and measured enjoyment of things temporal so as to attain the full enjoyment of God eternally.[56] Indebted to that, Hooker recognises a hierarchy of 'good things' that we desire and use both as means and even as ends in the course of mere temporal life; yet he reminds his readers that there remains a further end to which they are referred, and a sense of a more perfect satisfaction of desires yet to come.[57] In that ordering of use and enjoyment the power of the virtues is essential.

Hooker accepts that the natural virtues provide the foundation for the supernatural theological virtues of faith, hope and love which St Paul describes so beautifully in 1 Corinthians 13. He assumes too that the natural virtues require grace for their fully effective operation.[58] He knows as well on the basis of revelation that the law of human being requires the perfecting power of the infused theological virtues of faith, hope and love. Precisely through the ordered and disciplined immersion in the way of grace, that is, the contemplation of the two books and the striving to perform the laws and duties supernatural, the Christian is illumined in knowledge and understanding of self, God and the world. This stage of illumination extends throughout the life of sanctification for most

---

54. Surlis, 'Natural Law': 177.
55. This I deduce from II, viii, 5 [II, pp. 332-3], as well as from the entire course of Hooker's argument against non-conformist biblicism.
56. I owe this insight to Ingalls, 'Scriptures', pp. 159-60.
57. I, xi, 1-2 [I, p. 254-5]; on use and enjoyment see John Burnaby, *Amor Dei* (Norwich, 1991), p. 10ff.
58. We recall: 'Freedom of operation we have by nature, but the ability of virtuous operation by grace' (*DF*, V, App. I [II, p. 539]).

Christians. The knowledge attained, however, includes the awareness and sense of a perfection as yet unattained, beyond virtue itself, a last mark at which we aim, the possibility of a depth of participation in God as yet unreached. [59]

Union

The third and final stage of the threefold way is described by means of various complementary terms in the spiritual tradition. In the Greek tradition it is usually described as *theoria* to indicate a gifted, intuitive grasp of divine reality,[60] a stage *in via* of mystical union given to few. Of such experiences in the course of the temporal pilgrimage Hooker says nothing explicit, though we can deduce an appreciation for aspects of the spiritual posture that often characterises this third stage. In any case, any mystical experience of union with God, or *theoria*, is an anticipation of the glorifying grace that awaits all Christians in the end. On the character of that final goal Hooker is unequivocally clear: humankind has been created to enjoy God as the very substance of its spiritual perfection, what Hooker calls 'glorifying righteousness'.

Two points already made in previous chapters lay the foundation for this stage of the threefold way in Hooker's spiritual theology. First, although Hooker does not explicitly describe or offer practical guidance on inner stillness, he prizes and commends the way of stillness and wordlessness, or *apophasis*, as the most appropriate bearing of a Christian before the mystery of God. 'Dangerous it were for the feeble brain of man to wade far into the doings of the Most High', as we know; 'our safest eloquence concerning him is our silence, when we confess without confession that his glory is inexplicable, his greatness above our capacity and reach'.[61] Such negative theology is the only sound basis for the contemplative stillness, or *hesychia*, that is said to characterise this last stage of the threefold way. It goes hand in hand with a posture of unknowing, the passive receptivity to which intuitive spiritual 'sight' is given.[62]

The second point relates to the theme of 'union' by which this stage is commonly known in the west. Here we must remember how Hooker relates the end or final purpose of humankind to his foundational theme of participation. 'All things in the world', we have already observed him explain, 'are said in some sort to seek the highest, and to covet more or

---

59. I, xi, 1-2 [I, pp. 253-4].
60. Its meaning is not fixed in the developing spiritual tradition.
61. I, ii, 2 [I, p. 201].
62. The language of sight is, of course, metaphorical. Sight, however, was regarded in the medieval period as the highest of the senses, so it was natural to speak of the ultimate experience of God either mystically or in the end in terms of sight, the 'beatific *vision*'.

less the participation of God himself'.[63] Humankind above the rest of creation seeks its infinite, final good in 'participation and conjunction' in God, 'so that although we be men, yet by being unto God united we live as it were the life of God'.[64] While the fulfilment of such 'participation' and 'conjunction' awaits the full glorification of the Christian, it has its beginnings more or less in this life. Hooker's language and conceptual structure is not tight here, so we are left with the impression of a fluid transfer, as it were, between the stages of illumination and union, between sanctification and glorification.

All this points us back to the discussion of Hooker's theology of grace in chapter eight. Here, therefore, we need only to highlight how for Hooker believers' 'complete union', whether begun mystically in this life or not, fulfils humanity's law of being by perfecting all human powers and virtues, and above all the faculties of understanding and desire. 'Complete union' with God, Hooker explains,

> must be according unto every power and faculty of our minds apt to receive so glorious an object. Capable we are of God both by understanding and will: by understanding, as He is that sovereign Truth which comprehendeth the rich treasures of all wisdom; by will, as He is that sea of Goodness whereof whoso tasteth shall thirst no more. As the will doth now work upon that object by desire, which is as it were a motion towards the end as yet unobtained; so likewise upon the same hereafter received it shall work also by love. "Appetitus inhiantis fit amor fruentis," saith Augustine: "The longing disposition of them that thirst is changed into the sweet affection of them that taste and are replenished" . . . The soul being in this sort, as it is active, perfected by love of that infinite good, shall, as it is receptive, be also perfected with those supernatural passions of joy, peace, and delight. All this, endless and everlasting.[65]

Such is the 'last and highest estate of perfection' for the believer.[66] Yet those very words 'last' and 'highest' suggest the possibility of lesser anticipations of 'sweet affection', of active love and of receptive joy, peace and delight *in via*.

Although Hooker does not openly expound the threefold way, his theology provides the basis and even some superstructure for a traditional spiritual theology of ascetical journey and mystical ascent. In this he welds his distinctive English theology of nature and grace onto an established spiritual paradigm; he joins the worship and piety of the Prayer Book to a rich Catholic stock of spiritual concepts and aspirations.

---

63. I, v, 2 [I, p. 215].
64. I, xi, 2 [I, p. 255].
65. I, xi, 3 [I, pp. 255-6].
66. *Ibid.* 5 [I, p. 258].

Hooker and 'Anglican Devotion'

Hooker's *Laws* and other writings are not in any sense a devotional exposition of the sort that by his day had become a common feature on the English spiritual landscape. It is noteworthy that C. J. Stranks' classic study of 'Anglican devotion' nowhere mentions Hooker or cites his writings. Still, Stranks' work highlights two areas where, as this chapter has shown, Hooker's contribution is significant. First, it underlines the strong recollective tendency in English spirituality for which the *Laws* provide a firm theological basis. Second, Hooker's defence of the patterns of worship, sacraments and prayers of the *Book of Common Prayer* set a precedent for a rich devotional literature centred on the Prayer Book that characterised the seventeenth century and later periods.[67] In those ways, at least, Hooker enriched the spiritual culture of the reformed Church of England and gave it a resource from which subsequent churchmen would fashion a distinctly English spirituality that contemporised the great streams of ancient and medieval tradition.

---

67. Stranks, *Anglican Devotion*, pp. 26, and 149-73.

PART FIVE

APPLICATION

Chapter 15
'That Visible Mystical Body'
Ecclesiology

At the start of Book III Hooker declares the importance of the doctrine of the church in the overall apologetic argument of the *Laws*. For although the presenting issues in debate are of 'outward things', Hooker sees that 'forms of government' and 'polity' require consideration of the 'nature and being of the Church'.[1] To those concerns, which are the subject of this chapter, he turns at various points throughout the *Laws*, chiefly in Books III, V and VIII.

Insofar as Hooker's focus is 'polity' his attention is drawn mainly to the visible church. But as the quotation in the chapter heading indicates, there is far more to the doctrine of the church, in Hooker's view, than the visible aspects comprehended by the category of 'polity'. Ecclesiology, or the doctrine of the church, then, with its concern for the origin, nature and functions of the church in the economy of salvation, is distinguishable from polity, and it is in that way that we will explore it as an aspect of Hooker's theological vision.

Hooker, like others of his era, was aware of the evolution of ecclesiology into a distinct topic within the systematic exposition of sacred doctrine.[2] While he shared the general Reformation's general commitment to biblical categories, he joined that to a patristic tendency to hold conceptualisations about the church in close relation to Christology. As a result, we find in Hooker's ecclesiological thought a dynamic amalgam of sources and 'models'.[3]

An additional factor is, of course, the apologetic context in which he wrote. Here too various strands converge. One of the most fruitful lines in recent Hooker scholarship has been in plotting Hooker's contribution to the developing establishment defence of the Church of England. Peter Lake has shown how in the department of ecclesiology (as in other areas, as we have already seen) Hooker developed current apologetic trends in ways that set a new course for establishment religion.[4]

We can explore the contours and content of Hooker's ecclesiology with the aid of four thematic couplets: visible and invisible; natural and

---

1. III, i, 1 [I, p. 338].
2. It was in the late fourteenth and fifteenth centuries in the Latin west that the doctrine of the church became a distinct topic.
3. That is a modern term, of course, but a useful one in analysing the various guiding perspectives in Hooker's ecclesiology; see Avery Dulles, *Models of the Church* (New York, 1974).
4. See *Anglicans and Puritans?*, pp. 153-62.

supernatural; necessity and freedom; and particular and universal. To those we now turn as we seek to discover what Hooker means when he describes the church as 'that visible mystical body'.

Visible and Invisible

The first chapter of Book III opens with a description of the church as, on the one hand, a 'body mystical' and invisible, and, on the other, a body 'visible' through outward profession. Both expressions of the church of Christ are, Hooker insists, 'real', though they are not simply identical and coterminous.[5] While some have found in that tension inconsistency and irresolution in Hooker's thought,[6] I think it is rather the case that he is struggling to recapture the dynamism found in, say, Augustine and Aquinas, for whom the church, while a concrete reality in space and time, is chiefly defined in – for a lack of better words – invisible terms.[7] This couplet is, then, consistent with attempts elsewhere in Hooker's theology to reprise the Augustinian trajectory as mediated through Aquinas and other scholastics.

The 'body mystical' is invisible, Hooker explains, 'because the mystery of their conjunction [*viz.* to Christ] is removed altogether from sense'. They, he says,

> who are of this society have such marks and notes of distinction from all others, as are not object unto our sense; only unto God, who seeth their hearts and understandeth all their secret cogitations, unto him they are clear and manifest.[8]

In contrast to undue introspection as well as to church membership based on discernible signs and evidences of the sort sought for by non-conformists, Hooker sees in his understanding of the 'body mystical' an affirmation of the only ground of Christian confidence, namely, the compassionate, all-seeing pronouncement of God, 'the Searcher of all men's hearts' knows 'intuitively' who are his.[9]

While the promises of love, mercy and blessedness belong to that 'mystical Church', everything that pertains to individual and corporate duty to God belongs to the church 'as a sensibly known company'. That is the visible church spanning space and time; it is divided only in relation to Christ as first, those who preceded his Incarnation, and then those who were contemporary with and follow after it, termed properly 'the Church of Christ'.

5. III, i, 1, 4 [I, pp. 338-9].
6. So Thornton, for instance, *Hooker*, p. 74.
7. So, for Augustine the body of which Christ is the head 'is not essentially visible' owing to its inter-generational and trans-earthly membership, while for Aquinas the church 'essentially consists in a divinising communion with God'; so Dulles, *Models*, pp. 46-7.
8. III, i, 2 [I, p. 338].
9. *Ibid.* [I, p. 339]. Harrison makes the important point that 'invisible' and 'mystical' are not simply equivalent in Hooker's usage; 'mystical' carries other connotations ('The Church', *CRH*, p. 307)

A Wide Definition of the Visible Church

It is at this point in Book III that we find Hooker's foundational definition of the visible church. Interpreting Paul's affirmation in 1 Corinthians 12.13 that believers are 'all incorporated into one company', Hooker then explains with recourse to Ephesians 4.5:

> The unity of which visible body and Church of Christ consisteth in that uniformity which all several persons thereunto belonging have, by reason of that *one Lord* whose servants they all profess themselves, that *one Faith* which they all acknowledge, that *one Baptism* wherewith they are all initiated.[10]

That 'minimal' definition recognises the supernatural truths that form the essence of Christianity and, as Hooker explains his intent, focuses on the affirmation of the lordship of Christ as professed in baptism: 'entered we are not into the visible Church before our admittance by the door of Baptism'.[11] With that baptismal basis Hooker's is at once a 'large' definition insofar as he refuses to exclude schismatics, heretics, apostates and those whom others might simply view as corrupt, and a 'minimal' one insofar as the requirements of profession are only the creedal essentials.[12] Put simply, the visible church *is* wherever there is valid baptism.[13] All the baptised, whether profane or godly in practice, are part of the 'sensibly known company' of the church, and this mixture is not a defect of the church but an inevitable feature of its life *in via*.[14] Thus Hooker's ecclesiology has incarnational and sacramental sources: incarnational insofar as it 'pleaseth him [*viz.* Christ] in mercy to account himself incomplete and maimed without us'; sacramental insofar as that 'mystical conjunction' has its effectual beginning through baptism.[15] As we shall see, Hooker's 'almost indecent enthusiasm' for such a large definition of the church took his conformist ecclesiology in distinctive new directions.[16]

---

10. III, i, 3 [I, p. 339].

11. III, i, 6 [I, p. 341]; see Loyer's discussion, II, pp. 545-6.

12. See Hooker's remarks on those typically viewed as outside the church in III, I, xi [I, p. 348].

13. Loyer argues that Hooker's position combines Augustine's affirmation of heretical baptism with Cyprian's insistence that true baptism is only accomplished in the church; he argues that those two theologies 'which are to a considerable degree opposed' are affirmed in a surprising 'double loyalty' (*ibid.* pp. 548-9).

14. Lake, *Anglicans and Puritans?*, p. 161.

15. V, lvi, 7 [II, p. 249]. We recall that any eternal calling to grace and salvation must become effectual through the church; see above, pp. 138-9, 142. That is the 'point of connection' between Hooker's notions of 'invisible' and 'visible' which Thornton fails to see (*Hooker*, p. 77).

16. The phrase is Lake's, *Anglicans and Puritans?*, p. 160.

Natural and Supernatural

The title of this chapter with its tight compression of key terms – visible, mystical, body – uniquely expresses both the linkage and the coordination of nature and grace which characterises Hooker's theology. In his ecclesiology also a careful correlation of the two is at work. If the visible-invisible couplet suggested it, this second couplet takes it further, into a specific consideration of the church as at once a natural – what we might call a sociological – entity and at the same time a mystery and instrument of grace. At the centre of this discussion is 'polity', the sphere where the natural and supernatural are actually in play. How does Hooker understand the church as the locus of those two different aspects and energies?

Polity and 'Discipline'

'Polity', Hooker's preferred term for 'whatsoever belongeth to the ordering of the Church in public',[17] is a necessary feature of every church in its visible aspects even though no 'one certain form' is required throughout them all.[18] So in the church, like all visible societies ecclesiastical or otherwise, 'laws of polity it cannot want'.[19] Hooker's preference for the term 'polity', however, does not lack a controversial edge. In origin it was a Classical Greek term (*politeia*) without any essential Christian or theological significance; it referred simply to the public life of the city. It was very much a term of 'nature'.

In contrast, Puritans and non-conformists preferred their overtly Christian, morally-laden word 'discipline', and meant by it the comprehensive pastoral governance of the Christian community. Its aim was the spiritual integrity of the church in its members as well as corporately both through magisterial teaching and the maintenance of moral order. Non-conformists like Walter Travers, insofar as they used the word 'polity' at all, meant the external spiritual discipline of the church.[20] They preferred 'discipline' with its scriptural resonances and its implied understanding of the church as a fellowship set apart from the profane and ungodly. Needless to say, 'discipline' carried a strong exclusionary connotation in a way that 'polity' did not. It was very much a term of 'grace'.

However, that contrast is far too simple in interpreting Hooker's understanding of polity since Hooker's interest, as we have seen elsewhere, is

---

17. III, i, 14 [I, p. 352]; Hooker also uses the term 'regiment' and affirms its close link with 'government'. For Hooker 'Church-Polity' is a more inclusive terminology. It should be pointed out too, though, that Hooker does not exclude the concept or vocabulary of 'discipline' from his view of church life but, as we shall see, locates it elsewhere.

18. III, ii, 1 [I, p. 352].

19. III, xi, 14 [I, p. 406].

20. Loyer, II, pp. 552-3.

not to set grace apart from nature, but to build grace's edifice on the basis of nature. In the face of the non-conformist assertion that (as Hooker himself puts it) 'in Scripture there must be of necessity contained a form of church polity divinely and immutably fixed', Hooker responds not with an alternative divine and immutable polity but with an ecclesiology of synergy between nature and grace. What, then, is the natural basis of ecclesiastical polity with which the supernatural aspect of the church interacts as an instrument of grace?

A 'natural subject of power'

In the sixth chapter of Book VIII, where Hooker discusses the power of making ecclesiastical laws, he has occasion to expand upon a theme running through the *Laws*: that according to the law of nature the subject of power in any society resides in 'the body of the commonwealth'.[21] We will pick up that thread when we turn to Hooker's political theology. It is pertinent here to highlight Hooker's principle that, insofar as the church is a natural society, it too retains a power of self-determination in its corporate life. '[N]ature itself,' he insists, 'doth abundantly authorize the Church to make laws and orders for her children that are within her'.[22]

In asserting that, Hooker is far from arguing that the church is not accountable to Scripture. Rather, he is establishing one of the natural foundation blocks upon which the church's life is ordered, namely, that there are areas – and Hooker's tendency is to widen them as far as principles allow – where Christians are given broad guidance but no detail in Scripture, or given no explicit guidance at all, or are given guidance that is not immutable. In those instances the church has within itself power to decide.

Aspects of Polity that are 'of God'

In cases where the church acts as the natural subject of power to regulate its outward, public life, are those decisions 'of God'? This is an important point in the content of Hooker's case as he seeks to legitimise aspects of the Church of England's polity which have no scriptural basis or have evolved through a process of re-ordering and change.

It is obvious to Hooker that when the church orders itself it must be accountable to its twofold character as, on the one hand, a natural society, and, on the other, an instrument of grace. It must, in other words, be loyal to both reason and revelation. We have seen already what a high premium Hooker places on natural law and right reason; their voice is but God's instrument. On that account Hooker can view the determinations of the church, when properly settled on according to the dictates of legitimate theological method, rational method and due authority, as 'of God'.

---

21. VIII, vi, 1 [III, p. 396].
22. *Ibid*. See Paget's Laws made by a Body Politic 'which is spiritually joined' (p. 67).

At the same time, there are areas of church life where a dominical example or injunction may or may not be followed. The church's corporate judgment in those cases too can fairly be described as 'of God'. Beyond that, there are thoroughgoing supernatural verities which are unequivocally divine. Hooker, therefore, sidesteps the non-conformists' 'of God'/not 'of God' opposition by means of his synergic view of nature and grace within the saving economy. The church is no less faithful to its divine calling by relying on its natural powers than it is by obedience to supernatural influence.

Efficacious Instrument of Salvation

In words that might be taken from a patristic or medieval commentary Hooker affirms the inseparable link between Christ and the church as the locus of believers' mysterious 'coherence with Jesus Christ':

> The Church is in Christ as Eve was in Adam. Yea by grace we are every of us in Christ and in his Church, as by nature we are in those our first parents. God made Eve of the rib of Adam. And his Church he frameth out of the very flesh, the very wounded and bleeding side of the Son of Man. His body crucified and his blood shed for the life of the world, are the true elements of that heavenly being, which maketh us such as himself is of whom we come. For which cause the words of Adam may be fitly the words of Christ concerning his Church, "flesh of my flesh, and bone of my bones," a true native extract out of my own body. So that in him even as according to his manhood we according to our heavenly being are as branches in that root out of which they grow.[23]

Incorporation into Christ is by means of the church, his body. Here in suggestive terms rather than with hard theological rigor, Hooker links ecclesiology with the principle of participation which runs through the *Laws* like a silver thread. Hooker's 'church' in the passage cited, and in the exposition in Book V of which it is part, is unqualified by attributes like 'visible' or 'mystical' so that we might wonder of which he is speaking. But the thrust of his exposition is that we cannot, and should not, make such a distinction.[24] The church is an 'efficacious instrument of salvation' because life-giving, saving, invisible coherence with Christ by grace is mediated through the 'sensibly known company' and the polity that gives that company expression in the world.

We have noted more than once how Hooker understands God's gracious call to a believer: whatever its source may be in the eternal counsels of God, that call must be actualised by grace operating through real, visible

23. V, lvi, 7 [II, p. 250].
24. That is the thrust of Neelands' analysis too in 'Richard Hooker on the Identity of the Visible and Invisible Church', *RHER*, pp. 106-7.

instruments, Hooker's intermediate causes. Just as this is a foundation for Hooker's theology of sacraments so it is foundational for his theology of the church. It too is a visible instrument by which God's invisible grace is communicated. Hooker will go no further in plotting the secret influences of grace by means of the church's proclamation, sacraments and worship. His enduring sense of the freedom of God prevents him. But the fundamental point is clear: the church is not merely a gathering and sign of those secretly elected, called, and saved; rather, it is the effective instrumental means whereby the grace of election, justification and sanctification are mediated to believers. As an efficacious *instrument* of grace really given, it is also a sign of the hope of glory toward which its members, by drawing upon the means of grace, strive. And precisely because the efficacious working of grace is largely a secret affair and grace's efficacy in the life of a believer largely hidden from others' view, the church, as the 'mother of believers', extends its arms inclusively.[25]

Necessity and Freedom

The Reformers' assertion of the liberty of the Christian on account of the personally justifying grace of God had ecclesiological implications. What freedom in their corporate guise did Christians therefore have in ordering their common life as a society of public profession? Under the force of an unmediated justifying grace, how much of the hitherto necessary ecclesiastical edifice could give way or at least be substantially changed? Thus the theme of 'adiaphorism' arose.[26]

In the Reformers' usage, 'adiaphora'[27] referred to aspects of Christian thought and practise that were inconsequential *vis-à-vis* saving faith. In England such indifferent matters were sometimes described as 'accessory' as distinct from matters essential to the faith – a twofold distinction used by Archbishop Whitgift in his combat with non-conformist critics.[28] English non-conformist thought, however, carried within it a contradiction that Hooker sought to exploit. Whereas Calvin had argued that matters of polity were largely adiaphoral, why, Hooker wonders, do his non-conformist contemporaries seek, by contrast, to shrink the range of adiaphora and erect a polity by divine right?

For his part, Hooker develops the notion of adiaphora, what he

25. V, lxiv, 5 [II, p. 315].
26. For a careful survey of this theme in England before Hooker, see Bernard Verkamp, *The Indifferent Mean. Adiaphorism in the English Reformation to 1554* (Athens and Detroit, USA, 1977).
27. From the Greek word '*adiaphoros*' meaning something indifferent, neither good nor bad.
28. See *Works* [Parker Society], I, pp. 175ff.; and Richard Wilmer 'Hooker on Authority', *Anglican Theological Review*, XXXIII (1951): 107.

sometimes calls things 'arbitrary', in a way that supports his view of the relation between nature and grace, and, on that basis he uses it as an aid to his understanding of the church's power of determination in matters of faith, practice and polity.

Hooker's Taxonomy of Freedom and Necessity

For our purposes in this chapter, where we are interested in understanding the legitimate freedom of the church in ordering its public life, we can usefully delineate a threefold taxonomy of freedom and necessary. This taxonomy, a subset of the full taxonomy of laws described earlier in this study, describes the status of aspects of the church's life and, by implication, clarifies where the church has and has not power in itself to adapt and change.

Hooker is clear that the church is not free to alter every aspect of its faith, life and constitution as a visible society of profession. Supernatural law, which is by definition unchangeable – 'not capable of any diminution or augmentation at all by men'[29] –, includes evangelical doctrine and the sacraments. At the other end of the spectrum are matters discernible through reason and nature. While, as we saw, such matters can be described as 'of God', they are not by that mere fact necessarily immune from adaptation and change. Hooker includes in his category the substance of liturgical prayer and, in many regards, the ministry. (However, matters of natural law Hooker regards as fixed insofar as nothing can attain its properly designated end or purpose unless it honours those laws.) Whereas in the sphere of supernatural law the church is bound, in matters reasonable and natural the church has a wide scope for adaptation and change.

Between those two spheres lies a third and more ambiguous one which encompasses matters of divine or dominical origin that are, nonetheless, changeable. This area includes matters that pertain to the church as a supernatural instrument of grace where the church as a collective subject may still exercise its power to arbitrate. Probably the clearest example of this occurs in Hooker's discussion of spiritual jurisdiction in Book VI of the *Laws*. There Hooker asserts the supernatural origin, power and efficacy of the church's spiritual power, 'such as neither can be challenged by right of nature, nor could by human authority be instituted', and yet he acknowledges that Christ's 'commission to exercise' as well as his 'direction how to use' such power provide only a 'ground' and 'foundation'.[30] The implication is clear: the church must use its liberty to provide for what is lacking; it must build upon the dominical foundation. Likewise, there are matters where a dominical example in the Scriptures must of necessity be viewed differently owing to the change of times and circumstances. So, Hooker argues,

---

29. II, xi, 16 [I, p. 408].
30. VI, ii, 2 [III, p. 4].

[t]o think that no law, constitution, or canon, can be further made either for limitation or amplification in the practice of our Saviour's ordinances, whatsoever occupation be offered through variety of times and things, during the state of this unconstant world, which bringing forth daily new evils as must of necessity by new remedies be redrest, did both of old enforce our venerable predecessors, and will always constrain others, sometime to make, sometime to abrogate, sometime to augment, and again to abridge sometime; in sum, often to vary, alter, and change customs incident to the manner of exercising that power which doth itself continue always one and the same.[31]

Of course non-conformists did not argue that the church has *no* power to arbitrate things 'indifferent' or 'arbitrary'.[32] The difference between them and Hooker lay in the extent of that power. Hooker chose to cut a wide swathe indeed, and while it distanced him greatly from non-conformist critics, it also distanced him from many of his conformist predecessors and 'allies'.

'Traditions ecclesiastical'

The wide field that Hooker accorded to matters indifferent led inevitably to a reassessment of tradition in the life of the church. We have already touched on the theme in relation to the sources of theology. We complement that discussion now by location tradition and traditions within the church's power of self-determination.

In keeping with his Reformed credentials, Hooker typically regards 'traditions' negatively.[33] He has in mind, of course, the Council of Trent's espousal of a two-source theory of revelation in which saving truth is communicated by sacred tradition as well as by Scripture.[34] Hooker will have nothing to do with such a view. 'When the question therefore is, whether we be now to stand for any revealed law of God otherwise than only in the sacred scripture', he explains, 'whether we do now stand bound in the sight of God to yield to traditions urged by the Church of Rome the same obedience we do to his written law, honouring equally and adoring both as divine: our answer is, No.'[35]

It is hard for Hooker to leave things there, however. For one thing, Hooker discerns the basis of tradition and traditions in nature itself which, he observes, 'inclineth unto validities and preservations'. Against the natural tendency for customs to prevail, '[d]issolutions and nullities of things done, are not only not favoured, but hated when urged without cause, or extended

31. *Ibid.* [III, p. 5].
32. Lake, *Anglicans and Puritans?*, p. 19.
33. That negative view usually applies to 'traditions' in the plural.
34. On this see the discussion in chapter twelve.
35. See chapter twelve where this quotation is cited.

beyond their reach.[36] From that natural basis it was but a small step to affirm both the preservation of customs in the church and the evolution of received habits as expressions of its legitimate power of determination.

So Hooker defends, for instance, making the sign of the cross in baptism, a ceremony impugned by non-conformists on just that basis. In this passage it is notable how Hooker defends both 'tradition' and 'traditions'.

> Lest therefore the name of tradition be offensive to any, considering how far by some it hath been and is abused, we mean by traditions, ordinances made in the prime of Christian religion, established with the authority which Christ hath left to his Church for matters indifferent, and in that consideration requisite to be observed, till like authority see just and reasonable cause to alter them. So that traditions ecclesiastical are not rudely and in gross to be shaken off, because the inventor of them were men.[37]

In fact Hooker himself, like the non-conformists, interprets the 'prime' of the Christianity liberally, so it is no surprise to find Hooker's support for ecclesiastical traditions exceeding strictly primitivist parameters.[38] Throughout Hooker's theological and ecclesiological system, though, whether in the case of practical ordinances or of pious beliefs like the perpetual virginity of the Lord's mother, such traditions require no rationally necessary assent and have only a relative value as compared to the absolute value of Scripture's supernatural laws.

Particular and Universal

Hooker was, of course, aware of the Church of England's place in the wider spread of churches throughout Europe. If the mystical body of Christ is extensive in time, being 'in number as the stars of heaven' yet 'divided successively by reason of their mortal condition into many generations,'[39] the church in its visible form is likewise divided and extensive in space. Even among England's own population there remained a small number of loyal Roman Catholics who showed minimum conformity to the legally established religious settlement. So what was the Church of England's relationship to the other churches of the Reformation, on the one hand, and the Roman Catholic Church, on the other? This fourth couplet comprises comment on those and related matters.

---

36. V, lxii, 13 [II, p. 292].

37. V, lxv, 2 [II, p. 318].

38. See Hooker's critical comment on the non-conformists' primitivism in VII, xiii, 2 [III, p. 216]: 'the question is, how far they will have the prime to extend?'.

39. V, lvi, 11 [II, p. 254]; Hooker's use of 'mystical' here does not appear to exclude any members of the church who participate in the sacrament life with good intent; he uses 'saints' in this passage in its general, New Testament's sense.

'Particular' and National

The first chapter of Book III offers brief but pertinent definitions which form important structural components of Hooker's ecclesiology. One aspect of the context was a matter of translation with which Hooker, like other conformist divines, took issue and which had major ecclesiological implications.

In translating the New Testament's Greek term '*ekklesia*' as 'congregation', non-conformists thereby defined the church as the locally gathered 'assembly' of believers. 'The Church', then, was not an inclusive corporate body extensive in space but – if one had to speak of it in broader terms at all – a host of distinct, gathered fellowships. Hooker, for his part, rejects that translation and interpretation of the New Testament terminology. Their error, he argues, is to mistake the part for the whole; or rather, to define what the church *is* by an aspect of what it *does*. 'For although the name of the Church be given unto assemblies', Hooker acknowledges, 'although any multitude of Christian men congregated may be termed by the name of a Church, yet assemblies properly are rather things that belong to a Church.' Assemblies begin and end; the church persists. So, 'the Church' is not an assembly but a 'Society'. Such a society is specifically 'a number of men belonging unto some Christian fellowship, the place and limits whereof are certain. That wherein they have communion is the public exercise of such duties as those mentioned in the Apostles' Acts, "instruction, breaking of bread and prayer".'[40]

Can that 'society' be further defined?

In a well known passage from Book VIII Hooker comments on his understanding of the church as a visible society. Claiming that 'there is not any man of the Church of England but the same man is also a member of the commonwealth', he infers that no one is a member of the commonwealth 'which is not also of the Church of England'.[41] The whole society of Christians making up the Church of England forms, according to Hooker, a 'particular church'. Presuming a parallel between the city-state concept of the New Testament period and the nation-state of early modern Europe, Hooker likens the Church of Rome, or Corinth or Ephesus individually to the Church of England. In this he followed the lead of men like Whitgift who was clear that, when he spoke of 'particular churches' he meant, for instance, national churches like that of, say, Denmark or England.[42]

The Reformed Churches

Granting a conceptual parity with the 'society' of other reformed churches like those of Denmark, Germany or France (as distinct from the sectaries

---

40. III, i, 14 [I, p. 351].
41. VIII, i, 2 [III, p. 330].
42. *The Works of John Whitgift*, D.D., ed. J. Ayre (Cambridge, 1851-3), III, p. 198.

in England), was there anything more to be said about the relation of the Church of England to those churches? Through most of the sixteenth century there was little more to be said. In the interests of political alliance, and on the basis of a generous embrace of the adiaphoral principle as it pertained to church polity and order, little was made of differences between particular national churches. What did it matter if the Church of England, unlike most continental reformed churches, maintained the parochial structure, patterns of sacraments and habits of worship and ceremony harkening back to its pre-reformed days?

By the time Hooker was composing the *Laws*, however, circumstances had changed. If Peter Lake is right, the hardening of attitudes among non-conformists rushing to complete England's Reformation provoked an equivalent reaction among conformist divines of Hooker's generation.[43] There was argumentative pressure to advocate for the polity of the Church of England not on the basis of 'indifference' but on the basis of scriptural warrant.

Admittedly, Hooker is rightly described as constitutionally allergic to appeals of 'divine right';[44] still, we see the pressure of this change in his use of the adjective 'perfection' *vis-à-vis* matters of polity and order. In other words, Hooker has an interest in distinguishing the *esse* (being) and the *bene esse* (wellbeing) of the church. The wellbeing of the church lies in 'having that which best agreeth with Scripture'.

On the basis of his minimal definition of the church – one Lord, one Faith, one baptism – it is easy for Hooker to reckon other reformed churches unequivocally churches. When it comes to the 'perfection' of those churches, however, Hooker is equivocal. He is clear that by 'that which best agreeth with Scripture' the Church of England's polity possesses a perfection that the other reformed churches lack. Having fallen under a 'different regiment' lacking bishops, for instance, those reformed churches suffer 'defect' and 'imperfection'. Whether through a fault of their own or not, they have been driven 'to want that kind of polity or regiment which is best'.[45] In his attitude toward non-episcopal churches we see at work the more basic ecclesiological principle of economy, that is, concessions made by the church in view of human weakness. Hooker thinks of it in terms of equity;[46] by that he means an application of law adjusted to circumstances. In Book V he describes how the church has authority with discretion to mitigate its normative customs with 'favourable equity', just such a relaxing of 'rigour' shown in the Church of England's posture toward non-episcopal churches abroad.[47]

---

43. For instance, Saravia, Bilson, Bridges and Sutcliffe, see Lake, *Anglicans and Puritans?*, pp. 93-6.

44. *Ibid.* p. 222.

45. III, xi, 16 [I, p. 409].

46. See the discussion in chapter six, pp. 94-5.

47. V, x, 1 [II, p. 41]; on economy see also V, lxi, 5 [II, p. 280].

In that ecclesiological point we can see a broader attitude at work, namely Hooker's preference for continuity and thoughtful adaptation. Hooker admits the need from time to time to 'shear' the church but he refuses in the name of alleged 'imperfect reformation' to 'flay' it![48] It goes hand in hand with his appreciative but by no means slavish regard for the learned among the reformers, including John Calvin himself.[49]

The Roman Catholic Church

However that may be, the logic of Hooker's minimal definition of the church required re-evaluation of the inherited views of the Roman Catholic Church too. Here the issue was different: not whether Roman Catholics possessed the 'being' or 'wellbeing' of the church but whether they were a true church at all. English Reformers had early concluded that the Roman Church was no church because it had overthrown the very basis of Christian faith by denying or by irretrievably obscuring the unique mediatorial and expiatory work of Christ.

As early as his *Learned Discourse of Justification* Hooker had bravely argued that the Roman Catholic Church had not in fact overthrown the 'foundation of faith'. Although, as we have seen, the *Discourse* includes key points about Hooker's understanding of justification, sanctification and glorification, the bulk of the work involves careful analysis of Roman Catholic views on grace, faith and works. For our purposes here we need only grasp Hooker's main point, namely, '[s]alvation only by Christ is the true foundation whereupon true Christianity standeth'. In Hooker's analysis of their position it follows that whatever else might be added was *added* and so did not *displace* that foundation.[50]

A subtle distinction perhaps, but it carried important implications for the ecclesial self-definition. If Rome was a true church then the pre-Reformation inheritance need not be jettisoned lock, stock and barrel for the sake of reform. A more judicious and 'adaptive process' could be embraced.[51] Fundamentally, Hooker's inclusive definition of the church meant that the English Church was not under any ideological pressure to distance itself from its popish past. Far from it, Peter Lake contends: conformity with the pre-Reformation church could be desired in and for itself in that it emphasised how the Reformation in England was a judicious process of reform to remove corruptions and not the result of 'a wonton desire of innovation'.[52]

---

48. V, lxv, 1 [II, p. 317].
49. See the *Laws*' Preface, IV.6 [I, pp. 160-1].
50. *LDJ*, 29 [III, p. 528]; see Hooker's *Answer to Travers*. It contains important qualifications ameliorating the anti-Roman bias; for instance, sec. 13 [III, p. 583].
51. William Gregg's phrase ('Sacramental Theology ': 161).
52. Quoted by Lake, *Anglicans and Puritans?*, p. 157.

Catholicity

Catholicity was an important idea for Hooker, and his ecclesiology seeks to render the notion of the 'Catholic church' as professed in the Prayer Book's creed meaningful. Hooker's definition of a particular church as a visible society coterminous with a national polity forces him back to the original sense of the creedal note of 'Catholic' as universal. The Catholic church, therefore, is the sum of particular churches geographically dispersed. In asserting the twin features required of a church universal in extent – distinct as visible societies according to their national parameters yet having 'mutual fellowship' between them – Hooker invokes this image:

> [A]s the main body of the sea being one, yet within diverse precincts hath diverse names; so the Catholic Church is in like sort divided into a number of distinct Societies, every of which is termed a Church within itself.[53]

A serene, even beautiful image but one that fails to provide any concrete form for political association of the sort that effective polity requires. If, for example, polity requires laws and governance, then how does the 'Catholic Church' as Hooker describes it measure up? If, as we shall see in the chapter on political theology, the particular church possesses a visible head, can Hooker's Catholic Church, understood as a single ocean (albeit with distinct bodies of water with different names and shores), do without one? If supremacy of some kind is requisite for any visible polity, what sort of supremacy can operate through the 'Catholic Church'?

Conciliarity

In the end, Hooker affirms the need for a visible order for the 'Catholic church' without asserting the need for visible sovereignty. The basis of that order is law rather than any office or officer. In Book VIII, where Hooker considers issues of power and sovereignty in visible societies, he makes this pertinent remark: '[d]issimilitude in great things is such a thing which draweth great inconvenience after it'; he then explains that

> the way to prevent it is, not as some do imagine, the yielding up of supreme power over all churches into one only pastor's hands; but the framing of their government, especially for matters of substance, every where according to the rule of one only Law, to stand in no less force than the laws of nations doth, to be received in all kingdoms, all sovereign rulers to be sworn no otherwise unto it than some are to maintain the liberties, laws, and received customs of the country where they reign.[54]

---

53. III, i, 14 [I, p. 351].
54. VIII, iii, 5 [III, p. 366].

Here Hooker applies a general principle of political philosophy to the church: particularly and universally, the church is ruled and mutually bound by law.[55]

Behind that 'constitutionalism' lies the spirit of conciliarism.[56] Here it is not overt; but throughout the *Laws*, beginning in the Preface and then reiterated through various books, Hooker declares his conciliar hand and brings into public discourse from the theological quarter the burst of conciliar theorising that characterised the early Elizabethan period. In advocating thus Hooker has both a natural and a supernatural warrant.

On one hand, the concept of the law of nations, a department of human positive law, provided a paradigm for the laws which regulate the relations between particular churches within the Catholic Church. As the maintenance of communion between nations requires laws, 'so amongst nations Christian the like in regard even of Christianity hath always been judged needful.'[57] On the other hand, there was a supernatural warrant: the scriptural account of the Council of Jerusalem (Acts 15.6-29), a 'divine invention', the work of 'God's own blessed Spirit.'[58] Such councils, Hooker suggests, are part of the perfection of the church.[59] For this reason, and with Hooker's insistence that matters in debate in the church be reserved for discussion and consensus among the learned in divinity, Hooker advocates a conciliar form of discernment and decision

> whether it be for the finding out of any thing whereunto divine law bindeth us, but yet in such sort that men are not thereof on all sides resolved; or for the setting down of some uniform judgment to stand touching such things, as being neither way matters of necessity, are notwithstanding offensive and scandalous when there is open opposition about them; be it for the ending of strifes touching matters of Christian belief, wherein the one part may seem to have probable cause of dissenting from the other; or be it concerning matters of polity, order, and regiment in the church; I nothing doubt but that Christian men should much better frame themselves to those heavenly precepts, which our Lord and Saviour with so great instancy gave as concerning peace and unity, if we did all concur in desire to have the use of ancient councils again renewed.'[60]

Hooker is mindful of Article Twenty-One's hesitations about conciliar

---

55. An application of the principle '*Lex facit regem*'; so Loyer, II, p. 585.
56. On this theme in Hooker see the essay of W. B. Patterson, 'Hooker on Ecumenical Relations: Conciliarism in the English Reformation', *RHCCC*, pp. 283-303.
57. I, x, 14 [I, p. 252]. See Paget's Laws of Spiritual Communion between Christian Nations (p. 67).
58. *Ibid*.
59. 'That first perfection' is a phrase Hooker applies to the Jerusalem council.
60. I, x, 14 [I, 253].

authority and will not credit councils with anything like strict infallibility.[61] His advocacy of probable persuasion based on the reasonable consensus of the learned leads him to go beyond the article's hesitations in firm avowal not just of conciliar decisions but of conciliarity itself as the binding polity of the Catholic Church. In all of this the church has a magisterial function without an infallible character.[62]

Toward a 'Via Media'

The ecclesiology which this chapter has plotted is dynamic in the variety of models, images and concepts that Hooker brings into play. For that reason it may disappoint those wanting something less tense and more univocal. Certainly it is challenging for Hooker to hold in suitable balance the rightful claims of components of the four couplets by means of which we have described his doctrine of the church. However successful or unsuccessful Hooker may have been integrating the elements presented here, Hooker assembled and then generated with his unique alchemy a rich ecclesiology that took the doctrine of the church in English divinity to a new and distinctive place. Perhaps most important of all for the evolution of that theological tradition was the fact that, as Peter Lake rightly says, Hooker constructed an ecclesiological vision that effectively extracted the Church of England from a simplistic alliance with Reformed continental theology and located it somewhere else.[63] That 'somewhere else' has been negotiated and debated by Hooker's successors ever since. His inclusive understanding of the church was, as William Haugaard says, both untypical of his age and suggestive for conformist theologians thenceforth.[64] In ecclesiology, as elsewhere, Hooker opened up an alternative vision, a *via media*, of new possibilities of development and change which he himself could scarcely have imagined.

---

61. Patterson, 'Conciliarism': 285; see IV, xiv, 5 [I, p. 484]. On the interesting question of the influence on Hooker of Edwin Sandys' proposals for a Church of England ecumenical initiation among the chuches of Europe, and its conciliar spirit, see William Haugaard, 'Richard Hooker: Evidences of an Ecumenical Vision From A Twentieth-Century Perspective', *Journal of Ecumenical Studies*, 24: 3 (1987): 427-30.
62. Loyer, I, pp. 143-4.
63. *Anglicans and Puritans?*, pp. 159-60.
64. 'Ecumenical Vision': 432.

Chapter 16
'The Public Ministry of Holy Things'
The Christian Ministry

Because all Christian communities have office holders of some sort or another, ecclesiology and ministry go hand in hand.[1] Even if that were not the case conceptually, it was still true for Hooker in that a chief presenting issue that gave rise to the *Laws of Ecclesiastical Polity* was the kind of ministry serving the established church and its people. In his notes to the sixth book of the *Laws*,[2] George Cranmer pointed out to Hooker that, in his opinion, 'this question of lay elders and the next of bishops are the most essential points of all this controversy.'[3] Whether Hooker viewed those contentious issues of ministry as 'the most essential points' or not, he devotes considerable space to the Christian ministry in the *Laws*.

In taking up the matter of Christian ministry Hooker was by no means breaking new ground. It had been a matter of increasingly fierce debate from the time of the Marprelate tracts onwards, and despite harsh repressive measures under the successive archiepiscopal regimes the controversy had not abated. It may indeed be the case that the hardening of non-conformist views regarding the Genevan models of church and ministry – claims that moved such matters from the sphere of the 'indifferent' to that of 'divine right' – forced a comparable counter-move by the establishment. That controversial need, coupled with more evidence of ancient Christian practice through the expansion of available patristic sources, emboldened establishment divines to espouse a more intense and assured advocacy of episcopacy and the received array of ministries that accompanied it.[4] Hooker can be seen as part of that trend.

Still, the treatment of Christian ministry in the *Laws* is different. The most obvious difference lies in the fact that Hooker's treatment of Christian ministry comes within a wide compass of 'polity' generously defined. While an array of historical and liturgical sources support his argument,[5] Hooker's real interest is to locate and justify his vision of

---

1. Dulles, *Models*, p. 151.
2. The text actually comprises notes on books VI and VII; see Keble's edition, III, pp., 109-130.
3. *Ibid.* p. 125.
4. Loyer, II, p. 625.
5. The sort of evidence, that is, that appeared in works like his friend Saravia's *De Diversis Gradibus Ministrorum* (*On the Various Levels of Ministry*).

the Christian ministry within the bedrock of the *Laws*' fundamental concerns. For just that reason, I think, the treatment of Christian ministry does not come all at once. We are helpfully reminded that the broad shape of Hooker's view is laid out toward the end of his treatment of worship and sacraments in Book V, and that only then does Hooker move, in the subsequent 'books on power,'[6] to specific concerns relating to presbyteral spiritual jurisdiction and episcopacy in Books VI and VII respectively.[7]

The approach of this chapter reflects something of that order. First we will consider ministry in general, highlighting three aspects that inform Hooker's understanding. Then we will consider, first, episcopacy, and, second, the presbyterate, drawing attention to elements in Hooker's theology of ministry that the discussion of each of them throws up.

Ministry in General

Hooker's treatment of the Christian ministry must be unique in its point of departure. As we might expect, Hooker's teleological approach leads him to begin his consideration with the 'end' or 'scope' of ministry. Here, though, is the surprise: Hooker lays the foundation for his consideration low and wide, as low as earth itself and as wide as human nature and the nature of civil society.

Ministry's Roots in Nature

Reprising arguments we encountered in Book I, Hooker reminds us that as individuals, as well as in groups such as civil society, human beings seek happiness. He reminds us too that as happiness is twofold, so natural beatitude through 'sound and sincere virtues' is supported by religious belief as the wellspring of 'full joy and felicity'.[8] In such an account what we would call 'secular' concerns such as peace and prosperity, as well as most other aspects of social and political good, depend not just on religion but on *true* religion. Such blessings 'attend as handmaids upon religion'.[9]

For Hooker it is also axiomatic that religion requires a 'spiritual ministry' if it is to exercise its role in the pursuit of both temporal and eternal happiness. Such a ministry is essential in the work of religion in binding all together, natural as well as supernatural, in the service of the attainment of beatitude.[10] Hooker could easily declare, if it were not virtually self-evident,

---

6. That is, Books VI, VII and VIII.
7. See Loyer, II, pp. 597-8.
8. V, lxxxvi, 1 [II, p. 444].
9. *Ibid.* [II, p. 445].
10. '*Religio*' and the verb '*religo*' derive from a verb root to 'bind together'.

how all things which are of God he hath by wonderful art and wisdom sodered as it were together with the glue of mutual assistance, appointing the lowest to receive from the nearest to themselves what the influence of the highest yieldeth.

Then the work of both church and ministry begin, so that
the Church being the most absolute of all his works was in reason to be also ordered with like harmony, that what he worketh might no less in grace than in nature be effected by hands and instruments duly subordinated unto the power of his Spirit.[11]

So the Christian ministry labours for both earthly and heavenly beatitude.

A Divine Origin

Still, Hooker is clear that Christian ministry – the role of those entrusted with public performance of 'divine duties' in the church – has a divine origin. 'The ministry of things divine is a function which as God did himself institute, so neither may men undertake the same but by authority and power given them in lawful manner.'[12] The authority that ministry carries, whether it be transmitted 'immediately' by God or 'as the Church in his name investeth', is the same.[13]

The conveyance of that authority is through ordination. Hooker does not call it a sacrament since it does not fulfil the strict criteria that, as we have seen, he lays down for such nomenclature. Hooker is nonetheless clear that a charism is communicated, 'a gracious donation which the Spirit of God doth bestow', that provides perpetual 'assistance, aid, countenance and support' in the duties of ministry.[14] If it is not a sacrament in Hooker's strict sense, it is nonetheless a full-blown channel of grace. Thus the grace that is the power of ministry is, in Hooker's view, legitimately termed 'a kind of mark or character' and, in accord with the scholastic tradition, is 'indelible'.[15] On that account Hooker criticises the non-conformist insistence that every ordained person be 'tied to some certain parish', as though the exercise of the charism were place – or congregation – specific. With awareness of the gradual evolution of something like the parish system, Hooker cannot accommodate the non-conformist view to apostolic institution or practice. In origin and early practice the cure of souls was, as he reads the evidence, 'a charge in common', so that the power conveyed in ordination must likewise be not just indelible and perpetual but general in extent.[16]

---

11. V, lxxvi, 9 [II, p. 454].

12. V, lxxvii, 1 [II, p. 455].

13. *Ibid.*

14. V, lxxvii, 8 [II, p. 462]; Thornton is right to say that Hooker views ordination as a channel of grace with 'a sacramental function analogous to that of Baptism and the Eucharist' (*Hooker*, p. 79).

15. V, lxxvii, 2 [II, p. 456].

16. V, lxxx, 2-3 [II, pp. 500-1].

Ministerial Mediation

In looking for a broad concept that brings together the various strands of Hooker's discussion of Christian ministry we can profitably use the term *intermediary*. It applies throughout Book V, so its relevance to ministry is part of its wider application to all that pertains to Christian worship. If the church at worship is the occasion when angelic powers mediate between God's descending grace and worshippers' rising aspirations – 'Angels intermingled as our associates' – [17], the ministry takes a central place in that exchange.

Two subordinate concepts are at work here: hierarchy, and instrumentalism. The hierarchical principle was cited at the start of this study as a principle in Hooker's conceptual world. It informs Hooker's understanding of the Christian ministry in that the ordained, public ministry performs a key role as a ligature between the natural and the supernatural, between nature and grace. Corneliu Simuţ captures Hooker's sense well when he explains that the ministry occupies a key position in the constant interaction between the transcendent God and the natural order.[18] We have seen how Hooker relies on Dionysius' hierarchical model of reality by which there is constant movement between its higher and lower orders.[19] Hierarchy, as we have stressed, has as its aim not separation but connection and (to use another key concept for Hooker) participation. The clergy are enmeshed in this hierarchical order in that, joined by the people around them as well as by the 'intermingling angels', they convey divine blessing to the people and offer worshippers' intercession to God.[20]

This very function within the hierarchical order implies the second concept, namely, instrumentalism. We can locate such instrumentalism within the operation of secondary causes which, we have seen, play a key part in effecting God's purposes; and we have encountered instrumentalism specifically in Hooker's sacramental theology, so it is bound to operate in the analogous sphere of holy orders. It follows too from Hooker's repeated insistence on the bestowal of ministerial grace for the duties of ministerial service. Hooker explains:

> Knowing therefore that when we take ordination we also receive the presence of the Holy Ghost, partly to guide, direct and strengthen us in all our ways, and partly to assume unto itself for the more authority those actions that appertain to our place and calling, can our ears admit such a speech uttered

17. V, xxv, 2 [II, 119]; Hooker is rendering a text from St John Chrysostom on 1 Cor. 11. 10. Paget's Law of Angels (p. 66).
18. 'Orders of Ministry', *CRH*, p. 405.
19. See chapter two.
20. The intercessory prayers were spoken by the minister according to the rubrics of the *Book of Common Prayer*.

in the reverend performance of that solemnity, or can we at any time renew the memory and enter into serious cogitation thereof but with much admiration and joy? Remove what these foolish words do imply, and what hath the ministry of God besides wherein to glory? Whereas now, forasmuch as the Holy Ghost which our Saviour in his first ordinations gave doth no less concur with spiritual vocations throughout all ages, than the Spirit which God derived from Moses to them that assisted him in his government did descend from them to their successors in like authority and place, we have for the least and meanest duties performed by virtue of ministerial power, that to dignify, grace and authorise them, which no other offices on earth can challenge. Whether we preach, baptise, communicate, condemn, give absolution, or whatsoever, as disposers of God's mysteries, our words, judgements, acts and deeds are not ours but the Holy Ghost's.[21]

A rich passage worth citing in full so as to appreciate the wider spiritual dynamics of ministerial order in which instrumentalism is the crown.

Perhaps the most important thing is to appreciate the place of such instrumentalism within the over-arching pattern of humankind's return to God. The clergy's duties in preaching and teaching, as 'disposers of God's mysteries' and leaders of worship, are necessary instruments in the conveyance of sanctifying grace by which, through the gifts of grace, humankind journeys to glory.[22]

The Minister: 'God's most beloved'

Peter Lake credits Hooker above all among his contemporaries with advancing the cause of a 'conformist clericalism'.[23] Certainly Hooker attaches to his high doctrine of Christian ministry a lofty standard for the minister himself. Hooker's consideration of the clerical *persona* is focused on its importance in the church's worship. As the 'scenic apparatus' of worship is an important contextual factor in the stirring of devotion and godly thoughts and desires, the attitude of the minister is even more influential. 'The authority of his place, the fervour of his zeal, the piety and gravity of his whole behaviour must needs exceedingly both grace and set forward the service he doth.'[24]

As the sacraments have by definition a 'mixed nature',[25] so does ordered

---

21. V, lxxvii, 8 [II, pp. 462-3].
22. Neelands, 'Grace', p. 335.
23. *Anglicans and Puritans?*, p. 214; see Lake's discussion of the ministry generally, pp. 213-25.
24. V, xxv, 3 [II, p. 119].
25. V, lvii, 2 [II, p. 256].

public ministry. Hooker is aware of the fact that while the bestowal of grace is real and powerful, ministers still labour under their natural limitations. God's grace, though, is not circumscribed by the weakness and failings of his 'most beloved' ministers. Baptismal grace, for instance, 'cometh by donation from God alone'; the officiant's authority gives no 'being' nor does it 'add force' to the rite's efficacy.[26] Weakness in the minister, as in all believers, is the basis for more assurance in the inalienable divine source of grace.[27]

Episcopacy

Episcopacy was a debated issue in Hooker's day for a variety of reasons. There was, for instance, the non-conformists' assault on the Church of England's episcopal structure based chiefly on their exegesis of New Testament texts, and their determination to place issues of polity in the sphere of the scripturally 'necessary'. As has already been said, comparable response was forthcoming from the conformist quarter.

However, another issue lurked beneath the heat and smoke of the Elizabethan controversy. Even before the Reformation, the still-intact western church had no fixed theology of episcopacy.[28] There was scope for development at least in theological articulation. Elizabethan apologists, often inspired by their continental reformed experiences during the Marian Exile, argued for a pastoral and evangelical model.

In the 1590s Hooker may well have looked critically at the net effect of that model with several decades to show for it.[29] It would be consistent with the complementarity of nature and grace, and with his view of religion as a principal pillar in the natural beatitude which civil society promotes, for Hooker to hold up the role of bishops in the deliberations and councils of the realm. He does so. Since the founding of the 'commonweal' (a notable word given the thrust of the argument) the threefold 'conjunction of states', monarch, nobility and people, has included in its second estate of nobility lords temporal *and* spiritual, 'nobility and prelacy being by this mean twined together'. '[H]ow can it possibly be avoided,' he wonders, 'but that the tearing away of the one must needs exceedingly weaken the other, and by consequent impair greatly the good of all?'[30] So, Hooker clearly intends to set episcopacy on a new footing that is both accountable to scripture and tradition, and apt to meet contemporary needs of both church and society.

---

26. V, lxii, 19 [II, p. 300].
27. V, lvii, 2 [II, 256].
28. See Loyer, II, pp. 626-7; Louis Bouyer 'Bishops in the Church: The Catholic Tradition', in Peter Moore, ed., *Bishops But What Kind?* (London, 1982), p. 25-38.
29. Lake argues that Hooker rejected that pastoral model in favour of a more governmental, counsellor of state model, a 'man of affairs' (*Anglicans and Puritans?*, p. 218).
30. VII, xviii, 10 [III, p. 272].

Imparity within a Single Ministry

In relation to the argument of the *Laws*, however, it was chiefly the non-conformist assertion of the parity of all Christian ministers that focused the case to be made for episcopacy. The plot of that debate has been charted before and we will not repeat it here.[31] Turning, rather, to the issue itself, we want to know how Hooker understands the imparity that he ascribes to ministerial order.

In keeping with his correlation of nature and grace, Hooker's first line of argument recalls the principle of hierarchy invoked earlier in the chapter. Nature, he argues, is intrinsically hierarchical so that it is natural and therefore reasonable that a hierarchical distinction between, say, bishops, presbyters and deacons characterises ministerial order.[32] On that natural basis ministerial 'imparity', or inequality, in church order can rise.

It is important to notice that Hooker's doctrine of ministry asserts imparity *within a single ministry*. (It is a line of argument that may owe something to Hooker's appreciation of hierarchy as a principle of connection rather than separation.) The New Testament word 'presbyter', Hooker argues, refers to the generic ministry within which differentiation existed by dominical institution: 'For of presbyters some were greater some less in power, and that by our Saviour's own appointment; the greater they which received fulness of spiritual power, the less they to whom less was granted.'[33]

That 'fulness of spiritual power' Hooker understands as the power to 'ordain' and 'consecrate'; in all other respects bishops share the same spiritual power that 'inferior presbyters' exercise.[34]

Confirmation, while not an exercise of superior spiritual power like ordination, normally pertains to episcopal dignity too. Hooker defends this as an expression of the chief spiritual authority which a bishop exercises over his flock, an expressive act especially when members of the flock have not been baptised by the bishop himself. In so praying for and blessing members of his spiritual family the bishop expresses his role of spiritual fatherhood over those under his charge.[35]

In addition to their greater spiritual power bishops, possessing the fullness of the presbyterate, exercise the chief role of governance within the church. And this, Hooker insists, is as hard as it is necessary. Governance,

---

31. See the classic study by Norman Sykes, *Old Priests & New Presbyter* (Cambridge, 1956), especially chapters II and III. But see A. L. Peck's careful deconstruction of Sykes' argument regarding Hooker and others in *Anglicanism and Episcopacy* (London, 1958), pp. 17, 62-3.
32. Hooker says little about the diaconate, so it will not be treated in this chapter.
33. V, lxxviii, 4 [II, p. 473]. Does this not echo the relation between substance and person in his Trinitarian doctrine?
34. *Ibid*. This was a common medieval view.
35. V, lxvi, 1 [II, p. 337].

while not an expression of spiritual power in the strict sense, is the exercise of spiritual authority, and on that ground must be the careful study of a bishop. 'Yea a hard and toilsome thing it is for a bishop to know the things that belong unto a bishop', Hooker reflects. 'And for discharge of a bishop's office, to be well-minded is not enough, no not to be well learned also. Skill to instruct is a thing necessary, skill to govern much more necessary in a bishop.' Then, perhaps holding some of his episcopal contemporaries to the measure of an earlier era, he adds:

> It is not safe for the Church of Christ, when bishops learn what belongeth unto government, as empirics learn physic by the killing of the sick. Bishops were wont to be men of great learning in the laws both civil and of the Church; and while they were so, the wisest men in the land for counsel and governance were bishops.[36]

So, superiority through ordination and governance belonged to bishops' full presbyterate from their scriptural beginnings. A similar 'preeminence' was, argues Hooker, consistently taught by patristic writers like Augustine. 'First he excelled in latitude of the power of order, secondly in that kind of power which belongeth unto jurisdiction.'[37]

If, according to Hooker's account, episcopacy was no mere convenience devised over time for the effective running of the church, was it therefore *iure divino*, 'by divine right'? And if so, in what sense? Here we face a contested issue in the interpretation of Hooker's view of ecclesiastical polity.[38] Hooker, along with key figures defending the Elizabethan church establishment, views episcopacy as by divine right and of apostolic institution. 'The first Bishops in the Church of Christ were', in fact, 'his blessed Apostles',[39] and Hooker has no apparent difficulty squaring that view with St Jerome's troubling assertion about episcopacy arising from custom within the church.[40]

For all that, though, Hooker can still hold that episcopacy is not of perpetual necessity. Precisely as a matter of polity, episcopacy and the structure of ministerial imparity which it entails, falls in the category of divine laws which are not supernatural and so are open to change.[41] By

---

36. VII, xxiv, 5 [III, p. 306].

37. VII, vi, 1 [III, p. 168].

38. For an account of the various view points, see M. R. Sommerville's article 'Richard Hooker and his Contemporaries on Episcopacy: An Elizabethan Consensus', *Journal of Ecclesiastical History*, 35: 2 (1984): 177-87. I follow that interpretation of Hooker's views *vis-à-vis* his fellow supporters of the establishment.

39. VII, iv, 1 [III, p. 151].

40. On that interesting issue (which continued to arise in the debates about episcopacy) see VII, v, 8 [III, pp. 163-6].

41. Some of Hooker's contemporary defenders of episcopacy preferred to describe matters like episcopacy as 'regulation' rather than law; a noteworthy alternative in nomenclature; see Sommerville, 'Episcopacy': 181.

arguing thus we find a coherent line linking the arguments in Books III and VII, the former stressing the non-necessity and the discretion allowed in matters adiaphoral, with the latter putting to the fore episcopacy's scriptural and apostolic origin. In keeping with that approach, Hooker can espouse episcopacy not as a criterion for the *esse* of the church but for the *bene esse*, or perfection, of the church. In that sense Hooker cites with approval Cyprian's statement '*Ecclesia est in Episcopo*' ('the outward being of a church consisteth in the having of a bishop') and underlines its evidential and argumentative force by presenting it as 'the general received persuasion of the ancient Christian world'.[42] Indeed Hooker makes his case for episcopacy by a steady, correlated, triple appeal to reason, scripture, and tradition in such a way that each element of the argument is explicitly or implicitly in play.[43]

Presbyterate

It should not surprise us that when Hooker deals with the second order of ministry, those 'less in power', he prefers the term 'presbyter' to 'priest'.[44] Hooker in fact minimises issues of nomenclature: 'let them use what dialect they will, whether we call it a Priesthood, a Presbytership, or a Ministry it skillet not', while declaring the reason for his preference for 'presbyter':

> For what are they that embrace his Gospel but the sons of God? What are churches but his families? Seeing therefore we receive the adoption and state of sons by their ministry whom God hath chosen out for that purpose, seeing also that when we are the sons of God, our continuance is still under their care which were our progenitors, what better title could there be given to them than the reverend name of *Presbyters* or fatherly guides?[45]

The essence of presbyterate, Hooker affirms with patristic support, is 'the power of spiritual procreation'.[46] The procreational theme leads to a parental theme in that by the sacraments presbyters feed their families so that they may grow into their full spiritual stature.[47]

Building up the Body

In fact, the work of building up the 'visible mystical body' is central to Hooker's theology of the presbyterate. It is related to the twin concepts of order and jurisdiction as Hooker embraces and works with them in Books V and VI.

---

42. VII, v, 2 [III, p. 156].
43. Loyer makes this important point on behalf of Hooker's 'triple argument' (II, p. 630).
44. Simuț, I think, overstates Hooker's rejection of the term 'priest' ('Orders', *CRH*, p. 411).
45. V, lxxviii, 3 [II, p. 472].
46. *Ibid*. He cites Epiphanius' *Panarion*, or *Refutation of All the Heresies* (75.4).
47. V, lxii, 16 [II, p. 296].

What we may call the cultic function, tied to ministerial *order*, is primary. Its span is as wide as the privileges of blessing and intercession that constitute the 'office' of the presbyter, but its centre is the sacraments and chiefly the Eucharist.[48] Hooker is eloquent when he speaks of this privilege of ministerial order:

> The power of the ministry of God translateth out of darkness into glory, it raiseth men from the earth and bringeth God himself down from heaven, by blessing visible elements it maketh them invisible grace, it giveth daily the Holy Ghost, it hath to dispose of that flesh which was given for the life of the world and that blood which was poured out to redeem souls.[49]

We should notice in that passage how Hooker makes no mention of sacrifice. Perhaps in order to avoid any Roman Catholic connotations he is silent. While he is willing to make general links between the Eucharist and Christ's sacrifice, Hooker does not at any point take up that theme or the related theme of offering; nor does he apply them to the cultic office of the presbyter.[50]

Nevertheless, his sense of the link between presbyteral ministry and the Eucharist is rich. This ordered spiritual power is over 'that natural body which is himself', by which Hooker means the sacramental Body of Christ. In speaking thus he takes inspiration from Jerome's description of the eucharistic 'work' of persists and bishops 'which antiquity doth call', Hooker accurately renders, 'the making of Christ's body'.[51]

Importantly, though, Hooker will not disconnect that sacramental 'making of Christ's body' from the building up of the ecclesial body. Indeed, they cannot be separated since the logic of the Eucharist is that the sacramental body is given *in order to* build up the ecclesial body. That is why Hooker speaks of the 'natural body' of Christ – he means here his sacramental body – 'knitting' together his own body with the mystical body, the 'society of souls'. Both bodies together constitute the ecclesial body in its full reality.

It follows, then, that the cultic function of presbyters implies the complementary function of pastoral guidance. The building up of the 'society of souls' is another way to describe the range of pastoral duties for which presbyters are ordered. In this Hooker sees the essential link

---

48. V, xxv, 4 [II, p. 120].
49. V, lxxvii, 1 [II, p. 456].
50. See Stevenson, *Covenant of Grace*, pp. 30, 34.
51. *Ibid.* Jerome's phrase is '*Christi corpus . . . conficiunt*' ('make the Body of Christ'); that such is done '*sacro ore*' ('by the sacred mouth', or speech) of those '*qui apostolico gradu succedentes*' ('succeeding to the apostolic order') clearly refers to the act of eucharistic consecration (Epistle XIV, 8).

between spiritual order and spiritual jurisdiction. Precisely in that linkage lies the essence of Hooker's argument, as far as we can detect it, in the incomplete sixth book of the *Laws*.[52]

Repentance and Spiritual Jurisdiction

At the level of presenting issues Book VI of the *Laws* argues against the devolution of presbyteral jurisdiction in matters of penitential disciple to congregational lay elders, as non-conformists advocated.[53] As a 'virtue' of grace repentance operates primarily in the 'internal forum' of the Christian soul. In taking inspiration from Aquinas in describing repentance as a virtue, Hooker also embraces the traditional understanding of the stages of repentance. Insofar as repentance involves a process that may begin with attrition but then must move to contrition, confession, and finally to satisfaction, spiritual jurisdiction applies to that 'internal forum'.[54]

Here Hooker protects the inalienable role of the presbyter as absolver and guide.[55] It is no small work to engender contrition in souls, that is, by educating reason and will so that it 'abhors' and 'shuns' what it previously had taken delight in. That, in fact, is central to the exercise of his spiritual jurisdiction. The key to absolution from sin is the penitent's contrition which, in the case of significant sin, then leads the penitent on to the subsequent stages of confession and satisfaction, all aspects of the ritualised side of repentance which Hooker views as instituted by Christ and practiced throughout the ancient church. In this Dean Kernan acutely observes how Hooker seems to place the Church of England at a 'midpoint' between ecclesial poles, with a medieval Catholic jurisdictional system expressing the magisterial Reformation's emphasis on justification by grace through faith.[56] It seems contradictory at first until we remember that for Hooker the virtue of faith is linked to hope and love, and that justification itself is authenticated in sanctification's 'faith working in love'.

---

52. See Lee Gibbs' article 'Richard Hooker's *Via Media* Doctrine of Repentance', *Harvard Theological Review*, 84: 1 (1991): 61-3 especially, where he discusses the shape of Book VI. In contrast, see Rudolph Almasy, 'Book VI and the "Tractate on Penance:" do they belong together?', *RHER*, pp. 263-83.
53. Hooker defines jurisdiction as the power to command and judge according to law; spiritual jurisdiction is that same power in spiritual affairs according to spiritual laws; so Dean Kernan in his essay 'Jurisdiction and the Keys', *CRH* p. 435.
54. On the components of the traditional western theology of repentance see Gibbs, 'Repentance': 66-7.
55. See Gibbs' essay 'Hooker and Andrewes on Priestly Absolution', *SRH*, pp. 261-74.
56. 'Jurisdiction', *CRH*, p. 479.

The Return to God

In his study of Hooker Neelands points out that in the foundational structure of *exitus* and *reditus*, journey from God and return to God, the Christian ministry plays a pivotal role. We saw as we began this chapter that in Hooker's account the very natural desire for happiness looks for a ministry that supports the means of natural beatitude even as it offers the means, and points the way toward, supernatural beatitude. 'Ministry', Neelands explains, 'takes its place as a moment' – and we should add cause or 'instrument' – in humankind's movement of return to God through grace.'[57]

In that we see how Hooker has adroitly moored his doctrine of ministry in both nature and grace. Equally, we can see how, amid debates about polity, sacraments, and ministry Hooker was able to use the controversial occasion to integrate the meaning and purpose of 'the public ministry of holy things'[58] into his vision of the visible mystical body of Christ on its spiritual journey to the homeland of the blessed Trinity.

---

57. 'Grace', p. 335.
58. V, lxxvi, 1 [II, p. 444].

Chapter 17
'The Laws by Which We Live'
Political Theology

Given the canvass painted so far, it would be extraordinary if Hooker's theological brush did not at least sketch views on what today we would call political theology, that is, in Hooker's context, reflection on the relation of church, state and the exercise of political power. Indeed, even if Hooker were disinclined in that direction, consideration of the connections between Christian faith and life, society and civil power and laws was pressed upon him by his context as well as by apologetic pressure.[1] The overview of Hooker's life at the start of this study indicates why that was so.

In fact, Hooker was keenly interested in issues of power and law both theoretically and practically. Part of that interest surely was to support a civil order that was felt to be fragile – hence claims of Hooker's Erastianism.[2] But in Hooker's case there is far more to it.[3] The system of laws that Hooker describes in Book I includes the positive laws of communities. Insofar as the first book's conceptualisation of laws grounds the entire exposition of the *Laws* Hooker was bound to respond to the culture of complaint and challenge against the Church of England in its established guise with a rationale that had the power to convince. Indeed, if Stephen McGrade is right, Hooker's political theology even seeks to move the Elizabethan *status quo* on in important respects, and in so doing to show why non-conformist and Roman Catholic critiques had a positive stake in it.[4] Hooker is therefore justly described as the philosopher of the 'politic society'.[5] But Hooker's motivations were not merely metaphysical,

1. Richard Helgerson, for instance, argues that Hooker's defence was part of 'a large and deliberate movement of reaction and repression led by Archbishop Whitgift' (*Forms of Nationhood: The Elizabethan Writing of England* [Chicago, 1992], p. 272); but Shuger sees Hooker writing more independently without strict partisan alliance; hence the 'ideologically diverse' audience that read the *Laws* ('Society supernatural', p. 117).

2. Morris, 'Introduction', p. xii.

3. One of the strength's of Loyer's analysis of Hooker is his sensitivity to the context of legal theory and practice for Hooker; see his 'Contrat Social et Consentement chez Richard Hooker', *Revue de Sciences philosophiques et théologiques*, 59 (1973): 369-98.

4. So he argues at points in his 'Introduction to Book VIII', *FLE*, VI: I, pp. 337-83; see in particular p. 378.

5. The phrase is that of W. D. J. Cargill Thompson in his essay 'The Philosopher of the "Politic Society": Richard Hooker as a Political Thinker', pp. 3-76.

and he was not simply concerned with plotting a coherent theoretical course between the foundations of Book I and their expression in the so-called 'books on power'. As the Preface to the *Laws* makes clear, Hooker was sharply aware of the historical evolution and context of the views that eventually provoked non-conformist criticism of the established church's posture *vis-à-vis* the crown and what we would call the 'state'. In other words, Hooker was aware that, as Rowan Williams puts it, 'communities of religious meaning do not live in a timeless world of ideas and vision; they have political and structural histories, and their relation to the sacred is invariably bound up with ways in which power and control are exercised'.[6] Hooker' political theology recognises this and works in terms of it.

It is all the more frustrating, therefore, that the tortuous publishing history and incomplete form of Book VIII, devoted to 'the power of Ecclesiastical Dominion or Supreme Authority', have complicated the book's status and analysis.[7] This chapter will not wade into those contested waters. Instead we will take up Book VIII's nine chapters, the last of the three so-called 'books on power' and 'capstone' of the *Laws*,[8] as from Hooker's hand, and will explore the theological strands in Hooker's argument as he applies his principles to his vision of the Elizabethan settlement of church and state.[9] Yet just on account of the inter-relation of the books of the *Laws*, we will need to glance back at Books I and V as well to appreciate their out-workings in Book VIII.[10]

Hooker's 'final persuasion', clearly set down in his Preface to the *Laws*, is this: 'Surely the present form of church-government which the laws of this land have established is such, as no law of God nor reason of man hath hitherto been alleged of force sufficient to prove they do ill'.[11] Yet if the non-conformists' case left much still to be said, so did that of the conformists. In defending Elizabeth's settlement of 1559 in the course of the Admonition controversy Whitgift, for instance, had asserted the Queen's royal authority in 'indifferent' church affairs without explaining how monarch, political power and church were connected.[12] Hooker's

---

6. *Theology*, p. 98.

7. On these questions see the introduction to Book VIII cited in note 4 above.

8. So McGrade describes it ('Book VIII', p. 337).

9. We should recall Hooker's own insistence in Book I: 'I have endeavoured throughout the body of this whole discourse, that every former part might give strength unto all that follow, and every later bring some light unto all before' (I, i, 2 [I, p. 199]).

10. Aspects of these concerns appear as well, for instance, in the fragmentary 'Sermon on Civil Obedience' (VIII, App. 1 [III, pp. 456-60]).

11. I, 2 [I, p. 127]. It is important to note the limitation of Hooker's claim; 'His avowed intent was only to show that there was "great reason" to observe the ecclesiastical laws of the land and "no necessity" to impugn them (Preface, 7.1)' (A. S. McGrade, ed., *Hooker Of the Laws of Ecclesiastical Polity* [Cambridge, 1989], p. xxx).

12. McGrade, 'Book VIII', p. 347.

Book VIII seeks to fill that gap. In this chapter, then, we will explore how Hooker legitimates the established church's relation to the nation, its laws and its monarch on the basis of revelation and reason.

The Origins of Society and of Polity

In keeping with his approach throughout, Hooker's political theology is firmly grounded in nature and reason. In his view of the origin of human society in chapter one of Book VIII Hooker embraces the received tradition of interpretation; however, he is deft in choosing and organising traditional insights to fit his purpose.[13] Clear from the start is Hooker's debt to Aristotle and, to a lesser extent, to his pre-eminent Christian interpreter, Aquinas.[14] In Book I Hooker follows Aristotle's concept of politics as an intentional association for the sake of living well: 'politic society' arises naturally out of humans' need for their material good, that is, the practicalities required for life 'fit for the dignity of man'.[15] For that reason the 'good life' is by practical necessity a social one; indeed, our 'social instinct'[16] includes a desire for the 'good life'. According to Aristotle and Hooker, that 'good life' is not satisfied merely by the corporate provision of material goods. It needs to enlist people's intellectual and moral capacities. Through those comes the formation of a particular character (in Greek *ethos*) in its members by means of the practice of virtue, a 'perfection' excelling mere material provision in a community striving for the 'good life'.[17] To knowledge and virtue 'belongeth the law of moral and civil perfection'.[18]

Of course, writing in the tradition of Christian Aristotelianism as developed by Aquinas, Hookers knows too that, as important as natural virtue and perfection are, the human person also has a capacity for supernatural virtue and perfection through the exercise of spiritual life and the appropriation of grace. The 'good life' in a Christian society, therefore, involves the provision first of material needs, then of means of formation in natural moral and civic goods, and finally the means

13. So says Loyer, I, p. 269.
14. Moore argues that Hooker is part of a Renaissance neo-Aristotelian revival, and notes the preponderance of citations from Aristotle in laying the groundwork of his political theory in Book I ('Recycling Aristotle: The Sovereignty Theory of Richard Hooker', *History of Political Thought*, XIV: 3 [1993]: 347-8, 350).
15. McGrade, *Hooker*, p. xxvii; I, x, 1 [I, p. 239]; the inspiration is chiefly from the *Nicomachean Ethics*.
16. Loyer's excellent phrase (I, p. 270); note too the teleological aspect of this stress on human 'dignity' as intrinsic end or purpose of the social instinct.
17. F. J. Shirley is helpful on this aspect of Hooker's Aristotelianism (*Richard Hooker and Contemporary Political Ideas* [London, 1949], p. 93).
18. I, xi, 4 [I, p. 257].

to access supernatural, engraced virtues tending toward the *summum bonum*, or highest good, participation in God – a 'triple perfection' that is by necessity a social endeavour and experience.[19]

Staying with the natural foundation of that 'triple perfection', the argument in Book I follows Aristotle's line of thought in two ways. First, Hooker argues that social groups naturally devise 'an order expressly or secretly agreed upon touching the manner of their union in living together.'[20] There lies the origin of social order, including the source of power and the exercise of governance, what Hooker means by 'polity', the 'order of things and persons in public societies'.[21] So polity is both natural and good. Second, whereas the first impulse toward social union expresses a natural law within humankind, the devising of an actual polity through an agreement or social compact (to use a somewhat technical phrase) is the deliberative consequence of a consensual decision by the whole group.

We can now see that societies and the polities by which they order themselves derive from two kinds of laws working together. On the one hand, natural law inclines toward fellowship aiming toward the 'good life'; on the other, a group's positive, human laws give form to their concrete 'union together' in pursuit of their 'good'.

In addition to Aristotle's influence, however, there is another strand of thought that accounts for the necessary role of polity and positive law. Church fathers such as Irenaeus and Augustine located the motivation for polity, with its elements of law, governance and sanction, in the consequences of humankind's fall. That more cynical explanation, tied to notions of 'depravity', influences Hooker too.[22] On balance, though, the overall stress of the political theory in Book I is on political association as a blessing that enables the pursuit of humankind's triple perfection.

Consent, Polity and Power

Beyond Aristotle, Augustine and Aquinas, other more proximate sources affected Hooker's political theory. The ideas of the Renaissance Italian Marsiglio of Padua, for instance, were especially important as Hooker nuanced his understanding of the source and exercise of political power. The issue of political 'contract' between ruler and ruled was a lively and relevant topic during the period of the emergence of nation-states throughout Europe in the wake of the demise of the Holy Roman Empire

---

19. Aristotle contended, and Aquinas repeated, that 'the good of the people as a whole is more divine than that of one man' ('*Bonum gentis est divinius quam bonum unius hominis*') (from the *Summa contra Gentiles*, cited by Loyer, I, p. 271).
20. I, x, 1 [I, p. 239].
21. VIII, ii, 2 [III, p. 342].
22. Loyer, I, pp. 274-5. See Paget's Human laws or Laws Politic (p. 66).

and the ruptures of the Reformation. Under Marsiglio's influence, Hooker developed a theory not of contract but of *consent* in the relation between ruler and ruled.[23]

We have seen in Book I that for Hooker the form of polity that a group chooses is a self-determined act, an expression of positive law: '[A]ll public regiment of what kind soever seemeth evidently to have arisen from deliberate advice, consultation, and composition between men, judging it convenient and behoveful.'[24] This emphasis on consent in the formation of polity has two consequences key to the polemics in which the *Laws* was involved: the locus of sovereign power, and the constituents of the deliberative body. To the first point we will return shortly. The second point deserves further comment now, since it clarifies how Hooker views the actual operation of consent within a body politic.

Hooker is clear that, as with the discernment of theological truths, so in political decision-making, 'wise men' alone are responsible for framing the laws that give shape to a particular polity. There remains, however, a critical caveat: the *source* of the power to frame and give laws acceptation resides first and fundamentally in the 'whole politic society'.[25] Hooker puts it like this:

> That which we spake before concerning the power of government must here be applied unto the power of making laws whereby to govern; which power God hath over all: and by the natural law, whereunto he hath made all subject, the lawful power of making laws to command whole politic societies of men belongeth so properly unto the same entire societies, that for any prince or potentate of what kind soever upon earth to exercise the same of himself, and not either by express commission immediately and personally received from God, or else by authority derived at the first from their consent upon whose persons they impose laws, it is no better than mere tyranny.[26]

Those are hardly the words of a mere apologist for the Elizabethan political status quo;[27] still less are they a support to the creeping absolutism of the

---

23. Loyer, I, p. 285. McGrade contends that Marsiglio's was the only 'well-articulated' late-medieval theory of *lay* political supremacy ('Book VIII', p. 355).

24. I, x, 4 [I, p. 243].

25. I, x, 8 [I, p. 245].

26. *Ibid* [I, pp. 245-6].

27. Hence we must reject R. Eccleshall's view that Book VIII's argument was not a novel venture but mere window-dressing for a church co-opted into the state's authoritarian control ('Richard Hooker and the Peculiarities of the English: The Reception of the *Ecclesiastical Polity* in the Seventeenth and Eighteenth Centuries', *History of Political Thought*, 2 [1981]: 83). On Hooker's departure from the absolutist tendencies of conformist colleagues, see J. P. Sommerville, 'Richard Hooker, Hadrian Saravia, and the

Stuart age. So, it seems likely that Hooker was first in his formulation of consent as the historical and legal basis of civil power in England.[28] Stephen McGrade goes so far as to claim that, in Hooker's account, the crown's executive power in religious, as in all other affairs, is *directly dependent* on the consent of the community as given in Parliament.[29]

The 'Mixed' Subjects of Polity

It is relevant to the unfolding of Hooker's political theology to ask now: who are the subjects of the English polity? This is a key issue for Hooker as he brings his principles to bear on the particulars of England's civil and ecclesiastical polity which he wants to commend. It is clear in Book VIII that Hooker fashions a response to the criticisms of non-conformists and Roman Catholics alike. On both sides Hooker had detected a slip of judgment *vis-à-vis* the subjects of England's polity. His interest, therefore, is not to deny a difference but instead to clarify 'the kind of distinction' between commonwealth and church in the English context. 'In their opinion,' Hooker explains, thinking of non-conformists and Roman Catholics alike, 'the church and the commonwealth are corporations, not distinguished only in nature and definition, but in subsistence perpetually severed.'[30] That so-called dualist view regarded civil society and church each in itself as a 'perfect society' (*societas perfecta*), each possessing in itself all the components, powers and officers to fulfil its appointed end, and ever divided one from the other by 'walls of separation'.[31]

In contrast, Hooker advances an understanding of England's polity that is mixed.[32] In other words, England's two polities, civil and ecclesiastical, are inhabited by the same people; each polity, therefore, involves the same people expressing themselves in different modes of action and differently defined according to those modes. 'A church and commonwealth we grant are things in nature the one distinguished from the other', Hooker insists.[33] The theme of diversity in unity derived from the Trinitarian and

---

Advent of the Divine Right of Kings', *History of Political Thought*, IV: 2 (1983): 229-45.

28. And not, as Shirley claims, 'compact' (*Political Ideas*, p. 96).

29. *Hooker*, p. xxvii; he notes too how the Elizabethan Act of Supremacy, as distinct from the Henrician one, made the Queen supreme governor 'by the authority of this present Parliament' (*ibid.*).

30. VIII, i, 2 [III, pp. 328-9].

31. *Ibid.* [III, p. 330]. On mixed laws see Paget's Laws Politic (p. 66).

32. Hooker himself does not use the word; it was used instead by Hooker's friend and critic in his preparation of the *Laws*, Edwin Sandys; see his comments on Book VI where he speaks of various causes to be adjudicated as 'mixt' [III, p. 132].

33. VIII, i, 2 [VIII, p. 328].

Christological discourses in Books I and V inform Hooker's approach, which is at one and the same time 'dualist' and 'monist', that is, respectively affirming the differences between commonwealth and church *vis-à-vis* 'nature' and 'accidents', *and* affirming their indivisible union in the subjects who constitute the polity.[34]

The very notion of 'church', Hooker suggests, informed by the mystery of unity and diversity in God and in Christ, is defined in terms that promote this mixed character. 'With us [*viz.* the English] therefore,' he explains, 'the name of a Church importeth only a society of men, first united unto some public form of regiment, and secondly distinguished from other societies by the exercise of Christian religion.'[35] In one of the most famous passages in the *Laws* Hooker applies the notion of personal union to the English people generally:

> We hold, that seeing there is not any man of the Church of England but the same man is also a member of the commonwealth; nor any man a member of the commonwealth, which is not also a member of the Church of England; therefore as in a figure triangular the base doth differ from the sides thereof, and yet one and the selfsame line is both a base and also a side; a side simply, a base if it chance to be the bottom and underlie the rest: so, albeit properties and actions of one kind do cause the name of a commonwealth, qualities and functions of another sort the name of a Church to be given unto a multitude, yet one and the selfsame multitude may in such sort be both, and is so with us, that no person appertaining to the one can be denied to be also of the other.[36]

Various 'properties', 'accidents', 'qualities', 'actions', and 'natures' – Hooker uses all those terms, echoing Chalcedonian doctrine, to highlight distinguishing features of the civil and ecclesiastical spheres – subsist within one and the same population.

'The whole body of the realm'

Hooker supports the representative structures of the English commonwealth, Parliament's Lords and Commons, on the one hand, and the Convocations of the clergy, the 'ecclesiastical senate', on the other.[37] There are found the differentiated actions, accidents and natures that

---

34. Loyer points out the unavoidable tension in holding these two aspects together (II, p. 652).

35. VIII, i, 2 [III, p. 329].

36. *Ibid.* [III, p. 330]. The basic argument, though, is taken from Bp Stephen Gardiner's apology for the Henrician break, *De vera obedientia* (*On True Obedience*) of 1535.

37. VIII, v, 2 [III, p. 395]. Hooker 'stretches' the make-up of Parliament to include the Convocation of clergy (McGrade, *Hooker*, p. xxvii).

constitute the commonwealth. As hierarchies of representation giving voice to their respective constituencies, they, together with the sovereign, form the whole body of the realm. While Hooker shares a political thought that included the sovereign in a broad definition of 'parliament', the challenge was to explicate a meaningful relationship within that compass. So how was that relationship to be understood? Hooker draws upon various conceptual strands and sources to explicate the relation of the supreme governor to both the other estates of the realm and to the realm as a whole.

Head and Body

It is in the person of the monarch that the body of the realm has its head. What, then, is the relationship between the head and the body? Admittedly, Hooker is less interest in the language used to explain 'chiefty' and 'dominion' and more interested in the principle that a lay person might lay claim to such dominion in spiritual affairs. Still, Hooker's rebuttal to non-conformist and Roman Catholic critics had to take up the specific term 'head' as applied to the monarch. That discussion forms a considerable part of the most thoroughly theological part of Book VIII, its fourth chapter.[38]

Hooker makes use of scholastic discourse on polity where the notions of 'head' and 'body' commonly described the components of any society or realm, and he is emphatic that the monarch's title as 'head' is reconcilable with Christ's role both as head of the civil regiment *and* of the ecclesiastical regiment. 'The two regiments', Torrance Kirby explains, 'are invisibly unified in Christ, their source; they are visibly unified through the Royal Supremacy'.[39] There are distinctions in Hooker's explanation to which we will return below; here we should note Hooker's insistence that the monarch's headship is wholly derivative, and distinguished from Christ's own headship in 'order', 'measure' and 'kind'.[40] The monarch is an 'under and subordinate head of Christ's people'. At the same time, for Hooker the language of head and body highlights two important ideas in his world-view that we have noted before: hierarchy and unity. Through the monarch's relation to Parliament and Convocation head and body are knit together in mutual regard; indeed, through those representative houses the social hierarchy operates: 'the lowest be knit to the highest by that which being interjacent may cause each to cleave to the other, and so all to continue one'.[41]

---

38. Elizabeth had, of course, opted for the less offending title 'supreme *governor* of this realm' as a concession to critics early in her reign; but the content of her power in ecclesiastical affairs was to no degree lessened (Loyer, II, pp. 646-7).

39. *Richard Hooker's Doctrine of the Royal Supremacy* (Leiden, 1990), p. 113; see his chapter on Hooker's theology of the supremacy (pp. 92-125). Kirby credits this aspect of Hooker's critique of Cartwright's *Second Reply* to Whitgift to his Trinitarian theology in Book V.

40. VIII, iv, 5 [III, p. 373].

41. VIII, ii, 2 [III, p. 342].

Other Paradigms: Israel, Rome and Byzantium

While Hooker's argumentative context required him to justify the term 'head', he furthered his argument on behalf of the monarch's relation to the spirituality of the realm and dominion in ecclesiastical affairs with biblical examples and historical precedents.[42]

The precedent for a sovereign's exercise of dominion in spiritual affairs is, in Hooker's account, amply supplied by the sacred history of the monarchy and forms of government in ancient Israel.[43] No sooner does Hooker begin Book VIII than he remarks: 'It was not thought fit in the Jews' commonwealth, that the exercise of supremacy ecclesiastical should be denied unto him, to whom the exercise of chiefty civil did appertain'.[44] David, Asa, Jehoshaphat and Josiah fill the witness box on behalf of Hooker's case so that by the 'pattern' of that example 'the like power in causes ecclesiastical is by the laws of this realm annexed unto the crown'.[45] The principle of shared clerical and lay involvement in the affairs of the commonwealth was also exemplified in the Jewish Council of Seventy. That useful strand of evidence in Hooker's argument of Book VI has, alas, been lost; we can appreciate, though, how directly it fed into the argument that Hooker develops in his last book.

On the basis of both a fascination with Christian antiquity, and its imperial pretensions, Tudor apologists looked to Byzantium for inspiration and example. Hooker read Eusebius' *Life of Constantine*, the first Christian emperor, carefully and appreciatively.[46] He knew of the emperor's solicitude for the church, his involvement in many practical aspects of the church's life and doctrine, and his self-styled quasi-episcopal role outside the strictly canonical spheres of church life.[47] The Byzantines viewed their empire in terms of the salvific interaction of nature and grace of which Christ himself was the consummate expression; even that, though, was but a fulfilment of Old Testament prefigurations of the godly prince exercising

---

42. Thus Hooker invokes revelation and reason, grace and nature in support of his case, as we have come to expect throughout.

43. In this Hooker followed the lead of other defenders of the Elizabethan settlement; Hooker's use is perhaps less prominent, though still significant. Hooker is not arguing that a royal supremacy is the *only* biblically legitimate form of supreme power (Daniel Eppley, 'Royal Supremacy', *CRH*, p. 511).

44. VIII, i, 1 [III, p. 327].

45. VIII, i, 2 [III, p. 328].

46. See, for example, VII, xxii, 6 [III, p. 287].

47. See Eusebius' *Life of Constantine* IV, 23 (cited in *Laws* VIII, viii, 8 [III, p. 441]), where the emperor styles himself 'a bishop appointed by God over those outside [the church]'. Eusebius comments: 'In accordance with this saying, he exercised a bishop's supervision over all his subjects, and pressed them all, as far as lay in his power, to lead the godly life' (text in Averil Cameron and Stuart Hall, trans., *Life of Constantine* (Oxford, 1999) p. 161).

dominion in affairs sacred and secular alike.[48] The sovereign's solicitude for the 'purity', 'comeliness' and 'fervor' of the clergy, and by implication the whole institutional church, the *sacerdotium*, was necessary to sustain and further the well-being of *imperium*.[49] We should not suppose that any of this was lost on Hooker; it was solid ground on which to build.

The Christological Paradigm

It was, as Torrance Kirby has argued, the person and work of Christ above all that provided Hooker with a theological basis for the kind of 'dominion' in ecclesiastical affairs that he commends.[50] That is not surprising in view of Hooker's intention that former, general parts of the *Laws* contribute to later arguments. We have seen already how Book I set the stage for elements in Book VIII. Now we encounter the long reach of Book V where Hooker treated the doctrines of the Trinity and the Incarnation. There are two chief ways in which Hooker applies the orthodox doctrine of the person of Christ to his argument in this last book of the *Laws*.

Christ's Twofold Lordship

English non-conformists like Thomas Cartwright built upon Calvin's 'complaint' against the power of England's monarch in ecclesiastical affairs by distinguishing, and indeed separating, two forms of lordship.[51] In chapter four, perhaps Book VIII's key chapter, Hooker rehearses Cartwright's argument and refutes it. The argument at its simplest is this: Christ exercises two distinct lordships according to his two natures. As 'Son of Man', that is, in his humanity, he exercises an immediate lordship over the church; as 'Son of God', that is, as eternal Word, lordship applies to the kingdoms of the world. In consequence, whereas the clergy derive their authority from Christ as man, monarchs and magistrates derive authority from his divinity alone.[52]

---

48. For Old Testament fulfilment as a feature of Eusebius' theology of history as applied to Constantine, see Averil Cameron, *Christianity and the Rhetoric of Empire: the Development of Christian Discourse* Berkeley, USA, 1991), pp. 54-5.

49. A view Hooker espouses supported by another Byzantine source, Justinian's sixth-century legal *Code* (the terms here are taken from Hooker's Latin text of *Law 34 de Episcopali Auctoritate*). The sixth Novella, or supplement to the *Code*, drew the distinction equally between *imperium* and *sacerdotium* while regarding them as closely interdependent. The whole set of Justinian's legal documents constituted the *Corpus Juris Civilis* which widely influenced the western medieval canonical tradition; Hooker knew it well.

50. Hooker's treatment in Book VIII, he concludes, needs to be examined 'in the full light of his theological assumptions' (p. 126); for Kirby those assumptions are identified with magisterial Reformed doctrine.

51. For Hooker's citation of Calvin's criticism see VIII, iv. 8 [III, pp. 385-6].

52. I follow Loyer in this part of the exposition (II, pp. 653-4).

Hooker is unhappy with that distinction, even confusion; it is based, he thinks, on a faulty Christology.[53] Earlier in Book VIII Hooker pointed out the 'error of personal separation' afflicting his non-conformist critics; now he identifies that same error at the heart of their political theology.[54] It divides the work of Christ by short-changing the personal union. The upshot, according to Hooker, is a sharp divide between the officers and the authority in church and commonwealth.

In rejoinder, Hooker uses the Johannine Christological theme of the 'Word', or *Logos*, to stress the unified and unifying person and work of Christ. 'For there is no necessity', he says, 'that all things spoken of Christ should agree unto him *either* as God, *or else* as man; but some things as he is the consubstantial Word of God, some things as he is that Word incarnate.' And so, bringing that reasoning to the issue at hand: 'The works of supreme dominion which have been since the first beginning wrought by the power of the Son of God [i.e. the consubstantial Word], are now most truly and properly the works of the Son of man [i.e. the incarnate Word]: the Word made flesh doth sit for ever, and reign as sovereign Lord over all.'[55]

Hooker's use of the term '*logos*' places Christ at the centre of God's creative and redemptive work. As a result, Christ's lordship applies as much to the natural sphere of lordship over commonwealths – what Cartwright, for instance, would ascribe to God directly – as it does to the gracious and redemptive sphere of lordship within the church. By implication, the lordship or dominion that derives from Christ cannot in principle be restrained to this sphere or that. Specifically, then, there can be no *a priori* exclusion of the exercise of derivative lordship from the ecclesiastical sphere.

Christ's Personal Union

Such an argument as applied to church and commonwealth is, in Hooker's view, wholly consistent with the Chalcedonian doctrine of two natures in one person. Just as the 'error of personal separation' is disallowed as applied to the subjects of polity generally, since '[t]he Church and the commonwealth . . . are personally one society', all the more so in the case of the monarch. In the monarch above all temporality and spirituality are related in a personal union.[56]

It is a question, then, according to Hooker's line of thought, whether commonwealth and church cannot be segregated on the basis of human

53. And by implication, Kirby argues, a false ecclesiology where the invisible and visible realms and regiments are conflated (*Royal Supremacy*, pp. 122-3).
54. VIII, i, 4 [III, p. 332].
55. VIII, iv, 6 [III, p. 376]; emphases in the first quotation are mine.
56. Or, to use Edwin Sandys language in his notes on the sixth book, the prince too is 'a mixt person' [III, p. 132].

and divine, nature and grace, or the 'two kingdoms' of Luther and Calvin.[57] While in nature distinct, the two coinhere and, in keeping with Hooker's theology of the grace of unction, actually interpenetrate in some respects. Just as grasping the exact inter-relation of human and divine in Christ and of nature and grace in the Christian involves ambiguities *vis-à-vis* their points of contact and influence, so there are ambiguities in the relation of temporality and spirituality. This tension is an unavoidable feature of the structure of Hooker's political theology because it is unavoidable in Christology too.

The Exercise of Derived Lordship: Two Necessary Distinctions

To make his case on behalf of the crown's involvement in ecclesiastical affairs, Hooker invokes two sets of distinctions. First, he distinguishes invisible and visible components in the exercise of lordship; second, he clarifies the use of two key terms, 'dominion' and 'jurisdiction'.

Invisible and Visible

In a critical part of chapter four of Book VIII, where Hooker nuances his understanding of Christ's headship, he describes the constituents of 'spiritual regiment'. '[W]e make the spiritual regiment of Christ', Hooker explains, ' to be generally that whereby his Church is ruled and governed in things spiritual.'[58] He then distinguishes within spiritual regiment 'two distinct kinds'. First and foremost there is 'one invisibly exercised by Christ himself in his own person'. Hooker explains this as the inward working of the Spirit that marks and seals believers.[59] There is then a second, visible, and outward order 'administered by them whom Christ doth allow to be the rulers and guiders of his Church'. This second sphere of spiritual regiment concerns the means of grace flowing into the church and the world. It involves, says Hooker, a power of administration concerned with word, sacraments and discipline, 'or whatsoever be the mean whereby it [grace] floweth'.[60]

---

57. Kirby's study rightly highlights, as I have indicated, the centrality of Christology in Hooker's argument in Book VIII. However, his claim that Hooker simply relies on the magisterial Reformers' doctrine of the 'two kingdoms', with its sharp divide between nature and grace (depraved and justified), seems to me to be unconvincing and unnecessary. What is missing in his account based on Reformed doctrine, it seems to me, is the 'grace of unction' by which there is an overcoming of the strict boundary between nature and grace and, most especially, depraved and sanctified.
58. VIII, iv, 10 [III, p. 389].
59. In this regard Christ is uniquely 'head' as the 'fountain' and source. Hooker's language here is consistent with his sacramental discourse in Book V where he disallows the sacramental elements to be in themselves, that is, in their natures, *sources* of grace; rather, they are means or instruments.
60. *Ibid*. This distinction is the basis of Kirby's appeal to the Reformer's 'two kingdoms' dichotomy.

Hooker then distinguishes in this outward category of spiritual regiment two powers of administration. First, there is the power of order. Can it really be viewed as part of Christ's spiritual regiment? Yes, insists Hooker. While admittedly this power is not exercised inwardly and invisibly by Christ 'in his own person', that is, without mediation, yet it is 'both Spiritual and His [i.e. Christ's]' since the outward forms of this administration are both instituted by Christ and concern the working of his Spirit.[61]

To that first and chief element of spiritual regiment which is external and visible Hooker adds a second, namely the 'power of dominion'[62] This too is spiritual 'in regard of the matter about which it dealeth' and is Christ's, even though, as in the power of order, Christ does not administer this external dominion 'in his own person'. Whereas the power of order is the inalienable right and responsibility of the clergy, the power of dominion is a right and responsibility shared by the monarch.[63]

'Jurisdiction' and 'Dominion'

It is important to grasp that amid the broad philosophical brush strokes of Book VIII some qualification of terminology is going on. Hooker, for instance, is careful to distinguish the terms 'dominion' and 'jurisdiction' and in so doing both clarifies inherited ambiguities of usage and gives subtlety to understanding the monarch's derived lordship in relation to spiritual affairs.[64] In contrast to interchangeable applications of words like authority, superiority and jurisdiction in discussions of these matters from the era of Henrician reform, Hooker's treatment through the three 'books on power' distinguishes ministerial 'jurisdiction', treated in Books VI and VII,[65] from supreme royal 'ecclesiastical *dominion*' addressed in Book VIII.

Having begun Book VIII by declaring how '[i]t was not thought fit in the Jews' commonwealth, that the exercise of supremacy ecclesiastical should be denied unto him, to whom the chiefty of dominion did pertain',[66] Hooker argues that in some sense the monarch *does* exercise jurisdiction in spiritual affairs. A critical clarification comes chapters later from an interpretation of Hebrews 5.1. With reference to the grant of power to the

---

61. *Ibid.* See Paget's Laws made by a Body Politic 'which is civilly united' (p. 67).
62. VIII, iv, 10 [III, pp. 389-90]; 'which is indeed the point of this controversy'.
63. Loyer conveniently lays this scheme out (II, pp. 935-6; note 17).
64. See George Cranmer's and Edwyn Sandys' clarification of these terms in their notes on Hooker's Book VI, App. [III, pp. 113, 133]; Loyer's discussion (II, pp. 649-51; note 11 (pp. 934-5) points up the ambiguities inherited from the Henrician era).
65. Book VI on episcopacy concerns a specific form of ministerial jurisdiction, which Hooker terms 'dignity'.
66. VIII, i, 1 [III, p. 327].

high-priest 'in things pertaining to God', Hooker distinguishes the powers of order not just 'given' but 'restrained unto priests only' (e.g. offering gifts and sacrifices for sins; that is, pastoral, liturgical and sacramental), from the 'power of jurisdiction and ruling authority' given to the clergy 'but not them alone'.[67]

An important final distinction is added in the same part of Book VIII. The monarch's exercise of jurisdiction in spiritual affairs is 'in far other sort than such as have ordinary spiritual power'; it is qualitatively different, that is, from the power of order and of jurisdiction canonically given to the clergy.[68]

So Hooker, with the help of Cranmer and Sandys, establishes a general distinction between order, jurisdiction and dominion. A threefold classification is thereby constructed. First, the power of order pertains to the clergy alone; second, the power of ordinary spiritual jurisdiction belongs to the clergy, and in restricted, non-ordinary forms to lay people beginning with the monarch; thirdly, the power of dominion in spiritual affairs belongs exclusively to the monarch.

Limitations on the Exercise of 'spiritual dominion'

The discussion above points to limitations in the exercise of the royal prerogative. In chapter two of Book VIII Hooker lays out three sources of limitation on the sovereign's exercise of 'spiritual dominion':God, law and the body politic.[69]

We have already encountered the first limitation in Hooker's discussion of headship: the monarch's headship is derived, in relation to the absolute headship of Christ. When defenders of the established Church say, therefore, that the monarch has 'spiritual dominion' or 'supreme power in ecclesiastical affairs' it is understood that such supremacy is under God.[70] Hooker, McGrade reminds us, stops far short of divinising the basis and the nature of royal authority.[71]

'Spiritual dominion' is, second, limited by law. This is the basis for what

67. VIII, viii, 6 [III, pp. 436]; emphasis mine.
68. Elizabeth's royal injunctions had, in fact, prohibited her subjects from interpreting the Oath of Allegiance by the clergy to imply that the crown might challenge authority and power of ministry in divine offices of the Church (McGrade, 'Book VIII', p. 341, note 7).
69. This is one point where the text of the FLE clarifies Hooker's argument in an important way. Its shortening of chapter 2 to sections 1-3 and the movement of the remaining sections to chapter 3 means that Hooker's second chapter is a focused discussion of the factors limiting spiritual dominion, a presentation somewhat obscured in the longer format of chapter 2 in the Keble edition; see McGrade's discussion, 'Book VIII', pp. 360-75.
70. 'For what man is there so brain-sick, as not to except in such speeches God himself, the King of all the kings of the earth?' (VIII, ii, 3 [III, p. 342].
71. 'Book VIII', p. 361.

some describe as Hooker's 'constitutionalism', that is, his bounding all authority by the rule of law.[72] Here Hooker stands in a formidable line of English legal theorists. When he asks 'where the law doth give him [*viz.* the monarch] dominion, who doubteth but that the king who received it must hold it of and under the law?' he stands on the axiom of Henry Bracton: 'Let the king grant to the law what the law has granted to him, namely power and dominion'. So, in keeping with these first two limitations, the monarch is 'under God and under law'.[73] 'Where the king doth guide the state, and the law the king, that commonwealth is like an harp or melodious instrument, the strings whereof are tuned and handled all by one, following as laws the rules and canons of musical science.'[74] In so limiting royal authority by law – 'an indifferent rule' – Hooker stood alone among his fellow defenders of the establishment.[75]

The third source of limitation is the community itself. Again, chapter two includes a key passage justifying the view 'that kings, even inheritors, do hold their right to the power of dominion, with dependency upon the body politic as a whole over which they rule as kings'.[76] Behind that assertion stands the legal maxim that the king is 'greater than any individual but less than the whole entire body'.[77] It is important to note, however, that Hooker does not mean by this that the monarch serves at the recurrent will of the body politic through time: 'the cause of dependency is in that *first original conveyance*, when power was derived by the whole into one'.[78] The enduring factor is the king's dependence on the laws and the structures of polity that fashion and assess the mind of the whole.[79]

With those constraints in mind, then, Hooker defines the power of spiritual dominion in causes ecclesiastical as 'that ruling authority, which neither any foreign state, nor yet any part of that politic body at home, wherein the same is established, can lawfully overrule'.[80]

Royal Prerogatives

In chapters four to nine of Book VIII Hooker describes and defends five particular prerogatives attached to the crown in relation to ecclesiastical affairs. The fourth chapter, treating the claim of 'headship' and the role

---

72. *Ibid.*
73. VIII, ii, 3 [III, p. 342]: "*Attribuat rex legi, quod lex attribuit ei, potestatem et dominium*'; '*sub Deo et lege*' (from his *de Leg. Angl.* I.8).
74. VIII, ii, 12 [III, p. 352].
75. So McGrade contends, 'Book VIII', pp. 364-5.
76. VIII, ii, 9 [III, p. 349].
77. 'The king', says Hooker, 'is "*major singulis, universis minor*"' (VIII, ii, 7 [III, p. 347]).
78. VIII, ii, 9 [III, p. 349]; emphasis mine.
79. 'Dependence' is a not wholly satisfactory word; in Hooker's thinking it does not mean subservience; the monarch is, rather, an active participate in the expression and action of the corporate mind.
80. VIII, ii, 3 [III, p. 343].

as 'supreme governor', has already been discussed and forms a bridge from the generalities of the first three chapters to those that follow. The succeeding chapters each treat one of the five specific prerogatives.

Chapter five, taking up the first such prerogative, concerns the calling of ecclesiastical councils for which, again as we have seen, Constantinian imperial examples provided important precedents. In the Elizabethan church this related chiefly to the calling and dissolving of the Convocations of the clergy. The second prerogative concerns the making of ecclesiastical laws.[81] The third involves the 'making of ecclesiastical governors', that is, the process of episcopal election and consecration, and granting of sees to bishops. The fourth prerogative concerns the monarch's involvement in the ecclesiastical courts and their judgments. Hooker draws here an important distinction between 'ordinary' judges, namely 'Ordinaries' or bishops, and 'commissionary' judges, who may be lay persons.[82] Beyond that, he wants to defend the role of the monarch's delegates, or commissionary judges, as the last court of appeal in ecclesiastical causes. Fifthly and finally, Hooker defends the monarch's exemption from excommunication, a clear and robust rejection of 'the platform of Reformed Discipline'.[83]

The 'Supreme Head', Parliament and Convocation

In keeping with his concept of the original derivation of sovereign power from the whole body politic, and recognising that body as the fashioner of law for the whole, Hooker affirms the coordinated roles of Parliament and Convocation. On them, says Hooker, 'the very essence of all government within the Kingdom doth depend' since together they form 'even the whole body of the realm'. That 'whole body', Hooker insists, 'consisteth of the king, and of all that within the land are subject unto him; for they are there present, either in person or by such as they voluntarily have derived their very personal right unto'.[84]

In purely temporal affairs the monarch acts with Parliament alone. In ordinary spiritual matters the monarch acts with the Convocation of

81. McGrade describes this sixth chapter as 'long and tangled' ('Book VIII', p. 376).
82. 'In spiritual causes, a lay person may be no ordinary; a commissionary judge there is not but that he may' (VIII, viii, 4 [III, p. 433]). This points up the fact that others beside the monarch him or herself operate as 'mixt' persons in Hooker's theology of polity.
83. VIII, ix, 6 [III, p. 455].
84. VIII, iv, 11 [III, pp. 408-9]. An interesting question we do not address here is this: how does the functioning of royal authority in a national church relate to the pan-Christian discernment of truth beyond the realm's borders? Hooker needs to say more about the relation of the monarch and indeed the Convocation and Parliament in relation to his conciliar ecclesiology. Daniel Eppley broaches this issue in 'Richard Hooker and Christopher St. German: Biblical Hermeneutics and Princely Power', *RHER*, pp. 287-94.

clergy; from that source legislation pertaining to the ecclesiastical sphere originates. Initiatives from Convocation require the concurrence of Parliament adding the temporality's assent to such matters. Finally, the royal assent confirms and moves the matter as binding upon the whole body politic. We have here, then, an exercise of supremacy that is, as G. V. Bennett once described it, constitutional and conciliar in character.[85]

Hierarchy, Community, Integrity

In light of Hooker's highly nuanced presentation of themes in the rich and complex sphere of political philosophy and theology it is understandable that supporters of the Restoration monarchy would impugn the authenticity of parts of Book VIII.[86] This suggests that Hooker wrote Book VIII, like the rest of the *Laws*, more as an outsider than as an unhesitating establishment partisan, and that he really did want to move the terms of the Elizabethan settlement on. We have said enough about the political theology of Book VIII to suspect how that could be so.

However Hooker's political theology may have sat with the realities of the period in which he wrote, or whether it was indeed effectively dead after England's political reforms of the early 1830s,[87] four themes of his political theology continue to speak from the pages of the *Laws*. The first, arising from the theology of personal union, is what John Booty describes as 'the essential connection between personal belief and public policy'. Hooker offered his contemporaries a way to recognise and affirm how religious and political convictions coexist and interact *within* and therefore *between* people.[88] The eighth book of the *Laws* gives that concrete, structured political expression; it shines a light on an area of political motivation which a secular world ignores at its peril.

Hooker's second theme is the understanding of political association and action in terms of 'the good'. He argues that the social and political project has to do with the nurture of a social 'ethos' – ethic – and the formation of both communal and personal virtue. Political life, in other words, is necessarily bound up with life that strives for virtue: the nurture of character that prospers common life and that fulfils legitimate human potentials.

Hooker's third theme, in line with long-standing Christian thought, is

---

85. 'The Royal Supremacy', in *To the Church of England* (Worthing, 1988), p. 54.
86. In the early 1680s Sir William Dugdale, for instance, reviewing the 'late troubles' in England, claimed that Hooker could not have asserted 'that though the king were singulis major, yet he was universis minor' (quoted in Raymond Houk, ed., *Book VIII Hooker's Ecclesiastical Polity* [New York, 1931], p. 87).
87. 'Effectively dead' is Diarmaid MacCulloch's phrase ('Richard Hooker's Reputation', *CRH*, p. 605).
88. See his chapter 'The Church and the Commonweal' in *Reflections*, pp. 160-1.

that public good has a transcendent goal. The satisfaction of natural goods, material and moral, while the first business of polity, are insufficient by themselves. The public sphere must be one where humankind's intrinsic spiritual capacities and aspirations are recognised and honoured. They crown the common good, for which public association and polity exist in the first place, with beatitude as the spiritual end of humankind and the fulfilment of all forms of human association. So the positive laws of a Christian commonwealth coincide with the laws of revelation and reason, both 'secular' and sacred.

Finally, Hooker implies throughout the argument of Book VIII that matters of personal religious conviction are only tenable to the extent that they offer what Stephen McGrade describes as 'a suitable focus of public devotion'.[89] That is another way of saying that the individual accesses truth among and with the many, and that spiritual truth is authenticated in no small measure by the extent to which it enhances the 'good life' of all. And that 'good life' is not for Hooker (nor for his predecessors in political thought) a merely individual goal or attainment. The undoubted correspondence between the whole body of the realm and of the whole Christ, head and body, signals a political, and therefore social, vision which is inter-connected and communitarian. In all those respects Hooker's political theology still has much to teach us.

---

89. 'Book VIII', p. 383.

Part Six

Conclusion

Summing Up
Hooker, 'Anglicanism' and Us

Where does all this leave us? Given that the purpose of this study has been to orientate readers to understand Hooker's particular theological 'voice', both in his own context and as a present-day interlocutor, the following conclusion can take up each of the angles discussed in a summary.

Hooker and 'Anglicanism'

A persistent feature of the analysis and assessment of Hooker's contribution in recent decades has been the attempt to place Hooker more accurately on the map of sixteenth- and early seventeenth- century ecclesiastical trends and movements. It has gone hand in hand with closer study of the extent and kinds of 'Calvinism' in the Elizabethan church, and the diverse nomenclatures employed both at the time and in subsequent writings about the period. This study is built upon the main insights of such scholarship. Two preliminary conclusions follow. First, we can assuredly lay to rest a view of the established Elizabethan Church of England as 'Anglican', standing against Calvinist and Puritan extremes. Certainly as to nomenclature C. S. Lewis is right: Hooker had never heard of a religion called 'Anglicanism'.[1] A broadly Calvinist atmosphere suffused the religious culture of Elizabethan England.[2] Hooker was formed theologically within that atmosphere.

Second, and following from that, we must describe Hooker as standing unhesitatingly in the Reformation tradition. That is, he defended the jurisdictional break with the See of Rome;[3] and he accepted the theological nomenclature forged by Luther and Calvin concerning 'justification' and 'sanctification' respectively. In response to the attack of *A Christian Letter* Hooker made no effort to disassociate himself from or disclaim the self-description of 'certain English *Protestants*'.[4]

However, studies of the Elizabethan situation have revealed two factors which further clarify Richard Hooker's place within the mainstream English

---

1. *English Literature*, p. 454.
2. We might, though, question the legitimacy of the phrase 'Calvinist consensus', wondering what 'consensus' actually refers to.
3. We could translate it: 'The civil magistrate determines the religion his people profess and practice'.
4. *FLE*, IV, p. 6; emphasis mine.

religious tradition of the sixteenth century. First, the Calvinist atmosphere, precisely because of its diffuse quality, varied; there was a spectrum extending from conformist episcopal Calvinists to non-conformist, hard-core double-predestinarians.[5] Second, whatever may have prevailed in the period of Edward Tudor and immediately afterward, by the 1580s and 1590s the ecclesiastical and theological atmosphere smelled rather different. Anti-puritanism created a watershed in the later Elizabethan Church: an opening, as Peter Lake has put it, 'to think new thoughts and say in public things that had previously been virtually unsayable'.[6]

It was within such dynamic ideological, political and theological currents that Hooker formulated his theological vision. For that reason, if for no others, we cannot expect that Hooker's vision of God and, by implication, the structure and content of theology that flows from that vision, would look just like that of his admired English predecessors (John Jewel, for instance) or even of his contemporaries (such as Archbishop John Whitgift). So, beyond recognising Hooker's own avowed and intentional embrace of the general Calvinism of the Elizabethan church, there is little else that we can predictably say *a priori* about Hooker's theology.

This study has drawn attention to Hooker's notable historical sense, an awareness of the development of theological ideas in relation to historical contexts. As to the Reformation agenda, we know that Hooker appreciated the 'moderate kind' of reform taken by the English Church in contrast to 'that other more extreme and rigorous which certain churches elsewhere have better liked'.[7] We can reasonably suppose, I think, that Hooker recognised the movement within the English Church from Lutheran dominance to Calvinist since the 1530s; we can suppose too that Hooker viewed the Reformation legacy itself as an evolving project. Had he himself not said it in so many words: 'The wisdom which is learned by tract of time, findeth the laws that have been in former ages established, needful in later to be abrogated'?[8] Indeed, Hooker's tackling the 'new question' concerning the authority of Scripture clearly shows his awareness of the Reformation's own unfinished business not so much with regard to issues of outward polity, as non-conformist critics insisted, but with regard to central, defining doctrines.

Hooker's answer to that 'new question' reveals, as we have said at points throughout this study, a mind 'on the move' and no more so than in the sources and conceptual apparatus that he felt free to bring to his project to define

---

5. Peter Lake's works describe this spectrum.
6. 'The "Anglican Moment"? Richard Hooker and the Ideological Watershed of the 1590s', in Stephen Platten, ed., *Anglicanism and the Western Tradition* (Norwich, 2003) p. 108.
7. IV, xiv, 6 (I, pp. 486-7). Hooker refers to the Henrician and Edwardian reforms; see McGrade, 'Book VIII', p. 345.
8. IV, xiv, 1 [I, pp. 480-1].

belief and practice for his own generation. As a beneficiary of Humanist interest in pagan philosophers, historical study and the philology of the learned languages; with his interest in scholasticism and especially Thomism in both its pristine and sixteenth-century resurgent forms; through access to more and better patristic texts; with a sharp eye on the pastoral and practical consequences of nearly half a century of reform within the life of the English Church; and above all with his distinctive 'speculative breadth',[9] Hooker was ready and able to say what had hitherto been unsayable. However much he sought to honour his Reformation credentials, however honest his desire to preserve the intentions of the early Reformers, his theological vision as it appears in the *Laws* and his other, and especially his final writings, was not just a qualitatively more sophisticated rebuttal to English non-conformists; it in fact implied a new kind of tradition.

Hooker's new tradition of course used much of the terminology and concepts which were the prizes forged out of bitter debates of earlier decades. Hooker was no isolate, so it could not have been otherwise. The very preference in the English Reformation for outward conformity in practice over a narrow form of doctrinal subscription, gave Hooker intellectual space to nuance language, re-position ideas, and, perhaps most important of all, to re-ground and re-proportion the edifice of philosophical and theological ideas. That dynamic intrinsic to the English situation is highlighted by *A Christian Letter* and Hooker's rebuttal. In Hooker's case the resulting theological plan and adornment is far more like an English mediaeval church than a Genevan one.[10]

A brief recollection of what some of the preceding chapters have described may help substantiate that claim. Hooker's main conceptual tool is the idea of law. His particular understanding and use of it indicate that theology, and the knowledge of God that it articulates, has deep moorings in nature, indeed in the very structure of reality, as a necessary complement to the insights borne of revelation and grace.[11] Even God behaves lawfully insofar as God's reason determines God's will and action. At the root of God's posture toward what He has created is his own goodness. God's predestinating will is that all things, and especially humankind, function, grow and move toward the enjoyment of their appointed goodness. Christians' use of Scripture itself relies on the complementarity of nature and grace summed up in Hooker's Augustinian and Thomistic axiom:

9. McGrade, 'Hooker', p.xxx.

10. And so we must agree with Lee Gibbs' critique of the 'revisionist' approach which seeks to align Hooker securely with the continental 'magisterial' Reform ('Richard Hooker: Prophet of Anglicanism or English Magisterial Reformer', *Anglican Theological Review*, 88:2 [2006]: 952-8)

11. In different terms but to the same end, Gibbs says that Hooker stands in the rationalist-realist-essentialist tradition of Aristotle and Aquinas tempered by the English common law tradition ('Book I', p. 113).

'Nature hath need of grace' and 'grace hath use of nature'.[12] In Hooker's case it is no "throw away line"; rather, it is a principle that informs Hooker's whole theological vision.

Hooker's intellectualist strain prizes reason both in God and in God's image, humankind; for Hooker that faculty, however damaged by sin, retains enough power to legitimate the enquiries of natural reason and natural theology, and, as restored by grace, guides the spiritual ascent. In his understanding of theological science it is the basis for a scholastic-style analogical method that enhances his biblical theology. In his anthropology Hooker's emphasis falls on human freedom; and his ethics are thoroughly *eudaimonistic* in a way that honours the natural 'ground' of ethical insight and endeavour while complementing it with a theocentric goal. The natural, the intellectual and the spiritual cooperate and converge in pursuit of law's end: happiness and perfection.

In his soteriology Hooker works with terms that Luther and Calvin, in their different ways, had bequeathed to their heirs. The conceptual triad of justification, sanctification and glorification echoes Calvin's creative complement to Luther's insights. Whereas Luther's emphasis fell on justification, and Calvin's on sanctification, it can be argued that Hooker's falls on glorification. The very fact that he moves that concept in the direction of the language of deification and the import of 2 Peter 1.4 supports that claim although Hooker does not embrace the language or the concept as forcefully as some of his contemporaries.[13] There we see a new vision of the entire theological edifice of the economy of salvation in favour of participation in divine life. The implications can be seen then in Hooker's theology of sacraments as effectual instruments of a real participation in the person of the deified God-Man, Christ, and in his understanding of prayer and worship. As necessary intermediate causes they become in Hooker's account necessary transformational experiences through which the human person, in body, mind, imagination, and spirit ascends to a more intense communion with God even as God, through his appointed means, descends to his world and to humankind. In that exchange in time – and only in that willed, enacted exchange – does eternal election become actual.

The sacramental experience is also a communal experience. Indeed, the entire journey Godward is a communal project and experience so that 'church' can never be adequately defined by or experienced in closed meetings of the self-described 'godly'. Hooker is profoundly wary of isolated, subjective claims, a 'methinketh' approach to Christian truth and authenticating experience. The Spirit's compelling testimony is never solitary and unreasonable (though it may be more than that), and 'right reason' is always moored to the insights of the community of faith. Theology, like

---

12. III, viii. 6 (I, p. 367).
13. We can note, for instance, Hooker's contemporary Lancelot Andrewes.

scriptural interpretation, which is basic to theology's integrity, is a task in company, possible through the influence of healing and transforming grace, and accountable to the Church as a whole both in space and in time. Because grace has use of nature and nature has need of grace, the public, social life of whole peoples, societies and nations, expressed in polity, are the field in which the seeds of grace are planted, tended, and grow. The thrust of such a theology is not retreat and enclosure but expansion and inculturation. The Church's boundaries are, by implication, meant to extend so that a whole society genuinely becomes what, in Hooker's reckoning of England's polity, it already is, Christ's Church, the fellowship of believers who are themselves living members of his glorious body. In this vision the godly prince, or supreme governor, together with Parliament and Convocation, fashion and execute laws that have as their final purpose the formation of individual characters and social relations oriented toward a common good of body, mind and spirit defined and understood according to the testimonies of the two books of nature and grace, reason and revelation.

Such the Christian vision of God became in Hooker's hands. Is it any wonder that some of his contemporaries doubted whether he really stood with them as *bone fide* members of the Church of England when his avowed combat in defence of the church seemed instead to sow tares to 'hinder the good corne of the Church'?[14] Precisely because it was borne of controversy and in response to a particular situation, and despite Hooker's disposition toward the articulation of principles, it was not and is not a 'fully-articulated system of scientific divinity'.[15] It contained gaps; it had fissures; ambiguities and irresolutions remained; and an astonishingly diverse audience could and did over time claim Hooker, or at least a part of Hooker, for themselves.[16]

That notwithstanding, Hooker gives us enough theological sub-structure, structure and super-structure, proportion and sensibility, to recognise a church reformed in a way different from what he and his generation had received. In that sense Hooker, whether he intended to or not, has given to the Christian world the origins of 'Anglianisme' or, as others later came to call it, 'Anglicanism'.

Hooker, Theology and Us

Hooker's valued witness to theology will in no small part be determined according to the needs and preoccupations of a given age, as a recent study of Hooker's reception through the centuries shows.[17] So, what of us? John Booty is surely right to look beyond the appeal to Scripture, reason and tradition in assessing Hooker's most important and enduring witness to

14. *ACL, FLE*, IV, p. 6.
15. McAdoo, *Structure*, p. 14.
16. Lake, 'Anglican Moment', pp. 120-1.
17. See Brydon's *Evolving Reputation, passim*.

theology.[18] In our situation at the start of the third millennium more is needed. Does this study help us grasp what that 'more' might be? Bearing in mind that we cannot simply and simplistically appropriate Hooker's apologetic for ourselves,[19] here I want to draw attention to a triad of characteristics in Hooker's theology that constitute an enduring legacy to Christian theological culture.

First, Hooker's theology articulates a vision of *wholeness*. For Hooker theology is an integrating project, and it is so because it attends to reality whose source and end are marked by union, communion and mutual participation. He writes in his *Sermon on Pride*,

> God hath created nothing simply for itself: but each thing in all things, and of every thing each part in other hath such interest, that in the whole world nothing is found whereunto any created can say, 'I need thee not.'[20]

In relating parts to a whole, the one to the many, and vice-versa, this theology does not just describe but elucidates and articulates the 'interest', the mutual relations, that did, do, or might exist. Such a theology aims at what the New Testament terms *pleroma*, or fullness.[21] Hooker's theology is, in its broadest sense, a 'quest for Catholicity' not simply because it reintroduced some of the 'great fundamentals' of the Catholic tradition, as Lionel Thornton once claimed,[22] but because it prefers relation, balance and fullness. Theology's fundamental paradigm, we could therefore say, is the life of the triune God, the sublime reality to which those theological attributes analogically point.

Hooker's theology is therefore a theology of *wisdom*.[23] It is useful to recall Hooker's invocation of the biblical concept of wisdom in Book II as he describes the mediation of divine truth. 'Whatsoever either men on earth or the Angels of heaven do know, it is as a drop of that unemptiable fountain of wisdom; which wisdom hath diversely imparted her treasures unto the world.' He continues:

> As her ways are of sundry kinds, so her manner of teaching is not merely one and the same. Some things she [*viz*. Wisdom] openeth by the sacred books of Scripture; some things by the glorious works of Nature: with some things she imparteth them from above by spiritual influence; in some things she leadeth and traineth them only by worldly experience and practice. We

18. *Reflections*, p. 186.
19. Williams, 'Philosopher, Anglican, Contemporary', p. 382.
20. *LSNP*, II [III, p. 617]; see Booty, *Reflections*, p. 187.
21. The origins, it can be argued, of the later term 'Catholicity' (Dulles, *Catholicity*, pp. 13-15).
22. *Hooker*, p. 101.
23. Williams describes a 'sapiential model' inhering in Hooker's intellectual posture ('Philosopher, Anglican, Contemporary', p. 383).

may not so in any one special kind admire her, that we disgrace her in any other, but let all her ways be according unto their place and degree adored.[24]

Its fullness of vision involves a search for insight, understanding and truth that scans widely over the terrain of metaphysics, human experience and natural phenomena. One of the most formidable twentieth-century theologians, himself a practitioner of such wisdom theology, has written, 'God's truth is, indeed, great enough to allow an infinity of approaches and entryways'.[25] Hooker's is a wisdom theology in that sense. It was, in fact, just that aspect which, if Izaac Walton is to believed, captivated Pope Clement VIII after reading Cardinal Stapleton's Latin translation of Book I, and elicited the astonished declaration: 'There is no learning that this man hath not searched into'.[26]

One consequence of that is a three-fold integration. First, there is the integration of metaphysics and biblical theology as a particular expression of the coordination of and interplay between reason and revelation. Second, and in continuity with that, Hooker's theology does not opt either for transcendence or immanence, and with that it strives to hold in balance the objective and the subjective. The Liberal Roman interpretation of Hooker, insofar as it favoured the 'immanentalist impulse' of the late-nineteenth and early twentieth centuries,[27] required the transcendentalist correction of revisionist Evangelical, 'Protestantising' interpretations in more recent decades.[28] In the end, though, Hooker's theological style seeks to integrate those poles. Third, Hooker's theology holds together the three great transcendentals, truth, goodness, and beauty, and his theological construction proceeds on the basis of their 'inseparable relation to one another'.[29] One consequence is the expectation that truth is attractive, and that from truth's radiant beauty ethical implications follow as we are drawn to conformity with the truth that attracts. Hooker's vision of theology's object as truth, goodness and beauty in the face of Jesus Christ constitutes both a return to and a revolution in theological discourse, an embrace of a commonplace of earlier Christian epochs, and a silent rebellion in the soul of English theology in most of its early-modern and modern forms.

Following from that Hooker's theology is, thirdly, a theology of *worship*; it is, to use a current term, doxological. It is another expression of Hooker's preference for wholeness that (as John Booty reminds us) he knew no hard and fast divisions between theology and liturgy, between pastoral care and

24. II, i, 4 [I, p. 290].
25. Hans Urs Von Balthasar, *The Glory of the Lord* (San Francisco, 1982), vol. I, p. 17.
26. Walton, *Life*, p. 212.
27. Stanley Grenz and Roger Olson, *20th-Century Theology* (Carlisle, 1992), p. 62.
28. I would count Atkinson's treatment as an example of that.
29. von Balthasar, *Glory*, pp. 18-9.

devotion.[30] God-talk and 'reverence' go hand in hand for Hooker. Theology is the mind's liturgy, and the mind's 'reasonable worship' (Romans 12.1) is the fruit of the ascetic disposition of the whole person. The foundations of that intellectual liturgy lie in the soil of repentance and awe, the two postures most characteristic of Hooker's spiritual *attrait*.[31] Not only does this remind us that theology is one of the fruits of repentance – that is, the turning of the whole person Godward in Christ and (as John of Damascus put it) nature's return to a proper accord with nature[32] – but that, as another great twentieth-century theologian has put it, the experience of public worship links the theologian with Christians' 'living dialogue with Christ' where prayer, praise and adoration expands the mind's capacity to see and take in the reality of God in Christ.[33] The objective and the subjective meet and move toward integration; immanent, personal faith and the transcendent personal Word connect in a dynamic commerce between heaven and earth.

In all of this we find, as John Marshall so aptly reminds us, 'a design of strange beauty and magnificent variety'.[34] And here, I think, is Hooker's continuing testimony to Christian theology and to the vision of ecclesial life that he advocated. His writings, and his *Laws* above all, are 'classic' since, in their context, the theological vision they expressed maintained an extraordinary balance between past and present; they bore fruit in insightful, even daring novelty with deep and intentional roots in what had gone before and been validated through time.[35] It has been said of a great theologian of the twentieth century (whose own inspiration from biblical, patristic and scholastic sources reminds us of Hooker) that in the face of the 'problems' of theology he never lost sight of the 'living realities' with which they are concerned, the Mystery behind them. Hooker teaches us that too.[36]

Whatever the future of 'Anglicanism' may be, Hooker's vision of God and of theology has much to say still. Our generation may fruitfully take note so that his witness to Anglicans and, indeed, to all Christians, does not 'pass away as in a dream'.[37]

---

30. *Reflections*, p. 190.
31. Walton's description of Hooker's last days, when he made his confession of sin to his colleague Dr Saravia and, near death, was 'meditating the number and nature of Angels', illustrates those two postures; but they recur throughout Hooker's writings (*Life*, pp. 224-5). *Attrait* refers to the innate predisposition of a person to a particular kind of spirituality.
32. *On the Orthodox Faith*, II, 30.
33. So the Orthodox theologian Dumitru Staniloae, quoted by Miller, *Gift of the World*, pp. 48-9.
34. 'Hooker's Theory of Church and State', *Anglican Theological Review*, XXVII: 3 (1945): 151.
35. So John Polkinghorne describes a 'classic' in *Reason and Reality* (London, 1991), p. 66.
36. So Cornelius Ernst in his Foreword to Schillebeeckx's *Christ the Sacrament*, p. xviii.
37. Preface, I [I, p. 125].

Further Reading

A useful bibliography is provided by Egil Grislis and W. Speed Hill in 'Richard Hooker: An Annotated Bibliography' in W. Speed Hill, ed., *Studies in Richard Hooker: Essays Preliminary to an Edition of His Works*, pp. 279-320. A current and very thorough 'Select Bibliography' by Egil Grislis and John K. Stafford is found in W. J. Torrance Kirby, ed., *Companion to Richard Hooker*, pp. 613-38.

Volumes 5 and 6 of the *Folger Library Edition of the Works of Richard Hooker* provide highly readable introductions to the *Laws* and Hooker's other works. With that material understood, the student could then profitably turn to the wide-ranging essays in *Richard Hooker and the English Reformation* and the *Companion to Richard Hooker*.

Stephen McGrade provides a very useful 'Guide to Hooker's sources and to the Elizabethan debate about religion and society' in his edition of *Hooker Of the Laws of Ecclesiastical Polity*, pp. 227-40. This gives short descriptions of the writers upon whom Hooker draws in the course of his argument. This volume includes the texts of the Preface, and Books I and VIII of the *Laws*.

For those without access to any edition of the *Laws* a selection of texts is available in Raymond Chapman, ed., *Law and Revelation: Richard Hooker and His Writings*.

Appendix
A Selection of Texts from Hooker's Works

The Emergence of the Genevan Discipline
and the Critique of the English Church

Preface to the Laws, chapter ii

[In this brilliantly understated passage from the Preface Hooker puts the Genevan Discipline for church order into historical perspective and at the same time subtly undercuts Calvin's authority by likening it to a papal magisterium. See chapter 1 of this book.]

[7.] The present inhabitants of Geneva, I hope, will not take it in evil part, that the faultiness of their people heretofore is by us so far forth laid open, as their own learned guides and pastors have thought necessary to discover it unto the world. For out of their books and writings it is that I have collected this whole narration, to the end it might thereby appear in what sort amongst them that discipline was planted, for which so much contention is raised amongst ourselves. The reason which moved Calvin herein to be so earnest, was, as Beza himself testifieth, 'For that he saw how needful these bridles were, to be put in the jaws of that city.' That which by wisdom he saw to be requisite for that people, was by as great wisdom compassed.

But wise men are men, and the truth is truth. That which Calvin did for establishment of his discipline, seemeth more commendable than that which he taught for the countenancing of it established. Nature worketh in us all a love to our own counsels. The contradiction of others is a fan to inflame that love. Our love set on fire to maintain that which once we have done, sharpeneth the wit to dispute, to argue, and by all means to reason for it. Wherefore a marvel it were if a man of so great capacity, having such incitements to make him desirous of all kind of furtherances unto his cause, could espy in the whole Scripture of God nothing which might breed at the least a probable opinion of likelihood, that divine authority itself was the same way somewhat inclinable. And all which the wit even of Calvin was able from thence to draw, by sifting the very utmost sentence and syllable, is no more than that certain speeches there are which to him did seem to intimate that all Christian churches ought to have their elderships endued with power of excommunication, and that a part of those elderships every where should be chosen out from amongst the laity, after that form which himself had framed Geneva unto. But what argument are ye able to shew, whereby it was ever proved by Calvin, that any one sentence of Scripture doth necessarily enforce these things, or the rest wherein your opinion concurreth with his against the orders of your own church?

[8.] We should be injurious unto virtue itself, if we did derogate from them whom their industry hath made great. Two things of principal moment there are which have deservedly procured him honour throughout the world: the one his exceeding pains in composing the Institutions of Christian religion; the other his no less industrious travails for exposition of holy Scripture according unto the same Institutions. In which two things whosoever they were that after him bestowed their labour, he gained the advantage of prejudice against them, if they gainsayed; and of glory above them, if they consented. His writings published after the question about that discipline was once begun omit not any the least occasion of extolling the use and singular necessity thereof. Of what account the Master of Sentences was in the church of Rome, the same and more amongst the preachers of reformed churches Calvin had purchased; so that the perfectest divines were judged they, which were skilfullest in Calvin's writings. His books almost by the very canon to judge both doctrine and discipline by. French churches, both under others abroad and at home in their own country, all cast according to that mould which Calvin had made. The church of Scotland in erecting the fabric of their reformation took the selfsame pattern. Till at length the discipline, which was at the first so weak, that without the staff of their approbation, who were not subject unto it themselves, it had not brought others under subjection, began now to challenge universal obedience, and to enter into open conflict with those very churches, which in desperate extremity had been relievers of it.

[9.] To one of those churches which lived in most peaceable sort, and abounded as well with men for their learning in other professions singular, as also with divines whose equals were not elsewhere to be found, a church ordered by Gualter's discipline, and not by that which Geneva adoreth; unto this church, the church of Heidelburgh, there cometh one who craving leave to dispute publicly defendeth with open disdain of their government, that 'to a minister with his eldership power is given by the law of God to excommunicate whomsoever, yea even kings and princes themselves.' Here were the seeds sown of that controversy which sprang up between Beza and Erastus about the matter of excommunication, whether there ought to be in all churches an eldership having power to excommunicate, and a part of that eldership to be of necessity certain chosen out from amongst the laity for that purpose. In which disputation they have, as to me it seemeth, divided very equally the truth between them; Beza most truly maintaining the necessity of excommunication, Erastus as truly the non-necessity of lay-elders to be ministers thereof.

[10.] Amongst ourselves, there was in King Edward's days some question moved by reason of a few men's scrupulosity touching certain things. And beyond seas, of them which fled in the days of Queen Mary, some contenting themselves abroad with the use of their own service-book at home authorized before their departure out of the realm, others liking better the Common Prayer-book of the Church of Geneva translated, those smaller contentions before begun were by this means somewhat increased. Under the happy reign of her Majesty which now is, the greatest matter awhile contended for was the wearing of the cap and surplice, till there came Admonitions directed unto the high court of Parliament, by men who concealing their names thought it glory enough to discover their minds and affections, which now were universally bent even against all the orders and laws, wherein this church is found uncomformable to the platform of Geneva. Concerning the Defender of which Admonitions, all that I mean to say is but this: *there will come a time when three words uttered with charity and meekness shall receive a far more blessed reward than three thousand volumes written with disdainful sharpness of wit.* But the manner of men's writing must not alienate our hearts from the truth, if it appear they have the truth; as the followers of the same defender do think he hath; and in that persuasion they follow him, no otherwise than himself doth Calvin, Beza and others, with the like persuasion that they in this cause had the truth. We being as fully persuaded otherwise, it resteth that some kind of trial be used to find out which part is in error.

God, Law and Laws

Laws, I, chapter i

[With noteworthy concision Hooker links the presenting issues which called forth the Laws to theological-philosophical foundations. He provides a working definition of law, rooting it in the character of God's being and working. See chapters 2 and 3 of this book.]

[3.] The Laws of the Church, whereby for so many ages together we have been guided in the exercise of Christian religion and the service of the true God, our rites, customs, and orders of ecclesiastical government, are called in question: we are accused as men that will not have Christ Jesus to rule over them, but have wilfully cast his statutes behind their backs, hating to be reformed and made subject unto the sceptre of his discipline. Behold therefore we offer the laws whereby we live unto the general trial and judgement of the whole world; heartily beseeching Almighty God, whom we desire to serve according to his own will, that both we and others (all kind of partial affection being clean laid aside) may have eyes to see and hearts to embrace the things that in his sight are most acceptable.

And because the point about which we strive is the quality of our laws, our first entrance hereinto cannot better be made, than with consideration of the nature of law in general, and of that law which giveth life unto all the rest, which are commendable, just, and good; namely the law whereby the Eternal himself doth work. Proceeding from hence to the law, first of Nature, then of Scripture, we shall have the easier access unto those things which come after to be debated, concerning the particular cause and question which we have in hand.

II. All things that are, have some operation not violent or casual. Neither doth any thing ever begin to exercise the same, without some fore-conceived end for which it worketh. And the end which it worketh for is not obtained, unless the work be also fit to obtain it by. For unto every end every operation will not serve. That which doth assign unto each thing the kind, that which doth moderate the force and power, that which doth appoint the form and measure, of working, the same we term a Law. So that no certain end could ever be attained, unless the actions whereby it is attained were regular; that is to say, made suitable, fit and correspondent unto their end, by some canon, rule or law. Which thing doth first take place in the works even of God himself.

[2.] All things therefore do work after a sort according to law: all other things according to a law, whereof some superior, unto whom they are subject, is author; only the works and operations of God have Him both for their worker, and for the law whereby they are wrought. The being of God is a kind of law to his working: for that perfection which God is, giveth perfection to that he doth. Those natural, necessary, and internal operations of God, the Generation of the Son, the Proceeding of the Spirit, are without the compass of my present intent: which is to touch only such operations as have their beginning and being by a voluntary purpose, wherewith God hath eternally decreed when and how they should be. Which eternal decree is that we term an eternal law.

God the Trinity

Laws, V, chapter li

[Hooker prefaces his discussion of sacraments with a succinct statement of Trinitarian theology. While his treatment is, in western terms, seemingly favouring 'substance' over 'person', we see suggestions of the perichoresis characterizing the Trinitarian relations. See chapter 3 of this book.]

[1.] 'The Lord our God is but one God.' In which indivisible unity notwithstanding we adore the Father as being altogether of himself, we glorify that consubstantial Word which is the Son, we bless and magnify that co-essential Spirit eternally proceeding from both which is the Holy Ghost. Seeing therefore the Father is of none, the Son is of the Father and the Spirit is of both, they are by these their several properties really distinguishable each from other. For the substance of God with this property *to be of none* doth make the Person of the Father; the very selfsame substance in number with this property *to be of the Father* maketh the Person of the Son; the same substance having added unto it the property of *proceeding from the other two* maketh the Person of the Holy Ghost. So that in every Person there is implied both the substance of God which is one, and also that property which causeth the same person really and truly to differ from the other two. Every person hath his own subsistance from which no other besides hath, although there be others besides that are of the same substance. As no man but Peter can be the person which is Peter is, yet Paul hath the selfsame nature which Peter hath. Again, angels have every of them the nature of pure and invisible spirits, but every angel is not that angel which appeared in a dream to Joseph.

God's Goodness, Wisdom and Will

The Dublin Fragments

[Hooker describes the relation of reason to will in God in relation to God's goodness, and establishes a line between God's justice and reason, on the one hand, and the human capacity to perceive its own 'laws of action', on the other. 'Nature' and 'Scripture' have complementary roles as 'true interpreters of God's wisdom'. See chapters 3, 4 and 6 of this book.]

We are therefore to note certain special differences in God's will. God being of infinite goodness by nature, delighteth only in good things: neither is it possible that God should alter in himself this desire, because that without it he were not himself. But from this natural inclination of his will, unless it be some way or other determined, there cometh no certain particular effect. Wherefore, as God hath a natural bent only, and infinitely, unto good; and hath likewise a natural power to effect whatsoever himself willeth: so there is in God an incomprehensible wisdom, according to the reasonable disposition whereof his natural or general will restraineth itself as touching particular effects. So that God doth determine of nothing that it shall come to pass, otherwise than only in such manner as the law of his own wisdom hath set down within itself. Many things proceed from the will of God, the reasons whereof are oftentimes to us unknown. But unpossible it is that God should will any thing unjust, or unreasonable, any thing against those very rules whereby himself hath taught us to judge what equity requireth: for out of all peradventure there are no antinomies with God. The laws of action which he teacheth us, and the laws which his own wisdom chooseth to follow, are not the one repugnant to the other. The concealed causes of his secret intents overthrow not the principles which Nature or Scripture, the true interpreters of his wisdom, have disclosed to the whole world: and by virtue whereof, to our great contentment of mind, yea to his everlasting praise and glory, we are able in many things to yield abundantly sufficient reason for the works of God, why and how it is most just which God willeth.

Humankind: the Image of God

Laws, I, chapter vii

[In interpreting Genesis 1.26 Hooker asserts that, properly, human action is free and flows from understanding's perception of goodness and the will's desire for it, even in the case of many behaviours which seem neither reasoned nor actively chosen. See chapter 5 and 13 of this book.]

[2.] Man in perfection of nature being made according to the likeness of his Maker resembleth him also in the manner of working; so that whatsoever we work as men, the same we do wittingly work and freely; neither are we according to the manner of natural agents any way so tied, but that it is in our power to leave the things we do undone. The good which either is gotten by doing, or which consisteth in the very doing itself, causeth not action, unless apprehending it as good we so like and desire it: that we do unto any such end, the same we choose and prefer before the leaving of it undone. Choice there is not, unless the thing which we take be so in our power that we might have refused and left it. If fire consume the stubble, it chooseth not so to do, because the nature thereof is such that it can do no other. To choose is to will one thing before another. And to will is to bend our souls to the having or doing of that which they see to be good. Goodness is seen with the eye of the understanding. And the light of that eye, is reason. So that two principal fountains there are of human action, Knowledge and Will; which Will, in things tending towards any end, is termed Choice. Concerning Knowledge, 'Behold (saith Moses,) I have set before you this day good and evil, life and death.' Concerning Will, he addeth immediately, 'Choose life;' that is to say, the things that tend unto life, them choose.
    [3.] But of one thing we must have special care, as being a matter of no small moment; and that is, how the Will, properly and strictly taken, as it is of things which are referred unto the end that man desireth, differeth

greatly from that inferior natural desire which we call Appetite. The object of Appetite is whatsoever sensible good may be wished for; the object of Will is that good which Reason doth lead us to seek. Affections, as joy, and grief, and fear, and anger, with such like, being as it were the sundry fashions and forms of Appetite, can neither rise at the conceit of a thing indifferent, nor yet choose but rise at the sight of some things. Wherefore it is not altogether in our power, whether we will be stirred with affections or no: whereas actions which issue from the disposition of the Will are in the power thereof to be performed or stayed. Finally, Appetite is the Will's solicitor, and the Will is Appetite's controller; what we covet according to the one by the other we often reject; neither is any other desire termed properly Will, but that where Reason and Understanding, or the show of Reason, prescribeth the thing desired.

It may be therefore a question, whether those operations of men are to be counted voluntary, wherein that good which is sensible provoketh Appetite, and Appetite causeth action, Reason being never called to counsel; as when we eat or drink, and betake ourselves unto rest, and such like. The truth is, that such actions in men having attained to the use of Reason are voluntary. For as the authority of higher powers hath force even in those things, which are done without their privity, and are so of mean reckoning that to acquaint them therewith it needeth not; in like sort, voluntarily we are said to do that also, which the Will if it listed might hinder from being done, although about the doing thereof we do not expressly use our reason or understanding, and so immediately apply our wills thereunto. In cases therefore of such facility, the Will doth yield her assent as it were with a kind of silence, by not dissenting; in which respect her force is not so apparent as in express mandates or prohibitions, especially upon advice and consultation going before.

Humankind's Natural Desire for Union with God

Laws, I, chapters x and xi

[Owing to its fall into sin a 'new foundation' is required if humankind is to attain its supernatural goal. Diverse goods contribute to the various perfections of which humankind is capable. Hooker suggests the idea of humankind's 'transcendental openness'. See chapters 5 and 14 of this book.]

[15.] It followeth therefore that a new foundation being laid, we now adjoin hereunto that which cometh in the next place to be spoken of; namely, wherefore God hath himself by Scripture made known such laws as serve for direction of men.

[1.] All things, (God only excepted,) besides the nature which they have in themselves, receive externally some perfection from other things, as hath been shewed. Insomuch as there is in the whole world no one thing great or small, but either in respect of knowledge or of use it may unto our perfection add somewhat. And whatsoever such perfection there is which our nature may acquire, the same we properly term our Good; our Sovereign Good or Blessedness, that wherein the highest degree of all our perfection consisteth, that which being once attained unto there can rest nothing further to be desired; and therefore with it our souls are fully content and satisfied, in that they have they rejoice, and thirst for no more. Wherefore of good things desired some are such that for themselves we covet them not, but only because they serve as instruments unto that for which we are to seek: of this sort are riches. Another kind there is, which although we desire for itself, as health, and virtue, and knowledge, nevertheless they are not the last mark whereat we aim, but have their further end whereunto they are referred, so as in them we are not satisfied as having attained the utmost we may, but our desires do still proceed. These things are linked and as it were chained one to another; we labour to eat, and we eat to live, and we live to do good, and the good which we do is as seed sown with reference to a future harvest. But we must come at length to some pause. For, if every thing were to be desired for some other without any stint, there could be no certain end proposed unto our actions, we should go on we know not whither; yea, whatsoever we do were in vain, or rather nothing at all were possible to be done. For as to take away the first efficient of our being were to annihilate utterly our persons, so we cannot remove the last final cause of our working, but we shall cause whatsoever we work to cease. Therefore something there must be desired for itself simply and for no other. That is simply for itself desirable, unto the nature whereof it is opposite and repugnant to be desired with relation unto any other. The ox and the ass desire their food, neither propose they unto themselves any end wherefore; so that of them this is desired for itself; but why? By reason of their imperfection which cannot otherwise desire it; whereas that which is desired simply for itself, the excellency thereof is such as permitteth it not in any sort to be referred to a further end.

[2.] Now that which man doth desire with reference to a further end, the same he desireth in such measure as is unto that end convenient; but what he coveteth as good in itself, towards that his desire is ever infinite. So that unless the last good of all, which is desired altogether for itself, be also infinite, we do evil in making it our end; even as they who placed their felicity in wealth or honour or pleasure or any thing here attained; because in desiring any thing as our final perfection which is not so, we do amiss. Nothing may be infinitely desired but that good which indeed is infinite; for the better the more desirable; that therefore most desirable wherein there is infinity of goodness: so that if any thing desirable may be infinite, that must needs be the highest of all things that are desired. No good is infinite but only God; therefore He our felicity and bliss. Moreover, desire tendeth unto union with that it desireth. If then in him we be blessed, it is by force of participation and conjunction with Him. Again, it is not the possession of any good thing can make them happy which have it, unless they enjoy the thing wherewith they are possessed. Then are we happy therefore when fully we enjoy God, as an object wherein the powers of our souls are satisfied even with everlasting delight: so that although we be men, yet by being unto God united we live as it were the life of God.

[3.] Happiness therefore is that estate whereby we attain, so far as possibly may be attained, the full possession of that which simply for itself is to be desired, and containeth in it after an eminent sort the contention of our desires, the highest degree of all our perfection. Of such perfection capable we are not in this life. For while we are in the world, subject we are unto sundry imperfections, griefs of body, defects of mind; yea the best things we do are painful, and the exercise of them grievous, being continued without intermission; so as in those very actions whereby we are especially perfected in this life we are not able to persist; forced we are with very weariness, and that often, to interrupt them: which tediousness cannot fall into those operations that are in the state of bliss, when our union with God is complete. Complete union with him must be according unto every power and faculty of our minds apt to receive so glorious an object. Capable we are of God both by understanding and will: by understanding, as He is that sovereign Truth which comprehendeth the rich treasures of all wisdom; by will, as He is that sea of Goodness whereof whoso tasteth shall thirst no more. As the will doth now work upon that object by desire, which is as it were a motion towards the end as of yet unobtained; so likewise upon the same hereafter received it shall work also by love. 'Appetitus inhiantis fit amor fruentis,' saith St. Augustine: 'The longing disposition of them that thirst is changed into the sweet affection of them that taste and are replenished.' Whereas we now love the thing that is good, but good especially in respect of benefit unto us; we shall then love the thing that is good, only or principally for the goodness of beauty in itself. The soul being in this sort, as it is active, perfected by love of that infinite good, shall, as it is receptive, be also perfected with those supernatural passions of joy, peace, and delight. All this endless and everlasting. Which perpetuity, in regard whereof our blessedness is termed 'a crown which withereth not,' doth neither depend upon the nature of the thing itself, nor proceed from any natural necessity that our souls should so exercise themselves for ever in beholding and loving God, but from the will of God, which doth both freely perfect our nature in so high a degree, and continue it so perfected. Under Man, no creature in the world is capable of felicity and bliss. First, because their chiefest perfection consisteth in that which is best for them, but not in that which is simply best, as ours doth. Secondly, because whatsoever external perfection they tend unto, it is not better than themselves, as ours is. How just occasion have we therefore even in this respect with the Prophet to admire the goodness of God? 'Lord, what is man, that thou shouldst exalt him above the works of thy hands,' so far as to make thyself the inheritance of his rest and the substance of his felicity?

Humankind's Fall

The Certainty and Perpetuity of Faith in the Elect

[Hooker asserts that, owing to the fall, no knowledge or love can lead to beatitude without grace through Christ. The 'faith' this requires is a virtue, which means that it must grow and develop through time and experience. See chapters 5 and 11 in this book.]

Now the minds of all men being so darkened as they are with the foggy damp of original corruption, it cannot be that any man's heart living should be either so enlightened in the knowledge, or so established in the love of that wherein his salvation standeth, as to be perfect, neither doubting nor shrinking at all. If any such were, what doth let why man should not be justified by his own inherent righteousness? For righteousness inherent being perfect will justify. And perfect faith is a part of perfect righteousness inherent; yea, a principal part, the root and the mother of all the rest: so that if the fruit of every tree be such as the root is, faith being perfect, as it is if it be not at all mingled with distrust and fear, what is there to exclude other Christian virtues from the like perfections? And then what need we the righteousness of Christ? His garment is superfluous: we may be honourably clothed with our own robes, if it be thus. But let them beware who challenge to themselves a strength which they have not, lest they lose the comfortable support of that weakness which indeed they have.

Holy Scripture

Laws, II, chapter i

[Hooker describes the 'epistemological lapse' into which non-conformists have fallen: Scripture's 'universal jurisdiction'. By contrast, he argues, the 'law of Scripture' requires the 'law of Reason'. See chapter 6 in this book.]

[2.] Unto which scope that our endeavour may the more directly tend, it seemeth fittest that first those things be examined, which are as seeds from whence the rest that ensue have grown. And of such the most general is that wherewith we are here to make our entrance: a question not moved (I think) any where in other churches, and therefore in ours the more likely to be soon (I trust) determined. The rather for that it hath grown from no other root, than only a desire to enlarge the necessary use of the Word of God; which desire hath begotten an error enlarging it further than (as we are persuaded) soundness of truth will bear. For whereas God hath left sundry kinds of laws unto men, and by all these laws the actions of men are in some sort directed; they hold that one only law, the Scripture, must be the rule to direct in all things, even so far as the 'taking up of a rush or straw.' About which point there should not need any question to grow, and that which is grown might presently end, if they but yield these two restraints: the first is, not to extend the actions whereof they speak so low as that instance doth import of taking up a rush, but rather keep themselves at the least within the compass of moral actions, actions which have in them vice or virtue: the second, not to exact at our hands for every action the knowledge of some place of Scripture out of which we stand bound to deduce it, as by diverse testimonies they seek to enforce; but rather as the truth is, so to acknowledge, that it sufficeth if such actions be framed according to the law of Reason; the general axioms, rules, and principles of which law being so frequent in Holy Scripture, there is no let but in that regard even out of Scripture such duties as may be that even all truth out of any truth may be deduced by some kind of consequence...howbeit no man bound in such sort to deduce all his actions out of Scripture, as if either the place be to him unknown whereon they may be concluded, or the reference unto that place not presently considered of, the action shall in that respect be condemned as unlawful. In this we dissent, and this we are presently to examine.

Scripture's Perfection

Laws, II, chapter viii

[Hooker determines the exact meaning of Hooker's 'perfection' in relation to Roman Catholic and non-conformist views: it relates to Scripture's end or purpose. See chapter 6 in this book.]

[5.] . . . . Howbeit that we swerve not in judgment, one thing especially we must observe, namely that the absolute perfection of Scripture is seen by relation unto that end whereto it tendeth. And even hereby it cometh to pass, that first such as imagine the general and main drift of the body of sacred Scripture not to be so large as it is, nor that God did thereby intend to deliver, as in truth he doth, a full instruction in things unto salvation necessary, the knowledge whereof man by nature could not otherwise in this life attain unto: they are by this very mean induced either to look for new revelations from heaven, or else dangerously to add to the word of God uncertain tradition, that so the doctrine of man's salvation might be complete; which doctrine we constantly hold in all respects without any such thing added to be so complete, that we utterly refuse as much as once to acquaint ourselves with any further thing. Whatsoever to make up the doctrine of man's salvation is added, as in supply of the Scripture's unsufficiency, we reject it. Scripture purposing this, hath perfectly and fully done it.

Again the scope and purpose of God in delivering the Holy Scripture such as do take more largely than behoveth, they on the contrary side, racking and stretching it further than by him was meant, are drawn into sundry as great inconveniences. These pretending the Scripture's perfection infer thereupon, that in Scripture all things lawful to be done must needs be contained. We count those things perfect which want nothing requisite for the end whereunto they were institutued . . . so the Scripture, yea every sentence thereof, is perfect, and wanteth nothing requisite unto the purpose for which God delivered the same.

The Person of Christ

Laws, V, chapter li

[Hooker strives to maintain the Chalcedonian balance between personal distinction and shared divine nature in the Incarnation. Notice Hooker's use of the word 'consonant', an Anselmic and scholastic turn of phrase ('It was fitting . . . '). See chapter 7 in this book.]

[2.] Now when God became man, lest we should err in applying this to the Person of the Father, or of the Spirit, St. Peter's confession unto Christ was, 'Thou art *the Son* of the living God,' and St. John's exposition thereof was plain, that it is *the Word* which was made Flesh. 'The Father and the Holy Ghost (saith Damascen) have no communion with the incarnation of the Word otherwise than only by approbation and assent.'

Notwithstanding, forasmuch as the Word and Deity are one subject, we must beware we exclude not the nature of God from incarnation, and so make the Son of God incarnate not to be very God. For undoubtedly even the nature of God itself in the only person of the Son is incarnate, and hath taken to itself flesh. Wherefore incarnation may neither be granted to any person but only one, nor yet denied to that nature which his common unto all three.

[3.] Concerning the cause of which incomprehensible mystery, forasmuch as it seemeth a thing unconsonant that the world should honour any other as the Saviour but him whom it honoureth as the Creator of the world, and in the wisdom of God it hath not been thought convenient to admit any way of saving man but by man himself, though nothing should be spoken of the love and mercy of God towards man, which this way are become such a spectacle neither men nor angels can behold without a kind of heavenly astonishment, we may hereby perceive there is cause sufficient why divine nature should assume human, so that God might be in Christ reconciling to himself the world. And if some cause be likewise required why rather to this end and purpose the Son than either the Father or the Holy Ghost should be made man, could we which are born the children of wrath be adopted the sons of God through grace, any other than the natural Son of God being Mediator between God and us? It became therefore him by whom all things are to be the way of salvation to all, that the institution and restitution of the world might be both wrought by one hand. The world's salvation was without the incarnation of the Son of God a thing impossible, not simply impossible, but impossible it being presupposed that the will of God was no otherwise to have it saved than by the death of his own Son. Wherefore taking to himself our flesh, and by his incarnation making it his own flesh, he had now of his own although from us what to offer unto God for us.

And as Christ took manhood that by it he might be capable of death whereunto he humbled himself, so because manhood is the proper subject of compassion and feeling pity, which maketh the sceptre of Christ's regency even in the kingdom of heaven amiable, he which without our nature could not on earth suffer for the sins of the world, doth now also by means thereof both make intercession to God for sinners and exercise dominion over all men with a true, a natural, and a sensible touch of mercy.

The Work of Christ

A Learned Discourse of Justification, 31

[Hooker expresses his understanding of Christ's unique and unrepeatable redemptive work through his sacrifice on the cross, while asserting the necessity of cooperation with the Spirit within the fellowship of the Church for the actual receipt of the divine gift. See chapter 7 in this book.]

How then is our salvation wrought by Christ alone? Is it our meaning that nothing is requisite to man's salvation, but Christ to save, and he to be saved quietly without any more to do? No, we acknowledge no such foundation. As we have received, so we teach that besides the bare and naked work, wherein Christ, without any other associate, finished all the parts of our redemption, and purchased salvation himself alone; for conveyance of this eminent blessing unto us, many things are required, as, to be known and chosen of God before the foundations of the world; in the world to be called, justified, sanctified; after we have left the world, to be received into glory; Christ in every of these hath somewhat which he worketh alone. Through him, according to the eternal purpose of God before the foundation of the world, born, crucified, buried, raised, &c., we were in a gracious acceptation known unto God long before we were seen of men: God knew us, loved us, was kind towards us in Christ Jesus, in him we were elected to be heirs of life. Thus far God through Christ hath wrought in such sort alone, that ourselves are mere patients, working no more than dead and senseless matter, wood, or stone, or iron, doth in the artificer's hand, no more than the clay, when the potter appointeth it to be framed for an honourable use; nay, not so much. For the matter whereupon the craftsman worketh he chooseth, being moved by the fitness which is in it to serve his turn; in us no such thing. Touching the rest, that which is laid for the foundation of our faith, importeth further, that by him we be called, that we have redemption, remission of sins through his blood, health by his stripes; justice by him; that he doth sanctify his Church, and make it glorious to himself; that entrance into joy shall be given us by him; yea, all things by him alone. Howbeit, not so by him alone, as if in us, to our vocation, the hearing of the gospel; to our justification, faith; to our sanctification, the fruits of the spirit; to our entrance into rest, perseverance in hope, in faith, in holiness, were not necessary.

Christ's Atoning Work

Laws, VI, chapter v

[Hooker's properly Anselmic doctrine of satisfaction comes to the fore: it is by recompense not by punishment. A derivative kind of satisfaction characterizes 'repentance' and 'works' done in faith by Christians. See chapters 7 and 11 in this book.]

[2.] Satisfaction is a work which justice requireth to be done for contentment of persons injured: neither is it in the eye of justice a sufficient satisfaction, unless it fully equal the injury for which we satisfy. Seeing then that sin against God eternal and infinite must needs be an infinite wrong; justice in regard thereof doth necessarily exact an infinite recompense, or else inflict upon the offender infinite punishment. Now because God was thus to be satisfied, and man not able to make satisfaction in such sort, his unspeakable love and inclination to save mankind from eternal death ordained in our behalf a Mediator, to do that which had been for any other impossible. Wherefore all sin is remitted in the only faith of Christ's passion, and no man without belief thereof justified. Faith alone maketh Christ's satisfaction ours; howbeit that faith alone which after sin maketh us by conversion his. For inasmuch as God will have the benefit of Christ's satisfaction both thankfully acknowledged and duly esteemed of all such as enjoy the same, he therefore imparteth so high a treasure unto no man, whose faith hath not made him willing by repentance to do even that, which of itself how unavailable soever, yet being required and accepted with God, we are in Christ made thereby capable and fit vessels to receive the fruit of his satisfaction: yea, we so far please and content God, that because when we have offended he looketh but for repentance at our hands, our repentance and the works thereof are therefore termed satisfactory, not for that so much is thereby done as the justice of God can exact, but because such actions of grief and humility in a man after sin are *illices divinae misericordiae* (as Tertullian speaketh of them) they draw that pity of God towards us, wherein he is for Christ's sake contented upon our submission to pardon our rebellion against him; and when that little which his law appointeth is faithfully executed, it pleaseth him in tender compassion and mercy to require no more.

Grace Defined

The Dublin Fragments

[In relating the doctrinal controversy over grace in the western Church during and following Augustine's life-time, Hooker firmly maintains the necessity of prevenient grace, and even locates this insight within the sphere of 'the Book of Nature', that is, what 'the diviner sort of the heathens themselves saw . . . ' See chapter 8 in this book.]

And lest ignorance what I mean by the name of grace should put into your head some new suspicion, know that I do understand grace so as all the ancient Fathers did in their writings against *Pelagius*. For whereas the grace of Almighty God signifieth either his undeserved love and favour; or his offered means of outward instruction and doctrine; or thirdly, that grace which worketh inwardly in men's hearts; the scholars of Pelagius denying original sin did likewise teach at the first, that in all men there is by nature ability to work out their own salvation. And although their profession soon after was, that without the grace of God, men can neither begin, proceed, nor continue in any good thing available unto eternal life, yet it was perceived that by grace they only meant those external incitements unto faith and godliness, which the Law, the Prophets, the Ministers, the works of God do offer; that is to say the second grace, whereby being provoked and stirred up, it is, as they supposed, in our own power to assent to seek after God, and to labour for that, which then in regard of such our willingness, God willingly doth bestow, so that partly holpen by his grace, but principally through the very defect ['desert' or 'effect'?] of our own travel we obtain life.

Touching natural sufficiency without grace, Pelagius generally was withstood, and the necessity of that third kind of grace which moved the heart inwardly, they all maintained against Pelagius. Only in this, there were a number of the French especially, who went not so far, as to think with St. Augustine that God would bestow his grace upon any, which did not first procure and obtain it by labour proceeding from that natural ability which yet remaineth in all men. Hilary therefore, informing St. Augustine what the French churches thought thereof, declareth their steadfast belief to have been, that in Adam *all men were utterly lost*, and that to deliver them which never could have risen by their own power *the way of obtaining life is offered: that they which desire health, and believe that they may be cured, do thereby obtain augmentation of faith, and the whole effect of safety. For in that it is said, 'believe and live,' the one of these is required at our hands, and the other so offered, that in lieu of our willingness, if we perform what God requireth, that which He offereth is afterwards bestowed. That freedom of will we have so far only, as thereby to be able without grace to accept the medicine which God doth offer. But, saith he, we worthily abhor and condemn them which think that in any man there is remaining any spark of ability to proceed but the least step further than this, to the recovery of health.*

Now although they did well maintain that we cannot finish our salvation without the *assistance of inward grace*; yet because they held that of ourselves by assenting to grace externally first offered, we may begin and thereby obtain the grace which perfecteth our raw and unsufficient beginnings, the French were herein as *Demipelagians* by St. Augustine, Prosper, Fulgentius, and sundry others gainsayed, at length also condemned by the Arausican Council, as the Council of Millevis had before determined against that first opinion of Pelagius which the French themselves did condemn. So that the whole question of grace being grown amongst the ancient unto this issue, *whether man may without God seek God, and without grace either desire or accept grace first offered*, the conclusion of the catholic part was No, and therefore in all their writings, the point still urged is grace, *both working inwardly, and preventing the very first desires, or motion of man to goodness.* Which unless we every where diligently mark, there is no man but may be abused by the words whereby Pelagians and Demipelagians seem to magnify the grace of God, the one meaning only *external grace*, the other *internal*, but only to perfect that which our own good desires without grace have begun. The diviner sort of the heathens themselves saw, that their own more eminent perfections in knowledge, wisdom, valour, and other the like qualities, for which sundry of them were had in singular admiration, did grow from more than the ordinary influence which that supreme cause instilleth into things beneath.

Justifying and Sanctifying Grace

A Learned Discourse of Justification

[This is a passage from one of the most important discussions in Hooker's theology: the nature of justifying grace and the righteousness it confers. Hooker seeks to correlate the apparently divergent claims of Paul and James regarding grace, faith, and works. See chapters 8 and 11 in this book.]

[3.] This openeth a way to the plain understanding of that grand question, which hangeth yet in controversy between us and the Church of Rome, about the matter of justifying righteousness.

[4.] First, although they imagine that the mother of our Lord and Saviour Jesus Christ were, for his honour, and by his special protection, preserved clean from all sin, yet touching the rest, they teach as we do, that all have sinned; that infants which did never actually offend, have their natures defiled, destitute of justice, and averted from God. They teach as we do, that God doth justify the soul of man alone, without any other coefficient cause of justice; that in making man righteous, none do work efficiently with God, but God. They teach as we do, that unto justice no man ever attained, but by the merits of Jesus Christ. They teach as we do, that although Christ as God be the efficient, as man the meritorious cause of our justice; yet in us also there is something required. God is the cause of our natural life; in him we live: but he quickeneth not the body without the soul in the body. Christ hath merited to make us just: but as a medicine which is made for health, doth not heal by being made, but by being applied; so, by the merits of Christ there can be no justification, without the application of his merits. Thus far we join hands with the Church of Rome.

[5.] Wherein then do we disagree? We disagree about the nature of the very essence of the medicine whereby Christ cureth our disease; about the manner of applying it; about the number and the power of means, which God requireth in us for the effectual applying thereof to our soul's comfort. When they are required to shew, what the righteousness is whereby a Christian man is justified, they answer, that it is a 'divine spiritual quality'; which quality received into the soul, doth first make it to be one of them who are born of God: and, secondly, endue it with power to bring forth such works, as they do that are born of him; even as the soul of man being joined unto his body, doth first make him to be in the number of reasonable creatures, and secondly enable him to perform the natural functions which are proper to his kind; that it maketh the soul gracious and amiable in the sight of God, in regard whereof it is termed Grace; that it purgeth, purifieth, washeth out, all the stains and pollutions of sin; that by it, through the

merit of Christ we are delivered as from sin, so from eternal death and
condemnation, the reward of sin. This grace they will have to be applied
by infusion; to the end, that as the body is warm by the heat which is in the
body, so the soul might be righteous by inherent grace: which grace they
make capable of increase; as the body may be more and more warm, so the
soul more and more justified, according as grace shall be augmented; the
augmentation whereof is merited by good works, as good works are made
meritorious by it. Wherefore, the first receipt of grace is in their divinity
the first justification; the increase thereof, the second justification. As grace
may be increased by the merit of good works; so it may be diminished by
the demerit of sins venial; it may be lost by mortal sin. Inasmuch, therefore,
as it is needful in the one case to repair, in the other to recover, the loss
which is made; the infusion of grace hath her sundry after-meals; for which
cause they make many ways to apply the infusion of grace. It is applied
unto infants through baptism, without either faith or works, and in them it
really taketh away original sin, and the punishment due unto it; it is applied
unto infidels and wicked men in their first justification through baptism,
without works, yet not without faith; and it taketh away both sin actual
and original, together with all whatsoever punishment eternal or temporal
thereby deserved. Unto such as have attained the first justification, that is
to say, the first receipt of grace, it is applied further by good works to the
increase of former grace, which is the second justification. If they work
more and more, grace doth more and more increase, and they are more and
more justified. To such as have diminished it by venial sins, it is applied by
holy water, Ave Marias, crossings, papal salutations, and such like, which
serve for reparations of grace decayed. To such as have lost it through
mortal sin, it is applied by the sacrament (as they term it) of penance;
which sacrament hath force to confer grace anew, yet in such sort, that
being so conferred, it hath not altogether so much power as at the first. For
it only cleanseth out the stain or guilt of sin committed, and changeth the
punishment eternal into a temporal satisfactory punishment, here, if time
do serve, if not, hereafter to be endured, except it be either lightened by
masses, works of charity, pilgrimages, fasts, and such like; or else shortened
by pardon for term, or by plenary pardon quite removed and taken away.
This is the mystery of the man of sin. This maze the Church of Rome doth
cause her followers to tread, when they ask her the way of justification. I
cannot stand now to unrip this building, and to sift it piece by piece; only I
will set a frame of apostolical erection by it in few words, that it may befall
Babylon, in presence of that which God hath builded, as it happened unto
Dagon before the ark.

'Doubtless,' saith the Apostle, 'I have counted all things loss, and I do
judge them to be dung, that I may win Christ; and be found in him, not
having mine own righteousness, but that which is through the faith of
Christ, the righteousness which is of God through faith.' Whether they

speak of the first or second justification, they make the essence of it a divine quality inherent, they make it righteousness which is in us. If it be in us, then it is ours, as our souls are ours, though we have them from God, and can hold them no longer than pleaseth him; for if he withdraw the breath of our nostrils, we fall to dust: but the righteousness wherein we must be found, if we will be justified, is not our own; therefore we cannot be justified by any inherent quality. Christ hath merited righteousness for as many as are found in him. In him God findeth us, if we be faithful; for by faith we are incorporated into Him. Then, although in ourselves we be altogether sinful and unrighteous, yet even the man which in himself is impious, full of iniquity, full of sin; him being found in Christ through faith, and having his sin in hatred through repentance; him God beholdeth with a gracious eye, putteth away his sin by not imputing it, taketh quite away the punishment due thereunto, by pardoning it; and accepteth him in Jesus Christ, as perfectly righteous, as if he had fulfilled all that is commanded him in the law: shall I say more perfectly righteous than if himself had fulfilled the whole law? I must take heed what I say: but the Apostle saith, 'God made him which knew no sin, to be sin for us; that we might be made the righteousness of God in him.' Such we are in the sight of God the Father, as is the very Son of God himself. Let it be counted folly, or phrensy, or fury, or whatsoever. It is our wisdom, and our comfort; we care for no knowledge in the world but this, that man hath sinned, and God hath suffered; that God hath made himself the sin of men, and that men are made the righteousness of God.

You see therefore that the church of Rome, in teaching justification by inherent grace, doth pervert the truth of Christ; and that by the hands of His Apostles we have received otherwise than she teacheth. Now concerning the righteousness of sanctification, we deny it not to be inherent; we grant, that unless we work, we have it not; only we distinguish it as a thing in nature different form the righteousness of justification: we are righteous the one way, by the faith of Abraham; the other way, except we do the works of Abraham, we are not righteous. Of the one St. Paul, 'To him that worketh not, but believeth, faith is counted for righteousness.' Of the other, St. John, 'Qui facit justitiam Justus est: - He is righteous which worketh righteousness.' Of the one, St. Paul doth prove by Abraham's example, that we have it of faith without works. Of the other, St. James by Abraham's example, that by works we have it, and not only by faith. St. Paul doth plainly sever these two parts of Christian righteousness one from the other. For in the sixth to the Romans thus he writeth, 'Being freed from sin, and made servants to God, ye have your fruit in holiness, and the end everlasting life.' 'Ye are made free from sin, and made servants unto God;' this is the righteousness of justification: 'Ye have your fruit in holiness;' this is the righteousness of sanctification. By the one we are interested in the right of inheriting; by the other we are brought to the actual possessing of eternal bliss, and so the end of both is everlasting life.

The Sacraments Defined

Laws, V, chapter l

[Hooker defines 'sacrament' both widely and narrowly. As a 'visible sign of invisible grace' he rejects memorialism and emphasises the sacraments' role in effecting what Christ makes possible for believers: 'the union of the soul with God'. See chapter 10 in this book.]

[1.] Instruction and Prayer whereof we have hitherto spoken, are duties which serve as elements, parts, or principles, to the rest that follow, in which number the Sacraments of the Church are chief. The Church is to us that very mother of our new birth, in whose bowels we are all bred, at whose breasts we receive nourishment. As many therefore as are apparently to our judgement born of God, they have the seed of their regeneration by the ministry of the Church which useth to that end and purpose not only the Word, but the Sacraments, both having generative force and virtue.

[2.] As oft as we mention a Sacrament properly understood, (for in the writings of the ancient Fathers all articles which are peculiar to Christian faith, all duties of religion containing that which sense or natural reason cannot of itself discern, are most commonly named Sacraments,) our restraint of the word to some few principal divine ceremonies importeth in every such ceremony two things, the substance of the ceremony itself which is visible, and besides that somewhat else more secret in reference whereunto we conceive that ceremony to be a Sacrament. For we all admire and honour the holy Sacraments, not respecting so much the service which we do unto God in receiving them, as the dignity of that sacred and secret gift which we thereby receive from God. Seeing that Sacraments therefore consist altogether in relation to some such gift or grace supernatural as only God can bestow, how should any but the Church administer those ceremonies as Sacraments which are not thought to be Sacraments by any but by the Church?

[3.] There is in Sacraments to be observed their force and their form of administration. Upon their force their necessity dependeth. So that how they are necessary we cannot discern till we see how effectual they are. When Sacraments are said to be visible signs of invisible grace, we thereby conceive how grace is indeed the very end for which these heavenly mysteries were instituted, and besides sundry other properties observed in them, the matter whereof they consist is such as signifieth, figureth, and representeth their end. But still their efficacy resteth obscure to our understanding, except we search somewhat more distinctly what grace in particular that is whereunto they are referred, and what manner of operation they have towards it.

The use of sacraments is but only in this life, yet so that here they concern a far better life than this, and are for that cause accompanied with 'grace which worketh Salvation.' Sacraments are the powerful instruments of God to eternal life. For as our natural life consisteth in the union of the body with the soul; so our life supernatural in the union of the soul with God. And forasmuch as there is no union of God with man without that mean between both which is both, it seemeth requisite that we first consider how God is in Christ, then how Christ is in us, and how the Sacraments do serve to make us partakers of Christ. In other things we may be more brief, but the weight of this requireth largeness.

The Trinitarian Basis of the Sacraments

Laws, V, chapters lvi and lvii

[The sacraments are described as fashioning 'mystical association' with Christ by the operation of the Holy Spirit; in so doing they involve a sensory and imaginative kind of religious experience appropriate to diverse human capacities and sensibilities. See chapter 10 in this book.]

[13.] Thus therefore we see how the Father is in the Son, and the Son in the Father; how they both are in all things, and all things in them; what communion Christ hath with his Church, how his Church and every member thereof is in him by original derivation, and he personally in them by way of mystical association wrought through the gift of the Holy Ghost, which they that are his receive from him, and together with the same what benefit soever the vital force of his body and blood may yield, yea by steps and degrees they receive the complete measure of all such divine grace, as doth sanctify and save throughout, till the day of their final exaltation to a state of fellowship in glory, with him whose partakers they are now in those things that tend to glory. As for any mixture of the substance of his flesh with ours, the participation which we have of Christ includeth no such kind of gross surmise.

LVII. It greatly offendeth, that some, when they labour to shew the use of the holy Sacraments, assign unto them no end but only *to teach* the mind, by other senses, that which the Word doth teach by hearing. Whereupon, how easily neglect and careless regard of so heavenly mysteries may follow, we see in part by some experience had of those men with whom that opinion is most strong. For where the word of God may be heard, which teacheth with much more expedition and more full explication any thing we have to learn, if all the benefit we reap by sacraments be instruction, they which at all times have opportunity of using the better mean to that purpose, will surely hold the worse in less estimation. And unto infants which are not capable of instruction, who would not think it a mere superfluity that any sacrament is administered, if to administer the sacraments be but to teach receivers what God doth for them? There is of sacraments therefore undoubtedly some other more excellent and heavenly use.

The Sacramental, Personal Presence of Christ

Chapter lxvii

[The key to sacrament presence lies in a proper theological grasp of 'the Person of Christ', who in his person comprehends both created and uncreated natures. Hooker makes the case for sacramental instrumentalism by which Christ 'imparts' himself to the recipient. See chapter 10 in this book.]

[4.] If then the presence of Christ with them did so much move, judge what their thoughts and affections were at the time of this new presentation of Christ not before their eyes but within their souls. They had learned before that his flesh and blood are the true cause of eternal life; that this they are not by the bare force of their own substance, but through the dignity and worth of his Person which offered them up by way of sacrifice for the life of the whole world, and doth make them still effectual thereunto; finally that to us they are life in particular, by being particularly received. Thus much they knew, although as yet they understood not perfectly to what effect or issue the same would come, till at the length being assembled for no other cause which they could imagine but to have eaten the Passover only that Moses appointeth, when they saw their Lord and Master with hands and eyes lifted up to heaven first bless and consecrate for the endless good of all generations till the world's end the chosen elements of bread and wine, which elements made for ever the instruments of life by virtue of his divine benediction they being the first that were commanded to receive from him, the first which were warranted by his promise that not only unto them at the present time but to whomsoever they and their successors after them did duly administer the same, those mysteries should serve as conducts of life and conveyances of his body and blood unto them, was it possible they should hear that voice, 'Take, eat, this is my body; drink ye all of this, this is my blood;' possible that doing what was required and believing what was promised, the same should have present effect in them, and not fill them with a kind of fearful admiration at the heaven which they saw in themselves? They had at that time a sea of comfort and joy to wade in, and we by that which they did are taught that this heavenly food is given for the satisfying of our empty souls, and not for the exercising of our curious and subtile wits.

[5.] If we doubt what those admirable words may import, let him be our teacher for the meaning of Christ to whom Christ was himself a schoolmaster, let our Lord's Apostle be his interpreter, content we ourselves with his explication, My body, *the communion of my body*, My blood, *the communion of my blood*. Is there any thing more expedite, clear, and easy, than that as Christ is termed our life because through him we obtain life, so the parts of this sacrament are his body and blood for that they are so to us who receiving them receive that by them which they are termed? The bread and cup are his body and blood because they are causes instrumental upon the receipt whereof the *participation* of his body and blood ensueth. For that which produceth any certain effect is not vainly nor improperly said to be that very effect whereunto it tendeth. Every cause is in the effect which groweth from it. Our souls and bodies quickened to eternal life are effects the cause whereof is the Person of Christ, his body and blood are the true wellspring out of which this life floweth. So that his body and blood are in that very subject whereunto they minister life not only by effect or operation, even as the influence of the heavens is in plants, beasts, men, and in every thing they quicken, but also by a far more divine and mystical kind of union, which maketh us one with him even as he and the Father are one.

[6.] The real presence of Christ's most blessed body and blood is not therefore to be sought for in the sacrament, but in the worthy receiver of the sacrament.

And with this the very order of our Saviour's words agreeth, first 'take and eat;' then 'this is my Body which was broken for you:' first 'drink ye all of this;' then followeth 'this is my Blood of the New Testament which is shed for many for the remission of sins.' I see not which way it should be gathered by the words of Christ, when and where the bread is His body or the cup His blood, but only in the very heart and soul of him which receiveth them. As for the sacraments, they really exhibit, but for aught we can gather out of that which is written of them, they are not really nor do they really contain in themselves that grace which with them or by them it pleaseth God to bestow.

If on all sides it be confessed that the grace of Baptism is poured into the soul of man, that by water we receive it although it be neither seated in the water nor the water changed into it, what should induce men to think that the grace of the Eucharist must needs be in the Eucharist before it can be in us that receive it?

The fruit of the Eucharist is the participation of the body and blood of Christ. There is no sentence of Holy Scripture which saith that we cannot by this sacrament be made partakers of his body and blood except they be first contained in the sacrament or the sacrament converted into them. 'This is my body,' and 'this is my blood,' being words of promise, sith we all agree that by the sacrament Christ doth really and truly in us perform his promise, why do we vainly trouble ourselves with so fierce contentions whether by consubstantiation, or else by transubstantiation the sacrament itself be first possessed with Christ, or no? A thing which no way can either further or hinder us howsoever it stand, because our participation of Christ in this sacrament dependeth on the co-operation of his omnipotent power which maketh it his body and blood to us, whether with change or without alteration of the element such as they imagine we need not greatly to care nor inquire.

[7.] Take therefore that wherein all agree, and then consider by itself what cause why the rest in question should not rather be left as superfluous than urged as necessary. It is on all sides plainly confessed, first that this sacrament is a true and real participation of Christ, who thereby imparteth himself even his whole entire Person *as a mystical Head* unto every soul that recevieth him, and that every such receiver doth thereby incorporate or unite himself unto Christ as *a mystical member of* him, yea of them also whom he acknowledgeth to be his own; secondly that to whom *the person of Christ* is thus communicated, to them he giveth by the same sacrament his Holy Spirit to sanctify them as it sanctifieth him which is their head; thirdly that what *merit, force or virtue soever there is in his sacrificed body and blood,* we freely fully and wholly have it by this sacrament; fourthly that *the effect thereof in us is a real transmutation of our souls and bodies* from sin to righteousness, from death and corruption to immortality and life; fifthly that because the sacrament being of itself but a corruptible and earthly creature must needs be thought an unlikely instrument to work so admirable effects in man, we are therefore to rest ourselves altogether upon *the strength of his glorious power* who is able and will bring to pass that the bread and cup which he giveth us shall be truly the thing he promiseth.

[8.] It seemeth therefore much amiss that against them whom they term Sacramentaries so many invective discourses are made all running upon two points, that the Eucharist is not a bare sign or figure only, and that the efficacy of his body and blood is not all we receive in this sacrament. For no man having read their books and writings which are thus traduced can be ignorant that both these assertions they plainly confess to be most true. They do not so interpret the words of Christ as if the name of his body did import but the figure of his body, and to be were only to signify his blood. They grant that these holy mysteries received in due manner do instrumentally both make us partakers of the grace of that body and blood which were given for the life of the world, and besides also impart unto us even in true and real though mystical manner the very Person of our Lord himself, whole, perfect, and entire, as hath been shewed.

Chapter lvii

[2.] Sacraments, by reason of their mixed nature, are more diversely interpreted and disputed of than any other part of religion besides, for that in so great store of properties belonging to the selfsame thing, as every man's wit hath taken hold of some especial consideration above the rest, so they have accordingly seemed one to cross another as touching their several opinions about the necessity of sacraments, whereas in truth their disagreement is not great. For let respect be had to the duty which every communicant doth undertake, and we may well determine concerning the use of sacraments, that they serve as bonds of obedience to God, strict obligations to the mutual exercise of Christian charity, provocations to godliness, preservations from sin, memorials of the principal benefits of Christ; respect the time of their institution, and it thereby appeareth that God hath annexed them for ever unto the New Testament, as other rites were before with the old; regard the weakness which is in us, and they are warrants for the more security of our belief; compare the receivers of them with such as receive them not, and sacraments are marks of distinction to separate God's own from strangers: so that in all these respects, they are found to be most necessary.

[3.] But their chiefest force and virtue consisteth not herein so much as in that they are heavenly ceremonies, which God hath sanctified and ordained to be administered in his Church, first, as marks whereby to know when God doth impart the vital or saving grace of Christ unto all that are capable thereof, and secondly as means conditional which God requireth in them unto whom he imparteth grace. For sith God in himself is invisible, and cannot by us be discerned working, therefore when it seemeth good in the eyes of his heavenly wisdom, that men for some special intent and purpose should take notice of his glorious presence, he giveth them some plain and sensible token whereby to know what they cannot see. For Moses to see God and live was impossible, yet Moses by fire knew where the glory of God extraordinarily was present. The angel, by whom God endued the waters of the pool called Bethesda with supernatural virtue to heal, was not seen of any, yet the time of the angel's presence known by the troubled motions of the waters themselves. The Apostles by fiery tongues which they saw, were admonished when the Spirit, which they could not behold, was upon them. In like manner it is with us, Christ and his Holy Spirit with all their blessed effects, though entering into the soul of man we are not able to apprehend or express how, do notwithstanding give notice of the times when they use to make their access, because it pleaseth Almighty God to communicate by sensible means those blessing which are incomprehensible.

[4.] Seeing therefore that grace is a consequent of sacraments, a thing which accompanieth them as their end, a benefit which he that hath receiveth from God himself the author of sacraments, and not from any other natural or supernatural quality in them, it may be hereby both understood that sacraments are necessary, and that the manner of their necessity to life supernatural is not in all respects as food unto natural life, because they contain *in themselves* no vital force or efficacy, they are not physical but *moral instruments* of salvation, duties of service and worship, which unless we perform as the Author of grace requireth, they are unprofitable. For all receive not the grace of God which receive the sacraments of his grace. Neither is it *ordinarily* his will to bestow the grace of sacraments on any, but by the sacraments; which grace also they that receive by sacraments or with sacraments, receive it from him and not from them. For of sacraments the very same is true which Solomon's wisdom observeth in the brazen serpent, 'He that turned towards it was not healed by the thing he saw, but by thee, O Saviour of all.'

[5.] This is therefore the necessity of sacraments. That saving grace which Christ originally is or hath for the general good of his whole Church, by sacraments he severally deriveth into every member thereof. Sacraments serve as the instruments of God to that end and purpose, moral instruments, the use whereof is in our hands, the effect in his; for the use we have his express commandment, for the effect his conditional promise: so that without our obedience to the one, there is of the other no apparent assurance, as contrariwise where the signs and sacraments of his grace are not either through contempt unreceived, or received with contempt, we are not to doubt but that they really give what they promise, and are what they signify. For we take not baptism nor the eucharist for bare *resemblances* or memorials of things absent, neither for *naked signs* and testimonies assuring us of grace received before, but (as they are indeed and in verity) for means effectual whereby God when we take the sacraments delivereth into our hands that grace available unto eternal life, which grace the sacraments represent or signify.

[6.] There have grown in the doctrine concerning sacraments many difficulties for want of distinct explication what kind or degree of grace doth belong unto each sacrament. For by this it hath come to pass, that the true immediate cause why Baptism, and why the Supper of our Lord is necessary, few do rightly and distinctly consider. It cannot be denied but sundry the same effects and benefits which grow unto men by the one sacrament may rightly be attributed unto the other. Yet then doth baptism challenge to itself but the inchoation of those graces, the consummation whereof dependeth on mysteries ensuing. We receive Christ Jesus in baptism once as the first beginner, in the eucharist often as being by continual degrees the finisher of our life. By baptism therefore we receive Christ Jesus, and from him that saving grace which is proper unto baptism, By the other sacrament we receive him also, imparting therein himself and that grace which the eucharist properly bestoweth. So that each sacrament having both that which is general or common, and that also which is peculiar unto itself, we may hereby gather that participation of Christ which properly belongeth to any one sacrament, is not otherwise to be obtained but by the sacrament whereunto it is proper.

Faith and Works

The Dublin Fragments

[Hooker presents the basis of congruous merit: God's gracious condescension 'unto favourable conditions'. Cooperation and effort – 'works' – are needful in the life of grace, which restores and enhances humankind's 'ability' to live into its supernatural perfection. See chapter 11 in this book.]

But lest only wrath and justice should take effect, love and mercy be without exercise, by reason of sin, God hath not suffered the preparations of eternal life to be thus frustrated altogether as concerning man, but chosen rather to remit on his own part much of that, which extremity and rigour of justice might require, being contented to condescend unto favourable conditions: and except it be where incurable malice, on the part of the sinful themselves, will not suffer mercy with such conditions to take place, leadeth still to eternal life, by an amiable course, framed even according to the very state wherein we now are. He is not wanting to the world in any necessary thing for the attainment of eternal life, though many things be necessary now, which according to our first condition we needed not. He bestoweth now eternal life as his own free and undeserved gift; together also with that general inheritance and lot of eternal life, great varieties of rewards proportioned to the very degrees of those labours, which to perform he himself by his grace enableth. He leaveth us not as Adam in the hands of our own wills, at once endued with ability to stand of our own accord, but because that ability is altogether lost, he putteth into our souls continually new strength, the paths of our duty he layeth before us, and directeth our steps therein, he giveth warning whereby to know, and wisdom also whereby to prevent the fearful hazards whereinto our souls, being left to themselves, would assuredly fall....

It followeth therefore, I. That God hath predestined certain men, not all men. 2. That the cause, moving him hereunto, was not the foresight of any virtue in us at all. 3. That to him the number of the elect is definitely known. 4. That it cannot be but their sins must condemn them, to whom the purpose of his saving mercy doth not extend. 5. That to God's foreknown elect final continuance of grace is given. 6. That inward grace, whereby to be saved, is deservedly not given unto all men. 7. That no man cometh unto Christ, whom God, by the inward grace of his Spirit, draweth not. 8. And that it is not in every, no not in any man's own mere ability, freedom, and power, to be saved, no man's salvation being possible without grace. Howbeit, God is no favourer of sloth; and therefore, there can be no such absolute decree, touching man's salvation, as on our part includeth no necessity of care and travail, but shall certainly take effect, whether we ourselves do wake or sleep.

Theology: Faith and Reason

Laws, III, chapter viii

[Scripture's unique status is set within a rich bed of knowledge gained outside of Scripture itself. Indeed, such knowledge is necessary in appreciating Scripture as Scripture. See chapter 12 in this book.]

[11.] . . . . The whole drift of the Scripture of God, what is it but only to teach Theology? Theology, what is it but the science of things divine? What science can be attained unto without the help of natural discourse and reason? 'Judge you of that which I speak,' saith the Apostle. In vain it were to speak anything of God, but that by reason men are able somewhat to judge of that they hear, and by discourse to discern how consonant it is to truth.

[12.] Scripture indeed teacheth things above nature, things which our reason by itself could not reach unto. Yet those things also we believe, knowing by reason that the Scripture is the word of God . . .

[13.] Because we maintain that in Scripture we are taught all things necessary unto salvation; hereupon very childishly it is by some demanded, what Scripture can teach us the sacred authority of the Scripture, upon the knowledge whereof our whole faith and salvation dependeth? As though there were any kind of science in the world which leadeth men into knowledge without presupposing a number of things already known. No science doth make known the first principles whereupon it buildeth, but they are always either taken for plain and manifest in themselves, or as proved and granted already, some former knowledge having made them evident.

Human Actions

Laws, II, chapter viii

[The relation between reason and will is highlighted in this account of moral agency. Noteworthy is the threefold gradation – 'sundry degrees' – of goodness of which humankind is capable, and the resultant grades of heavenly 'reward' which God gives to believers; it provides the basis for Hooker's implicit theology of sainthood. See chapter 13 in this book.]

[1.] But to the end it may more plainly appear what we are to judge of their sentences, and of the cause itself wherein they are alleged; first, it may not well be denied, that all actions of men endued with the use of reason are generally either good or bad. For although it be granted that no action be properly termed good or evil unless it be voluntary; yet this can be no let to our former assertion, That all actions of men endued with the use of reason are generally either good or evil; because even those things are done voluntarily by us which other creatures do naturally, inasmuch as we might stay our doing of them if we would. Beasts naturally do take their food and rest when it offereth itself unto them. If men did so too, and could do no otherwise of themselves, there were no place for any such reproof as that of our Saviour Christ unto his disciples, 'Could ye not watch with me one hour?' That which is voluntarily performed in things tending to the end, if it be well done, must needs be done with deliberate consideration of some reasonable cause wherefore we should rather do it than not. Whereupon it seemeth, that in such actions only those are said to be good or evil which are capable of deliberation; so that many things be hourly done by men, wherein they need not use with themselves any manner of consultation at all, it may perhaps hereby seem that well or ill-doing belongeth only to weightier affairs, and to those deeds which are of so great importance that they require advice. But thus to determine were perilous, and peradventure unsound also. I do rather incline to think, that seeing all the unforced actions of men are voluntary, and all voluntary actions tending to the end have choice, and all choice presupposeth the knowledge of some cause wherefore we make it: where the reasonable cause of such actions so readily offereth itself that it needeth not to be sought for; in those things though we do not deliberate, yet they are of their nature apt to be deliberated on, in regard of the will, which may incline either way, and would not any one way bend itself, if there were not some apparent motive to lead it. Deliberation actual we use, when there is doubt what we should incline our wills unto. Where no doubt is, deliberation is not excluded as impertinent unto the thing, but as needless in regard of the agent, which seeth already what to resolve upon. It hath no apparent absurdity therefore in it to think, that all actions of men endued with the use of reason are generally either good or evil.

[2.] Whatsoever is good, the same is also approved of God: and according unto the sundry degrees of goodness, the kinds of divine approbation are in like sort multiplied. Some things are good, yet in so mean a degree of goodness, that men are only not disproved or allowed of God for them. 'No man hateth his own flesh'. 'If ye do good unto them that do so to you, the very publicans themselves do as much.' 'They are worse than infidels that have no care to provide for their own.' In actions of this sort, the very light of Nature alone may discover that which is so far forth in the sight of God allowed.

[3.] Some things in such sort are allowed, that they be also required as necessary unto salvation, by way of direct immediate and proper necessity final; so that without performance of them we cannot by ordinary course be saved, nor by any means by excluded from life by observing them. In actions of this kind our chiefest direction is from Scripture, for Nature is no sufficient teacher what we should do that we may attain unto life everlasting. The unsufficiency of the light of Nature is by the light of Scripture so fully and so perfectly herein supplied, that further light than this hath added there doth not need unto that end.

[4.] Finally some things, although not so required of necessity that to leave them undone excludeth from salvation, are notwithstanding of so great dignity and acceptation with God, that most ample reward in heaven is laid up for them. Hereof we have no commandment either in Nature or Scripture which doth exact them at our hands; yet those motives there are in both which draw most effectually our minds unto them. In this kind there is not the least action but it doth somewhat make to the accessory augmentation of our bliss. For which cause our Saviour doth plainly witness, that there shall not be as much as a cup of water bestowed for his sake without reward. Hereupon dependeth whatsoever difference there is between the states of saints in glory; hither we refer whatsoever belongeth unto the highest perfection of man by way of service towards God; hereunto that fervour and first love of Christians did bend itself, causing them to sell their possessions, and lay down the price at the blessed Apostles' feet. Hereat St. Paul undoubtedly did aim in so far abridging his own liberty, and exceeding that which the bond of necessary and enjoined duty tied him unto.

Spiritual Life

Prayer

Laws, V, chapter xxiii

[In describing prayer Hooker employs his principle of hierarchy, and describes an angelic interchange between heaven and earth. He suggests too that the spiritual aspirations of prayer express our deepest human desire, a Good beyond all others. See chapter 14 in this book.]

XXIII. Between the throne of God in heaven and his Church upon earth here militant if it be so that Angels have their continual intercourse, where should we find the same more verified than in these two ghostly exercises, the one Doctrine, and the other Prayer? For what is the assembling of the Church to learn, but the receiving of Angels descended from above? What to pray, but the sending of Angels upward? His heavenly inspirations and our holy desires are as so many Angels of intercourse and commerce between God and us. As teaching bringeth us to know that God is our supreme truth; so prayer testifieth that we acknowledge him our sovereign good.

Besides, sith on God as the most high all inferior causes in the world are dependent; and the higher any cause is, the more it coveteth to impart virtue unto things beneath it; how should any kind of service we do or can do find greater acceptance than prayer, which sheweth our concurrence with him in desiring that wherewith his very nature doth most delight?

Is not the name of prayer usual to signify even all the service that ever we do unto God? And that for no other cause, as I suppose, but to shew that there is in religion no acceptable duty which devout invocation of the name of God doth not either presuppose or infer. Prayers are those 'calves of men's lips;' those most gracious and sweet odours; those rich presents and gifts, which being carried up to heaven do best testify our dutiful affection, and are for the purchasing of all favour at the hands of God the most undoubted means we can use.

Sanctifying Times and Seasons

Laws, V, chapter lxx

[Hooker's advocacy of the liturgical calendar shows how his theology links creation and redemption in the Incarnate Word of God. See chapters 9 and 14 in this book.]

LXX. The sanctification of days and times is a token of that thankfulness and a part of that public honour which we owe to God for admirable benefits, whereof it doth not suffice that we keep a secret calendar, taking thereby our private occasions as we list ourselves to think how much God hath done for all men, but the days which are chosen out to serve as public memorials of such mercies as ought to be clothed with those outward robes of holiness whereby their difference from other days must be made sensible. But because time in itself as hath already been proved can receive no alteration, the hallowing of festival days must consist in the shape or countenance which we put upon the affairs that are incident into those days.

[2.] 'This is the day which the Lord hath made,' saith the prophet David; 'let us rejoice and be glad in it.' So that generally offices and duties of religious *joy* are that wherein the hallowing of festival times consisteth. The most natural testimonies of our rejoicing in God are first His praises set forth with cheerful alacrity of mind, secondly our comfort and delight expressed by a charitable largeness of somewhat more than common bounty, thirdly sequestration from ordinary labours, the toils and cares whereof are not meet to be companions of such gladness. Festival solemnity therefore is nothing but the due mixture as it were of these three elements, Praise, and Bounty, and Rest.

Penitential Days and Seasons

Laws, V, chapter lxxii

[The treatment of fasting reveals a biblical and traditional spirituality in which intense supplication to God and bodily self-denial go hand-in-hand. In Hooker's age those disciplines were still largely communal experiences, and Hooker affirms the importance of that as the body politic honours its spiritual dimension. The rhythm of feast and fast also reflects the spectrum of joy and grief in human lives. See chapter 14 in this book.]

LXXII. The matching of contrary things together is a kind of illustration to both. Having therefore spoken thus much of festival days, the next that offer themselves to hand are days of pensive humiliation and sorrow. Fastings are either of men's own free and voluntary accord as their particular devotion doth move them thereunto; or else they are publicly enjoined in the Church and required at the hands of all men. There are which altogether disallow not the former kind, and the latter they greatly commend, so that it be upon extraordinary occasions only, and after one certain manner exercised. But yearly or weekly fasts such as ours in the church of England they allow no further than as the temporal state of the land doth require the same for the maintenance of seafaring men and preservation of cattle, because the decay of the one and the waste of the other could not well be prevented but by a politic order appointing some such usual change of diet as ours is.

We are therefore rather to make it manifest in all men's eyes, that set times of fasting appointed in spiritual considerations to be kept by all sorts of men took not their beginning either from Montanus or any other whose heresies may prejudice the credit and due estimation thereof, but have their ground in the law of nature, are allowable in God's sight, were in all ages heretofore, and may till the world's end be observed not without singular use and benefit.

[2.] . . . . The affections of Joy and Grief are so knit unto all the actions of man's life, that whatsoever we can do or may be done unto us, the sequel thereof is continually the one or the other affection. Whereof considering that they which grieve and joy as they ought cannot possibly otherwise than as they should, the Church of Christ, the most absolute and perfect school of all virtue, hath by the special direction of God's good Spirit hitherto always inured men from their infancy partly with days of festival exercise for the framing of one affection, and partly with times of a contrary sort for the perfecting of the other. Howbeit over and besides this, we must note that as resting so fasting likewise attendeth sometimes no less upon the actions of the higher, than upon the affections of the lower part of the mind. Fasting (saith Tertullian) is a work of reverence towards God. The end sometimes elevation of mind; sometimes the purpose thereof clean contrary. The cause why Moses in the Mount did so long fast was mere divine speculation, the cause why David, humiliation. Our life is a mixture of good with evil. When we are partakers of good things we joy, neither can we but grieve at the contrary. If that befall us which maketh glad, our festival solemnities declare our rejoicing to be in him whose mere undeserved mercy is the author of all happiness; if any thing be either imminent or present which we shun, our watchings, fastings, cries and tears are unfeigned testimonies, that ourselves we condemn as the only causes of our own misery, and do all acknowledge him no less inclinable than able to save.

The Church – A Mystical, and Mixed Body

Laws, III, chapter i

[Hooker's ecclesiology strives to hold the 'mystical' and 'sensible', invisible and visible Church together. His generous definition of the Church, eschewing hard parameters of inclusion and exclusion, is appropriate for a national Church and stands against the sectarian ecclesiology of the various non-conforming groups. See chapter 15 in this book.]

I. Albeit the substance of those controversies whereinto we have begun to wade be rather of outward things appertaining to the Church of Christ, than of any thing wherein the nature and being of the Church consisteth, yet because the subject or matter which this position concerneth is, *A Form of Church Government* or *Church Polity*, it therefore behoveth us so far forth to consider the nature of the Church, as is requisite for men's more clear and plain understanding in what respect Laws of Polity or Government are necessary thereunto.

[2.] That Church of Christ, which we properly term his body mystical, can be but one; neither can that one be sensibly discerned by any man, inasmuch as the parts thereof are some in heaven already with Christ, and the rest that are on earth (albeit their natural persons be visible) we do not discern under this property, whereby they are truly and infallibly of that body. Only our minds by intellectual conceit are able to apprehend, that such a real body there is, a body collective, because it containeth an huge multitude; a body mystical, because the mystery of their conjunction is removed altogether from sense. Whatsoever we read in Scripture concerning the endless love and the saving mercy which God sheweth to his Church, the only proper subject thereof is this Church. Concerning this flock it is that our Lord and Saviour hath promised, 'I give unto them eternal life, and they shall never perish, neither shall any pluck them out of my hands.' They who are of this society have such marks and notes of distinction from all others, as are not object unto our sense; only unto God, who seeth their hearts and understandeth all their secret cogitations, unto him they are clear and manifest. All men knew Nathanael to be an Israelite. But our Saviour piercing deeper giveth further testimony of him than men could have done with such certainty as he did, 'Behold indeed an Israelite in whom is no guile.' If we profess, as Peter did, that we love the Lord, and profess it in the hearing of men, charity is prone to believe all things, and therefore charitable men are likely to think we do so, as long as they see no proof to the contrary. But that our love is sound and sincere, that it cometh from 'a pure heart and a good conscience and a faith unfeigned,' who can pronounce, saving only the Searcher of all men's hearts, who alone intuitively doth know in this kind who are His?

[3.] And as those everlasting promises of love, mercy, and blessedness belong to the mystical Church; even so on the other side when we read of any duty which the Church of God is bound unto, the Church whom this doth concern is a sensibly known company. And this visible Church in like sort is but one, continued from the first beginning of the world to the last end. Which company being divided into two moieties, the one before, the other since the coming of Christ; that part, which since the coming of Christ partly hath embraced and partly shall hereafter embrace the Christian Religion, we term as by a more proper name the Church of Christ. And therefore the Apostle affirmeth plainly of all men Christian, that be they Jews or Gentiles, bond or free, they are all incorporated into one company, they all make but *one body*. The unity of which visible body and Church of Christ consisteth in that uniformity which all several persons thereunto belonging have, by reason of that *one Lord* whose servants they all profess themselves, that *one Faith* which they all acknowledge, that *one Baptism* wherewith they are all initiated.

[4.] The visible Church of Jesus Christ is therefore one, in outward profession of those things, which supernaturally appertain to the very essence of Christianity, and are necessarily required in every particular Christian man. 'Let all the house of Israel know for certainty,' saith Peter, 'that God hath made him both Lord and Christ, even this Jesus whom you have crucified.' Christians therefore they are not, which call him not their Master and Lord. And from hence it came that first at Antioch, and afterwards throughout the whole world, all that are of the Church visible were called Christian even amongst the heathen. Which name unto them was precious and glorious, but in the estimation of the rest of the world even Christ Jesus himself was execrable; for whose sake all men were so likewise which did acknowledge him to be their Lord. This himself did foresee, and therefore armed his Church, to the end they might sustain it without discomfort. 'All these things they will do unto you for my name's sake; yea, the time shall come, that whosoever killeth you will think that he doth God good service. These things I tell you, that when the hour shall come, ye may then call to mind how I told you beforehand of them.'

[5.] But our naming of Jesus Christ the Lord is not enough to prove us Christians, unless we also embrace that faith, which Christ hath published unto the world. To shew that the angel of Pergamus continued in Christianity, behold how the Spirit of Christ speaketh, 'Thou keepest my name, and thou hast not denied my faith.' Concerning which faith, 'the rule thereof,' saith Tertullian, 'is one alone, immovable, and no way possible to be better framed anew.' What rule that is he sheweth by rehearsing those few articles of Christian belief. And before Tertullian, Ireney; 'The Church though scattered through the whole world unto the utmost borders of the earth, hath from the Apostles and their disciples received belief.' The parts of which belief he also reciteth, in substance the very same with Tertullian, and thereupon inferreth, 'This faith the Church being spread far and wide preserveth as if one house did contain them: these things it equally embraceth, as though it had even one soul, one heart, and no more: it publisheth teacheth and delivereth these things with uniform consent, as if God had given it but one only tongue wherewith to speak. He which amongst the guides of the Church is best able to speak uttereth no more than this, and less than this the most simple doth not utter, when they make profession of their faith.'

[6.] Now although we know the Christian faith and allow of it, yet in this respect we are but entering; entered we are not into the visible Church before our admittance by the door of Baptism. Wherefore immediately upon the acknowledgement of Christian faith, the Eunuch (we see) was baptized by Philip, Paul by Ananias, by Peter an huge multitude containing three thousand souls, which being once baptized were reckoned in the number of souls added to the visible Church.

[7.] As for those virtues that belong unto moral righteousness and honesty of life, we do not mention them, because they are not proper unto Christian men, as they are Christian, but do concern them as they are men. True it is, the want of these virtues excludeth from salvation. So doth much more the absence of inward belief of heart; so doth despair and lack of hope; so emptiness of Christian love and charity. But we speak now of the visible Church, whose children are signed with this mark, 'One Lord, one Faith, one Baptism.' In whomsoever these things are, the Church doth acknowledge them for her children; them only she holdeth for aliens and strangers, in whom these things are not found. For want of these it is that Saracens, Jews, and Infidels are excluded out of the bounds of the Church. Others we may not deny to be of the visible Church, as long as these things are not wanting in them. For apparent it is, that all men are of necessity either Christians or not Christians. If by external profession they be Christians, then are they of the visible Church of Christ: and Christians by external profession they are all, whose mark of recognizance hath in it those things which we have mentioned, yea, although they be impious idolaters, wicked heretics, persons excommunicable, yea, and cast out for notorious improbity. Such withal we deny not to be the imps and limbs of Satan, even as long as they continue such.

[8.] Is it then possible, that the selfsame men should belong both to the synagogue of Satan and to the Church of Jesus Christ? Unto that Church which is his mystical body, not possible; because that body consisteth of none but only true Israelites, true sons of Abraham, true servants and saints of God. Howbeit of that visible body and Church of Jesus Christ those may be and oftentimes are, in respect of the main parts of their outward profession, who in regard of their inward disposition of mind, yea, of external conversation, yea, even of some parts of their very profession, are most worthily both hateful in the sight of God himself, and in the eyes of the sounder part of the visible Church most execrable. Our Saviour therefore compareth the kingdom of heaven to a net, whereunto all which cometh neither is nor seemeth fish: his Church he compareth unto a field, where tares manifestly known and seen by all men do grow intermingled with good corn, and even so shall continue till the final consummation of the world. God hath had ever and ever shall have some Church visible upon earth. When the people of God worshipped the calf in the wilderness; when they adored the brazen serpent; when they served the gods of nations; when they bowed their knees to Baal; when they burnt incense and offered sacrifice unto idols: true it is, the wrath of God was most fiercely inflamed against them, their prophets justly condemned them, as an adulterous seed and a wicked generation of miscreants, which had forsaken the living God, and of him were likewise forsaken, in respect of that singular mercy wherewith he kindly and lovingly embraced his faithful children. Howbeit retaining the law of God and the holy seal of his covenant, the sheep of his visible flock they continued even in the depth of their disobedience and rebellion. Wherefore not only *amongst* them God always had his Church, because he had thousands which never bowed their knees to Baal; but whose knees were bowed unto Baal, even they were also of that visible Church of God. Nor did the Prophet so complain, as if that Church had been quite and clean extinguished; but he took it as though there had not been remaining in the world any besides himself, that carried a true and an upright heart towards God with care to serve him according unto his holy will.

The Church - Conciliar

Laws, I, chapter x

[Patristic sources guide Hooker's advocacy of a conciliar model of Church governance and decision-making both within the nation and, equally, between Christian nations. See chapter 15 in this book.]

[14.] Now as there is great cause of communion, and consequently of laws for the maintenance of communion, amongst nations; so amongst nations Christian the like in regard even of Christianity hath been always judged needful.

And in this kind of correspondence amongst nations the force of general councils doth stand. For as one and the same law divine, whereof in the next place we are to speak, is unto all Christian churches a rule for the chiefest things; by means whereof they all in that respect make one church, as having all but 'one Lord, one faith, and one baptism:' so the urgent necessity of mutual communion for preservation of our unity in these things, as also for order in some other things convenient to be every where uniformly kept, maketh it requisite that the Church of God here on earth have her laws of spiritual commerce between Christian nations; laws by virtue whereof all churches may enjoy freely the use of those reverend, religious, and sacred consultations, which are termed Councils General. A thing whereof God's own blessed Spirit was the author; a thing practised by the holy Apostles themselves; a thing always afterward kept and observed throughout the world; a thing never otherwise than most highly esteemed of, till pride, ambition, and tyranny began by factious and vile endeavours to abuse that divine invention unto the furtherance of wicked purposes. But as the just authority of civil courts and parliaments is not therefore to be abolished, because sometime there is cunning used to frame them according to the private intents of men over potent in the commonwealth; so the grievous abuse which hath been of councils should rather cause men to study how so gracious a thing may again be reduced to that first perfection, than in regard of stains and blemishes sithence growing be held for ever in extreme disgrace.

To speak of this matter as the cause requireth would require very long discourse. All I will presently say is this: whether it be for the finding out of any thing whereunto divine law bindeth us, but yet in such sort that men are not thereof on all sides resolved; or for the setting down of some uniform judgement to stand touching such things, as being neither way matters of necessity, are notwithstanding offensive and scandalous when there is open opposition about them; be it for the ending of strifes touching matters of Christian belief, wherein the one part may seem to have probable cause of dissenting from the other; or be it concerning matters of polity, order, and regiment in the church; I nothing doubt but that Christian men should much better frame themselves to those heavenly precepts, which our Lord and Saviour with so great instancy gave as concerning peace and unity, if we did all concur in desire to have the use of ancient councils again renewed, rather than these proceedings continued, which either make all contentions endless, or bring them to one only determination, and that of all other the worst, which is by sword.

Episcopal Ministry

Laws, VII, chapter vi

[This text exemplifies Hooker's use of biblical, patristic, and even 'secular' sources in advocacy of the bishop's pre-eminence in both order and jurisdiction. Hooker cleverly cites his opponents' authority, John Calvin, to support ancient episcopal authority, and implies inconsistency in Calvin's own ecclesiological posture. See chapter 16 in this book.]

[7.] . . . . The thing is true, that indeed high priests were figures of Christ, yet this was in things belonging unto their power of order; they figured Christ by entering into the holy place, by offering for the sins of all the people once a year, and by other the like duties: but that to govern and to maintain order amongst those that were subject to them, is an office figurative and abrogated by Christ's coming in the ministry; that their exercise of jurisdiction was figurative, yea figurative in such sort, that it had no other cause of being instituted, but only to serve as a representation of somewhat to come, and that herein the Church of Christ ought not to follow them; this article is such as must be confirmed, if any way, by miracle, otherwise it will hardly enter into the heads of reasonable men, why the high priest should more figure Christ in being a Judge than in being whatsoever he might be besides. St. Cyprian deemed it no wresting of Scripture to challenge as much for Christian bishops as was given to the high priest amongst the Jews, and to urge the law of Moses as being most effectual to prove it. St. Jerome likewise thought it an argument sufficient to ground the authority of bishops upon. 'To the end,' saith he, 'we may understand Apostolical traditions to have been taken from the Old Testament; that which Aaron and his sons and the Levites were in the temple, Bishops and Presbyters and Deacons in the Church may lawfully challenge to themselves.'

[8.] In the office of a Bishop Ignatius observeth these two functions, *hierateuein kai archein*: concerning the one, such is a [the?] pre-eminence of a bishop, that he only hath the heavenly mysteries of God committed originally unto him, so that otherwise than by his ordination, and by authority received from him, others besides him are not licensed therein to deal as ordinary ministers of God's Church. And touching the other part of their sacred function, wherein the power of their jurisdiction doth appear, first how the Apostles themselves, and secondly how Titus and Timothy had rule and jurisdiction over presbyters, no man is ignorant. And had not Christian bishops afterwards the like power? Ignatius bishop of Antioch being ready by blessed martyrdom to end his life, writeth unto his presbyters, the pastors under him, in this sort: *Hoi presbuteroi, poimanate to en umin poimnion, heōs anadeiksi o Theos ton mellonta apchein hēmōn. Ego gar ēdē spendomai.* After the death of Fabian bishop of Rome, there growing some trouble about the receiving of such persons into the Church as had fallen away in persecution, and did now repent their fall, the presbyters and deacons of the same church advertised St. Cyprian thereof, signifying 'That they must of necessity defer to deal in that cause till God did send them a new bishop which might moderate all things.' Much we read of extraordinary fasting usually in the Church. And in this appeareth also somewhat concerning the chiefty of bishops. 'The custom is,' saith Tertullian, 'that bishops do appoint when the people shall all fast.' 'Yea, it is not a matter left to our own free choice whether bishops shall rule or no, but the will of our Lord and Saviour is,' saith Cyprian, 'that every act of the Church be governed by her bishops.' An argument it is of the bishop's high preeminence, rule and government over all the rest of the clergy, even that the sword of persecution did strike, especially, always at the bishop as at the head, the rest by reason of their lower estate being more secure, as the selfsame Cyprian noteth; the very manner of whose speech unto his own both deacons and presbyters who remained safe, when himself then bishop was driven into exile, argueth likewise his eminent authority and rule over them. 'By these letters,' saith he, 'I both exhort and *command* that ye whose presence there is not envied at, nor so much beset with dangers, supply my room in doing those things which the exercise of religion doth require.' Unto the same purpose serve most directly those comparisons, than which nothing is more familiar in the books of the ancient Fathers, who as oft as they speak of the several degrees in God's clergy, if they chance to compare presbyters with Levitical priests of the law, the bishop they compare unto Aaron the high priest; if they compare the one with the Apostles, the other they compare (although in a lower proportion) sometime to Christ, and sometime to God himself, evermore shewing that they placed the bishop in an eminent degree of ruling authority and power above other presbyters. Ignatius comparing bishops with deacons, and with such ministers of the word and sacraments as were but presbyters, and had no authority over presbyters; 'What is,' saith he, 'the bishop, but one which hath all principality and power over all, so far forth as man may have it, being to his power a follower even of God's own Christ?'

[9.] Mr. Calvin himself, though an enemy unto regiment by bishops, doth notwithstanding confess, that in old time the ministers which had charge to teach, chose of their company one in every city, to whom they appropriated the title of bishop, lest equality should breed dissension. He added farther, that look what duty the Roman consuls did execute in proposing matters unto the senate, in asking their opinions, in directing them by advice, admonition, exhortation, in guiding actions by their authority, and in seeing that performed which was with common consent agreed on, the like charge had the bishop in the assembly of other ministers. Thus much Calvin being forced by the evidence of truth to grant, doth yet deny the bishops to have been so in authority at the first as to bear rule over other ministers: wherein what rule he doth mean, I know not. But if the bishops were so far in dignity above other ministers, as the consuls of Rome for their year above other senators, it is as much as we require. And undoubtedly if as the counsuls of Rome, so the bishops in the Church of Christ had such authority, as both to direct other ministers, and to see that every of them should observe that which their common consent had agreed on, how this could be done by the bishop not bearing rule over them, for mine own part I must acknowledge that my poor conceit is not able to comprehend.

[10.] One objection there is of some force to make against that which we have hitherto endeavoured to prove, if they mistake it not who allege it. St. Jerome, comparing other presbyters with him unto whom the name of bishop was then appropriate, asketh, 'What a bishop by virtue of his place and calling may do more than a presbyter, except it be only to ordain?' In like sort Chrysostom having moved a question, wherefore St. Paul should give Timothy precept concerning the quality of bishops, and descend from them to deacons, omitting the order of presbyters between, he maketh thereunto this answer, 'What things he spake concerning bishops, the same are also meet for presbyters, whom bishops seem not to excel in any thing but only in the power or ordination.' Wherefore seeing this doth import no ruling superiority, it follows that bishops were as then no rulers over that part of the clergy of God.

Whereunto we answer, that both St. Jerome and St. Chrysostom had in those their speeches an eye no further than only to that function for which presbyters and bishops were consecrated unto God. Now we know that their consecration had reference to nothing but only that which they did by force and virtue of the power of order, wherein sith bishops received their charge, only by that one degree, to speak of, more ample than presbyters did theirs, it might be well enough said that presbyters were that way authorized to do, in a manner, even as much as bishops could do, if we consider what each of them did by virtue of solemn consecration: for as concerning power of regiment and jurisdiction, it was a thing withal added unto bishops for the necessary use of such certain persons and people, as should be thereunto subject in those particular churches whereof they were bishops, and belonged to them only as bishops of such or such a church; whereas the other kind of power had relation indefinitely unto any of the whole society of Christian men, on whom they should chance to exercise the same, and belonged to them absolutely, as they were bishops, wheresoever they lived.

Ministry – The Cure of Souls

Laws, VI, chapter ii

[Hooker lays down a most important ecclesiological principle: on the one hand, the Church's obligation to protect and maintain Christ's inalienable right to her of spiritual power; on the other, her need and freedom to 'limit' and 'amplify' the practice of divine ordinances according to circumstances. See chapters 15 and 16 in this book.]

[2.] The spiritual power of the Church being such as neither can be challenged by right of nature, nor could by human authority be instituted, because the forces and effects thereof are supernatural and divine; we are to make no doubt or question, but that from him which is the Head it hath descended unto us that are the body now invested therewith. He gave it for the benefit and good of souls, as a mean to keep them in the path which leadeth unto endless felicity, a bridle to hold them within their due and convenient bounds, and if they do go astray, a forcible help to reclaim them. Now although there be no kind of spiritual power, for which our Lord Jesus Christ did not give both commission to exercise, and direction how to use the same, although his laws in that behalf recorded by the holy evangelists be the only ground and foundation, whereupon the practice of the Church must sustain itself; yet, as all multitudes, once grown to the form of societies, are even thereby naturally warranted to enforce upon their own subjects particularly those things which public wisdom shall judge expedient for the common good; so it were absurd to imagine the Church itself, the most glorious amongst them, abridged of this liberty; or to think that no law, constitution, or canon, can be further made either for limitation or amplification in the practice of our Saviour's ordinances, whatsoever occasion be offered through variety of times and things, during the state of this unconstant world, which bringing forth daily such new evils as must of necessity by new remedies be redrest, did both of old enforce our venerable predecessors, and will always constrain others, sometime to make, sometime to abrogate, sometime to augment, and again to abridge sometime; in sum, often to vary, alter, and change customs incident into the manner of exercising that power which doth itself continue always one and the same. I therefore conclude, that spiritual authority is a power which Christ hath given to be used over them which are subject unto it for the eternal good of their souls, according to his own most sacred laws and the wholesome positive constitutions of his Church.

In doctrines referred unto action and practice, as this is which concerneth spiritual jurisdiction, the first step towards sound and perfect understanding is the knowledge of the end, because thereby both use doth frame, and contemplation judge all things.

Contrition and the Discipline of Penance

Laws, VI, chapters iii and iv

[Hooker addresses a key issue prompting the Laws: the locus of spiritual jurisdiction. Against non-conformists' grant of such authority to lay people, Hooker argues that such jurisdiction is an apostolic gift, passed to episcopal successors and to those with whom they share it. Hooker's 'contritionist' credentials appear in his description of the interior disposition in penitence and its relation to the outward act of absolution. Noteworthy is Hooker's startling appraisal of the spiritual importance of repentance: to make a sinner 'just'. See chapter 16 in this book.]

[5.] . . . . But forasmuch as we cannot hate sin in ourselves without heaviness and grief, that there should be in us a thing of such hateful quality, the will averted from sin must needs make the affection suitable; yea, great reason why it should so do: for sith the will by conceiving sin hath deprived the soul of life; and of life there is no recovery without repentance, the death of sin; repentance not able to kill sin, but by withdrawing the will from it; the will unpossible to be withdrawn, unless it concur with a contrary affection to that which accompanied it before in evil: is it not clear that as an inordinate delight did first begin sin, so repentance must begin with a just sorrow, a sorrow of heart, and such a sorrow as renteth the heart; neither a feigned nor a slight sorrow; not feigned, lest it increase sin; nor slight, lest the pleasures of sin overmatch it.

[6.] Wherefore of Grace, the highest cause from which man's penitency doth proceed; of faith, fear, love, hope, what force and efficiency they have in repentance; of parts and duties thereunto belonging, comprehended in the schoolmen's definitions; finally, of the first among those duties, contrition, which disliketh and bewaileth iniquity, let this suffice.

And because God will have offences by repentance not only abhorred within ourselves, but also with humble supplication displayed before him, and a testimony of amendment to be given, even by present works, worthy repentance, in that they are contrary to those we renounce and disclaim: although the virtue of repentance do require that her other two parts, confession and satisfaction, should here follow; yet seeing they belong as well to the discipline as to the virtue of repentance, and only differ for that in the one they are performed to man, in the other to God alone; I had rather distinguish them in joint handling, than handle them apart, because in quality and manner of practice they are distinct.

IV. Our Lord and Saviour in the sixteenth of St. Matthew's Gospel giveth his Apostles regiment in general over God's Church. For they that have the keys of the kingdom of heaven are thereby signified to be stewards of the house of God, under whom they guide, command, judge, and correct his family. The souls of men are God's treasure, committed to the trust and fidelity of such as must render a strict account for the very least which is under their custody. God hath not invested them with power to make a revenue thereof, but to use it for the good of them whom Jesus Christ hath most dearly bought.

And because their office herein consisteth of sundry functions, some belonging to doctrine, some to discipline, all contained in the name of the Keys; they have for matters of discipline, as well as litigious as criminal, their courts and consistories erected by the heavenly authority of his most sacred voice, who hath said, *Dic Ecclesiae*, Tell the Church: against rebellious and contumacious persons which refuse to obey their sentence, armed they are with power to eject such out of the Church, to deprive them of the honours, rights, and privileges of Christian men, to make them as heathen and publicans, with whom society was hateful.

Furthermore, lest their acts should be slenderly accounted of, or had in contempt, whether they admit to the fellowship of saints or seclude from it, whether they bind offenders or set them again at liberty, whether they remit or retain sins, whatsoever is done by way of orderly and lawful proceeding, the Lord himself hath promised to ratify. This is that grand original warrant, by force whereof the guides and prelates in God's Church, first his Apostles, and afterwards others following them successively, did both use and uphold that discipline, the end whereof is to heal men's consciences, to cure their sins, to reclaim offenders from iniquity, and to make them by repentance just.

Neither hath it of ancient time for any other respect been accustomed to bind by ecclesiastical censures, to retain so bound till tokens of manifest repentance appeared, and upon apparent repentance to release, saving only because this was received as a most expedient method for the cure of sin.

The Ministry of Reconciliation

Laws, VI, chapter iv

[Hooker's understanding of spiritual jurisdiction related to ministerial order leads him to support the Prayer Book's provision for 'private confession and absolution' by a priest. See chapter 16 in this book.]

[15.] And for private confession and absolution it standeth thus with us:
The minister's power to absolve is publicly taught and professed, the Church not denied to have authority either of abridging or enlarging the use and exercise of that power, upon the people no such necessity imposed of opening their transgressions unto men, as if remission of sins otherwise were impossible; neither any such opinion had of the thing

itself, as though it were either unlawful or unprofitable, saving only for these inconveniences, which the world hath by experience observed in it heretofore. And in regard thereof, the Church of England hitherto hath thought it the safer way to refer men's hidden crimes unto God and themselves only; howbeit, not without special caution for the admonition of such as come to the holy Sacrament, and for the comfort of such as are ready to depart the world.

First, because there are but few that consider how much that part of divine service which consisteth in partaking the holy Eucharist doth import their souls; what they lose by neglect thereof, and what by devout practice they might attain unto: therefore, lest carelessness of general confession should, as commonly it doth, extinguish all remorse of men's particular enormous crimes; our custom (whensoever men present themselves at the Lord's Table) is, solemnly to give them very fearful admonition what woes are perpendicularly hanging over the heads of such as dare adventure to put forth their unworthy hands to those admirable mysteries of life, which have by rare examples been proved conduits of irremediable death to impenitent receivers; whom therefore as we repel being known, so being not known as we can but terrify. Yet with us, the ministers of God's most holy word and sacraments, being all put in trust with the custody and dispensation of those mysteries, wherein our communion is and hath been ever accounted the highest grace that men on earth are admitted unto, have therefore all equally the same power to withhold that sacred mystical food from notorious evil livers, from such as have any way wronged their neighbours, and from parties between whom there doth open hatred and malice appear, till the first sort have reformed their wicked life, the second recompensed them unto whom they were injurious, and the last condescended unto some course of Christian reconciliation, whereupon their mutual accord may ensue. In which cases, for the first branch of wicked life, and the last which is open enmity, there can arise no great difficulty about the exercise of his power: in the second, concerning wrongs, there may, if men shall presume to define or measure injuries according to their own conceits, depraved oftentimes as well by error as partiality, and that no less in the minister himself, than in any other of the people under him. The knowledge therefore which he taketh of wrongs must rise as it doth in the other two, not from his own opinion or conscience, but from the evidence of the fact which is committed; yea, from such evidence as neither doth admit denial nor defence. For if the offender having either colour of law to uphold, for any other pretence to excuse his own uncharitable and wrongful dealings, shall wilfully stand in defence thereof, it serveth as a bar to the power of the minister in this kind. Because (as it is observed by men of very good judgment in these affairs) 'although in this sort our separating of them be not to strike them with the mortal wound of excommunication, but to stay them rather from running desperately headlong into their own harm; yet in us it is not to sever from the holy communion but such as are either found capable by their own confession, or have been convicted in some public secular, or ecclesiastical court. For who is he that dare take upon him to be any man's both accuser and judge? Evil persons are not rashly, and as we list, to be thrust from communion with the Church; insomuch that, if we cannot proceed against them by any orderly course of judgement, they are rather to be suffered for the time than molested. Many there are reclaimed, as Peter; many, as Judas, known well enough, and yet tolerated; many, which must remain undescried till the day of His appearance, by whom the secret corners of darkness shall be brought into open light.'

Leaving therefore unto his judgement them whom we cannot stay from casting their own souls into so great hazard, we have in the other part of penitential jurisdiction, in our power and authority to release sin, joy on all sides, without trouble or molestation unto any. And if to give be a thing more blessed than to receive, are we not infinitely happier in being authorized to bestow the treasure of God, than when necessity doth constrain to withdraw the same?

The Monarch, 'Head' of the Church

Laws, VIII, chapter iv

[This firm rebuttal to non-conformists' criticism of the role of the monarch in ecclesiastical affairs centres on the idea of headship. In a deft argumentative move, Hooker cites Calvinist Theodore Beza against the Church of England's hyper-Calvinist critics as Hooker distinguishes headships according to 'order', 'measure' and 'kind'. See chapter 17 in this book.]

[IV. 1.] These things being thus first considered, it will be the easier to judge concerning our own estate, whether by force of ecclesiastical dominion with us kings have any other kind of prerogative than they may lawfully hold and enjoy. It is as some do imagine too much, that kings of England should be termed Heads, in relation to the Church. That which we understand by headship, is their only supreme power in ecclesiastical affairs or causes. That which lawfully princes are, what should make it unlawful for men by special styles or titles to signify? If the having of supreme power be allowed, why is the expressing thereof by the title of head condemned? They seem in words, at the leastwise some of them, now at the length to acknowledge that kings may have supreme government even over all, both persons and causes. We in terming our princes *heads of the Church*, do but testify that we acknowledge them such governors.

[2.] Against this peradventure it will be replied, that howsoever we interpret ourselves, it is not fit for a mortal man, and therefore not fit for a civil magistrate, to be entitled head of the Church. Why so? First, 'this title, Head of the Church, was given unto our Saviour Christ, to lift him above all powers, rules, and dominions, either in heaven or in earth. Where if this title belong also to the civil magistrate, then it is manifest that there is a power in earth whereunto our Saviour Christ is not in this point superior. Again, if the civil magistrate may have this title, he may be also termed the first-begotten of all creatures, the first-begotten of the dead, yea the Redeemer of his people. For these are alike given him as dignities whereby he is lifted up above all creatures. Besides this, the whole argument of the Apostle in both places doth lead to shew that this title, Head of the Church, cannot be said of any creature. And further, the very demonstrative article, among the Hebrews especially, whom S. Paul doth follow, serveth to tie that which is verified of one, unto himself alone: so that when the Apostle doth say that Christ is *hē kaphalē*, the Head; it is as much as if he should say, Christ, and no other, is the Head of the Church.'

[3.] Thus have we against the entitling of the highest magistrates, Head, with relation unto the Church, four several arguments, gathered by strong surmise out of words marvellous unlikely to have been written for any such purpose as that whereunto they are now urged. To the Ephesians, the Apostle writeth, 'That Christ, God hath seated on his own right hand in the heavenly places, above all regency, and authority, and power, and dominion, and whatsoever name is named, not in this world only, but in that which shall be also: and hath under his feet set all things, and hath given him head above all things unto the Church, which is his body, even the complement of him which accomplisheth all in all.' To the Colossians in like manner, 'That He is the head of the body of the Church, who is a first-born regency out of the dead, to the end he might be made amongst them all such an one as hath the chiefty:' he meaneth, amongst all them whom before he mentioned, saying, 'In him all things that are, were made; the things in the heavens, and the things in the earth, the things that are visible, and the things that are invisible, whether they be thrones, or dominations, or regencies,' &c.

Unto the fore-alleged arguments therefore we answer: first, that it is not simply the title of the Head, which lifteth our Saviour above all powers, but the title of Head in such sort understood, as the Apostle himself meant it: so that the same being imparted in another sense unto others, doth not any way make those others therein his equals; inasmuch as diversity of things is usual to be understood, even when of words there is no diversity; and it is only the adding of one and the selfsame thing unto diverse persons, which doth argue equality in them. If I term Christ and Cæsar lords, yet this is no equalling of Cæsar with Christ, because it is not thereby intended. 'To term the emperor Lord,' saith Tertullian, 'I for mine own part will not refuse, so that I be not required to term him Lord in the same sense that God is so termed.'

. . . . As for the force of the article, whereby our Lord and Saviour is named the Head, it serveth to tie that unto him by way of excellency, which in a meaner degree is common to others; it doth not exclude any other utterly from being termed Head, but from being entitled as Christ is, the Head, by way of the very highest degree of excellency. Not in the communication of names, but in the confusion of things, is error.

[4.] Howbeit, if Head were a name which well could not be, or never had been used to signify that which a magistrate may be in relation unto some church, but were by continual use of speech appropriated unto that only thing which it signifieth, being applied unto Jesus Christ; then, although we might carry in ourselves a right understanding, yet ought we otherwise rather to speak, unless we interpret our own meaning by some clause of plainer speech; because we are else in manifest danger to be understood according to that construction and sense wherein such words are usually taken. But here the rarest construction, and most removed from common sense, is that which the word doth import being applied unto Christ; that which we signify by it in giving it unto the magistrate, is a great deal more familiar in the common conceit of men. The word is so fit to signify all kinds of superiority, pre-eminence, and chiefty, that no one thing is more ordinary than so to use it even in vulgar speech, and in common understanding so to take it. If therefore a Christian king may have any pre-eminence or chiefty above all other in the Church, (albeit it were less than Theodore Beza giveth, who placeth kings amongst the principal members whereunto public function in the Church belongeth, and denieth not, but that of them which have public function, the civil magistrate's power hath all the rest at commandment, in regard of that part of his office, which is to procure that peace and good order be especially kept in things concerning the first Table;) even hereupon to term him *the Head of that Church*, which is *his kingdom*, should not seem so unfit a thing: which title surely we would not communicate to any other, no not although it should at our hands be exacted with torments, but that our meaning herein is made known to the whole world, so that no man which will understand can easily be ignorant, that we do not impart to kings, when we term them *Heads*, the honour which properly is given to our Lord and Saviour Christ, when the blessed Apostles in the Scripture do term him *the Head of the Church*.

[5.] The power which we signify by that name, differeth in three things plainly from that which Christ doth challenge.

It differeth in order, measure, and kind. In order because God hath given him to his Church for the Head, *huper panta*, above all, *huperanō pasēs tēs archēs*, 'far above all principality, and power, and might, and dominion, and every name that is named, not in this world only, but also in that which is to come:' whereas the power which others have is subordinate unto his.

Again, as he differeth in order, so in measure of power also; because God hath given unto him the ends of the earth for his possession; unto him, dominion from sea to sea; unto him, all power in heaven and in earth; unto him, such sovereignty, as doth not only reach all over places, persons, and things, but doth rest in his one only person, and is not by any succession continued: He reigneth as Head and King for ever, nor is there any kind of law which tieth him, but his own proper will and wisdom: his power is absolute, the same jointly over all which it is severally over each; not so the power of any other's headship. How kings are restrained, and in what sort their authority is limited, we have shewed before. So that unto him is given by the title of *Headship over the Church*, that largeness of power, wherein neither man nor angel can be matched or compared with him.

The last and the weightiest difference between him and them, is in the very kind of their power. The head being of all other parts of man's body the most divine, hath dominion over all the rest: it is the fountain of sense, of motion; the throne where the guide of the soul doth reign; the court from whence direction of all things human proceedeth, Why Christ is called *Head of his Church*, these causes they themselves do yield. As the head is the highest part of a man, above which there is none, always joined with the body; so Christ is the highest in his Church, inseparably knit with it. Again, as the head giveth sense and moving to all the body, so he quickeneth, and together with understanding of heavenly things, giveth strength to walk therein. Seeing therefore, that they cannot affirm Christ sensibly present, or always visibly joined unto his body the Church which is on earth, inasmuch as his corporal residence is in heaven; again, seeing they do not affirm (it were intolerable if they should) that Christ doth personally administer the external regiment of outward actions in the Church, but by the secret inward influence of his grace, giveth spiritual life and the strength of ghostly motions thereunto: impossible it is, that they should so close up their eyes, as not to discern what odds there is between that kind of operation which we imply in the headship of princes, and that which agreeth to our Saviour's dominion over the Church. The headship which we give unto kings is altogether visibly exercised, and ordereth only the external frame of the Church's affairs here amongst us; so that it plainly differeth from Christ's, even in very nature and kind. To be in such sort united unto the Church as he is; to work as he worketh, either on the whole Church, or on any particular assembly, or in any one man; doth neither agree, nor hath possibility of agreeing, unto any besides him.

Whereunto the sum of our answer is, first, that as Christ being Lord or Head over all, doth by virtue of that sovereignty rule all; so he hath no more a superior in governing his Church, than in exercising sovereign dominion upon the rest of the world besides. Secondly, that all authority, as well civil as ecclesiastical, is subordinate unto his. And thirdly, that the civil magistrate being termed Head, by reason of that authority in ecclesiastical affairs which it hath been already declared that themselves do in word acknowledge to be lawful; it followeth that he is an Head even subordinated of, and to Christ.

Kings, Christ's Ministers over His Church

Laws, VIII, chapter iv

[In contrast to non-conformists' rigid distinction between invisible and visible, spiritual and temporal, Hooker argues that Christ's invisible headship requires a visible, temporal expression. References to Roman Catholic apologists (Harding and Pighius) remind us that they too are implicated in Hooker's argument and rebuttal. See chapter 17 in this book.]

[7.] .... Now although there be not in Christ any such defect or weakness, yet other causes there may be diverse, more than we are able to search into, wherefore it might seem to him expedient to divide his kingdom into many portions, and to place many heads over it, that the power which each of them hath in particular with restraint, might illustrate the greatness of his unlimited authority. Besides, howsoever Christ be spiritually always united unto every part of his body, which is the Church; nevertheless we do all know, and they themselves who allege this will, I doubt not, confess also, that from every church here visible, Christ, touching visible and corporal presence, is removed as far as heaven from earth is distant. Visible government is a thing necessary for the Church; and it doth not appear how the exercise of visible government over such multitudes every where dispersed throughout the world should consist without sundry visible governors; whose power being the greatest in that kind so far as it reacheth, they are in consideration thereof termed so far heads. Wherefore, notwithstanding that perpetual conjunction, by virtue whereof our Saviour remaineth always spiritually united unto the parts of his mystical body; Heads endued with supreme power, extending unto a certain compass, are for the exercise of visible regiment not unnecessary.

.... A Church perfect without Christ, I know not which way a man should imagine; unless there may be either Christianity without Christ, or else a Church without Christianity. If magistrates be heads of the Church, they are of necessity Christians; if Christians, then is their Head Christ.

The adding of Christ the universal Head over all unto the magistrate's particular headship, is no more superfluous in any church than in other societies it is to be both severally each subject unto some head, and to have also a head general for them all to be subject unto. For so in armies and in civil corporations we see it fareth. A body politic in such respects is not like to a natural body; in this, moe heads than one are superfluous; in that, not.

It is neither monstrous nor as much as uncomely for a church to have different heads: for if Christian churches be in number many, and every of them a body perfect by itself, Christ being Lord and Head over all; why should we judge it a thing more monstrous for one body to have two heads, than one head so many bodies? Him God hath made the supreme Head of the whole Church; the Head, not only of that mystical body which the eye of man is not able to discern, but even of every Christian politic society, of every visible Church in the world.

Laws, VIII, chapters iv

[9.] . . . . But as for this distinction of headship, spiritual and mystical in Jesus Christ, ministerial and outward in others besides Christ; what cause is to dislike either Harding, or Pighius, or any other besides for it? That which they have been reproved for is, not because they did herein utter an untruth, but such a truth as was not sufficient to bear up the cause which they did thereby seek to maintain. By this distinction they have both truly and sufficiently proved that the name of head, importing power of dominion over the Church, might be given unto others besides Christ, without prejudice unto any part of his honour. That which they should have made manifest was, that the name of Head, importing the power of universal dominion over the whole Church of Christ militant, doth, and that by divine right, appertain unto the pope of Rome. They did prove it lawful to grant unto others besides Christ the power of headship in a different kind from his; but they should have proved it lawful to challenge, as they did to the bishop of Rome, a power universal in that different kind. Their fault was therefore in exacting wrongfully so great power as they challenged in that kind, and not in making two kinds of power, unless some reason can be shewed for which this distinction of power should be thought erroneous and false.

[10.] A little they stir, although in vain, to prove that we cannot with truth make any such distinction of power, whereof the one kind should agree unto Christ only, and the other be further communicated. Thus therefore they argue: 'If there be no head but Christ, in respect of the spiritual government, there is no head but he in respect of the word, sacraments, and discipline, administered by those whom he hath appointed, forasmuch as that is also his spiritual government.' Their meaning is, that whereas we make two kinds of power, of which two, the one being spiritual is proper unto Christ; the other men are capable of, because it is visible and external: we do amiss altogether, they think, in so distinguishing, forasmuch as the visible and external power of regiment over the Church, is only in relation unto the word, the sacraments, and discipline, administered by such as Christ hath appointed thereunto, and the exercise of this power is also his spiritual government: therefore we do but vainly imagine a visible and external power in the Church differing from his spiritual power.

Such disputes as this do somewhat resemble the wonted practising of well-willers upon their friends in the pangs of death, whose manner is even then to put smoke in their nostrils, and so to fetch them again, although they know it a matter impossible to keep them living. The kind affection which the favourers of this labouring cause bear towards it will not suffer them to see it die, although by what means they should be able to make it live, they do not see. But they may see that these wrestlings will not help. Can they be ignorant how little it booteth to overcast so clear a light with some mist of ambiguity in the name of spiritual regiment?

To make things therefore so plain that henceforth a child's capacity may serve rightly to conceive our meanings: we make the spiritual regiment of Christ to be generally that whereby his Church is ruled and governed in things spiritual. Of this general we make two distinct kinds; the one invisibly exercised by Christ himself in his own person; the other outwardly administered by them whom Christ doth allow to be the rulers and guiders of his Church. Touching the former of these two kinds, we teach that Christ in regard thereof is peculiarly termed the Head of the Church of God; neither can any other creature in that sense and meaning be termed head besides him, because it importeth the conduct and government of our souls by the hand of that blessed Spirit wherewith we are sealed and marked, as being peculiarly his. Him only therefore we do acknowledge to be that Lord, which dwelleth, liveth, and reigneth in our hearts; him only to be that Head, which giveth salvation and life unto his body; him only to be that fountain, from whence the influence of heavenly grace distilleth, and is derived into all parts, whether the word, or sacraments, or discipline, or whatsoever by the mean whereby it floweth. As for the power of administering these things in the Church of Christ, which power we call the power of order, it is indeed both Spiritual and His; Spiritual, because such duties properly concern the Spirit; His, because by him it was instituted. Howbeit neither spiritual, as that which is inwardly and invisibly exercised; nor his, as that which he himself in person doth exercise.

Legislation naturally belongs to the whole Church

Laws, VIII, chapter vi

[This is a key text in Hooker's political theology where he advances the view that 'the body of the commonwealth' is the original subject of power. The principle he applies to both civil and ecclesiastical bodies. However, in both cases that power is exercised irrevocably by particular constituencies within the body, monarchs and bishops, for instance. See Chapter 17 in this book.]

VI. [1.] The natural subject of power civil all men confess to be the body of the commonwealth: the good or evil estate whereof dependeth so much upon the power of making laws, that in all well settled states, yea though they be monarchies, yet diligent care is evermore had that the commonwealth do not clean resign up herself and make over this power wholly into the hands of any one. For this cause William, whom we call the Conqueror, making war against England in right of his title to the crown, and knowing that as inheritor thereof he could not lawfully change the laws of the land by himself, for that the English commonwealth had not invested their kings before with the fullness of so great power; therefore he took the style and title of a conqueror. Wherefore, as they themselves cannot choose but grant that the natural subject of power to make laws civil is the commonwealth; so we affirm that in like congruity the true original subject of power also to make church-laws is the whole entire body of that church for which they are made. Equals cannot impose laws and statues upon their equals. Therefore neither may any one man indifferently impose canons ecclesiastical upon another, nor yet one church upon another. If they go about at any time to do it, they must either shew some commission sufficient for their warrant, or else be justly condemned of presumption in the sight both of God and men. But nature itself doth abundantly authorize the Church to make laws and orders for her children that are within her. For every whole thing, being naturally of great power than is any part thereof, that which a whole church will appoint may be with reason exacted indifferently of any within the compass of the same church, and so bind all unto strict obedience.

[5.] The greatest agents of the bishop of Rome's inordinate sovereignty strive against no one point with such earnestness as against this, that jurisdiction (and in the name of jurisdiction they also comprehend the power of dominion spiritual) should be thought originally to be the right of the whole Church; and that no person hath or can have the same, otherwise than derived from the body of the Church.

The reason wherefore they can in no wise brook this opinion is, as friar Soto confesseth, because they which make councils above popes do all build upon this ground, and therefore even with teeth and all they that favour the papal throne must hold the contrary. Which thing they do. For, as many as draw the chariot of the Pope's preeminence, the first conclusion which they contend for is: The power of jurisdiction ecclesiastical doth not rest derived from Christ immediately into the whole body of the Church, but into the prelacy. Unto the prelacy alone it belongeth; as ours also do imagine, unto the governors of the Church alone it was first given, and doth appertain, even of very divine right, in every church established to make such laws concerning orders and ceremonies as occasion doth require.

[3.] Wherein they err, for want of observing as they should, in what manner the power whereof we speak was instituted. One thing it is to ordain a power, and another thing to bestow the same being ordained: or, to appoint the special subject of it, or the person in whom it shall rest. Nature hath appointed that there should be in a civil society power to make laws; but the consent of the people (which are that society) hath instituted the prince's person to be the subject wherein supremacy of that power shall reside. The act of instituting such power may and sometimes doth go in time before the act of conferring or bestowing it. And for bestowing it there may be order two ways taken: namely, either by appointing thereunto some certain person, one or many; or else, without any personal determination, and with appointment only of some determinate condition touching the quality of their persons (whosoever they be that shall receive the same), and for the form or manner of taking it.

Now God himself preventeth sometimes these communities, himself nominateth and appointeth sometimes the subject wherein their power shall rest, and by whom either in whole or in part it shall be exercised; which thing he did often in the commonwealth of Israel. Even so Christ having given unto his Church the power whereof we speak, what she doth by her appointed agents, that duty though they discharge, yet is it not theirs peculiarly, but hers; her power it is which they do exercise. But Christ hath sometimes prevented his Church, conferring that power and appointing it unto certain persons himself, which otherwise the Church might have done. Those persons excepted which Christ himself did immediately bestow such power upon, the rest succeeding have not received power as they did, Christ bestowing it upon their persons; but the power which Christ did institute in the Church they from the Church do receive, according to such laws and canons as Christ has prescribed, and the light of nature or Scripture taught men to institute.

But in truth the whole body of the Church being the first original subject of all mandatory and coercive power within itself, in case a monarch of the world together with his whole kingdom under him receive Christianity, the question is whether the monarch of that commonwealth may without offence or breath of the law of God have and exercise power of dominion ecclesiastical within the compass of his own territories, in such ample sort as the kings of this land may do by the laws thereof.

The Church's Power to Order its Life

Laws, VIII, chapter vi

[The Church's care for humankind's beatitude, both natural and spiritual, means that it needs to fashion laws and ordinances pertaining to the spheres of nature and grace, and that some laws will relate to both spheres at once. Therefore, some areas of legislation must involve the civil as well as the ecclesiastical spheres. See Chapters 15 and 16 in this book.]

[5.] . . . . Laws may be requisite to be made either concerning things that are only to be known and believed in, or else touching that which is to be done by the Church of God. The law of nature and the law of God are sufficient for declaration in both what belongeth unto each man separately, as his soul is the spouse of Christ, yea so sufficient, that they plainly and fully shew whatsoever God doth require by way of necessary introduction unto the state of everlasting bliss. But as a man liveth joined with others in common society, and belongeth unto the outward politic body of the Church, albeit the same law of nature and scripture have in this respect also made manifest the things that are of greatest necessity; nevertheless, by reason of new occasions still arising which the Church having care of souls must take order for as need requireth, hereby it cometh to pass, that there is and ever will be great use even of human laws and ordinances, deducted by way of discourse as conclusions from the former divine and natural, serving for principles thereunto.

No man doubteth, but that for matters of action and practice in the affairs of God, for the manner of divine service, for order in ecclesiastical proceedings about the regiment of the Church, there may be oftentimes cause very urgent to have laws made: but the reason is not so plain wherefore human laws should appoint men what to believe. Wherefore in this we must note two things: First, That in matter of opinion, the law doth not make that to be truth which before was not, as in matter of action it causeth that to be duty which was not before, but it manifesteth only and giveth men notice of that to be truth, the contrary whereunto they ought not before to have believed. Secondly, That as opinions do cleave to the understanding, and are in heart assented unto, it is not in the power of any human law to command them, because to prescribe what men shall think belongeth only unto God. 'Corde creditur, ore fit confessio,' saith the Apostle. As opinions are either fit or inconvenient to be professed, so man's law hath to determine of them. It may for public unity's sake require men's professed assent, or prohibit contradiction to special articles, wherein, as there haply hath been controversy what is true, so the same were like to continue still, not without grievous detriment to a number of souls, except law to remedy that evil should set down a certainty which no man is to gainsay. Wherefore as in regard of divine laws, which the Church receiveth from God, we may unto every man apply those words of Wisdom in Solomon, 'Conserva fili mi præcepta patris tui:' 'My son, keep thou thy father's precepts;' even so concerning the statutes and ordinances which the Church itself maketh, we may add thereunto the words that follow, 'Et ne dimittas legem matris tuæ,' 'And forsake not thou thy mother's law.'

[6.] It is undoubtedly a thing even natural, that all free and independent societies should themselves make their own laws, and that this power should belong to the whole, not to any certain part of a politic body, though haply some one part may have greater sway in that action than the rest: which thing being generally fit and expedient in the making of all laws, we see no cause why to think otherwise in laws concerning the service of God; which in all well-ordered states and commonwealths is the first thing that law hath care to provide for. When we speak of the right which naturally belongeth to a commonwealth, we speak of that which needs must belong to the Church of God. For if the commonwealth be Christian, if the people which are of it do publicly embrace the true religion, this very thing doth make it the Church, as hath been shewed. So that unless the verity and purity of religion do take from them which embrace it, that power wherewith otherwise they are possessed; look what authority, as touching laws for religion, a commonwealth hath simply, it must of necessity being Christian, have the same as touching laws for Christian religion.

[7.] It will be therefore perhaps alleged, that a part of the verity of Christian religion is to hold the power of making ecclesiastical laws a thing appropriated unto the clergy in their synods; and that whatsoever is by their only voices agreed upon, it needeth no further approbation to give unto it the strength of a law: as many plainly appear by the canons of that first most venerable assembly, where those things which the Apostles and James had concluded, were afterward published and imposed upon the churches of the Gentiles abroad as laws, the records thereof remaining still in the book of God for a testimony, that the power of making ecclesiastical laws belongeth to the successors of the Apostles, the bishops and prelates of the Church of God.

To this we answer, that the council of Jerusalem is no argument for the power of the clergy alone to make laws. For first, there hath not been sithence any council of like authority to that in Jerusalem: secondly, the cause why that way of such authority came by a special accident: thirdly, the reason why other councils being not like unto that in nature, the clergy in them should have no power to make laws by themselves alone, is in truth so forcible, that except some commandment of God to the contrary can be shewed, it ought notwithstanding the foresaid example to prevail.

The decrees of the council of Jerusalem were not as the canons of other ecclesiastical assemblies, human, but very divine ordinances: for which cause the churches were far and wide commanded every where to see them kept, no otherwise than if Christ himself had personally on earth been the author of them.

The cause why that council was of so great authority and credit above all others which have been sithence, is expressed in those words of principal observation, 'Unto the Holy Ghost and to us it hath seemed good:' which form of speech, though other councils have likewise used, yet neither could they themselves mean, nor may we so understand them, as if both were in equal sort assisted with the power of the Holy Ghost; but the later had the favour of that general assistance and the presence which Christ doth promise unto all his, according to the quality of their several estates and callings; the former, that grace of special, miraculous, rare, and extraordinary illumination, in relation whereunto the apostle, comparing the Old Testament and the New together, termeth the one a Testament of the letter, for that God delivered it written in stone, the other a Testament of the Spirit, because God imprinted it in the hearts and declared it by the tongues of his chosen Apostles through the power of the Holy Ghost, framing both their conceits and speeches in most divine and incomprehensible manner.

Select Bibliography

Primary Sources

Hooker, Richard, *The Works of that Learned and Judicious Divine Mr Richard Hooker with an account of His Life and Death by Isaac Walton*, John Keble, (2nd edn, Oxford, 1841).

—, *The Folger Library Edition of the Works of Richard Hooker*, 6 vols, ed. W. Speed Hill (Cambridge, MA/London, 1977)

Augustine, *On Faith and Works*, vol. 48 in the Ancient Christian Writers series, translated and annotated by Gregory Lombardo (New York/Mahwah, USA, 1988).

Calvin, John, *Institutes of the Christian Religion*, 2 vols, eds John T McNeil & trans. Lewis Ford Battles [Library of Christian Classics edn] (Westminster, PA, 1960).

Eusebius, *Life of Constantine*, trans. Averil Cameron and Stuart G. Hall (Oxford, 1999).

Scupoli, Lorenzo, *The Spiritual Combat*, anon. trans. (London, 1890).

Walton, Izaac, *The Lives of John Donne, Sir Henry Wotton, Richard Hooker, George Herbert and Robert Sanderson*, reprinted (London, 1962).

Whitgift, John, *The Works of John Whitgift, D.D.*, ed. J. Ayre, Parker Society (Cambridge, 1851-3), vol. III.

Secondary Sources

Addleshaw, G.W.O., *The High Church Tradition: A Study in the Liturgical Thought of the Seventeenth Century* (London, 1941).

Allen, Diogenes, *Spiritual Theology* (Cambridge, MA 1997).

Allchin, A. M., *The Kingdom of Love and Knowledge: The Encounter between Orthodoxy and the West* (London, 1979).

—, *Participation in God. A Forgotten Strand in Anglican Tradition* (London, 1988).

Almasy, Rudolph, 'Book VI and the "Tractate on Penance:" do they belong together?', in *RHER*, pp. 263-83.

Atkinson, Nigel, *Richard Hooker and the Authority of Scripture, Tradition and Reason: Reformed Theologian of the Church of England?* (Carlisle, 1997).

Bainton, Roland, *Erasmus of Christendom* (New York, 1969).

Bauckham, Richard, 'Hooker, Travers and the Church of Rome in the 1580s', *Journal of Ecclesiastical History*, vol. 29, no. 1 (January 1978): 37-50.

—, 'Richard Hooker and John Calvin: A Comment', *Journal of Ecclesiastical History*, vol. 32, no. 1 (January 1981): 20-33.

Bennett, G. V., 'The Royal Supremacy' in *To the Church of England* (Worthing, 1988), pp. 47-60.

Bonhoeffer, Dietrich, *Christ the Center* (San Francisco, CA, 1978).

Booty, John E., 'Contrition in Anglican Spirituality: Hooker, Donne and Herbert', in Wolf, William, ed., *Anglican Spirituality* (Wilton, USA, 1982), pp. 25-48.

—, 'Hooker's Understanding of the Presence of Christ in the Eucharist' in John

Booty, ed., *The Divine Drama in History and Liturgy* (Allison Park, USA, 1984), pp. 131-148.

—, 'The Judicious Mr. Hooker and Authority in the Elizabethan Church', in Stephen Sykes, ed., *Authority in the Anglican Communion: Essays Presented to Bishop John Howe* (Toronto, 1987), pp. 94-115.

—, 'Hooker and Anglicanism', in *SRH*, pp. 207-39.

—, 'The Spirituality of Participation in Richard Hooker', *Sewanee Theological Review*, vol. 38, no. 1 (1994): 9-20.

—, 'Introduction to Book V', *FLE*, VI, I, pp. 183-231.

—, *Reflections on the Theology of Richard Hooker* (Sewanee, USA, 1998).

Bouyer, Louis, 'Bishops in the Church: The Catholic Tradition', in Moore, Peter, ed., *Bishops. But What Kind?* (London, 1982), pp. 25-40.

Brown, David., *Choices. Ethics and the Christian* (Oxford, 1983).

Brydon, Michael, *The Evolving Reputation of Richard Hooker. An Examination of Responses, 1600-1714* (Oxford, 2006).

Burnaby, John, *Amor Dei: A Study of the Religion of St. Augustine*, reprinted (Norwich, 1991).

Cameron, Averil, *Christianity and the Rhetoric of Empire: The Development of Christian Discourse* (Berkeley, CA, 1991).

Chapman, Mark, 'The Theology of Richard Hooker', in *Anglican Theology* (Edinburgh, 2012), pp. 103-25.

Chapman, Raymond, ed., *Law and Revelation: Richard Hooker and His Writings* (Norwich, 2009).

Church, R. W., *Introduction to the First Book of Hooker's Treatise of the Laws of Ecclesiastical Polity* (Oxford, 1896).

Compier, Don. H., 'Hooker on the Authority of Scripture in Matters of Morality', in Arthur S. McGrade, ed., *Richard Hooker and the Construction of Christian Community*, Medieval & Renaissance Texts and Studies (Tempe, AR, 1997), pp. 251-9.

Curran, Charles E., 'Conscience in the Light of the Catholic Moral Tradition', in Charles E. Curran, ed., *Conscience* (New York, 2004).

Davies, Brian, *The Thought of Thomas Aquinas* (Oxford, 1992).

Davies, Julian, *The Caroline Captivity of the Church. Charles I and the Remoulding of Anglicanism* (Oxford, 1992).

Deme, Dániel, *The Christology of Anselm of Canterbury* (Aldershot, 2003).

Dent, Christopher M., *Protestant Reformers in Elizabethan Oxford*, reprinted (Oxford, 1983).

Dix, Gregory, 'The Origins of the Epiclesis', *Theology*, vol. 28, no. 165 (1934): 125-37.

Dugmore, W.C., *Eucharistic Doctrine from Hooker to Waterland* (London, 1942).

—, *The Mass and the English Reformers* (London, 1958).

Dulles, Avery, S.J., *Models of the Church* (New York, 1974).

Eccleshall, Robert, 'Richard Hooker and the Peculiarities of the English: The Reception of the Ecclesiastical Polity in the Seventeenth and Eighteenth Centuries', *History of Political Thought*, vol. II, no. 1 (1981): 63-117.

Emery, Gilles, O.P., *The Trinitarian Theology of St. Thomas Aquinas* (Oxford, 2007).

Eppley, Daniel, 'Richard Hooker on the Un-conditionality of Predestination', in *RHER*, pp. 63-77.

—, 'Richard Hooker and Christopher St. German: Biblical Hermeneutics and Princely Power, in *RHER*, pp. 285-94.

—, 'Royal Supremacy', in *CRH*, pp. 503-34.

Farrer, Austin, *The Triple Victory* (London & New York, 1965).

Faulkner, Robert F., 'Reason and Revelation in Hooker's Ethics', *The American Political Science Review*, vol. 59, no. 3 (September, 1965): 680-90.

Florovsky, George, 'The Idea of Creation in Christian Philosophy', *Eastern Churches Quarterly*, vol. 8 (1949): 53-77.

Gibbs, Lee W., 'Theology, Logic, and Rhetoric in the Temple Controversy Between Richard Hooker and Walter Travers', *Anglican Theological Review*, vol. LXV, no. 2 (1963): 177-88.

—, 'Hooker and Andrewes on Priestly Absolution', in *SRH*, pp. 261-74.

—, 'Richard Hooker's *Via Media* Doctrine of Repentance', *Harvard Theological Review*, vol. 84, no. 1 (1991): 59-74.

—, 'Introduction to Book I', in *FLE*, VI, I, pp. 81-124.

—, 'Life of Hooker', in *CRH*, pp. 1-25

—, 'Richard Hooker: Prophet of Anglicanism or English Magisterial Reformer', *Anglican Theological Review*, vol. LXXXIII, no. 2 (2006): 943-60.

Green, I.M., *The Re-Establishment of the Church of England 1660-1663*(Oxford, 1978).

Gregg, William, 'Sacramental Theology in Hooker's *Laws*: A Structural Perspective', *Anglican Theological Review*, vol. LXXIII, no. 2 (1995): 155-76.

Grenz, Stanley, and Olson, Roger, *20th-Century Theology* (Carlisle, 1992).

Grislis, Egil, 'Richard Hooker's Image of Man', *Renaissance Papers 1963* (The Southeastern Renaissance Conference, 1964), pp. 73-84.

—, 'The Role of Consensus in Richard Hooker's Method of Theological Inquiry', in R. E. Cushman and E. Grislis, eds, *The Heritage of Christian Thought: Essays in Honour of Robert Lowry Calhoun* (New York, 1965), pp. 64-88.

—, 'The Hermeneutical Problem in Richard Hooker', in *SRH*, pp. 159-206.

—, 'The Anglican Spirituality of Richard Hooker', *Toronto Journal of Theology*, vol. 12 (1996): 35-45.

—, 'The Role of Sin in the Theology of Richard Hooker', *Anglican Theological Review*, vol. LXXXIV, no. 4 (2002): 881-96.

—, 'Providence, Predestination, and Free Will in Richard Hooker's Theology', in *RHER*, pp. 79-95.

—, 'Richard Hooker among the Giants: the Creativity and Continuity of Richard Hooker's Doctrine of Justification', *Cithara*, XLIII, no. 2 (2004): 3-15.

—, 'Jesus Christ – The Centre of Theology in Richard Hooker's *Of the Laws of Ecclesiastical Polity*', *Journal of Anglican Studies*, vol. 5, no. 2 (2007), pp. 227-52

Harries, Richard, *Art and the Beauty of God* (London, 1993).

Harrison, William H., 'Prudence and Custom: Revisiting Hooker on Authority', *Anglican Theological Review*, LXXXIV, 4 (2002), 897-913

—, 'The Church', *CRH*, pp. 305-36

Harton, F. P., *Elements of the Spiritual Life*, reprinted (London, 1932).

Haugaard, William P., 'Richard Hooker: Evidence of an Ecumenical Vision From A Twentieth-Century Perspective', *Journal of Ecumenical Studies*, vol. 24, no. 3 (1987): 427-39.

—, 'The Scriptural Hermeneutics of Richard Hooker: Historical Contextualization and Teleology', in Armentrout, Donald S., ed., *This Sacred History: Anglican Reflections for John Booty* (Cambridge, MA, 1990), pp. 161-74.

—, 'Introduction: Books II, III & IV', *FLE*, VI, I, pp. 125-81.

Helgerson, Richard, *Forms of Nationhood: The Elizabethan Writing of England* (Chicago, IL, 1992).

Hill, W. Speed, ed., *Studies in Richard Hooker: Essays Preliminary to an Edition of his Works* (Cleveland, USA/London, 1972); cited as *SRH*.

—, 'The Evolution of Hooker's *Laws of Ecclesiastical Polity*', in *SRH*, pp. 117-158.

Holmgren, Stephen, *Ethics After Easter* (Cambridge, MA, 2000).

Houk, Raymond Aaron, *Hooker's Ecclesiastical Polity Book VIII* (New York, 1931).

Ingalls, L. Ranall, 'Richard Hooker on the Scriptures: Saint Augustine's Trinitarianism and the Interpretation of *Sola Scriptura*', Doctor of Philosophy Thesis (University of Wales, Lampeter, 2004).

—, 'Sin and Grace', in CRH, pp. 151-83

—, 'Richard Hooker as Interpreter of the Reformed Doctrine of *Sola Scriptura*', *Anglican & Episcopal History*, vol. 77, no. 4 (December 2008): 351-78.

Jordan, Mark, 'Theology and Philosophy' in N. Kretzman and E. Stump, eds, *The Cambridge Companion to Aquinas* (Cambridge, 1993), pp. 232-51

Joyce, J. A., *Richard Hooker and Anglican Moral Theology* (Oxford, 2012).

Kelly, J. N. D., *Early Christian Doctrines* (5th edn, London, 1977).

Kendell, R. T., *Calvin and English Calvinism to 1649* (Oxford, 1979).

Kenny, Anthony, *Aquinas on Mind* (Oxford, 1991).

Kernan, Dean, 'Jurisdiction', *CRH*, pp. 435-79.

Kirby, W. J. Torrance, *Richard Hooker's Doctrine of the Royal Supremacy* (Leiden, 1990).

—, 'The Neo-Platonic Logic of Richard Hooker's Generic Division of Law', *Renaissance et Réforme/Renaissance and Reform*, vol. 22, no. 4 (1998) 49-67.

—, ed., *Richard Hooker and the English Reformation*, Studies in Early Modern Religious Reform, vol. 2 (Dordrecht/Boston/London, 2003).

—, 'Angels descending and ascending: Hooker's "double motion" of Common Prayer', in *RHER*, pp. 111-30.

—, 'Grace and Hierarchy: Richard Hooker's Two Platonisms', in *RHER*, pp. 25-40.

—, *Richard Hooker Reformer and Platonist* (Aldershot, 2005).

—, ed., *A Companion to Richard Hooker*, vol. 8 in Brill's Companions to the Christian Tradition (Leiden/Boston, 2008).

Kirk, Kenneth, *Some Principles of Moral Theology and their Application* (London, 1920).

Lake, Peter, *Moderate Puitans and the Elizabethan Church* (Cambridge, 1982).

—, *Anglicans and Puritans? Presbyterianism and English Conformist Thought from Whitgift to Hooker* (London, 1988).

—, 'The "Anglican Moment"? Richard Hooker and the Ideological Watershed of the 1590s', in Stephen Platt, ed., *Anglicanism and the Western Christian Tradition*, pp. 90-121.

Lamirande, Émilien, *Études sur l'Écclesiologie de saint Augustin* (Ottawa, 1969).

Lewis, C. S., *English Literature in the Sixteenth Century, Excluding Drama* (Oxford, 1954).

Lossky, Vladimir, *The Mystical Theology of the Eastern Church*, reprinted (Crestwood, NY, 1976).

Louth, Andrew, *The Origins of the Christian Mystical Tradition* (Oxford, 1981).

—, *Denys the Areopagite* (London & Wilton, USA, 1989).

—, *St John of Damascus: Tradition and Originality in Byzantine Theology* (Oxford, 2002).

Loyer, Olivier, *L'Anglicanisme de Richard Hooker*, 2 vols (Lille, 1979).

Luoma, John K., 'Restitution Or Reformation? Cartwright And Hooker On The Elizabethan Church', *Historical Magazine of the Protestant Episcopal Church*, vol. XLVI, no. 1 (1977): 85-106.

—, 'Who Owns the Fathers? Hooker and Cartwright on the Authority of the Primitive Church', *Sixteenth Century Journal*, vol. VIII, no. 3 (1977): 45-59.

Malone, Michael T., 'The Doctrine of Predestination in the Thought of William Perkins and Richard Hooker', *Anglican Theological Review*, vol. LII, no. 2 (1970): 103-117.

MacCulloch, Diarmaid, 'Richard Hooker's Reputation', in *CRH*, pp. 563-610.

Macquarrie, John, *Principles of Christian Theology* (New York, 1966).

Marot, D. H., 'Aux origines de la Théologie anglicane', *Irénikon*, vol. XXXIII (1960): 321-43.

Marshall, John S., 'Hooker's Theory of Church and State', *Anglican Theological Review*, vol. XXVII, no. 3 (1945): 151-60.

Marshall, John S., 'Freedom and Authority in Classical Anglicanism', *Anglican Theological Review*, vol. XLV (1963): 54-73.

Marshall, John, *Hooker and the Anglican Tradition: An Historical and Theological Study of Hooker's Ecclesiastical Polity* (London, 1963).

Mascall, E. L., *Grace and Glory* (New York, 1961).

—, *The Openness of Being: Natural Theology Today* (Philadelphia, PA, 1971).

Mason, A. J., 'Richard Hooker', in W. E. Collins, ed., *Typical English Churchmen from Parker to Maurice* (London, 1903), pp. 25-34.

McAdoo, Henry R., *The Structure of Caroline Moral Theology* (London, 1949).

—, *The Spirit of Anglicanism. A Survey of Anglican Theological Method in the Seventeenth Century* (London, 1965).

—, 'Richard Hooker', in Geoffrey Rowell, ed., *The English Religious Tradition and the Genius of Anglicanism* (Wantage, 1992), pp. 105-126.

McGinn, Bernard, 'The Development of the Thought of Thomas Aquinas on the Reconciliation of Divine Providence and Contingency', *The Thomist*, vol. XXXIX, no. 4 (1975): 741-52.

McGrade, Arthur S., 'The Coherence of Hooker's Polity: The Books on Power', *Journal of the History of Ideas*, vol. XXIV, no. 2 (April-June 1963): 163-82.

—, ed., *Richard Hooker and the Construction of Christian Community* [Medieval & Renaissance Texts & Studies] (Tempe, AR, 1997).

—, *Hooker Of the Laws of Ecclesiastical Polity* [Cambridge Texts in the History of Political Thought], reprinted (Cambridge, 1989).

—, 'Introduction to Book VIII', *FLE*, VI, I, pp. 337-83.

McGrath, Alistair, *Reformation Thought: An Introduction*, 2nd edn (Oxford, 1993).

McIntyre, John, *St. Anselm and His Critics* (Edinburgh, 1954).

Menzies, Lucy, ed., *Collected Papers of Evelyn Underhill* (London, 1946).

Meyendorff, John, *Christ in Eastern Christian Thought* (Crestwood, NY, 1975).

—, *Living Tradition* (Crestwood, NY, 1978).

—, *Byzantine Theology. Historical Trends & Doctrinal Themes* (New York, 1979).

Miller, E.C., *Toward A Fuller Vision: Orthodoxy and the Anglican Experience* (Wilton, CT, 1985).

Miller, Charles, *For the Gift of the World: An Introduction to the Theology of Dumitru Staniloae* (Edinburgh, 2000).

Moore, Tod, 'Recycling Aristotle: The Sovereignty Theory of Richard Hooker', *History of Political Thought*, vol. XIV, issue 3 (1993): 345-59.

Morris, Christopher, 'Introduction' in *Of the Laws of Ecclesiastical Polity*, 2 vols [Everyman's Library ed., reprinted] (London, 1965).

Munz, Peter, *The Place of Hooker in the History of Thought* (London, 1952).

Neelands, W. David, 'The Theology of Grace of Richard Hooker', Doctor of Theology Thesis (University of Toronto, 1988).

—, 'Hooker on Scripture, Reason and "Tradition"', in *RHCCC*, pp. 75-94.

—, 'Crime, Guilt, and the Punishment of Christ: Traveling Another Way with Anselm of Canterbury and Richard Hooker', *Anglican Theological Review*, vol. LXXXIII, no. 2 (2006): 197-213.

—, 'Richard Hooker and the Debates about Predestination, 1580-1600', in *RHER*, pp. 43-61.

—, 'Richard Hooker on the Identity of the Visible and the Invisible Church', in *RHER*, pp. 99-110.

—, 'Christology and the Sacraments', in *CRH*, pp. 369-401.

—, 'Predestination', in *CRH*, pp. 185-219.

Nockles, Peter, 'Survivals or New Arrivals? The Oxford Movement and the Historical Reconstruction of Anglicanism', in Stephen Platten, ed., *Anglicanism and the Western Christian Tradition*.

Paget, Francis, *Introduction to the Fifth Book of Hooker's Treatise of the Laws of Ecclesiastical Polity* (Oxford, 1894).

Parris, J. R., 'Hooker's Doctrine of the Eucharist', *Scottish Journal of Theology*, vol. 16 (1963): 151-65.

Parry, Graham, *The Arts of the Anglican Counter-Reformation: Glory, Laud and Honour* (Woodbridge, 2006).

Patterson, Patrick, D. M., 'Hooker's Apprentice: God, Entelechy, Beauty and Desire in Book One of Richard Hooker's *Lawes of Ecclesiasticall Politie*', *Anglican Theological Review*, vol. LXXXIV, no. 4 (2002): 961-88.

Patterson, W. B., 'Hooker on Ecumenical Relations: Conciliarism in the English Reformation', in *RHCCC*, pp. 283-303.

Peck, A. L., *Anglicanism and Episcopacy: A Re-examination of Evidence with special reference to Professor Norman Sykes'* Old Priest and New Presbyter *together with an essay on Validity* (London/New York,1958).

Pelikan, Jaroslav, *Reformation of Church and Dogma (1300-1700)*, vol. 4 of *The Christian Tradition. A History of the Development of Doctrine* (Chicago/London, 1984).

Piolanti, Antonio, 'Il mistero del "Cristo totale" in St. Agostino', in *Agostino Magister* [Congrés International Augustinien](Paris, 1954), pp. 453-69.

Piper, Joseph, *Scholasticism* (New York, 1964).

Platten, Stephen, ed., *Anglicanism and the Western Christian Tradition: Continuity, Change and the Search for Communion* (Norwich, 2003).

Polkinghorne, John, *Reason and Reality* (London, 1991).

Porter, H. C., *Reformation and Reaction in Tudor Cambridge* (Cambridge, 1958).

—, 'Hooker, the Tudor Constitution, and the *Via Media*', *SRH*, pp. 77-116

Radner, Ephraim and Turner, Philip, eds, *The Fate of Communion: The Agony of Anglicanism and the Future of a Global Church* (Grand Rapids, MI, 2006).

Ramsey, Michael, *The Anglican Spirit*, Dale Coleman, ed. (Cambridge, MA, 1991).

Rasmussen, Barry G., 'Richard Hooker's Trinitarian Hermeneutic of Grace', *Anglican Theological Review*, vol. LXXXIV, no. 4 (2002): 929-41.

—, 'Presence and Absence: Richard Hooker's Sacramental Hermeneutic', in *RHER*, pp.151-64.

Reardon, B. M. G., 'Richard Hooker's Apology for Anglicanism', *The Hibbert Journal*, vol. LII, no. 2 (April 1954): 278-85.

Rolt, C. E., trans., *Dionysius the Areopagite: The Divine Names and the Mystical Theology* (London, 1940).

Rowell, Geoffrey, ed., *The English Religious Tradition and the Genius of Anglicanism* (Wantage, 1992).

Russell, Norman, *The Doctrine of Deification in the Greek Patristic Tradition* (Oxford, 2004).

Schillebeeckx, Edward, O.P., *Christ the Sacrament of encounter with God* (London, Melbourne and New York, 1963).

Schoek, R. J., 'From Erasmus to Hooker: An Overview', in Arthur McGrade, ed., *RHCCC*, pp. 59-73

Secor, Philip B., *Richard Hooker Prophet of Anglicanism* (Toronto and Tunbridge Wells, 1999).

Sherry, Patrick, *Spirit and Beauty: An Introduction to Theological Aesthetics* (Oxford, 1992).

Shuger, Deborah, '"Society supernatural": the imagined community of Hooker's Laws', in C. McEachern and D. Shuger, eds, *Religion and Culture in Renaissance England* (Cambridge, 1997), pp. 116-41.

Shapiro, Barbara, *Probability and Certainty in Seventeenth-Century England* (Princeton, NJ, 1983).

Shirley, F. J., *Richard Hooker and Contemporary Political Ideas* (London, 1949).

Simuţ, Corneliu C., *Richard Hooker and His Early Doctrine of Justification. A Study of His Discourse of Justification* (Aldershot, 2005).

—, 'Orders of Ministry', in *CRH*, pp. 404-34.

Sisson, C. J., *The Judicious Marriage of Mr. Hooker and the Birth of the 'Laws of Ecclesiastical Polity'* (Cambridge, 1940).

Sommerville, J. P., 'Richard Hooker, Hadrian Saravia, and the Advent of the Divine Right of Kings', *History of Political Thought*, vol. IV, no. 2 (1983): 229-45.

Sommerville, M. R., 'Richard Hooker and his Contemporaries on Episcopacy: An Elizabethan Consensus', *Journal of Ecclesiastical History*, vol. 35, no. 2 (1984): 177-87.

Spinks, Bryan D., *Two Faces of Elizabethan Anglican Theology. Sacraments and Salvation in the Thought of William Perkins and Richard Hooker* (Lanham, PA and London, 1999).

Stafford, John K., 'Grace, Sin, and Nature: Richard Hooker's Theology of Baptism', in *RHER*, pp. 185-205.

—, 'Practical Divinity', in *CRH*, pp. 535-61.

Stevenson, Kenneth, *Covenant of Grace Renewed. A Vision of the Eucharist in the Seventeenth Century* (London, 1994).

—, *The Mystery of Baptism in the Anglican Tradition* (Norwich, 1998).

Stranks, C. J., *Anglican Devotion: Studies in the Spiritual Life of the Church of England between the Reformation and the Oxford Movement* (London, 1961).

Surlis, Paul, 'Natural Law in Richard Hooker (c. 1554-1600)', *The Irish Theological Quarterly*, vol. XXXV, no. 2 (n.s.) (April, 1968): 173-85.

Sykes, Norman, *Old Priest and New Presbyter* (Cambridge, MA 1956).

Sykes, Stephen, Booty, John, Knight, Jonathan, *The Study of Anglicanism* (London, 1998).

Targoff, Ramie, 'Performing Prayer in Hooker's *Lawes*: The Efficacy of Set Forms', in *RHCCC*, pp. 275-82.

Tavard, George H., *Holy Writ or Holy Church* (London, 1959).

Thornton, L. S., *Richard Hooker. A Study of His Theology* (London, 1924).

Thornton, Martin, *Christian Proficiency* (London, 1959).

—, *English Spirituality: An Outline of Ascetical Theology According to the English Pastoral Tradition,* reprinted (Cambridge, MA, 1986).

Tillyard, E. M. W., *The Elizabethan World Picture* (New York, n.d.).

Thompson, W.D. J., Cargill, 'The Philosopher of the "Politic Society": Richard Hooker as a Political Thinker', in *SRH*, pp. 3-76.

Turrell, James F., 'Uniformity and Common Prayer', in *CRH*, pp. 337-66.

Thunberg, Lars, *The Vision of St. Maximus the Confessor* (Crestwood, NY, 1985).

Urban, Linwood, 'A Revolution in English Moral Theology', *Anglican Theological Review*, vol. LIII, no.1 (January, 1971): 5-20.

Verkamp, Bernard, *The Indifferent Mean: Adiaphorism in the English Reformation to 1554* (Athens and Detroit, MI, 1977),

Voak, Nigel, *Richard Hooker and Reformed Theology. A Study of Reason, Will, and Grace* (Oxford, 2003).

Von Balthasar, Hans Urs, *The Glory of the Lord*, vol. 1 (San Francisco, CA, 1982).

Wendle, Francois, *Calvin. The Origins and Development of his Religious Thought,* trans. Philip Mairet (London, 1963).

Westberg, Daniel, 'Thomistic Law and the Moral Theory of Richard Hooker', *American Catholic Philosophical Quarterly*, vol. 68, supplement (1994): 203-14.

Williams, A. N., *The Ground of Union: Deification in Aquinas and Palamas* (New York, 1999).

Williams, Rowan, *On Christian Theology* (Oxford, 2000).

—, 'Christology and Inter-Religious Dialogue' at http.//www.archbishopofcanterbury. org/articles.php/2279/the-future-of-interfaith-dialogue-archbishop-speaks-at-presence-of-faith-conference.

Wilmer, Richard H., 'Hooker on Authority', *Anglican Theological Review*, vol. XXXIII, (1951): 102-8.

Index

Words in quotation marks are Hooker's own terms and have what might be called a technical function in his theological vocabulary.

Modern Authors Cited

BV - #0004 - 260719 - C0 - 234/156/19 - PB - 9780227174005